Teacher's Resource Book

Houghton Mifflin

Spelling and Vocabulary

Level 8

Houghton Mifflin Company **Boston**

Atlanta **Dallas** **Geneva, Illinois** **Palo Alto** **Princeton** **Toronto**

Credits

Cover design: R.D. Brough
Design and Production: Kirchoff/Wohlberg, Inc.

Illustrations

Kirchoff/Wohlberg, Inc. pp. 10, 13, 32, 60, 88, 118, 140, 141, 146, 174
Susan Lexa pp. 5, 22
Jane McCreary pp. 7, 11, 14, 18, 25, 28, 33, 41, 45, 49, 53, 56, 62, 65, 67, 69, 74, 77, 81, 84, 93, 97, 100, 103, 104, 107, 111, 114, 120, 123, 124, 125, 129, 135, 139, 142, 149, 151, 152, 157, 167, 170

Photography

Front cover photograph: David Cavagnaro

ISBN: 0-395-48766-8

DEFGHIJ–CS–987654

How to Use This Resource Book

Introduction

This Resource Book provides a variety of student and teacher support materials that can be used with this level of *Houghton Mifflin Spelling and Vocabulary*.

Section 1
Unit Resources

Practice Masters

The materials for each Basic Unit include three Practice Masters designed to provide three levels of practice. These pages include meaning-based activities as well as many motivating gamelike activities that mix practice with fun.

- **Practice A** can be used for reteaching or practice. It includes the Summing Up statement from the Basic Unit and one activity that reinforces the unit spelling principle. Practice A pages deal with the first column of ten Basic Words listed on the Part A page. By dealing with half of the Basic Word list, this page provides an easy practice for students who may be having difficulty with the word list or who have limited English proficiency.
- **Practice B** provides extra practice for all of the Basic Words listed on the Basic Unit Part A page. Many Practice B masters use the Basic Words in proofreading activities to remind students of the importance of checking for correct spelling whenever they write.
- **Practice C** provides extra practice and extension activities for students who are working with the Challenge Words listed on the Part A page and with the Theme Vocabulary Words listed on the Part E page of each Basic Unit.

Tests

Placement

The **Prebook Test** can help you evaluate each student's general level of spelling ability. The test consists of twenty-five items that include one hundred Basic Words drawn from all Basic Units in this level. Students who score between 50 and 85 percent generally can be assigned the complete Basic Word list for each unit. Students who score above 85 percent might also attempt to work with the Challenge Words. Students who score below 50 percent could be assigned only the first column of Basic Words in each unit.

Note: You may also want to use the **Pretest** in your Teacher's Edition or the **Unit Test** in this Resource Book to determine each student's spelling assignment on a unit-by-unit basis.

Unit-by-Unit Evaluation

The **Unit** and **Review Tests** provide alternatives to the Pretest and the Unit Evaluation included in your Teacher's Edition. The Teacher's Resource Book Unit and Review Tests can help you evaluate your students' spelling skills as well as provide practice with many standardized test formats. They can be used as pretests or posttests.

Unit Tests: Each Unit Test evaluates every Basic Word in that unit. The words from the first column of the Basic Word list are tested first, followed by the words from the second column. The words are in a sequence different from that used in the student book word lists.

Review Tests: There are three Review Tests for each Review Unit.

- **Review Test A** evaluates Basic Words selected from the first column of each Basic Unit word list in that cycle. (One cycle comprises five Basic Units and the following Review Unit.)
- **Review Test B** evaluates Basic Words selected from the second column of each Basic Unit word list in that cycle.
- **Review Test C** evaluates Challenge Words selected from the Challenge Word lists in each Basic Unit in that cycle.

Note: Review Tests A, B, and C do not evaluate all of the Basic or Challenge Words in each cycle.

They do, however, test more words than those practiced in the pupil book Review Unit exercises. To review all of the Basic and Challenge Words that might be tested in Review Tests A, B, and C, have students complete the Extra Practice exercises in their pupil books as well as the Review Unit exercises.

Cumulative Tests

The **Midyear Test** and the **End-of-Year Test** are intended to be used after Review Units 18 and 36 respectively. Each test consists of twenty-five items that include one hundred Basic Words. The Midyear Test draws on Basic Words from all Basic Units in Cycles 1–3. The End-of-Year Test draws on Basic Words from all Basic Units in Cycles 1–6.

Bulletin Boards

A **Bulletin Board** suggestion has been provided for each cycle of units. Each bulletin board idea can be used with three or more units in that cycle.

Spelling Newsletters

A **Spelling Newsletter** for students and their families is available for each cycle of units. The letter appears in two languages, English and Spanish. Each letter includes a simple cooperative family activity that reinforces the importance of correct spelling in an enjoyable way.

Spelling Games

A **Spelling Game** master has been provided for each cycle of units. Some games work specifically with the spelling words in the cycle. Other games encourage students to work with any words that meet the game criteria in order to build their interest in words and language as a whole. Students can use these game masters independently.

When the game instructions direct students to use spelling words, they specify Basic Words. Depending on students' skills, you may want to direct some or all students to use Review, Challenge, or Theme Vocabulary Words as well.

Prewriting Ideas

A **Prewriting Ideas** master has been provided for use with Step 1 of the Writing Process assignment in the Literature and Writing lesson in each Review Unit. This master provides structured, yet open-ended, activities that will help students choose their writing topics and plan the organization and content of their compositions before they begin to write.

Section 2
Additional Resources

This section provides **Individual** and **Class Progress Charts** for record keeping. These charts are especially useful during meetings with parents or school administrators.

Note: The **Class Progress Chart** provides record-keeping space for one cycle of units. Make duplicate copies to cover all six cycles. You may want to write students' names on one copy and use that page to make the additional copies.

The **Proofreading Marks** and the **Proofreading Checklist** masters can be duplicated for each student to use as handy references for writing.

The **Handwriting Models** masters provide examples of four different handwriting styles. You may want to duplicate specific models for each student to use as a reference.

Section 3
Practice Master and
Test Answers

This section includes annotated copies of **Practice Masters A**, **B**, and **C**. It also includes annotated copies of the **Prebook**, **Midyear**, **End-of-Year**, **Unit**, and **Review Tests**. These materials are organized sequentially by unit.

Contents

Section 1
Unit Resources   1

Unit 1
Consonant Changes
Prebook Test   3
Practice A   5
Practice B   6
Practice C   7
Unit Test   8

Unit 2
Greek Word Parts I
Practice A   9
Practice B   10
Practice C   11
Unit Test   12

Unit 3
Latin Prefixes I
Practice A   13
Practice B   14
Practice C   15
Unit Test   16

Unit 4
Words from Names
Practice A   17
Practice B   18
Practice C   19
Unit Test   20

Unit 5
Homophones
Practice A   21
Practice B   22
Practice C   23
Unit Test   24

Unit 6
Review
Bulletin Board   25
Spelling Newsletter
(parent update)
English   26
Spanish   27
Spelling Game   28
Review Test A   29
Review Test B   30
Review Test C   31
Prewriting Ideas:
Personal Narrative   32

Unit 7
Absorbed Prefixes
Practice A   33
Practice B   34
Practice C   35
Unit Test   36

Unit 8
Greek Word Parts II
Practice A   37
Practice B   38
Practice C   39
Unit Test   40

Unit 9
Latin Prefixes II
Practice A   41
Practice B   42
Practice C   43
Unit Test   44

Unit 10
Words from Spanish
Practice A   45
Practice B   46
Practice C   47
Unit Test   48

Unit 11
Words Often Confused
Practice A   49
Practice B   50
Practice C   51
Unit Test   52

Unit 12
Review
Bulletin Board   53
Spelling Newsletter
(parent update)
English   54
Spanish   55
Spelling Game   56
Review Test A   57
Review Test B   58
Review Test C   59
Prewriting Ideas:
Comparison and Contrast   60

Unit 13
Vowel Changes I
Practice A   61
Practice B   62
Practice C   63
Unit Test   64

Unit 14
Latin Roots I
Practice A   65
Practice B   66
Practice C   67
Unit Test   68

Unit 15
Noun Suffixes I
Practice A   69
Practice B   70
Practice C   71
Unit Test   72

Unit 16
Words from French
Practice A   73
Practice B   74
Practice C   75
Unit Test   76

Unit 17
Words Often Misspelled I
Practice A   77
Practice B   78
Practice C   79
Unit Test   80

Unit 18
Review
Bulletin Board   81
Spelling Newsletter
(parent update)
English   82
Spanish   83
Spelling Game   84
Review Test A   85
Review Test B   86
Review Test C   87
Prewriting Ideas: Story   88
Midyear Test   89

Section 1
Unit Resources (continued)

Unit 19
Vowel Changes II

Practice A	91
Practice B	92
Practice C	93
Unit Test	94

Unit 20
Latin Roots II

Practice A	95
Practice B	96
Practice C	97
Unit Test	98

Unit 21
Noun Suffixes II

Practice A	99
Practice B	100
Practice C	101
Unit Test	102

Unit 22
Words from Other Languages

Practice A	103
Practice B	104
Practice C	105
Unit Test	106

Unit 23
Words Often Misspelled II

Practice A	107
Practice B	108
Practice C	109
Unit Test	110

Unit 24
Review

Bulletin Board	111
Spelling Newsletter (parent update)	
English	112
Spanish	113
Spelling Game	114
Review Test A	115
Review Test B	116
Review Test C	117
Prewriting Ideas: Description	118

Unit 25
Vowel Changes III

Practice A	119
Practice B	120
Practice C	121
Unit Test	122

Unit 26
Latin Roots III

Practice A	123
Practice B	124
Practice C	125
Unit Test	126

Unit 27
Adjective Suffixes

Practice A	127
Practice B	128
Practice C	129
Unit Test	130

Unit 28
Words from Places

Practice A	131
Practice B	132
Practice C	133
Unit Test	134

Unit 29
Single or Double Consonants

Practice A	135
Practice B	136
Practice C	137
Unit Test	138

Unit 30
Review

Bulletin Board	139
Spelling Newsletter (parent update)	
English	140
Spanish	141
Spelling Game	142
Review Test A	143
Review Test B	144
Review Test C	145
Prewriting Ideas: Persuasive Letter	146

Unit 31
Vowel Changes IV

Practice A	147
Practice B	148
Practice C	149
Unit Test	150

Unit 32
Latin Roots IV

Practice A	151
Practice B	152
Practice C	153
Unit Test	154

Unit 33
Number Prefixes

Practice A	155
Practice B	156
Practice C	157
Unit Test	158

Unit 34
Words New to English

Practice A	159
Practice B	160
Practice C	161
Unit Test	162

Unit 35
Words Often Mispronounced

Practice A	163
Practice B	164
Practice C	165
Unit Test	166

Unit 36
Review

Bulletin Board	167
Spelling Newsletter (parent update)	
English	168
Spanish	169
Spelling Game	170
Review Test A	171
Review Test B	172
Review Test C	173
Prewriting Ideas: Research Report	174
End-of-Year Test	175

Section 2
Additional Resources 177

Individual Progress Chart 179
Class Progress Chart 180
Scoring Chart 181
Proofreading Marks 183
Proofreading Checklist 184
Handwriting Models 185

Section 3
Practice Master and
Test Answers 189

Unit 1
Prebook Test 191
Practice A, Practice B 192
Practice C, Unit Test 193

Unit 2
Practice A, Practice B 194
Practice C, Unit Test 195

Unit 3
Practice A, Practice B 196
Practice C, Unit Test 197

Unit 4
Practice A, Practice B 198
Practice C, Unit Test 199

Unit 5
Practice A, Practice B 200
Practice C, Unit Test 201

Unit 6
Review Test A,
  Review Test B 202
Review Test C 203

Unit 7
Practice A 203
Practice B, Practice C 204
Unit Test 205

Unit 8
Practice A 205
Practice B, Practice C 206
Unit Test 207

Unit 9
Practice A 207
Practice B, Practice C 208
Unit Test 209

Unit 10
Practice A 209
Practice B, Practice C 210
Unit Test 211

Unit 11
Practice A 211
Practice B, Practice C 212
Unit Test 213

Unit 12
Review Test A 213
Review Test B,
  Review Test C 214

Unit 13
Practice A, Practice B 215
Practice C, Unit Test 216

Unit 14
Practice A, Practice B 217
Practice C, Unit Test 218

Unit 15
Practice A, Practice B 219
Practice C, Unit Test 220

Unit 16
Practice A, Practice B 221
Practice C, Unit Test 222

Unit 17
Practice A, Practice B 223
Practice C, Unit Test 224

Unit 18
Review Test A,
  Review Test B 225
Review Test C,
  Midyear Test 226
Midyear Test 227

Unit 19
Practice A 227
Practice B, Practice C 228
Unit Test 229

Unit 20
Practice A 229
Practice B, Practice C 230
Unit Test 231

Unit 21
Practice A 231
Practice B, Practice C 232
Unit Test 233

Unit 22
Practice A 233
Practice B, Practice C 234
Unit Test 235

Unit 23
Practice A 235
Practice B, Practice C 236
Unit Test 237

Unit 24
Review Test A 237
Review Test B,
  Review Test C 238

Unit 25
Practice A, Practice B 239
Practice C, Unit Test 240

Unit 26
Practice A, Practice B 241
Practice C, Unit Test 242

Unit 27
Practice A, Practice B 243
Practice C, Unit Test 244

Unit 28
Practice A, Practice B 245
Practice C, Unit Test 246

Unit 29
Practice A, Practice B 247
Practice C, Unit Test 248

Unit 30
Review Test A,
  Review Test B 249
Review Test C 250

Unit 31
Practice A 250
Practice B, Practice C 251
Unit Test 252

Unit 32
Practice A 252
Practice B, Practice C 253
Unit Test 254

Unit 33
Practice A 254
Practice B, Practice C 255
Unit Test 256

Unit 34
Practice A 256
Practice B, Practice C 257
Unit Test 258

Unit 35
Practice A 258
Practice B, Practice C 259
Unit Test 260

Unit 36
Review Test A 260
Review Test B,
  Review Test C 261
End-of-Year Test 262

Unit Resources

Placement and Cumulative Evaluation
Prebook Test (Unit 1)
Midyear Test (Unit 18)
End-of-Year Test (Unit 36)
Basic Units
Practice Masters
Practice A (Easy)
Practice B (Average)
Practice C (Challenging)
Unit Test
Review Units
Bulletin Board Idea
Spelling Newsletter (English and Spanish)
Spelling Game
Tests
Review Test A
Review Test B
Review Test C
Prewriting Ideas

Prebook Test

Find the word that is spelled incorrectly. Fill in the letter beside the misspelled word.

Sample:
- ⓐ succeed
- ● inevitible
- ⓒ cymbal
- ⓓ counterfeit

1. ⓐ synagogue
   ⓑ sensor
   ⓒ comedien
   ⓓ adjourn

2. ⓐ omelet
   ⓑ inference
   ⓒ embarass
   ⓓ calculator

3. ⓐ limuosine
   ⓑ exquisite
   ⓒ advertisement
   ⓓ hypnosis

4. ⓐ subscription
   ⓑ collaberate
   ⓒ anthology
   ⓓ mosquito

5. ⓐ familiarity
   ⓑ neutrality
   ⓒ kindergarden
   ⓓ avocation

6. ⓐ deprevation
   ⓑ abstention
   ⓒ acclamation
   ⓓ sacrifice

7. ⓐ monotonous
   ⓑ consede
   ⓒ descent
   ⓓ interchangeable

8. ⓐ consumption
   ⓑ conscientous
   ⓒ laboratory
   ⓓ synonym

9. ⓐ suburban
   ⓑ intrigue
   ⓒ accordian
   ⓓ persecute

10. ⓐ mannerism
    ⓑ recommend
    ⓒ transistor
    ⓓ extrordinary

11. ⓐ colleague
    ⓑ technology
    ⓒ savanna
    ⓓ hygeine

12. ⓐ sequential
    ⓑ contraversy
    ⓒ sensible
    ⓓ disastrous

13. ⓐ artificial
    ⓑ turquoise
    ⓒ sustenence
    ⓓ efficient

14. ⓐ monopoly
    ⓑ vegatation
    ⓒ disposal
    ⓓ anxiety

15. ⓐ sophomore
    ⓑ intravenous
    ⓒ pathological
    ⓓ sylabication

(continued)

Prebook Test (continued)

16. (a) remission
    (b) psychiatrist
    (c) summary
    (d) maintenence

17. (a) manipulate
    (b) diskett
    (c) allegiance
    (d) transition

18. (a) avacado
    (b) accede
    (c) camouflage
    (d) endeavor

19. (a) criticism
    (b) accomplice
    (c) strenuous
    (d) inturmural

20. (a) trillogy
    (b) canvass
    (c) alternative
    (d) preference

21. (a) democracy
    (b) conspiracy
    (c) grafitti
    (d) resumption

22. (a) miscelaneous
    (b) magenta
    (c) centennial
    (d) commission

23. (a) ascent
    (b) accesory
    (c) retention
    (d) dilemma

24. (a) illustrative
    (b) barbecue
    (c) accommodate
    (d) chauffer

25. (a) contageous
    (b) convenient
    (c) mathematics
    (d) pedestrian

PRACTICE A
Consonant Changes

Summing Up

Knowing how consonants change in one pair of words may help you predict changes in words with similar spelling patterns.

Basic Words
1. commit
2. commission
3. emit
4. emission
5. intercede
6. intercession
7. succeed
8. succession
9. submit
10. submission

Digging for Success 1–10. Professor Wyse dug up these pieces of pottery. On each one is a clue to the spelling of the letters missing from the Basic Words below. Fill in the missing letter or letters in each word on the shovels. Then write the Basic Word pairs under the correct category.

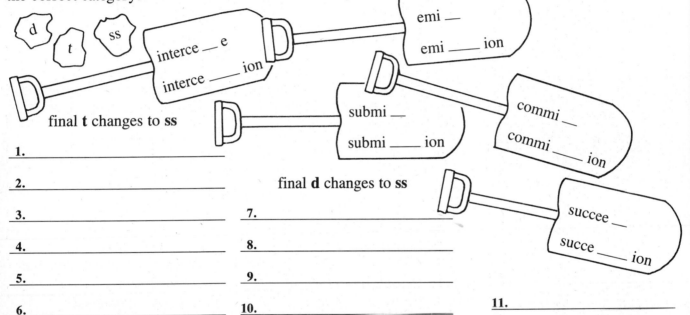

final t changes to ss

1. _____

2. _____

3. _____

4. _____

5. _____

6. _____

final d changes to ss

7. _____

8. _____

9. _____

10. _____

At the Dig Write the Basic Words to complete this reporter's story about Professor Wyse's expedition.

The crew broke the seal on the old door and stood back as the cave began to __(11)__ a strange odor. "Don't breathe that gas!" shouted someone from the archaeology __(12)__ . "The __(13)__ might be harmful."

Soon they could enter the cave. "Be careful, please," said the professor. "To damage anything would be to __(14)__ a terrible act. If we are to __(15)__ in our work, we must be very cautious."

The archaeologists entered several caves in __(16)__ . Some wall drawings told a story of a man who tried to __(17)__ for a friend who was in trouble because he would not __(18)__ to the law. His __(19)__ did not work, however. The last picture showed the friend kneeling in __(20)__ to the king.

11. _____

12. _____

13. _____

14. _____

15. _____

16. _____

17. _____

18. _____

19. _____

20. _____

Skill: Students will practice spelling word pairs with final consonant changes.

Home Use: Help your child practice the spelling words by having him or her complete the activities on this page. Check the completed page, and have your child practice saying and spelling any misspelled words.

Basic Words
1. commit
2. commission
3. emit
4. emission
5. intercede
6. intercession
7. succeed
8. succession
9. submit
10. submission
11. remit
12. remission
13. transmit
14. transmission
15. concede
16. concession
17. omit
18. omission
19. recede
20. recession

PRACTICE B

Consonant Changes

Crossword Puzzle   Complete the puzzle by writing the Basic Word that fits each clue.

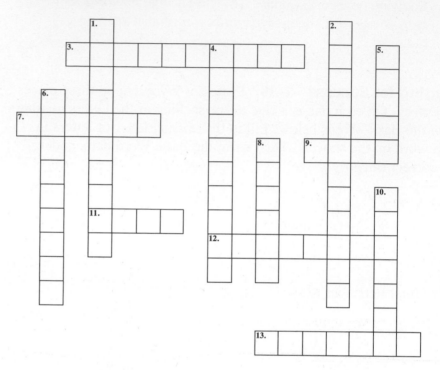

Across

3. a group with certain duties
7. to move back or away from
9. to give off
11. to leave out
12. the act of leaving something out
13. to follow or come next in order

Down

1. the act of yielding
2. something sent
4. the act of following in order
5. to send money
6. the act of going back
8. to yield to another's opinion
10. to admit as true

Proofreading   14–20. Find and cross out seven misspelled Basic Words in these headlines. Then write each word correctly. Remember to begin each word with a capital letter because it is an important word in the headline.

Rain Brings Remision of Hay Fever
Parents Committ to PTA
Prisoner Freed Through Friend's Intercesion
Cars Tested for Emmision and Transmission Problems
Boy's Poetry Submision Honored
Coach to Interseed with Commission
Ticks Transmitt Disease

14. _____

15. _____

16. _____

17. _____

18. _____

19. _____

20. _____

Skill: Students will practice spelling word pairs with final consonant changes.

Home Use: Help your child practice the spelling words by having him or her complete the activities on this page. Check the completed page, and have your child practice saying and spelling any misspelled words.

PRACTICE C
Consonant Changes

Super Analogies   Write the Challenge and Vocabulary Words that best complete each analogy.

1–2. irritate : _____ :: irritation : _____
3–4. protection : _____ :: dangerous : _____
5–6. remainder : _____ :: poisons : _____
7–8. cancel : _____ :: cancellation : _____

1. _____   5. _____

2. _____   6. _____

3. _____   7. _____

4. _____   8. _____

Earth Awareness   In the space below, design a two-page flier about an Earth Day seminar at your school. What will be the topics of the seminar sessions? Write a time, a title, and a brief description for each session. Use the Vocabulary Words *endangered, biodegradable, contaminate, aquifer,* and *conservation* and any other Challenge or Vocabulary Words you wish in your flier.

Challenge Words
1. revoke
2. revocation
3. provoke
4. provocation

Theme Vocabulary
5. conservation
6. endangered
7. contaminate
8. toxins
9. by-product
10. hazardous
11. biodegradable
12. aquifer

Skill: Students will practice spelling word pairs with final consonant changes and words related to the theme of ecology.

Home Use: Help your child practice the spelling words by having him or her complete the activities on this page. Check the completed page, and have your child practice saying and spelling any misspelled words.

7

Unit 1 Test: Consonant Changes

Each item below gives four possible spellings of a word. Fill in the letter beside the correct spelling.

Sample:
- ⓐ voilation
- ● violation
- ⓒ violashun
- ⓓ vialation

1. ⓐ comision
   ⓑ comission
   ⓒ commision
   ⓓ commission

2. ⓐ suceed
   ⓑ succede
   ⓒ succeed
   ⓓ sucseed

3. ⓐ emishun
   ⓑ emission
   ⓒ emmision
   ⓓ emmission

4. ⓐ submitt
   ⓑ submit
   ⓒ subbmit
   ⓓ subbmitt

5. ⓐ commit
   ⓑ committ
   ⓒ comitt
   ⓓ comit

6. ⓐ succesion
   ⓑ sucession
   ⓒ sucesion
   ⓓ succession

7. ⓐ submission
   ⓑ subbmission
   ⓒ submision
   ⓓ submmision

8. ⓐ emmit
   ⓑ emit
   ⓒ emitt
   ⓓ emmitt

9. ⓐ intercesion
   ⓑ interccesion
   ⓒ intercession
   ⓓ intircession

10. ⓐ intercede
    ⓑ intersede
    ⓒ interceed
    ⓓ interseed

11. ⓐ remision
    ⓑ remission
    ⓒ remmision
    ⓓ remmission

12. ⓐ remit
    ⓑ remitt
    ⓒ remmite
    ⓓ remmit

13. ⓐ concession
    ⓑ concesion
    ⓒ consesion
    ⓓ consession

14. ⓐ resesion
    ⓑ recession
    ⓒ resesion
    ⓓ recesion

15. ⓐ omitt
    ⓑ omite
    ⓒ ommit
    ⓓ omit

16. ⓐ trannsmit
    ⓑ transmit
    ⓒ transsmit
    ⓓ transmitt

17. ⓐ consede
    ⓑ conceed
    ⓒ concede
    ⓓ conceede

18. ⓐ transmission
    ⓑ transsmision
    ⓒ transmision
    ⓓ transsmission

19. ⓐ receed
    ⓑ receede
    ⓒ recede
    ⓓ reecede

20. ⓐ ommission
    ⓑ ommision
    ⓒ omision
    ⓓ omission

PRACTICE A
Greek Word Parts I

Summing Up

Many English words contain the Greek word parts *path, syn* (or *sym*), *gen*, and *prot*.

Basic Words
1. pathology
2. symptom
3. syndrome
4. synthetic
5. protein
6. oxygen
7. hydrogen
8. homogenized
9. synonym
10. sympathy

Word Part Match   1–11. Write each Basic Word under the Greek word part contained in that Basic Word. Write one Basic Word under two word parts.

path = disease; feeling   **syn/sym** = together; same

1. _____   4. _____

2. _____   5. _____   **gen** = born; produced

                                  6. _____   9. _____

prot = first   7. _____   10. _____

3. _____   8. _____   11. _____

Next to each Basic Word that you wrote, write the letter of its definition.

Definitions

A. a sign of illness
B. artificial
C. the study of disease
D. a set of symptoms
E. the lightest gas
F. a class of food

G. an understanding between persons
H. a word with a meaning similar to that of another word
I. spread evenly through a fluid
J. a gas needed for human life

Word Search   12–20. Circle the nine Basic Words hidden in this puzzle. The words may cross each other and may appear horizontally, vertically, or diagonally. Then write each word.

```
t s y m p a t h y d a y l g u s e t s
e y y p a r e p a t h o l o g y h h y
o n t m t o o s r y n o g o r y o v n
t d h e p y r e d o u l x l o r n e o
r r v o u t s o r j t u s y t p l a n
x o h y d r o g e n o e n b g o n i y
l m o u s t h m e y l a i c k e g e m
n e t e e l w a y s t e m n c i n j s
s y n t h e t i c r o r r a n s i m l
```

12. _____

13. _____

14. _____

15. _____

16. _____

17. _____

18. _____

19. _____

20. _____

Skill: Students will practice spelling words that have the Greek word parts *path, syn, gen,* and *prot.*

Home Use: Help your child practice the spelling words by having him or her complete the activities on this page. Check the completed page, and have your child practice saying and spelling any misspelled words.

Basic Words
1. pathology
2. symptom
3. syndrome
4. synthetic
5. protein
6. oxygen
7. hydrogen
8. homogenized
9. synonym
10. sympathy
11. pathetic
12. apathy
13. photogenic
14. synagogue
15. genealogy
16. empathy
17. pathological
18. symmetrical
19. protoplasm
20. syndicate

PRACTICE B
Greek Word Parts I

Code Load   While in Greece, Alex made up a code. Use his code to figure out and write the Basic Words. A △ stands for a vowel or *y*.

CODE:	5	7	10	3	12	1	9	2	11	8	4	6	△	△	△	△	△	△
LETTER:	c	d	g	h	l	m	n	p	r	s	t	z	a	e	i	o	u	y

1. 8-△-9-7-△-5-△-4-△   **6.** 2-△-4-3-△-12-△-10-△-5-△-12

2. 8-△-9-7-11-△-1-△   **7.** 3-△-7-11-△-10-△-9

3. 8-△-9-△-10-△-10-△-△   **8.** 3-△-1-△-10-△-9-△-6-△-7

4. 2-△-4-3-△-12-△-10-△   **9.** 2-11-△-4-△-2-12-△-8-1

5. △-1-2-△-4-3-△   **10.** 8-△-9-△-9-△-1

1. _____   6. _____

2. _____   7. _____

3. _____   8. _____

4. _____   9. _____

5. _____   10. _____

Greetings from Greece   Write ten Basic Words to complete the letter Alex sent from Greece to his friend Charlie.

Dear Charlie,

My study of family __(11)__ excited me so much that I had to explore my Greek background firsthand. Greece is wonderful! At first, I found the old buildings sad and __(12)__ because they were decayed, but now I find them magical. Many have beautiful columns that make the most uneven building look balanced and __(13)__ . I'm taking a lot of pictures of people because they are so __(14)__ . I bought clothes made of wool, not anything __(15)__ . The food is delicious. The lamb is a good source of __(16)__ .

Yesterday we climbed a mountain. The guide told us to report dizziness or any other __(17)__ that we might feel because there is less __(18)__ at higher altitudes.

I once felt __(19)__ for other cultures, but now I care very much about what goes on in the rest of the world. I feel __(20)__ for anyone who is unable to visit Greece.

See you soon,
Alex

11. _____

12. _____

13. _____

14. _____

15. _____

16. _____

17. _____

18. _____

19. _____

20. _____

Skill: Students will practice spelling words that have the Greek word parts *path*, *syn*, *gen*, and *prot*.

Home Use: Help your child practice the spelling words by having him or her complete the activities on this page. Check the completed page, and have your child practice saying and spelling any misspelled words.

PRACTICE C
Greek Word Parts I

Rights and Wrongs   Decide whether the underlined Challenge
or Vocabulary Word in each sentence is used correctly. If the word is
correct, write it on the answer line. If the word is incorrect, write
the correct Challenge or Vocabulary Word instead.

1. The doctor wore a <u>microbe</u> around her neck.
2. In the laboratory, scientists are working on the <u>biopsy</u> of
   separate elements to form a new substance.
3. Doctor Sinclair examined the <u>prognosis</u> through a high-powered
   microscope.
4. Kyle stayed home from school because he had caught the
   <u>diagnostic</u> disease that had spread through the town.
5. The <u>pathos</u> of the movie made Ernie cry.
6. The <u>synthesis</u> for Bob's immediate recovery looks very good.
7. The <u>inflammation</u> on Enid's knee caused the skin to redden.
8. The <u>protagonist</u> in that drama is a boy who saves a baby.
9. I saw an unusual x-ray in the <u>protocol</u> department today.
10. The doctor did a <u>biopsy</u> of the patient's muscle tissue.
11. The head nurse will <u>synthesis</u> her watch with the hospital clock
    to make sure that she is on time.
12. The interns followed proper <u>protocol</u> when greeting the visiting
    Count Von Diefendorf.
13. Dr. Klikka ran a series of <u>infectious</u> tests on the patient to
    identify the disease.

Challenge Words
1. synthesis
2. protocol
3. synchronize
4. pathos
5. protagonist

Theme Vocabulary
6. diagnostic
7. prognosis
8. stethoscope
9. biopsy
10. radiology
11. infectious
12. microbe
13. inflammation

1. _____   5. _____   9. _____
2. _____   6. _____   10. _____
3. _____   7. _____   11. _____
4. _____   8. _____   12. _____
                                              13. _____

Limericks   Write a Vocabulary Word to complete each limerick.
Then write three limericks of your own, using any three Challenge
or Vocabulary Words.

14. A lady who lived near the Rhine
    Collected x-rays of the spine.
    She made no apology.
    She loved _____ .
    She simply found x-rays divine!

15. A cartographer two inches tall
    Drew maps one could not see at all.
    He worked years on a globe
    The size of a _____
    Because he preferred the world small.

14. _____   15. _____

Skill: Students will practice spelling words that
have the Greek word parts *path, syn, gen,* and
prot and words related to the theme of medicine.

Home Use: Help your child practice the spelling words by having him
or her complete the activities on this page. Check the completed page,
and have your child practice saying and spelling any misspelled words.

11

Unit 2 Test: Greek Word Parts I

Find the correctly spelled word to complete each phrase. Fill in the letter beside the correct spelling.

Sample:

to conduct a _____
- (a) simphony
- ● symphony
- (c) symfony
- (d) symphuny

1. a food containing _____
   - (a) proteen
   - (b) protien
   - (c) protein
   - (d) protene

2. hydrogen and _____ gases
   - (a) oxigen
   - (b) oxegen
   - (c) oxygene
   - (d) oxygen

3. the treatment for the _____
   - (a) syndrome
   - (b) syndrom
   - (c) sindrome
   - (d) sindrom

4. to show _____ for
   - (a) simpathy
   - (b) sympethy
   - (c) symmpathy
   - (d) sympathy

5. a bottle of _____ milk
   - (a) homagenized
   - (b) homogenized
   - (c) homoginised
   - (d) hamogenized

6. the study of _____
   - (a) patholigy
   - (b) pathologie
   - (c) pathology
   - (d) pathalogy

7. a _____ for a word
   - (a) synanym
   - (b) synonim
   - (c) synomym
   - (d) synonym

8. a _____ fiber
   - (a) synthetick
   - (b) synthetic
   - (c) sinthetic
   - (d) synnthetic

9. a _____ atom
   - (a) hydrogen
   - (b) hydrogin
   - (c) hidrogen
   - (d) hydragen

10. a _____ of the disease
    - (a) simptom
    - (b) symmptom
    - (c) symptom
    - (d) symptum

11. two _____ sides
    - (a) symetrical
    - (b) symmetricel
    - (c) symmetricle
    - (d) symmetrical

12. the _____ of a cell
    - (a) protplasm
    - (b) protoplasm
    - (c) protoplasim
    - (d) protaplasm

13. a _____ sigh
    - (a) pethetic
    - (b) puthetic
    - (c) pathetic
    - (d) pathetick

14. to feel _____ for
    - (a) ampathy
    - (b) empathy
    - (c) empethy
    - (d) ampethy

15. people in a _____
    - (a) syndicate
    - (b) syndikit
    - (c) sindicate
    - (d) syndikat

16. a _____ smile
    - (a) fotogenic
    - (b) photogenic
    - (c) photogenik
    - (d) fotogennic

17. voter _____
    - (a) apethy
    - (b) appathy
    - (c) apathie
    - (d) apathy

18. a _____ condition
    - (a) pathological
    - (b) pathologicel
    - (c) pathalogical
    - (d) pathilogical

19. the congregation at the _____
    - (a) sinagogue
    - (b) synogogue
    - (c) synogog
    - (d) synagogue

20. to trace the _____
    - (a) geneology
    - (b) geniology
    - (c) genealogy
    - (d) genelogy

PRACTICE A
Latin Prefixes I

Basic Words
1. transportation
2. subway
3. transit
4. submerge
5. suburban
6. substance
7. translate
8. transplant
9. submarine
10. transform

Summing Up

A **prefix** is added to the beginning of a base word or a word root. *Trans-* and *sub-* are common Latin prefixes.

Over and Under **1–10.** The maze below has two paths. The *trans-* path always crosses over the *sub-* path. Follow each path to the end by writing the correct prefix beside each base word or word root to form Basic Words. Then write the Basic Words under the correct prefixes in the order in which they appeared in the maze.

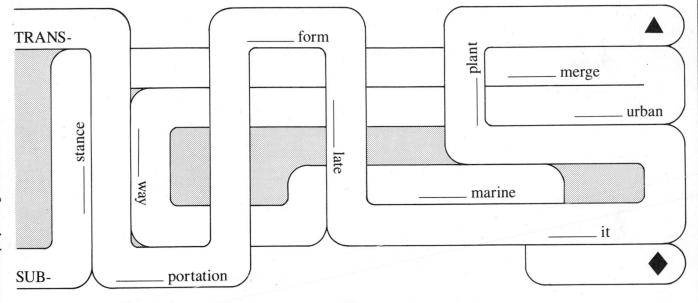

TRANS-

_____ form

_____ plant

_____ merge

_____ urban

_____ stance

_____ way

_____ late

_____ marine

_____ it

SUB-

_____ portation

trans-	sub-	
1. _____	6. _____	11. _____
2. _____	7. _____	12. _____
3. _____	8. _____	13. _____
4. _____	9. _____	14. _____
5. _____	10. _____	15. _____

Analogies Write the Basic Word that completes each analogy.
11. author : write :: interpreter : _____
12. toll : turnpike :: token : _____
13. turn : rotate :: change : _____
14. emit : submit :: emerge : _____
15. piece : part :: material : _____

Skill: Students will practice spelling words with the Latin prefixes *trans-* and *sub-*.

Home Use: Help your child practice the spelling words by having him or her complete the activities on this page. Check the completed page, and have your child practice saying and spelling any misspelled words.

Basic Words
1. transportation
2. subway
3. transit
4. submerge
5. suburban
6. substance
7. translate
8. transplant
9. submarine
10. transform
11. transfusion
12. subdivide
13. sublet
14. subscription
15. transparent
16. subtotal
17. transaction
18. subtitle
19. subside
20. transition

PRACTICE B
Latin Prefixes I

Prefix Time   Match each definition below with a Basic Word formed from the prefix *trans-* or *sub-* and a base word or a word root shown on the clock. Write the Basic Word. Then write the hour shown if the clock's hands were pointing to that Basic Word.

Example: to rent from a lease holder   *sublet*   6:00

1. the gist of something
2. to express in another language
3. to move something from one place to another
4. the act of carrying from one place to another
5. an underground railroad
6. to place under water
7. able to be seen through
8. of an area outside a city
9. an underwater ship
10. a business deal

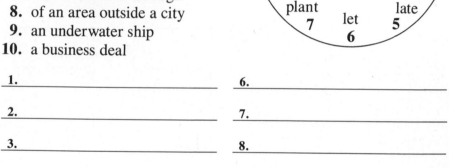

1. _____   6. _____

2. _____   7. _____

3. _____   8. _____

4. _____   9. _____

5. _____   10. _____

Movie Message   11–20. Read from left to right to find the Basic Words that appear on these strips of film. Circle and write the Basic Words. Then write the remaining letters to find a movie title. Remember to start each important word with a capital letter.

Example: a s j h a a m r e o s n ⟨t r a n
s c r i b e⟩ c m r a a r n o e s   *transcribe*

i t r a n s i t i o n w a s a s p s u b d i v i d e a t r a n s f o r m c e s u b

l e t s h t r a n s f u s i o n i p s u b s c r i p t i o n s t t r a n s i t

o w s u b t o t a l s u b t i t l e s u b s i d e a w a y

The name of the movie is __ __ __ __ __

__ __ __ __ __ __ __ __ __ __ __ __ __ __ __ __ .

11. _____

12. _____

13. _____

14. _____

15. _____

16. _____

17. _____

18. _____

19. _____

20. _____

Skill: Students will practice spelling words with the Latin prefixes *trans-* and *sub-*.

Home Use: Help your child practice the spelling words by having him or her complete the activities on this page. Check the completed page, and have your child practice saying and spelling any misspelled words.

PRACTICE C
Latin Prefixes I

Word Puzzle Write seven Challenge or Vocabulary Words so that the letters in the box spell a word that means "a group of four." Then write a clue for each numbered word.

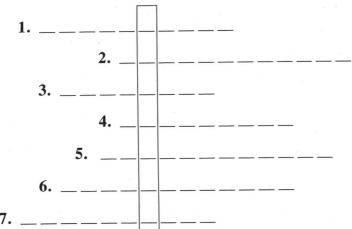

1. _ _ _ _ _ _ _ _

    2. _ _ _ _ _ _ _ _ _

3. _ _ _ _ _ _ _

    4. _ _ _ _ _ _ _ _

   5. _ _ _ _ _ _ _ _ _

6. _ _ _ _ _ _ _

7. _ _ _ _ _ _ _ _ _

1. _____

2. _____

3. _____

4. _____

5. _____

6. _____

7. _____

<table>
<tr><td colspan="2">Challenge Words</td></tr>
<tr><td>1.</td><td>subterranean</td></tr>
<tr><td>2.</td><td>transient</td></tr>
<tr><td>3.</td><td>subsequent</td></tr>
<tr><td>4.</td><td>subculture</td></tr>
<tr><td>5.</td><td>subconscious</td></tr>
<tr><td colspan="2">Theme Vocabulary</td></tr>
<tr><td>6.</td><td>metropolitan</td></tr>
<tr><td>7.</td><td>commuter</td></tr>
<tr><td>8.</td><td>intercity</td></tr>
<tr><td>9.</td><td>elevated</td></tr>
<tr><td>10.</td><td>trolley</td></tr>
<tr><td>11.</td><td>toll</td></tr>
<tr><td>12.</td><td>token</td></tr>
<tr><td>13.</td><td>turnstile</td></tr>
</table>

Rhyming Pairs Write a Challenge or Vocabulary Word and another rhyming word to answer each question.

Example: What do you call a foreigner who lives underground?
subterranean alien

8. What is a merry streetcar?

9. What is a shattered piece of stamped metal used as a substitute for currency?

10. What is a dish for a tax collected for passing over a bridge?

11. What is a simple song sung between towns?

12. What do you call a teacher of those who travel regularly between home and work?

13. What is a device for admitting people to an African river?

8. _____

9. _____

10. _____

11. _____

12. _____

13. _____

Skill: Students will practice spelling words with the Latin prefixes *trans-* and *sub-* and words related to the theme of transportation.

Home Use: Help your child practice the spelling words by having him or her complete the activities on this page. Check the completed page, and have your child practice saying and spelling any misspelled words.

Unit 3 Test: Latin Prefixes I

Each item below gives four possible spellings of a word. Fill in the letter beside the correct spelling.

Sample:
- ⓐ arival
- ● arrival
- ⓒ arrivel
- ⓓ arivil

1.
- ⓐ transform
- ⓑ transsform
- ⓒ transforem
- ⓓ transforme

2.
- ⓐ tranzplant
- ⓑ transplante
- ⓒ transplant
- ⓓ transplent

3.
- ⓐ substince
- ⓑ substense
- ⓒ substanse
- ⓓ substance

4.
- ⓐ submerge
- ⓑ submurge
- ⓒ submirge
- ⓓ submmerge

5.
- ⓐ sub-way
- ⓑ subway
- ⓒ subwaye
- ⓓ subbway

6.
- ⓐ transporrtation
- ⓑ transportashun
- ⓒ transportacion
- ⓓ transportation

7.
- ⓐ trannsit
- ⓑ transit
- ⓒ transitt
- ⓓ transsit

8.
- ⓐ suberban
- ⓑ suberben
- ⓒ suburban
- ⓓ suburben

9.
- ⓐ translate
- ⓑ translait
- ⓒ trenslate
- ⓓ translaite

10.
- ⓐ submurine
- ⓑ submerine
- ⓒ submarine
- ⓓ submarrine

11.
- ⓐ subdivid
- ⓑ subbdivide
- ⓒ subdevide
- ⓓ subdivide

12.
- ⓐ transfusion
- ⓑ trans-fusion
- ⓒ tranzfusion
- ⓓ transfiusion

13.
- ⓐ subscripshun
- ⓑ subscription
- ⓒ supscription
- ⓓ subscribtion

14.
- ⓐ sub-let
- ⓑ sublet
- ⓒ sublett
- ⓓ sublette

15.
- ⓐ transparrant
- ⓑ transparrent
- ⓒ transparent
- ⓓ transparant

16.
- ⓐ transaction
- ⓑ transsaction
- ⓒ transacsion
- ⓓ trensacssion

17.
- ⓐ subtotel
- ⓑ subtotal
- ⓒ subtotle
- ⓓ sub-total

18.
- ⓐ transision
- ⓑ transsition
- ⓒ trannsition
- ⓓ transition

19.
- ⓐ sub-title
- ⓑ subbtitle
- ⓒ subtitel
- ⓓ subtitle

20.
- ⓐ subside
- ⓑ sub-side
- ⓒ subsid
- ⓓ subcide

PRACTICE A
Words from Names

Houghton Mifflin Spelling and Vocabulary. Copyright © Houghton Mifflin Company. All rights reserved.

Summing Up

Some English words come from the names of mythological figures. Others come from the names of real people.

Basic Words
1. atlas
2. mercury
3. narcissus
4. psyche
5. odyssey
6. museum
7. hypnosis
8. Fahrenheit
9. czar
10. pasteurize

Crossword Puzzle   Complete the crossword puzzle by writing the Basic Word that fits each clue.

Across

4. a word from the name of a Greek maiden, meaning "soul"

7. a word from the name of the scientist Louis Pasteur

8. a word from the Latin word *Caesar,* meaning "emperor"

9. a word from the name of the giant who carried the world

10. a word from the name of the Greek warrior Odysseus

Down

1. a word from the name of the Muses of Greek myth

2. a word from the name of a German physicist

3. a word from the name of the Greek youth who loved himself

5. a word from the name of the Greek god of sleep

6. a word from the name of the Roman messenger god

Silly Book Titles   Write the Basic Word that completes each silly book title. Remember to use capital letters.

11. *Sleep Therapy Through* ____ by Z.Z.Z.

12. *My Days Among the Statues in the* ____ by Q. Ray Torr

13. *A Subject in the Court of the* ____ by Roy L. Tee

14. *Ninety Degrees* ____ by Hy Temps

15. *The Squirrel in the* ____ *Garden* by Flora N. Fauna

11. _____

12. _____

13. _____

14. _____

15. _____

Skill: Students will practice spelling words that come from names.

Home Use: Help your child practice the spelling words by having him or her complete the activities on this page. Check the completed page, and have your child practice saying and spelling any misspelled words.

Basic Words
1. atlas
2. mercury
3. narcissus
4. psyche
5. odyssey
6. museum
7. hypnosis
8. Fahrenheit
9. czar
10. pasteurize
11. fate
12. jovial
13. tantalize
14. hygiene
15. mentor
16. psychiatrist
17. mosaic
18. Celsius
19. fury
20. galvanized

PRACTICE B
Words from Names

Myth Mystery   Write the Basic Word that fits each clue. Then write the circled letters in order. Write a colorful mystery word that comes from the name of the Greek goddess of the rainbow.

1. full of fun   _ _ _ _ _ _

2. to kill germs   _ _ _ _ _ _ _ _ _ _

3. a sleeplike condition   _ _ _ _ _ _ _ _

4. an adventurous journey   _ _ _ _ _ _ _

5. destiny   _ _ _ _

6. a book of maps   _ _ _ _ _

7. a flower name   _ _ _ _ _ _ _ _ _

8. a building with exhibits   _ _ _ _ _ _

9. methods to promote good health   _ _ _ _ _ _ _

10. a Russian emperor   _ _ _ _

11. an advisor or counselor   _ _ _ _ _ _

Mystery Word: _ _ _ _ _ _ _ _ _ _

Proofreading   12–20. Find and cross out nine misspelled Basic Words in these advertisements. Then write each word correctly.

12. _____
13. _____
14. _____
15. _____
16. _____
17. _____
18. _____
19. _____
20. _____

Whether the merkury plunges in degrees Faranheit or Celcius, we have a down jacket to suit you!

Read *Odyssey of the Mind* by psychaitrist Jorge Ruiz.

Let us tentelize you with our newest line of cars featuring galvenized body panels.

Join Center East Crafts! Learn to work with mozaic tile.

Full of fewry and rage? Improve your psycke with a meditation course at Oak College. A lecture on hypnosis is included.

Skill: Students will practice spelling words that come from names.

Home Use: Help your child practice the spelling words by having him or her complete the activities on this page. Check the completed page, and have your child practice saying and spelling any misspelled words.

18

PRACTICE C
Words from Names

Word Merge   Use the clues below to write two words on each line. One word will be a Vocabulary Word. Letters at the end of the first word will also begin the second word. Circle the common letters. You may want to use a class dictionary.

Example: _n_ _e_ _m_ _e_ (_s_ _i_ _s_) _t_ _e_ _r_

1–2. _ _ _ _ _ _ _ _ _

3–4. _ _ _ _ _ _ _ _ _

5–6. _ _ _ _ _ _ _ _

7–8. _ _ _ _ _ _ _ _ _ _

9–10. _ _ _ _ _ _ _ _ _ _

11–12. _ _ _ _ _ _ _ _ _ _

13–14. _ _ _ _ _ _ _ _ _ _

15–16. _ _ _ _ _ _ _ _ _ _

Challenge Words
1. iridescent
2. nemesis
3. thespian
4. epicure
5. gargantuan
Theme Vocabulary
6. epic
7. immortal
8. phenomena
9. Muse
10. nectar
11. ambrosia
12. chariot
13. labyrinth

Clues

1. a long poem about heroes
2. an illustration
3. a Greek goddess of the arts and sciences
4. to establish residence
5. to join
6. the drink of the gods
7. a maze
8. to contemplate
9. to close loudly
10. the food of the gods
11. living forever
12. to count
13. a punctuation mark
14. facts perceived by the senses
15. the midday meal
16. a horse-drawn vehicle

Words and Names   Write the names of the characters described. Then write the Challenge Word that comes from each name. Use the etymologies in your Spelling Dictionary.

17–18. Greek goddess of the rainbow

19–20. Greek poet of the sixth century B.C., said to be the originator of Greek tragedy

21–22. fictional giant king noted for his huge appetite

23–24. Greek goddess of vengeance

25–26. Greek thinker who believed that the goal of life should be pleasure and luxurious living

17. _____

18. _____

19. _____

20. _____

21. _____

22. _____

23. _____

24. _____

25. _____

26. _____

Skill: Students will practice spelling words that come from names and words related to the theme of mythology.

Home Use: Help your child practice the spelling words by having him or her complete the activities on this page. Check the completed page, and have your child practice saying and spelling any misspelled words.

Unit 4 Test: Words from Names

Find the correctly spelled word to complete each phrase. Fill in the letter beside the correct spelling.

Sample:

to draw a _____
- ⓐ silouette
- ● silhouette
- ⓒ sillouette
- ⓓ silloette

---

1. to put under _____
- ⓐ hipnosis
- ⓑ hypnosis
- ⓒ hyppnosis
- ⓓ hypnosiss

2. the liquid metal _____
- ⓐ murcury
- ⓑ mercurie
- ⓒ mercury
- ⓓ mercuery

3. a person's _____
- ⓐ psyche
- ⓑ psiche
- ⓒ syche
- ⓓ psycke

4. ninety degrees _____
- ⓐ Farenheit
- ⓑ farenhiet
- ⓒ Fahrenheit
- ⓓ fahrenhiet

5. a map in the _____
- ⓐ atlis
- ⓑ atlas
- ⓒ atlass
- ⓓ attlas

6. to smell the _____
- ⓐ narsissus
- ⓑ narcisuss
- ⓒ narcisus
- ⓓ narcissus

7. to _____ the milk
- ⓐ pasteurize
- ⓑ pasturize
- ⓒ pasteruize
- ⓓ pastuerize

8. a visit to the _____
- ⓐ museum
- ⓑ museeum
- ⓒ musseum
- ⓓ museumm

9. the palace of the _____
- ⓐ zar
- ⓑ zarr
- ⓒ czarr
- ⓓ czar

10. the family's _____
- ⓐ odysey
- ⓑ oddyssey
- ⓒ oddisey
- ⓓ odyssey

11. a _____ manner
- ⓐ joviul
- ⓑ jovial
- ⓒ joviel
- ⓓ joviale

12. studied to be a _____
- ⓐ sychiatrist
- ⓑ psichiatrist
- ⓒ psykiatrist
- ⓓ psychiatrist

13. a type of _____ metal
- ⓐ galvinized
- ⓑ galvenized
- ⓒ galvanized
- ⓓ galvannized

14. to tempt _____
- ⓐ fate
- ⓑ fatte
- ⓒ fait
- ⓓ faet

15. a lesson on good _____
- ⓐ hygeine
- ⓑ hygiene
- ⓒ hygeen
- ⓓ hygeene

16. the _____ of the storm
- ⓐ furie
- ⓑ feury
- ⓒ fury
- ⓓ furee

17. a _____ of tiles
- ⓐ mosiac
- ⓑ mosaick
- ⓒ mosaic
- ⓓ mozaic

18. a teacher and a _____
- ⓐ mentor
- ⓑ mentorr
- ⓒ menter
- ⓓ menntor

19. on the _____ scale
- ⓐ Selsius
- ⓑ Selcius
- ⓒ Celcius
- ⓓ Celsius

20. to _____ the senses
- ⓐ tantilize
- ⓑ tantalize
- ⓒ tantulize
- ⓓ tantalise

PRACTICE A
Homophones

Basic Words
1. chord
2. cord
3. choral
4. coral
5. cymbal
6. symbol
7. aisle
8. isle
9. ascent
10. assent

Summing Up

Homophones are words that sound alike but differ in spelling and meaning.

Puzzling Pairs   Use the clues to complete each puzzle with a pair of homophones. Fill in any boxes that you do not need for letters.

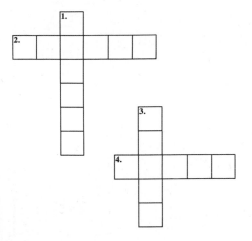  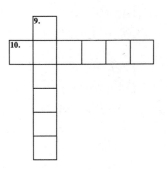

Clues
1. a substance formed from sea skeletons
2. of a choir
3. a passageway between rows
4. a small island
5. something that stands for something else
6. a percussion instrument
7. a combination of musical tones
8. a string or rope
9. an agreement
10. an upward climb

Hink Pinks   Write a Basic Word that rhymes with the given word to make a phrase that fits each clue.

Example: an uninterested piece of rope   bored ____ *cord*
11. a small island in an African river   Nile ____
12. flowered sea skeletons   floral ____
13. a quick percussion instrument   nimble ____
14. a heap of things in a passageway   ____ pile
15. a warped agreement   bent ____
16. a musical tone combination that is stashed away   stored ____

11. _____

12. _____

13. _____

14. _____

15. _____

16. _____

EXTRA!   Work with another student to think of other hink pinks using homophones. Use a class dictionary to check your spelling.

Skill: Students will practice spelling homophones.

Home Use: Help your child practice the spelling words by having him or her complete the activities on this page. Check the completed page, and have your child practice saying and spelling any misspelled words.

21

Basic Words
1. chord
2. cord
3. choral
4. coral
5. cymbal
6. symbol
7. aisle
8. isle
9. ascent
10. assent
11. stationary
12. stationery
13. site
14. cite
15. canvas
16. canvass
17. phase
18. faze
19. descent
20. dissent

PRACTICE B
Homophones

Homophone Cartoons   Write the Basic Words that correctly complete each speech balloon in the cartoons.

I will play that __(1)__ as soon as you plug in the __(2)__ .

Let me __(3)__ former Mayor Altman's remarks when he dedicated the first bridge on this __(4)__ .

1. _____   3. _____

2. _____   4. _____

Which Is Which?   Complete each sentence, using pairs of Basic Words that are homophones.

5–6. The mayor made the ____ down the stairs to express her ____ .
7–8. Jay will ____ the area in his new ____ sneakers.
9–10. Bud's latest ____ of behavior doesn't ____ his parents.
11–12. A gold ____ is the ____ of that marching band.
13–14. The ____ group sang on a boat near the ____ reef.
15–16. Keep your ____ ____ when writing a letter.
17–18. The rows of palm trees formed a lovely ____ on the ____ .
19–20. We need the ranger's ____ before we can make the ____ .

5. _____
6. _____
7. _____
8. _____
9. _____
10. _____
11. _____
12. _____
13. _____
14. _____
15. _____
16. _____

17. _____   19. _____

18. _____   20. _____

EXTRA!   Make up your own homophone cartoons, using as many words from this unit as possible. Then exchange cartoons with a classmate, and correctly complete each other's cartoons.

Skill: Students will practice spelling homophones.

Home Use: Help your child practice the spelling words by having him or her complete the activities on this page. Check the completed page, and have your child practice saying and spelling any misspelled words.

PRACTICE C
Homophones

Making Choices   Complete the answer to each question. First, write the correct Challenge Word. Then write an explanation telling why the word you chose is correct.

1. Might you find a callous or a callus on your hand?

   I might find a _____ because _____

   _____ .

2. Would a person more likely be callus or callous?

   A person would more likely be _____ because _____

   _____ .

3. Can a precious stone be bought by the carat or the caret?

   A precious stone can be bought by the _____ because ___

   _____ .

4. Would you more likely write a caret or a carat?

   I would more likely write a _____ because _____

   _____ .

Challenge Words
1. callous
2. callus
3. caret
4. carat

Theme Vocabulary
5. chorus
6. tenor
7. baritone
8. a cappella
9. octave
10. diva
11. aria
12. conservatory

Opera Lovers   Write the Vocabulary Words to complete these clues about four opera singers. Then complete the chart to match the singers with their parts and their favorite composers. Put a check mark in each correct box and an X in each incorrect box.

- Richard and the man who likes Wagner teach at the __(5)__ .
- The woman who likes Verdi is in the alto section of the __(6)__ .
- Lorenzo can sing almost an __(7)__ higher than Richard. He will play Lieutenant Pinkerton, the __(8)__ in *Madame Butterfly*.
- At a recent concert, Paula, a famous __(9)__ , sang an __(10)__ from *Madame Butterfly*. This opera is by her favorite composer, whose name begins with the same letter as Paula's. The bus carrying the orchestra broke down, and Paula was forced to sing __(11)__ .
- The __(12)__ saw *Amadeus*, a movie about his favorite composer.

	Paula	Beverly	Richard	Lorenzo
soprano				
tenor				
baritone				
alto				
Wagner				
Verdi				
Mozart				
Puccini				

5. _____   8. _____   11. _____

6. _____   9. _____   12. _____

7. _____   10. _____

Skill: Students will practice spelling homophones and words related to the theme of music.

Home Use: Help your child practice the spelling words by having him or her complete the activities on this page. Check the completed page, and have your child practice saying and spelling any misspelled words.

Unit 5 Test: Homophones

Read each sentence. Decide if the underlined word is the right word or the wrong word for that sentence. Fill in the circle for the correct answer in the answer column.

ANSWERS
Right Wrong

Sample:
Jen paid Rob a <u>compliment</u>. ● ○

1. Elsa wore the <u>coral</u> bracelet to the party. 1. ○ ○
2. You can find the carrots in the vegetable <u>isle</u>. 2. ○ ○
3. Jim wrote to Sharon on plain <u>stationery</u>. 3. ○ ○
4. Sara tied the boxes together with a thin <u>chord</u>. 4. ○ ○
5. Craig hit the <u>symbol</u> with his drumstick. 5. ○ ○
6. We voiced our <u>assent</u>. 6. ○ ○
7. Please exit down the center <u>aisle</u>. 7. ○ ○
8. My father gave me his <u>ascent</u>. 8. ○ ○
9. Fred joined the <u>choral</u> singing group. 9. ○ ○
10. Martina dropped her <u>cymbal</u> during the last song. 10. ○ ○
11. We voiced our <u>descent</u>. 11. ○ ○
12. Twelve carpenters were working at the building <u>cite</u>. 12. ○ ○
13. The sea is so calm that the water seems <u>stationary</u>. 13. ○ ○
14. Chet's sneakers were made of <u>canvas</u>. 14. ○ ○
15. The new procedure did not seem to <u>phase</u> Liza. 15. ○ ○
16. The <u>cord</u> was made of nylon. 16. ○ ○
17. The sails are made of a sturdy <u>canvass</u> fabric. 17. ○ ○
18. Next fall, we will begin a new <u>faze</u> of construction. 18. ○ ○
19. That grassy hill marks the <u>site</u> of the battle. 19. ○ ○
20. The elevator began its <u>dissent</u>. 20. ○ ○

BULLETIN BOARD

How to make: Provide a colored background and a border for the bulletin board. Cut out letters from contrasting colored paper to form the title "Cartoon Corner." Attach the title to the bulletin board.

How to use: Have students make up cartoons using two or more characters. The cartoon frames should be drawn on construction paper with speech balloons for each character. Students choose 2–4 Basic Words in one or more units in this cycle and use them in dialogue that they write for the characters. The dialogue may be a riddle or a joke and its answer, part of a conversation, or any other communication that comes to mind. Encourage students to be as imaginative as possible.

You may prefer to have students work together on one cartoon. Have one student draw a character, fill one speech balloon, and give the cartoon to another student to complete with another character and response. Both students should use at least one Basic Word in the cartoon.

Students should tack their completed cartoons to the Bulletin Board for the class to enjoy.

Use: For use with Units 1–5.

SPELLING NEWSLETTER
for Students and Their Families

Getting Started

This year your child is using *Houghton Mifflin Spelling and Vocabulary,* a program that promotes the most important spelling skills while building vocabulary through a wide variety of activities. A thematic approach in each unit permits students to learn and apply their spelling words in context.

Unit 1 focuses on related word pairs such as *commit* and *commission,* in which a spelling change occurs when the suffix *-ion* is added. Units 2 and 3 study words containing Greek word parts and prefixes from Latin. Unit 4 focuses on words that have come from the names of real people and of mythological figures. Finally, Unit 5 discusses homophones, words that sound alike but differ in spelling and meaning.

Word Lists

Here are some of the words your child has studied in Units 1–5.

UNIT 1	UNIT 2	UNIT 3	UNIT 4	UNIT 5
commit	syndrome	translate	narcissus	cymbal
commission	sympathy	transit	psyche	symbol
intercede	hydrogen	submerge	odyssey	aisle
intercession	synonym	suburban	Fahrenheit	isle
succeed	protein	substance	czar	ascent
succession	genealogy	subscription	hygiene	assent
remit	pathological	sublet	mentor	stationary
remission	symmetrical	transaction	Celsius	stationery
recede	protoplasm	transition	psychiatrist	descent
recession	synagogue	transfusion	mosaic	dissent

👪 *Family Activity*

Make word search puzzles with your child. You and your child should each draw a puzzle shape, such as a square or a rectangle. On graph paper or lined paper, write four to six words from the lists above to fit inside your puzzle outline. Arrange the words across, down, or diagonally. Fill in the spaces around the list words with other letters to complete your puzzle. Then exchange puzzles. Find and circle the list words in each other's puzzles.

b	n	l	t	o	s	a	h	r
o	a	p	r	o	t	e	i	n
f	g	h	a	m	c	r	k	l
s	e	g	n	o	b	z	u	v
c	m	o	s	a	i	c	a	n
r	e	m	i	t	i	g	l	r
d	c	o	t	z	n	s	g	f

Boletín de noticias de ortografía
para estudiantes y para sus familias

Para comenzar

Este año su hijo o hija está usando el libro *Houghton Mifflin Spelling and Vocabulary,* un programa que fortalece los conocimientos o destrezas más importantes de ortografía y que, al mismo tiempo, amplía el vocabulario mediante una gran variedad de actividades. En cada unidad, un enfoque temático permite a los estudiantes aprender sus palabras para ejercicios de ortografía y además usarlas en contexto.

Listas de palabras

Las siguientes son palabras para ejercicios de ortografía que su hijo o hija ha estado estudiando en las Unidades 1 a 5 del libro *Houghton Mifflin Spelling and Vocabulary.*

UNIDAD 1	UNIDAD 2	UNIDAD 3	UNIDAD 4	UNIDAD 5
commit	syndrome	translate	narcissus	cymbal
commission	sympathy	transit	psyche	symbol
intercede	hydrogen	submerge	odyssey	aisle
intercession	synonym	suburban	Fahrenheit	isle
succeed	protein	substance	czar	ascent
succession	genealogy	subscription	hygiene	assent
remit	pathological	sublet	mentor	stationary
remission	symmetrical	transaction	Celsius	stationery
recede	protoplasm	transition	psychiatrist	descent
recession	synagogue	transfusion	mosaic	dissent

Actividad para la familia

Preparen rompecabezas con su hijo o hija. Cada uno de ustedes debe dibujar un cuadrado o rectángulo por separado, que usarán para preparar un rompecabezas. Dibújenlo en papel cuadriculado o en papel a rayas, y escriban de cuatro a seis palabras de las que aparecen en las listas de arriba dentro de la figura que dibujaron. Escriban las palabras en sentido vertical, horizontal, o diagonal. Rellenen los espacios en blanco que están alrededor de las palabras con otras letras escogidas al azar, hasta completar el rompecabezas. Intercambien los rompecabezas. Encuentren las palabras, y dibujen un circulo alrededor de cada palabra.

b	n	l	t	o	s	a	h	r
o	a	p	r	o	t	e	i	n
f	g	h	a	m	c	r	k	l
s	e	g	n	o	b	z	u	v
c	m	o	s	a	i	c	a	n
r	e	m	i	t	i	g	l	r
d	c	o	t	z	n	s	g	f

27

ALPHABETWISE

SPELLING GAME

Players: any number

You need: paper, pencils

How to play: The object of this game is to make a sentence of words beginning with the letters in a Basic Word. The first player selects a Basic Word and starts a sentence with the first letter in that Basic Word. The next player adds a word beginning with the next letter of the Basic Word, and so on, until the sentence is completed or a player is stumped. Sentences must make some kind of sense.

Example: (*remit*) **R**alph's **e**mpathy **m**ight **i**nsult **T**ed.

The score is based on the number of words in the sentence. Score 1 point for each word. Add another point for each Basic Word used in the sentence. The score for the example above is 6 points: 1 point extra was given for the Basic Word *empathy*. When a player is stumped, no score is given, and that Basic Word is discarded.

When everyone knows how to play, choose teams of at least four players each. Have each team work on a sentence for no more than fifteen minutes. Share the results when time is up. The team with the highest score wins.

Other ways to play this game: You can make the game harder by making sentences in which each letter of the selected Basic Word begins two words in a row. Score 2 points for each word in the sentence and 1 point extra for any Basic Word used.

Example: (*remit*) **R**emember **R**yan, **E**ddie **E**arle's **m**ischievous **m**onkey, **i**s **i**n the **t**ree.

Use: For use with Units 1–5.

Unit 6 Review: Test A

Read each sentence. If one of the underlined words is misspelled, fill in the letter for that word in the answer column. If neither word is misspelled, fill in the letter for none in the answer column.

Sample:
Misha will <u>translate</u> his lines in the <u>choral</u> concert.   none
　　　　a　　　　　　　　　　　b　　　　　　　c

1. Alfred found a map of the <u>isle</u> in the <u>atlas</u>.　none
2. It was easy to <u>commit</u> the <u>odyssey</u> to memory.　none
3. Peasants had to <u>submitt</u> to the law of the <u>czar</u>.　none
4. The <u>substance</u> was found to contain <u>protien</u>.　none
5. A <u>comission</u> was formed to update the <u>transit</u> system.　none
6. Those plants <u>emit</u> healthy <u>quantities</u> of oxygen.　none
7. Pieces of <u>coral</u> were found on top of the <u>submerine</u>.　none
8. Quiet streets are a <u>symbol</u> of a <u>suberban</u> area.　none
9. The <u>pathology</u> department does not use <u>hypnosis</u>.　none
10. Do <u>transform</u> metric degrees to the <u>Farenheit</u> scale.　none
11. We made our <u>acsent</u> to the third floor of the <u>muscum</u>.　none
12. She will <u>intercede</u> for someone she has <u>simpathy</u> for.　none
13. He will <u>submerge</u> through a <u>succession</u> of air locks.　none
14. A <u>corde</u> of <u>synthetic</u> fiber is used in rock climbing.　none
15. The bride carried a <u>narcisus</u> down the <u>aisle</u>.　none
16. Someone has spilled <u>mercury</u> in the <u>subway</u> station.　none
17. The <u>transportation</u> of the <u>hydragen</u> gas was risky.　none
18. Amy hoped to <u>succede</u> in striking the right <u>chord</u>.　none
19. Inhaling a toxic <u>emision</u> may cause that <u>syndrome</u>.　none
20. Dr. Prichard gave his <u>assent</u> to treat the <u>symptom</u>.　none

1. ⓐ ⓑ ⓒ
2. ⓐ ⓑ ⓒ
3. ⓐ ⓑ ⓒ
4. ⓐ ⓑ ⓒ
5. ⓐ ⓑ ⓒ
6. ⓐ ⓑ ⓒ
7. ⓐ ⓑ ⓒ
8. ⓐ ⓑ ⓒ
9. ⓐ ⓑ ⓒ
10. ⓐ ⓑ ⓒ
11. ⓐ ⓑ ⓒ
12. ⓐ ⓑ ⓒ
13. ⓐ ⓑ ⓒ
14. ⓐ ⓑ ⓒ
15. ⓐ ⓑ ⓒ
16. ⓐ ⓑ ⓒ
17. ⓐ ⓑ ⓒ
18. ⓐ ⓑ ⓒ
19. ⓐ ⓑ ⓒ
20. ⓐ ⓑ ⓒ

Name _____

Unit 6 Review: Test B

Read each sentence. If one of the underlined words is misspelled, fill in the letter for that word in the answer column. If neither word is misspelled, fill in the letter for none in the answer column.

Sample:

Be jovial when you canvas the neighborhood.   none
    a   b   c

1. Please remit a check to renew your subscription.   none
    a   b   c
  1. ⓐ ⓑ ©
2. The psychietrist felt empathy for her patient.   none
  2. ⓐ ⓑ ©
3. It was pathetic to watch the captain consede defeat.   none
  3. ⓐ ⓑ ©
4. Jo had to transmit the message on plain stationary.   none
  4. ⓐ ⓑ ©
5. The transaction was made at the building site.   none
  5. ⓐ ⓑ ©
6. The subbtitle of May's book referred to her mentor.   none
  6. ⓐ ⓑ ©
7. In the first faze, they will subdivide the lot.   none
  7. ⓐ ⓑ ©
8. Make a concession to buy him a stationery bicycle.   none
  8. ⓐ ⓑ ©
9. A symmetrical pattern of mosiac tiles lined the pool.   none
  9. ⓐ ⓑ ©
10. The subtotal showed the omission of printing costs.   none
  10. ⓐ ⓑ ©
11. A transfusion involves the transmision of fluids.   none
  11. ⓐ ⓑ ©
12. With proper oral hygeine, gums should not recede.   none
  12. ⓐ ⓑ ©
13. Tom felt apathy for the fait of the prisoner.   none
  13. ⓐ ⓑ ©
14. A galvanized railing helped us in our descent.   none
  14. ⓐ ⓑ ©
15. His pathological symptoms did not phaze his doctor.   none
  15. ⓐ ⓑ ©
16. A canvas sheet covered some chairs in the synagogue.   none
  16. ⓐ ⓑ ©
17. Nora will site the scientist Celsius in her report.   none
  17. ⓐ ⓑ ©
18. The fury of the storm began to subbside.   none
  18. ⓐ ⓑ ©
19. The family geneology was found on transparent paper.   none
  19. ⓐ ⓑ ©
20. The syndicat will omit a name from its membership.   none
  20. ⓐ ⓑ ©

Unit 6 Review: Test C

Read each sentence. If one of the underlined words is misspelled, fill in the letter for that word in the answer column. If neither word is misspelled, fill in the letter for <u>none</u> in the answer column.

Sample:

The <u>eppicure</u> felt <u>pathos</u> in the soup line.   <u>none</u>
      a   **b**   **c**

ANSWERS
● ⓑ ⓒ

1. The <u>iridescent</u> gem weighed one <u>carat</u>.   <u>none</u>
         a   **b**   **c**
   1. ⓐ ⓑ ⓒ

2. The famous <u>thespien</u> played the film's <u>protagonist</u>.   <u>none</u>
              a   **b**   **c**
   2. ⓐ ⓑ ⓒ

3. Sal's <u>nemesis</u> wanted a <u>revacation</u> of the challenge.   <u>none</u>
          a   **b**   **c**
   3. ⓐ ⓑ ⓒ

4. Because of <u>provacation</u>, Mel will <u>revoke</u> his offer.   <u>none</u>
              a   **b**   **c**
   4. ⓐ ⓑ ⓒ

5. Try to <u>syncronize</u> all <u>subsequent</u> trips with us.   <u>none</u>
           a   **b**   **c**
   5. ⓐ ⓑ ⓒ

6. A tight shoe may give you a <u>gargantuan</u> <u>callous</u>.   <u>none</u>
                               a   **b**   **c**
   6. ⓐ ⓑ ⓒ

7. Ralph's <u>synthesis</u> into the <u>subculture</u> was not easy.   <u>none</u>
            a   **b**   **c**
   7. ⓐ ⓑ ⓒ

8. He tried to <u>provoke</u> a memory from her <u>subconcious</u>.   <u>none</u>
               a   **b**   **c**
   8. ⓐ ⓑ ⓒ

9. The <u>transient</u> was treated with <u>callus</u> indifference.   <u>none</u>
        a   **b**   **c**
   9. ⓐ ⓑ ⓒ

10. <u>Protacol</u> dictates that you use the <u>caret</u> as shown.   <u>none</u>
    a   **b**   **c**
    10. ⓐ ⓑ ⓒ

Prewriting Ideas: Personal Narrative

Choosing a Topic   Listed below are some topics that one student thought of for writing a story about a personal experience. What experiences of your own do they make you think of?

On the lines below *My Five Ideas*, list five funny, scary, or unforgettable experiences that you have had. Which ones do you remember most clearly? Which ones would your readers enjoy most? Circle the topic that you would like to write about.

Ideas for Writing

The Time I Was the Most Frightened
The Time I Breathed a Sigh of Relief
My Last Visit to the Doctor
The Time I Performed Music for an
   Audience
The Time I Saw a New Side of My Friend
The Biggest Risk I Ever Took
The Baby-sitting Job I Will Never Forget
The Time I Was Mistaken for Someone
   Famous

My Five Ideas

1. _____

2. _____

3. _____

4. _____

5. _____

Exploring Your Topic   Use the motion picture clapsticks below to plan your personal narrative. Write the topic you chose on the line above the clapsticks. Then answer the question What happens? by filling in the top bar of each clapstick with a different event in the order in which it will occur. On the bottom part of each clapstick, write details that will help you show the event to your readers.

Topic: _____

1. event / details

2. event / details

3. event / details

4. event / details

Houghton Mifflin Spelling and Vocabulary. Copyright © Houghton Mifflin Company. All rights reserved.

PRACTICE A
Absorbed Prefixes

Summing Up

The prefixes *ad-*, *in-*, and *con-* can be **absorbed prefixes**.

Basic Words
1. communication
2. announcer
3. commentary
4. accent
5. colleague
6. apparent
7. allude
8. aggressive
9. immerse
10. illusion

Absorb the Prefixes **1–9.** When the prefix in each puddle is added to the scrambled letters in each sponge, the prefix is absorbed to form a Basic Word. Unscramble the letters, and add the prefix to write a Basic Word. Then underline the letter that changes in the prefix.

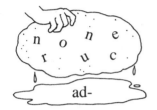
ad-

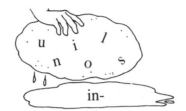
in-

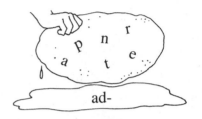
ad-

1. _____

2. _____

3. _____

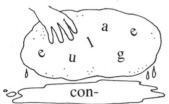
con-

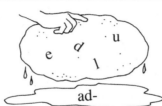
ad-

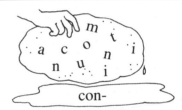
con-

4. _____

5. _____

6. _____

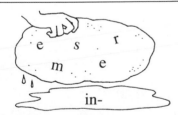
in-

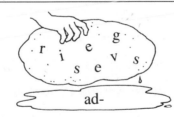
ad-

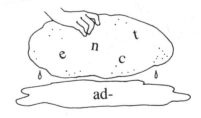
ad-

7. _____

8. _____

9. _____

Analogies Write the Basic Word that completes each analogy.

10. inform : tell :: hint : ____

11. story : narrator :: sports event : ____

12. sport : teammate :: work : ____

13. newspaper : editorial :: television : ____

14. rise : ascend :: submerge : ____

15. truth : reality :: deception : ____

16. clear : transparent :: obvious : ____

10. _____

11. _____

12. _____

13. _____

14. _____

15. _____

16. _____

Skill: Students will practice spelling words with absorbed prefixes for *ad-*, *in-*, and *con-*.

Home Use: Help your child practice the spelling words by having him or her complete the activities on this page. Check the completed page, and have your child practice saying and spelling any misspelled words.

Basic Words
1. communication
2. announcer
3. commentary
4. accent
5. colleague
6. apparent
7. allude
8. aggressive
9. immerse
10. illusion
11. collaborate
12. appliance
13. collision
14. accessory
15. immaculate
16. accumulate
17. allegiance
18. aggravate
19. collapse
20. illuminate

PRACTICE B
Absorbed Prefixes

Prefix Switch   Each word below begins with one of these prefixes: *re-, con-, inter-, trans-,* or *pro-*. Circle the prefix in each word. Then replace each prefix with a different prefix to form a Basic Word. Write each Basic Word.

1. recent
2. transparent
3. relapse
4. denouncer

5. interlude
6. collusion
7. compliance
8. progressive

1. _____   5. _____

2. _____   6. _____

3. _____   7. _____

4. _____   8. _____

Headline Completion   Write the Basic Word that completes each headline. Capitalize each word.

Cape Canaveral Reestablishes __(9)__ with Spacecraft

New Street Sweepers Make Roads __(10)__

Auction House Sells Antique Dress and __(11)__ for $1,000,000

Icy Roads Cause __(12)__ Near Bridge

Television Newscaster Broadcasts Controversial __(13)__

Train Staff Strike over Dismissal of __(14)__

Escape Artist Plans to __(15)__ Himself in Water for Two Days

Billionaire Shows Others How to __(16)__ Wealth

New Streetlights __(17)__ the City

General Crossfire Pledges __(18)__ to Republic of Oathia

Border Disputes __(19)__ Tension Between Neighboring States

Boris Vetlan and Buck Brady __(20)__ on New Musical

9. _____   13. _____   17. _____

10. _____   14. _____   18. _____

11. _____   15. _____   19. _____

12. _____   16. _____   20. _____

Skill: Students will practice spelling words with absorbed prefixes for *ad-, in-,* and *con-*.

Home Use: Help your child practice the spelling words by having him or her complete the activities on this page. Check the completed page, and have your child practice saying and spelling any misspelled words.

PRACTICE C
Absorbed Prefixes

Two-Step Crosswords   Fill in all the Challenge and Vocabulary Words in the puzzle. (There is only one way to arrange them.) Then write a short clue for each word.

Challenge Words
1. irrelevant
2. corroborate
3. commemorate
4. alliteration
5. commiserate
Theme Vocabulary
6. disc jockey
7. ad-lib
8. identification
9. prerecorded
10. cartridge
11. antenna
12. static
13. technician

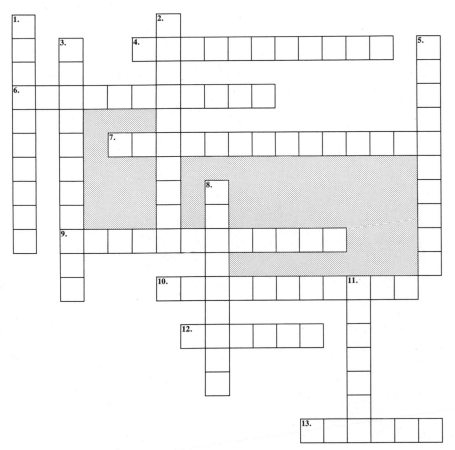

Across

4. _____

6. _____

7. _____

9. _____

10. _____

12. _____

13. _____

Down

1. _____

2. _____

3. _____

5. _____

8. _____

11. _____

Now write the Vocabulary Word that is written as two separate words.   14. _____

Skill: Students will practice spelling words with absorbed prefixes for *ad-*, *in-*, and *con-* and words related to the theme of radio broadcasting.

Home Use: Help your child practice the spelling words by having him or her complete the activities on this page. Check the completed page, and have your child practice saying and spelling any misspelled words.

Unit 7 Test: Absorbed Prefixes

Each item below gives four possible spellings of a word. Fill in the letter beside the correct spelling.

Sample:
- ⓐ apropriate
- ● appropriate
- ⓒ appropreate
- ⓓ appropriat

1. ⓐ communication
   ⓑ comunication
   ⓒ commumication
   ⓓ communacation

2. ⓐ aksent
   ⓑ akcent
   ⓒ accent
   ⓓ acsent

3. ⓐ aggressive
   ⓑ agressive
   ⓒ aggresive
   ⓓ agresive

4. ⓐ allude
   ⓑ alude
   ⓒ allood
   ⓓ alloode

5. ⓐ anouncer
   ⓑ announcer
   ⓒ annowncer
   ⓓ announser

6. ⓐ ilusion
   ⓑ ellusion
   ⓒ illussion
   ⓓ illusion

7. ⓐ aparent
   ⓑ apparant
   ⓒ aparrent
   ⓓ apparent

8. ⓐ commentery
   ⓑ comentary
   ⓒ commentary
   ⓓ comentairy

9. ⓐ colleag
   ⓑ coleague
   ⓒ colleague
   ⓓ coleag

10. ⓐ imerse
    ⓑ immerse
    ⓒ imerce
    ⓓ immerce

11. ⓐ apliance
    ⓑ appliance
    ⓒ applience
    ⓓ applyance

12. ⓐ acessory
    ⓑ accesory
    ⓒ accessory
    ⓓ accessery

13. ⓐ acumulate
    ⓑ acummulate
    ⓒ accummulate
    ⓓ accumulate

14. ⓐ iluminate
    ⓑ illuminate
    ⓒ illumenate
    ⓓ ilumenate

15. ⓐ immaculate
    ⓑ imaculate
    ⓒ immaculit
    ⓓ imaculat

16. ⓐ collappse
    ⓑ colapse
    ⓒ collapse
    ⓓ cullapse

17. ⓐ aggravate
    ⓑ agravate
    ⓒ aggrevate
    ⓓ aggrivate

18. ⓐ collaborrate
    ⓑ colaborate
    ⓒ collaborate
    ⓓ collaberate

19. ⓐ collision
    ⓑ colision
    ⓒ collission
    ⓓ collesion

20. ⓐ alegiance
    ⓑ alleggiance
    ⓒ allegience
    ⓓ allegiance

PRACTICE A
Greek Word Parts II

Summing Up
Some English words contain the Greek word parts *log* and *logy*.

Basic Words
1. chronology
2. terminology
3. catalog
4. technology
5. geology
6. zoology
7. logic
8. biology
9. apology
10. psychology

Word Riddles   Write the Basic Word that fits each clue.
1. This log helps you understand all living things.
2. This log teaches you about animals.
3. This log helps you understand rocks.
4. This log is full of regret.
5. This log will help you understand the mind.
6. This log gives you the words you need for a particular trade, science, or art.
7. This log is found in industry.
8. This log is a list.
9. This log is very rational.
10. This log always tells everything in order.

1. _____   6. _____

2. _____   7. _____

3. _____   8. _____

4. _____   9. _____

5. _____   10. _____

Now circle the Basic Words in which *log* or *logy* relate to the meaning "speech" or "reason." Underline the Basic Words in which *log* or *logy* relate to the meaning "science or study of."

Basic Word Mix-Up   Unscramble and write the Basic Word in each phrase.
11. a seed tolacag
12. the latest cogytholen
13. a sincere pogaloy
14. unquestionable golic
15. the study of loogyeg
16. proper trogonimely
17. the gryocholno of events
18. a yibloog class
19. child yogolchyps
20. a course in golzoyo

11. _____   15. _____

12. _____   16. _____

13. _____   17. _____   19. _____

14. _____   18. _____   20. _____

Skill: Students will practice spelling words with the Greek word parts *log* and *logy*.

Home Use: Help your child practice the spelling words by having him or her complete the activities on this page. Check the completed page, and have your child practice saying and spelling any misspelled words.

Basic Words
1. chronology
2. terminology
3. catalog
4. technology
5. geology
6. zoology
7. logic
8. biology
9. apology
10. psychology
11. dialogue
12. sociology
13. ecology
14. meteorology
15. theology
16. anthology
17. astrology
18. analogy
19. mythology
20. trilogy

PRACTICE B
Greek Word Parts II

Word Search   **1–10.** Find and circle ten Basic Words hidden in the puzzle. The words may appear horizontally, vertically, or diagonally. Then write the Basic Words.

```
d  l  a  a  n  a  l  o  g  y  n  b  d  o  i  f  r  l  t
i  d  a  b  s  u  t  h  e  s  o  c  i  o  l  o  g  y  e
a  w  y  e  o  t  n  f  t  a  g  t  h  o  e  w  a  l  r
l  l  m  f  t  l  r  e  f  s  e  h  e  a  l  n  l  d  m
o  e  i  e  n  h  t  o  e  p  o  r  o  e  v  o  r  b  i
g  i  a  d  c  l  u  s  l  t  l  g  o  o  g  s  g  h  n
u  l  y  l  g  o  e  e  l  o  o  a  s  y  i  t  r  y  o
e  b  l  t  y  a  l  b  h  e  g  l  t  i  d  e  u  e  l
e  j  a  d  u  e  t  o  i  f  y  y  u  l  r  a  l  f  o
a  m  m  e  e  s  h  c  g  r  t  a  s  n  a  e  w  r  g
t  e  c  h  n  o  l  o  g  y  a  n  t  r  i  l  o  g  y
```

1. _____   6. _____

2. _____   7. _____

3. _____   8. _____

4. _____   9. _____

5. _____   10. _____

Proofreading   **11–20.** Find and cross out ten misspelled Basic Words in this book review. Then write each word correctly.

BOOK NEWS

This season's catalogg from Cornell Publishing features Warner Workman's latest book, *Any Job Will Do,* an anthalogy of his earlier essays. Workman's previous accounts of trying to succeed in the fields of zoologie, pschyology, and meterology have been combined in this biography that describes his experiences in several other occupations as well.

Though Workman's job experiences are amusing, it is difficult to follow his job history because the book's chronalogy is so confusing. Also confusing are new essays that are included in the book for no apparent reason. In an essay on thelogy, Workman's theory lacks logick and wavers between mythalogy and astrology. Finally, Workman ends the book with scientific terminology when an apolagy to the reader would be more in order!

11. _____

12. _____

13. _____

14. _____

15. _____

16. _____

17. _____

18. _____

19. _____

20. _____

Skill: Students will practice spelling words with the Greek word parts *log* and *logy.*

Home Use: Help your child practice the spelling words by having him or her complete the activities on this page. Check the completed page, and have your child practice saying and spelling any misspelled words.

PRACTICE C
Greek Word Parts II

Word Change Follow the directions below to change Challenge or Vocabulary Words to other words. You may want to use a class dictionary.

1–2. Write the Challenge Word whose prefix means "before." Then change the prefix to write a word that names a long speech delivered by one actor on stage.

3–4. Write the Vocabulary Word that is a plural noun. Then replace the first three letters with one consonant to write a plural noun that means "information."

5–6. Write the Challenge Word that has a prefix meaning "ancient." Then change the prefix to write a word that means the study of animals.

7–8. Write the Vocabulary Word that means "a trip made by an organization." Then drop the suffix and add a vowel to write a word that means "to speed the progress of."

9–10. Write the Challenge Word that has a prefix meaning "on, upon, near, toward, or over." Then change the prefix to write a word that means "a discussion or conversation."

11–12. Write the Challenge Word that is a plural noun. Then change the Greek word part to write a word that means "a collection or set of numerical information."

13–14. Write the Challenge Word that means "the origin and development of a word." Then add a consonant and change the *y* to a vowel to write a word that means "the scientific study of insects."

15–16. Write a Vocabulary Word that means "a tool used in doing a task." Then change the prefix to write a word that means "something that completes."

Challenge Words
1. archaeology
2. logistics
3. etymology
4. prologue
5. epilogue
Theme Vocabulary
6. expedition
7. excavate
8. civilization
9. strata
10. relic
11. implement
12. shard
13. classification

1. _____

2. _____

3. _____

4. _____

5. _____

6. _____

7. _____

8. _____

9. _____

10. _____

11. _____

12. _____

13. _____

14. _____

15. _____

16. _____

Stop the Presses! Imagine that you are a journalist on an archaeological expedition. On the back of this paper, write at least three headlines that could accompany stories about your expedition. Use the Vocabulary Words *civilization*, *relic*, *shard*, *excavate*, and *classification*. Then write the first sentence of the news story that would follow each headline. Capitalize the first, last, and each important word in each headline.

Skill: Students will practice spelling words with the Greek word parts *log* and *logy* and words related to the theme of archaeology.

Home Use: Help your child practice the spelling words by having him or her complete the activities on this page. Check the completed page, and have your child practice saying and spelling any misspelled words.

Unit 8 Test: Greek Word Parts II

Find the correctly spelled word to complete each phrase. Fill in the letter beside the correct spelling.

Sample:

a _____ of glass
- ⓐ fraggment
- ⓑ fragmint
- ● fragment
- ⓓ fragmment

---

1. scientific _____
   - ⓐ terminalogy
   - ⓑ terminology
   - ⓒ termminology
   - ⓓ terminnology

2. to accept an _____
   - ⓐ apollogy
   - ⓑ appology
   - ⓒ apology
   - ⓓ appoligy

3. using _____
   - ⓐ logic
   - ⓑ loggic
   - ⓒ logick
   - ⓓ logik

4. an item in the _____
   - ⓐ catilog
   - ⓑ catalogg
   - ⓒ catilogue
   - ⓓ catalog

5. electronics _____
   - ⓐ tecknology
   - ⓑ technology
   - ⓒ technoligy
   - ⓓ tecnology

6. a _____ of events
   - ⓐ cronology
   - ⓑ chronnology
   - ⓒ chronology
   - ⓓ cronnology

7. the study of _____
   - ⓐ sychology
   - ⓑ psichology
   - ⓒ psychology
   - ⓓ psycology

8. a _____ class
   - ⓐ biology
   - ⓑ biulogy
   - ⓒ bioligy
   - ⓓ biologie

9. a professor of _____
   - ⓐ geologie
   - ⓑ geology
   - ⓒ geeology
   - ⓓ geoligy

10. to learn about _____
    - ⓐ zology
    - ⓑ zooology
    - ⓒ zooligy
    - ⓓ zoology

11. books in a _____
    - ⓐ trilogy
    - ⓑ trilogie
    - ⓒ trillogy
    - ⓓ triligy

12. to draw an _____
    - ⓐ analogy
    - ⓑ anallogy
    - ⓒ anelogy
    - ⓓ annalogy

13. the study of _____
    - ⓐ meterology
    - ⓑ meteorology
    - ⓒ meteoralogy
    - ⓓ meteorrology

14. a telephone _____
    - ⓐ dialogg
    - ⓑ dialoge
    - ⓒ diallog
    - ⓓ dialogue

15. to read books on _____
    - ⓐ theollogy
    - ⓑ theologie
    - ⓒ theeology
    - ⓓ theology

16. to read from an _____
    - ⓐ anthollogy
    - ⓑ annthology
    - ⓒ anthology
    - ⓓ enthology

17. ancient Greek _____
    - ⓐ mythology
    - ⓑ mythollogy
    - ⓒ mitholigy
    - ⓓ mythologie

18. the _____ of the ocean
    - ⓐ ecology
    - ⓑ ekology
    - ⓒ eecology
    - ⓓ ecollogy

19. an article on _____
    - ⓐ astralogy
    - ⓑ astrollogy
    - ⓒ astrology
    - ⓓ astrallogy

20. a _____ course
    - ⓐ sosiology
    - ⓑ sociology
    - ⓒ sociollogy
    - ⓓ socialogy

PRACTICE A
Latin Prefixes II

Basic Words
1. intramural
2. interstate
3. supervise
4. interference
5. intercept
6. counteract
7. intermediate
8. superlative
9. counterfeit
10. superficial

Summing Up

Inter-, intra-, super-, and *counter-* are common Latin prefixes.

Latin Prefix Prix   There are three bicycle races in the Latin Prefix Prix. They are the Super Speed, the Counter Contest, and the Inter/Intra Sprint. Determine which Basic Word placed first, second, etc., in each race by writing each word in alphabetical order under the race named for its prefix.

Super Speed

1. _____
2. _____
3. _____

Counter Contest

4. _____
5. _____

Inter/Intra Sprint

6. _____
7. _____
8. _____
9. _____
10. _____

Silly Book Titles   Write a Basic Word to complete each silly title. Remember to capitalize each word.

11. *How to Identify _____ Cash* by Bill Iz Fake
12. *Conversational German: _____ Level* by U. Ken Learn
13. *How to _____ the Effects of Sunburn* by Sonny Tan Lotion
14. *The History of the _____ Highway System* by Ty Urd Driver
15. *The Catskill College _____ Athletic Program* by Kip Fitt
16. *How to Treat _____ Wounds* by I. Ama Doctor
17. *Penalties for _____: A Referee's Handbook* by Les Playfair
18. *How to _____ the Ball* by Stan Dintheway
19. *Fabulous Main Courses and _____ Desserts* by Sue Perior Cook
20. *How to _____ Children* by I. Canteach

11. _____
12. _____
13. _____

14. _____
15. _____
16. _____

17. _____
18. _____
19. _____
20. _____

Skill: Students will practice spelling words with the Latin prefixes *inter-, intra-, super-,* and *counter-*.

Home Use: Help your child practice the spelling words by having him or her complete the activities on this page. Check the completed page, and have your child practice saying and spelling any misspelled words.

Basic Words
1. intramural
2. interstate
3. supervise
4. interference
5. intercept
6. counteract
7. intermediate
8. superlative
9. counterfeit
10. superficial
11. counterpart
12. intervention
13. intersection
14. intrastate
15. supermarket
16. interchangeable
17. superintendent
18. counterclockwise
19. interpret
20. intravenous

PRACTICE B
Latin Prefixes II

Synonym/Antonym **1–9.** Write the Basic Word that is a synonym for or an antonym of the clue word. Then circle *synonym* or *antonym* to show how the Basic Word and the clue word are related.

Clue Word	Basic Word	Synonym or Antonym
middle	1. _____	synonym antonym
unique	2. _____	synonym antonym
authentic	3. _____	synonym antonym
crossroads	4. _____	synonym antonym
deep	5. _____	synonym antonym
oversee	6. _____	synonym antonym
obstruction	7. _____	synonym antonym
support	8. _____	synonym antonym
explain	9. _____	synonym antonym

Proofreading **10–20.** Find and cross out eleven misspelled Basic Words in this sportscast. Then write each word correctly.

10. _____

11. _____

12. _____

13. _____

14. _____

15. _____

16. _____

17. _____

18. _____

19. _____

20. _____

Greetings, sports fans! The Babbleton Baboons finally left their intrestate league to cross the state border for the football championships. As the head coach was ill, the school superintendant asked Coach Ted Field to cancel his intamural college coaching activities to supervise the team. As it turned out, he more than matched the brilliant coaching of his countrapart, the Germville Gerbils' coach Bob Trophy.

The Baboons began badly. After losing their way in a supermarket parking lot, they took the wrong turn at an intersection on the interrstate near the state border and arrived late. In the first two quarters the Gerbils belted the Baboons, who were not able to intersept once.

In the second half the Baboons became brutal after a disagreement prompted the referee's intrevention. Coach Field's countarclockwise play exhausted the Gerbils, leaving them in need of intravenus injections of spirit. The Baboons bashed the Gerbils in the final minutes, closing with a score of Baboons 410, Gerbils 35. What a superlativ bunch of Baboons!

42

Skill: Students will practice spelling words with the Latin prefixes *inter-, intra-, super-,* and *counter-.*

Home Use: Help your child practice the spelling words by having him or her complete the activities on this page. Check the completed page, and have your child practice saying and spelling any misspelled words.

PRACTICE C
Latin Prefixes II

Challenge Words
1. interscholastic
2. superfluous
3. counterproductive
4. interrogate
5. intersperse

Theme Vocabulary
6. recreational
7. participant
8. competition
9. championship
10. varsity
11. scrimmage
12. defensive
13. offense

Word Substitution   Each pair of sentences includes an underlined word or phrase that is a synonym or a definition for a Challenge or Vocabulary Word. Write the Challenge or Vocabulary Word. Then write the letter of the sentence in which the Challenge or Vocabulary Word could be used.

1. **a.** The Westlake High School football team had a <u>practice game</u> before they played their first game of the season.
   b. Would you like to play a <u>practice game</u> of chess?
2. **a.** Sheila will <u>scatter</u> the birdseed on the ground.
   b. Let's <u>scatter</u> violets among the daffodils in the garden.
3. **a.** The police sergeant will <u>question</u> the suspect.
   b. The lost tourist will <u>question</u> the bus driver to get directions to the museum.
4. **a.** Manuel wished that he had brought <u>extra</u> food on the hike.
   b. Bring only necessities on the hike and nothing <u>extra</u>.
5. **a.** The <u>struggle</u> for the championship title was fierce.
   b. It was a <u>struggle</u> for Elena to solve the problem.
6. **a.** The farming technique had a <u>harmful</u> effect on the crops.
   b. Eating an imbalanced diet can be <u>harmful</u> to your health.
7. **a.** The Springfield Centaurs are the <u>best</u> team in the state.
   b. Our school's <u>best</u> team won top honors in the swim meet.
8. **a.** The semifinalists will compete in the <u>contest</u> next week.
   b. Jody wrote an essay on the application for the <u>contest</u>.

1. _____   4. _____   7. _____

2. _____   5. _____   8. _____

3. _____   6. _____

Word Relatives   Write a Challenge or Vocabulary Word and a word related in spelling and meaning to the Challenge or Vocabulary Word to complete each sentence. You may want to use a class dictionary.

9–10. The rival team took ____ when the captain of our soccer team was named the best ____ player in the state.
11–12. The lawyer's question made the ____ extremely ____ .
13–14. Every ____ in the tournament will ____ in the parade.
15–16. The park has many ____ facilities for all kinds of ____ .
17–18. Several ____ from different universities competed in an ____ math contest.
19–20. Clayton, a tough ____ , won the swimming ____ .

13. _____

14. _____

15. _____

16. _____

17. _____

18. _____

9. _____   11. _____   19. _____

10. _____   12. _____   20. _____

Skill: Students will practice spelling words with the Latin prefixes *inter-, intra-, super-,* and *counter-* and words related to the theme of intramural sports.

Home Use: Help your child practice the spelling words by having him or her complete the activities on this page. Check the completed page, and have your child practice saying and spelling any misspelled words.

Unit 9 Test: Latin Prefixes II

Each item below gives four possible spellings of a word. Fill in the letter beside the correct spelling.

Sample:
- ● athletic
- ⓑ athaletic
- ⓒ atheletic
- ⓓ athlettic

1. ⓐ interrstate
   ⓑ interstate
   ⓒ enterstate
   ⓓ intarstate

2. ⓐ interfeerence
   ⓑ interference
   ⓒ interferense
   ⓓ interrference

3. ⓐ counteracte
   ⓑ cownteract
   ⓒ counteract
   ⓓ counterract

4. ⓐ superlative
   ⓑ superllative
   ⓒ supperlative
   ⓓ superletive

5. ⓐ superfishal
   ⓑ superficial
   ⓒ sooperficial
   ⓓ suparficial

6. ⓐ intramural
   ⓑ interamural
   ⓒ interrmural
   ⓓ intramurel

7. ⓐ soopervise
   ⓑ superrvise
   ⓒ supervize
   ⓓ supervise

8. ⓐ interrcept
   ⓑ intersept
   ⓒ intercept
   ⓓ intircept

9. ⓐ intirmediate
   ⓑ intermmediate
   ⓒ interrmediate
   ⓓ intermediate

10. ⓐ counterfeit
    ⓑ counterfiet
    ⓒ counterfit
    ⓓ counterfet

11. ⓐ intervenntion
    ⓑ interventon
    ⓒ interrvention
    ⓓ intervention

12. ⓐ entrastate
    ⓑ intrestate
    ⓒ intrastate
    ⓓ intarstate

13. ⓐ interchangable
    ⓑ interrchangable
    ⓒ interrchangeable
    ⓓ interchangeable

14. ⓐ conterclockwise
    ⓑ counterclockwise
    ⓒ counter-clockwise
    ⓓ counter-clock-wise

15. ⓐ intervenous
    ⓑ intravenus
    ⓒ intravenous
    ⓓ intervenus

16. ⓐ counnterpart
    ⓑ counterparrt
    ⓒ counterpart
    ⓓ counterrpart

17. ⓐ intersection
    ⓑ interrsection
    ⓒ inter-section
    ⓓ interssection

18. ⓐ super-market
    ⓑ supermarket
    ⓒ supermarkett
    ⓓ supermarkette

19. ⓐ superinntendent
    ⓑ superintendant
    ⓒ superentendent
    ⓓ superintendent

20. ⓐ interpret
    ⓑ interprette
    ⓒ interrpret
    ⓓ interrprett

PRACTICE A
Words from Spanish

Basic Words
1. coyote
2. mesa
3. savanna
4. adobe
5. pueblo
6. stampede
7. lariat
8. bronco
9. barbecue
10. tornado

Summing Up
Many English words are borrowed from Spanish.

Word Chain   Complete the word chain by writing the Basic Word that matches each definition.

1. a small, wild horse
2. to rush suddenly
3. a lasso
4. a sun-dried brick
5. a small plateau
6. a flat-roofed dwelling
7. a flat, treeless grassland
8. a wolflike animal
9. a cyclone
10. a grill for roasting meat

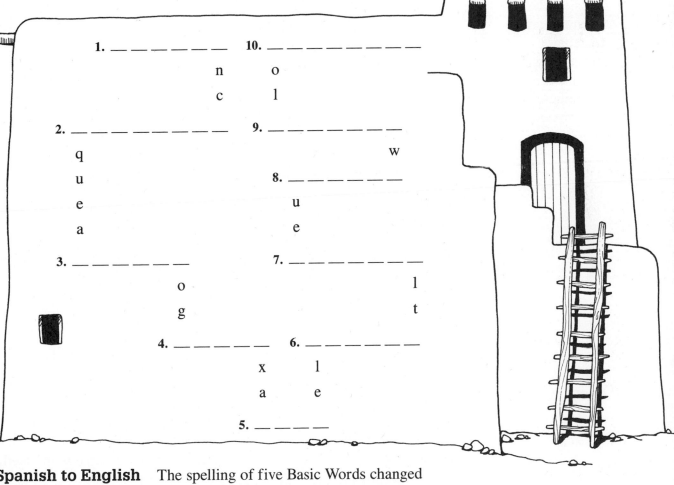

1. _ _ _ _ _ _   10. _ _ _ _ _ _ _
     n   o
     c   l

2. _ _ _ _ _ _   9. _ _ _ _ _ _ _
q   w
u
e   8. _ _ _ _ _ _
a   u
                      e

3. _ _ _ _ _ _   7. _ _ _ _ _ _
     o   l
     g   t

4. _ _ _ _ _   6. _ _ _ _ _ _
    x   l
    a   e

5. _ _ _ _ _

Spanish to English   The spelling of five Basic Words changed slightly when they were borrowed from Spanish. Write the Basic Words that match the Spanish spellings below.

11. tronada   13. estampida   15. la reata
12. zavana   14. barbacoa

13. _____

14. _____

11. _____   12. _____   15. _____

Skill: Students will practice spelling words that are borrowed from Spanish.

Home Use: Help your child practice the spelling words by having him or her complete the activities on this page. Check the completed page, and have your child practice saying and spelling any misspelled words.

PRACTICE B
Words from Spanish

Basic Words
1. coyote
2. mesa
3. savanna
4. adobe
5. pueblo
6. stampede
7. lariat
8. bronco
9. barbecue
10. tornado
11. indigo
12. jaguar
13. mosquito
14. sierra
15. avocado
16. alfalfa
17. cafeteria
18. mascara
19. pimento
20. armada

Crossword Puzzle   Complete the puzzle by writing the Basic Word that fits each clue.

Across
1. a meal for a cow
4. a mild pepper
5. a running herd of horses
7. a rope with a loop
11. a soft, green fruit
17. a tropical cat
18. a twister
19. a wild horse
20. a type of apartment building found in the Southwest

Down
2. clay used for building
3. eyelash darkener
6. a hill without a peak
8. a night sky color
9. a stinging insect
10. a howling predator
12. a mountain range with "teeth"
13. a mighty meadow
14. an army at sea
15. a place with tables and trays
16. a backyard grill

Skill: Students will practice spelling words that are borrowed from Spanish.

Home Use: Help your child practice the spelling words by having him or her complete the activities on this page. Check the completed page, and have your child practice saying and spelling any misspelled words.

PRACTICE C
Words from Spanish

Word Categories Cross out the word that does not belong in each group. Then write the Challenge or Vocabulary Word that belongs with each group. You may want to use a class dictionary.

1. fleet, yacht, armada
2. traitor, outlaw, nonconformist
3. cactus, tumbleweed, prickly pear
4. weasel, eel, elephant
5. praying mantis, black widow, tarantula
6. plateau, mountain, mesa
7. visitor, fan, admirer
8. mute, silent, rude
9. boastfulness, defiance, enthusiastic
10. canyon, cave, ravine

Challenge Words
1. bravado
2. renegade
3. incommunicado
4. flotilla
5. aficionado

Theme Vocabulary
6. mesquite
7. butte
8. scorpion
9. saguaro
10. gulch
11. armadillo
12. yucca
13. piñon

1. _____   6. _____

2. _____   7. _____

3. _____   8. _____

4. _____   9. _____

5. _____   10. _____

It Adds Up The code below has been used to determine the values of eight Challenge or Vocabulary Words. The vowels are each worth 1¢, 2¢, 3¢, 4¢, or 5¢, but not in that order. Use the code to help you figure out and write the eight words. (Hint: The number of letters in each word is given in parentheses.) Then figure out and write the value of each vowel in the code box.

CODE:	__	__	__	__	__	10¢	15¢	20¢	25¢	30¢	35¢	40¢
LETTER:	a	e	i	o	u	b	c	d	f	g	h	l

CODE:	45¢	50¢	75¢	$1.00	$1.50	$2.00	$3.00	$4.00	$5.00
LETTER:	m	n	p	q	r	s	t	v	y

11. $5.89 (7)   **14.** $6.17 (5)   **17.** $3.92 (7)
12. $6.57 (8)   **15.** $5.35 (5)   **18.** $1.81 (5)
13. $2.64 (8)   **16.** $1.23 (5)

11. _____   13. _____   15. _____

12. _____   14. _____   16. _____

17. _____

18. _____

Skill: Students will practice spelling words that are borrowed from Spanish and words related to the theme of the American Southwest.

Home Use: Help your child practice the spelling words by having him or her complete the activities on this page. Check the completed page, and have your child practice saying and spelling any misspelled words.

Unit 10 Test: Words from Spanish

Find the correctly spelled word to complete each phrase. Fill in the letter beside the correct spelling.

Sample:

a string ____
- (a) hamock
- (c) hammuck
- ● hammock
- (d) hamuck

---

1. invitation to a ____
- (a) barbacue
- (c) barbeque
- (b) barbicue
- (d) barbecue

2. to swing a ____
- (a) lariet
- (c) larriet
- (b) larriat
- (d) lariat

3. trees of the ____
- (a) savana
- (c) savvana
- (b) savanna
- (d) savannuh

4. atop the ____
- (a) maisa
- (c) mesa
- (b) masa
- (d) maysa

5. living in the ____
- (a) pweblo
- (c) pwebloh
- (b) puebblo
- (d) pueblo

6. a bucking ____
- (a) bronco
- (c) bronko
- (b) bronkoh
- (d) brawnco

7. a howling ____
- (a) kiyote
- (c) coyotee
- (b) coyote
- (d) kiotee

8. destruction caused by a ____
- (a) tornado
- (c) torrnado
- (b) tornadoh
- (d) tornaydo

9. a ____ of cattle
- (a) stampeed
- (c) stampede
- (b) stampeede
- (d) stammpede

10. bricks of ____
- (a) adobe
- (c) adobie
- (b) adobee
- (d) addobe

11. an ____ sprout
- (a) allfalfa
- (c) alfalfa
- (b) alphalfa
- (d) alfalpha

12. the color ____
- (a) inndigo
- (c) indiggo
- (b) indigo
- (d) inndigo

13. to eat in a ____
- (a) cafeteria
- (c) cafateria
- (b) caffeteria
- (d) cafeteeria

14. a bite from a ____
- (a) musquito
- (c) moskito
- (b) moskeeto
- (d) mosquito

15. a ____ stalking its prey
- (a) jagwar
- (c) jaggwar
- (b) jaguarr
- (d) jaguar

16. to apply ____
- (a) mascara
- (c) masscara
- (b) maskara
- (d) mascarra

17. a ripe ____
- (a) avacado
- (c) avocado
- (b) avocodo
- (d) avacodo

18. a ____ in a salad
- (a) pemento
- (c) pimmento
- (b) pimento
- (d) pimentto

19. a mountain in the ____
- (a) siarra
- (c) sierra
- (b) siera
- (d) searra

20. an ____ of ships
- (a) armadda
- (c) arrmada
- (b) armada
- (d) arrmadda

PRACTICE A
Words Often Confused

Summing Up

Be careful not to confuse words that have similar spellings or pronunciations.

Basic Words
1. immigrate
2. emigrate
3. adverse
4. averse
5. persecute
6. prosecute
7. accede
8. exceed
9. liable
10. libel

Write Right   1–10. Underline the correct Basic Word in each pair to complete the story. Then write the Basic Words on lines 1–10.

Tamal Finds a New Life

The Green Knights continued to (persecute/prosecute) the Blue Knights, bullying and mocking them. Still, many Blue Knights remained in Arburn. They were too loyal to (emigrate/immigrate) from their homeland, fearing (adverse/averse) times would befall the Arburnians without their protection.

Remaining in Arburn finally became impossible for Tamal, the historian for the Blue Knights, when he learned that the

Green Knights intended to (persecute/prosecute) him unjustly for (liable/libel). Because he would not (accede/exceed) to their demands to pay a large sum for his freedom, relatives in neighboring Carden persuaded him to (emigrate/immigrate) to their country.

Hurriedly Tamal went from merchant to merchant, trying not to (accede/exceed) the time left to him. He had to pay the bills for which he was (liable/libel), as he was (adverse/averse) to leaving debts behind.

At last Tamal mounted his steed and crossed Arburn's border. Once in Carden's forest, he knew he had found a place for a better life!

1. _____   4. _____   7. _____

2. _____   5. _____   8. _____

3. _____   6. _____   9. _____

                                               10. _____

Heads and Tails   Add the first syllable of the first word to the last syllable of the second word to write a Basic Word.

11. adventure + reverse   14. library + rebel   13. _____

12. excite + succeed   15. accept + precede

13. avert + diverse   14. _____

11. _____   12. _____   15. _____

Skill: Students will practice spelling words that are often confused.

Home Use: Help your child practice the spelling words by having him or her complete the activities on this page. Check the completed page, and have your child practice saying and spelling any misspelled words.

49

Basic Words
1. immigrate
2. emigrate
3. adverse
4. averse
5. persecute
6. prosecute
7. accede
8. exceed
9. liable
10. libel
11. rational
12. rationale
13. prospective
14. perspective
15. vocation
16. avocation
17. vial
18. vile
19. regimen
20. regiment

PRACTICE B
Words Often Confused

Rhyming Lines   Write a Basic Word that has the same meaning as the underlined word or phrase to make the two lines in each item rhyme.

1. I'm tired of living in New York state.
   I'll pack my bags and <u>leave a native region</u>.
2. I have always been <u>against</u>
   To skiing downhill in reverse!
3. Just because the suspect is of ill repute
   Does not mean the court will <u>conduct legal action</u>.
4. I made the mess; it's undeniable.
   You're right to say that I am <u>responsible</u>.
5. We thought our friendship was defective,
   Until we got a <u>new way of looking at something</u>.
6. Digging the foundation and pouring the cement
   Would take an enormous <u>group of soldiers</u>.
7. A pilot must practice navigation
   If she's to succeed at her chosen <u>profession</u>.
8. Do not befriend the crocodile!
   His smile is nice, but his breath is <u>disgusting</u>!

1. _____   5. _____

2. _____   6. _____

3. _____   7. _____

4. _____   8. _____

One Word Out   Cross out the word in each group that does not belong. Then write the Basic Word that belongs with the group.

9. shorten, slander, smear
10. obligation, plan, system
11. bottle, plate, container
12. bother, impress, oppress
13. detect, enter, settle
14. collect, outshine, surpass

15. hostile, negative, regal
16. expected, finished, possible
17. diversion, hobby, job
18. explanation, expense, reason
19. consent, yield, argue
20. logical, interesting, reasonable

9. _____   13. _____   17. _____

10. _____   14. _____   18. _____

11. _____   15. _____   19. _____

12. _____   16. _____   20. _____

Skill: Students will practice spelling words that are often confused.

Home Use: Help your child practice the spelling words by having him or her complete the activities on this page. Check the completed page, and have your child practice saying and spelling any misspelled words.

PRACTICE C
Words Often Confused

Making Choices Complete the answer to each question. First, write the correct Challenge Word. Then write an explanation telling why the word you chose is correct.

1. Would an eminent or imminent physician be given an award?

An _____ physician would be given an award

because _____ .

2. Would you warn someone of danger that is eminent or imminent?

I would warn someone of danger that is _____

because _____ .

3. Would one be likely to laugh at an antidote or an anecdote?

One would be more likely to laugh at an _____

because _____ .

4. Would you use an anecdote or an antidote for a snakebite?

I would use an _____ for a snakebite because

_____ .

Challenge Words
1. antidote
2. anecdote
3. eminent
4. imminent
Theme Vocabulary
5. asylum
6. aliens
7. quota
8. exile
9. refugee
10. assimilation
11. naturalized
12. citizenship

Newspaper Capers Help newspaper reporter Skip Scoop finish the first sentence of eight articles. Replace each wordy, underlined phrase with a Vocabulary Word. Then use the new, edited beginning to write the first sentence of a news article on another sheet of paper.

5. The maximum number that may be admitted to a country for imported watches is . . .
6. Several illegal persons living in one country though they are citizens of another . . .
7. Political activist Geoff Young may choose voluntary separation from his native country rather than . . .
8. One-hundred-year-old Juan Soledad received the status of a citizen with its duties, rights, and privileges today . . .
9. Studies have shown that foreigners who have been given full citizen status . . .
10. Soviet sailor Ivan Tartikov sought a place of refuge . . .
11. Living the life of a person who flees from his country to avoid oppression . . .
12. Many immigrants find the process of being taken into the cultural tradition of a group . . .

5. _____
6. _____
7. _____
8. _____
9. _____
10. _____
11. _____
12. _____

Skill: Students will practice spelling words that are often confused and words related to the theme of immigration.

Home Use: Help your child practice the spelling words by having him or her complete the activities on this page. Check the completed page, and have your child practice saying and spelling any misspelled words.

Unit **11** Test: Words Often Confused

Read each sentence. Decide if the underlined word is the right word or the
wrong word for that sentence. Fill in the circle for the correct answer in
the answer column.

ANSWERS
Right   Wrong

Sample:
Jim bought the old radio at the <u>bazaar</u>.   ●   ○

1. The harsh treatment was meant to <u>persecute</u> the prisoner.   1. ○   ○

2. Juan and his family want to <u>immigrate</u> from Chile.   2. ○   ○

3. We drove to the game under <u>averse</u> conditions.   3. ○   ○

4. Marcia is <u>liable</u> for service in the army.   4. ○   ○

5. Esther wants to <u>emigrate</u> to the United States.   5. ○   ○

6. That medicine had an <u>adverse</u> effect on the patient.   6. ○   ○

7. Please do not <u>exceed</u> the speed limit.   7. ○   ○

8. It is <u>libel</u> to rain today.   8. ○   ○

9. Mr. Craner is the lawyer who will <u>prosecute</u> the case.   9. ○   ○

10. The candidate plans to <u>accede</u> defeat tonight.   10. ○   ○

11. Josie has chosen a <u>vocation</u> in medicine.   11. ○   ○

12. What is the <u>rational</u> for your decision?   12. ○   ○

13. The <u>vial</u> contains grains of fine, black sand.   13. ○   ○

14. Dr. Teckman put his patient on a strict diet <u>regiment</u>.   14. ○   ○

15. Fran made a <u>rationale</u> decision about the repairs.   15. ○   ○

16. Owen's <u>avocation</u> is collecting post cards.   16. ○   ○

17. An army <u>regimen</u> marched through the town square.   17. ○   ○

18. <u>Prospective</u> employees should apply at the front desk.   18. ○   ○

19. Aunt Margaret always carried a <u>vile</u> of smelling salts.   19. ○   ○

20. From this <u>perspective</u>, the building looks slanted.   20. ○   ○

BULLETIN BOARD

CAREER WORDS

NEWSCASTER
communication
announcer
commentary
WAVR PROGRAM GUIDE
dialogue

COOK | DOCTOR | SCIENTIST | LAWYER

How to make: Divide the bulletin board into 7 sections as shown. Use a contrasting colored background for each section and border the sections in black. Title the sections with the career categories shown or with any other categories suggested by the Basic and Review Words. Cut out large letters for "Career Words" from contrasting colored paper.

How to use: Have students collect and display material related to each career: photos from magazines, want ads, and news or feature articles. Post Basic Words that fit the career categories from Units 7–11 and add other related words that students think of. Check out library books on the careers featured and display them by the bulletin board.

For extra credit, students might write reports on the different careers: why they would be interesting, what preparation is needed for entering them, and what the salary expectations are. Some students might interview people who have these jobs. Display any such reports and interviews.

Use: For use with Units 7–11.

SPELLING NEWSLETTER
for Students and Their Families

Moving Ahead

Unit 7 of your child's level of *Houghton Mifflin Spelling and Vocabulary* studies words such as *allude, immerse,* and *collapse,* in which the spelling of the prefixes *ad-, in-,* and *con-* has been changed. Unit 8 focuses on words with Greek word parts, while Unit 9 focuses on Latin prefixes. Unit 10 studies words of Spanish origin. Finally, Unit 11 studies pairs of words with similar spellings or pronunciations that are often confused with each other, such as *liable* and *libel.*

Word Lists

Here are some of the words your child has studied in Units 7–11.

UNIT 7	UNIT 8	UNIT 9	UNIT 10	UNIT 11
communication	catalog	intramural	coyote	immigrate
colleague	chronology	supervise	mesa	emigrate
apparent	technology	counterfeit	adobe	adverse
immerse	psychology	superficial	indigo	averse
aggressive	logic	intercept	barbecue	liable
allegiance	dialogue	intrastate	mascara	libel
accessory	meteorology	interpret	pimento	rational
appliance	sociology	counterpart	avocado	rationale
immaculate	astrology	superintendent	cafeteria	prospective
illuminate	trilogy	interchangeable	mosquito	perspective

👪 Family Activity

Play Think About a Word with your child. Choose a word from the lists above, and give your child a clue about the word's meaning. For example, if you chose the word *meteorology,* you might provide a clue such as "the science of weather." If your child correctly identifies and spells the word after one clue, he or she gets five points. Provide a second clue, if necessary. If your child correctly identifies and spells the word after two clues, award four points. Continue providing clues, but reducing possible points, until your child identifies the word. After your child has guessed and spelled the word, it is your child's turn to select a word, give you clues, and award points.

Boletín de noticias de ortografía
para estudiantes y para sus familias

Para continuar

Las siguientes son palabras para ejercicios de ortografía que su hijo o hija ha estado estudiando en las Unidades 7 a 11 del libro *Houghton Mifflin Spelling and Vocabulary*.

UNIDAD 7	UNIDAD 8	UNIDAD 9	UNIDAD 10	UNIDAD 11
communication	catalog	intramural	coyote	immigrate
colleague	chronology	supervise	mesa	emigrate
apparent	technology	counterfeit	adobe	adverse
immerse	psychology	superficial	indigo	averse
aggressive	logic	intercept	barbecue	liable
allegiance	dialogue	intrastate	mascara	libel
accessory	meteorology	interpret	pimento	rational
appliance	sociology	counterpart	avocado	rationale
immaculate	astrology	superintendent	cafeteria	prospective
illuminate	trilogy	interchangeable	mosquito	perspective

Actividad para la familia

Jueguen a adivinar una palabra con su hijo o hija. Escojan una palabra de las listas que aparecen arriba, y den a su hijo o hija un indicio o pista de su significado. Por ejemplo, si escogen la palabra *meteorology,* pueden dar una pista tal como "la ciencia del tiempo atmosférico". Si su hijo o hija identifica y deletrea correctamente la palabra después de una pista, recibe cinco puntos. Denle una segunda pista, si hace falta. Si su hijo o hija identifica y deletrea correctamente la palabra después de dos indicios, recibe cuatro puntos. Continúen dando pistas, pero reduciendo los puntos, hasta que su él o ella identifique la palabra. Después de que su hijo o hija haya adivinado y deletreado la palabra, le toca a él o ella escoger una palabra, dar pistas, y otorgar puntos.

SPELLING FOOTBALL

SPELLING GAME

 Players: any number

You need: Review and Basic Word lists, coin, chalkboard

How to play: Decide how much game time is available before play begins. Choose two teams. Pick one player as referee. The referee reads from three lists of words. These lists contain the Review Words, the Basic Words numbered 1–10, and the Basic Words numbered 11–20. The referee also keeps score on the chalkboard.

Flip a coin to see which side will "receive." The first player on the team receiving asks the referee for a word from one of the three lists.

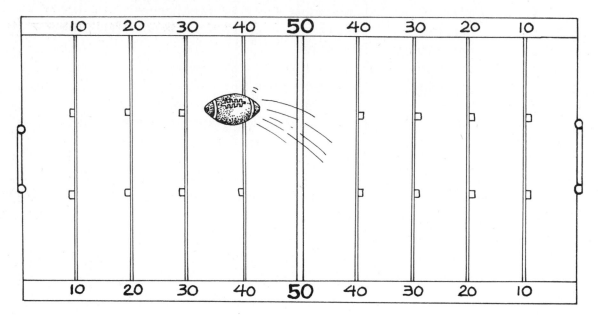

- A Review Word is worth 10 yards toward the end zone.
- A Basic Word numbered 1–10 is worth 20 yards.
- A Basic Word numbered 11–20 is worth 30 yards.

Play begins at the 50-yard line. As soon as a team has gone the necessary 50 yards to score a touchdown, it earns 6 points.

The first player spells the word given by the referee. If it is spelled correctly, the team earns the appropriate number of yards. Play then goes to the other team. Its first player chooses a Review or Basic Word to spell. If players on the same team misspell their words in two consecutive plays, their team loses its next turn as a penalty.

After a team scores a touchdown, a player on the team can score an extra point by spelling a Review Word that has not yet been spelled.

Teams continue taking turns this way until time is up. The team with the most points wins.

Use: For use with Units 7–11.

Unit 12 Review: Test A

Read each sentence. If one of the underlined words is misspelled, fill in the letter for that word in the answer column. If neither word is misspelled, fill in the letter for <u>none</u> in the answer column.

Sample:

High <u>technology</u> creates the <u>illusion</u> of order.   <u>none</u>
　　　　a　　　　　　　　**b**　　　　　**c**

ANSWERS
ⓐ ⓑ ●

1. Mike's <u>colleague</u> had to take a <u>psychology</u> course.   <u>none</u>
　　　　　a　　　　　　　　　**b**　　　　　**c**

2. Sara was the <u>announcer</u> at the <u>intermural</u> game.   <u>none</u>
　　　　　　a　　　　　**b**　　　　**c**

3. The <u>agressive</u> boy used to <u>persecute</u> the children.   <u>none</u>
　　　　a　　　　　　　**b**　　　　　**c**

4. A <u>geology</u> expert spoke on <u>adverse</u> soil conditions.   <u>none</u>
　　a　　　　　　　　**b**　　　　　　**c**

5. The surface of the <u>interstate</u> road was <u>imaculate</u>.   <u>none</u>
　　　　　　　a　　　　　　**b**　　　　**c**

6. Ann's <u>comentary</u> was on those who want to <u>immigrate</u>.   <u>none</u>
　　　a　　　　　　　　　　　**b**　　　　　**c**

7. Andrew plans to take an <u>intermediate</u> <u>biology</u> class.   <u>none</u>
　　　　　　　　　a　　　　　**b**　　　　**c**

8. Every teacher must <u>supervise</u> a mock <u>tornado</u> drill.   <u>none</u>
　　　　　　a　　　　　　**b**　　　　**c**

9. A <u>zooology</u> student studied animals of the <u>savanna</u>.   <u>none</u>
　a　　　　　　　　　　　　　**b**　　　　**c**

10. We found <u>counterfeit</u> money in the <u>peublo</u>.   <u>none</u>
　　　　a　　　　　　**b**　　　**c**

11. Try to <u>intercept</u> the <u>catalogg</u> before he sees it.   <u>none</u>
　　　a　　　**b**　　　　　　　　**c**

12. It was <u>apparent</u> that her <u>apology</u> was sincere.   <u>none</u>
　　　a　　　　　**b**　　　　　　**c**

13. The villagers were <u>averrse</u> to using <u>adobe</u> bricks.   <u>none</u>
　　　　　a　　　　　　**b**　　　　　**c**

14. Jim will not <u>prosicute</u> the man with the <u>accent</u>.   <u>none</u>
　　　　a　　　　　　　　　**b**　　**c**

15. You must <u>immerse</u> yourself in the math <u>terminalogy</u>.   <u>none</u>
　　　a　　　　　　　　　**b**　　　　**c**

16. Is there any <u>logic</u> in suing the magazine for <u>lible</u>?   <u>none</u>
　　　a　　　　　　　　**b**　　**c**

17. The length of her <u>lariat</u> seems to <u>exceed</u> the limit.   <u>none</u>
　　　　　a　　　　　**b**　　　　　**c**

18. Pam and Gary threw a <u>superlative</u> <u>barbecue</u> party.   <u>none</u>
　　　　　　　a　　　　**b**　　　**c**

19. Was anyone held <u>liable</u> for the <u>stampeed</u>?   <u>none</u>
　　　　a　　　**b**　　**c**

20. We heard radio <u>interfernce</u> on the <u>mesa</u>.   <u>none</u>
　　　a　　　　**b**　　**c**

1. ⓐ ⓑ ⓒ
2. ⓐ ⓑ ⓒ
3. ⓐ ⓑ ⓒ
4. ⓐ ⓑ ⓒ
5. ⓐ ⓑ ⓒ
6. ⓐ ⓑ ⓒ
7. ⓐ ⓑ ⓒ
8. ⓐ ⓑ ⓒ
9. ⓐ ⓑ ⓒ
10. ⓐ ⓑ ⓒ
11. ⓐ ⓑ ⓒ
12. ⓐ ⓑ ⓒ
13. ⓐ ⓑ ⓒ
14. ⓐ ⓑ ⓒ
15. ⓐ ⓑ ⓒ
16. ⓐ ⓑ ⓒ
17. ⓐ ⓑ ⓒ
18. ⓐ ⓑ ⓒ
19. ⓐ ⓑ ⓒ
20. ⓐ ⓑ ⓒ

Unit **12** Review: Test B

Read each sentence. If one of the underlined words is misspelled, fill in the letter for that word in the answer column. If neither word is misspelled, fill in the letter for <u>none</u> in the answer column.

Sample:
   The leader of the <u>armada</u> met the <u>praspective</u> sailor. <u>none</u>
                 a   **b**   **c**

ANSWERS
ⓐ ● ©

1. The uniforms of the <u>reggiment</u> were <u>immaculate</u>. <u>none</u>
         a   **b**   **c**

1. ⓐ ⓑ ©

2. I often <u>colaborate</u> with Tom's <u>counterpart</u> in sales. <u>none</u>
      a   **b**   **c**

2. ⓐ ⓑ ©

3. A <u>vial</u> of <u>indigo</u> fluid was drawn from the plant. <u>none</u>
    a   **b**   **c**

3. ⓐ ⓑ ©

4. A <u>collision</u> occurred at the main <u>interrsection</u>. <u>none</u>
      a   **b**   **c**

4. ⓐ ⓑ ©

5. The <u>superintendant</u> visited our <u>cafeteria</u> last week. <u>none</u>
       a   **b**   **c**

5. ⓐ ⓑ ©

6. The <u>sociology</u> expert offered <u>rational</u> explanations. <u>none</u>
      a   **b**   **c**

6. ⓐ ⓑ ©

7. The third book in the <u>trilogy</u> is hard to <u>interpret</u>. <u>none</u>
          a   **b**   **c**

7. ⓐ ⓑ ©

8. You can buy <u>astrology</u> charts at the <u>supermarkit</u>. <u>none</u>
        a   **b**   **c**

8. ⓐ ⓑ ©

9. The <u>jagaur</u> is sometimes found in folk <u>mythology</u>. <u>none</u>
     a   **b**   **c**

9. ⓐ ⓑ ©

10. Al's <u>vocation</u> combines <u>metorology</u> with acting. <u>none</u>
      a   **b**   **c**

10. ⓐ ⓑ ©

11. The blades on the <u>applience</u> are <u>interchangeable</u>. <u>none</u>
        a   **b**   **c**

11. ⓐ ⓑ ©

12. A tale of a <u>mosquito</u> swarm was in the <u>anthology</u>. <u>none</u>
        a   **b**   **c**

12. ⓐ ⓑ ©

13. From this <u>perspective</u>, the <u>sierra</u> looks purple. <u>none</u>
       a   **b**   **c**

13. ⓐ ⓑ ©

14. A <u>vile</u> odor rose from the <u>rotting</u> <u>avacado</u>. <u>none</u>
    a   **b**   **c**

14. ⓐ ⓑ ©

15. How did you <u>accumulate</u> so many kinds of <u>mascarra</u>? <u>none</u>
        a   **b**   **c**

15. ⓐ ⓑ ©

16. Toxic fumes will <u>agravate</u> damage to the <u>ecology</u>. <u>none</u>
        a   **b**   **c**

16. ⓐ ⓑ ©

17. Please <u>illuminate</u> the meaning of that <u>analogy</u>. <u>none</u>
      a   **b**   **c**

17. ⓐ ⓑ ©

18. The recovery <u>regemen</u> includes <u>intravenous</u> feedings. <u>none</u>
       a   **b**   **c**

18. ⓐ ⓑ ©

19. The crew's <u>intervention</u> halted the wall's <u>collapse</u>. <u>none</u>
       a   **b**   **c**

19. ⓐ ⓑ ©

20. Growing <u>alfalfa</u> has become Maeve's <u>avocation</u>. <u>none</u>
      a   **b**   **c**

20. ⓐ ⓑ ©

Unit 12 Review: Test C

Read each sentence. If one of the underlined words is misspelled, fill in the letter for that word in the answer column. If neither word is misspelled, fill in the letter for <u>none</u> in the answer column.

Sample:

Phil will <u>commemorate</u> the event in his <u>epilog</u>.   <u>none</u>
　　　　　a　　　　　　　　　　　b　　　　　c

ANSWERS
ⓐ ● ©

1. Charmaine used <u>alliteration</u> in her <u>anecdote</u>.   <u>none</u>
　　　　　　　　　a　　　　　　　b　　　　　c

2. A <u>flotilla</u> escorted the man carrying the <u>antedote</u>.   <u>none</u>
　　　a　　　　　　　　　　　　　　　b　　　　　c

3. Myles is an <u>aficianado</u> of <u>interscholastic</u> hockey.   <u>none</u>
　　　　　　　a　　　　　　　b　　　　　c

4. We spoke with an <u>eminent</u> professor of <u>archaeology</u>.   <u>none</u>
　　　　　　　　　a　　　　　　　　　b　　　　　c

5. Stu can <u>coroborrate</u> my sighting of the <u>renegade</u>.   <u>none</u>
　　　　　a　　　　　　　　　　　b　　　　　c

6. Please <u>intersperse</u> relevant quotes in the <u>prolog</u>.   <u>none</u>
　　　　　a　　　　　　　　　　　b　　　　　c

7. That <u>etymology</u> contains <u>superfluos</u> information.   <u>none</u>
　　　　　a　　　　　　　b　　　　　c

8. I could not <u>interogate</u> the <u>incommunicado</u> prisoner.   <u>none</u>
　　　　　　　a　　　　　　　b　　　　　c

9. The <u>logistics</u> of the move seem <u>irrelavant</u> to me.   <u>none</u>
　　　　a　　　　　　　　　b　　　　　c

10. We <u>commiserate</u> with you on his <u>imminent</u> departure.   <u>none</u>
　　　　a　　　　　　　　　　　b　　　　　c

1. ⓐ ⓑ ©
2. ⓐ ⓑ ©
3. ⓐ ⓑ ©
4. ⓐ ⓑ ©
5. ⓐ ⓑ ©
6. ⓐ ⓑ ©
7. ⓐ ⓑ ©
8. ⓐ ⓑ ©
9. ⓐ ⓑ ©
10. ⓐ ⓑ ©

Prewriting Ideas: Comparison and Contrast

Choosing a Topic   Listed below are some pairs of things that one
student thought of to compare and contrast. What ideas come to your
mind when you look at the list?

On the lines below *My Five Ideas*, list five pairs of things you could
compare and contrast. Which ones do you know the most about? Which
ones would your readers be most interested in? Circle the topic that you
would like to write about.

Ideas for Writing

Fish and sea mammals
Saltwater and freshwater sea life
The American Southwest and Northeast
Radio and television programs
Taking care of dogs and of cats
The city by day and by night
Having a sister and a brother
Living today and 100 years ago

My Five Ideas

1. _____

2. _____

3. _____

4. _____

5. _____

Exploring Your Topic   Use a diagram to plan what is alike and what
is different about the two parts of the topic you chose. Write the parts of
your topic on the blank lines above the circles, and list similarities and
differences between the two parts of your topic within the circles.

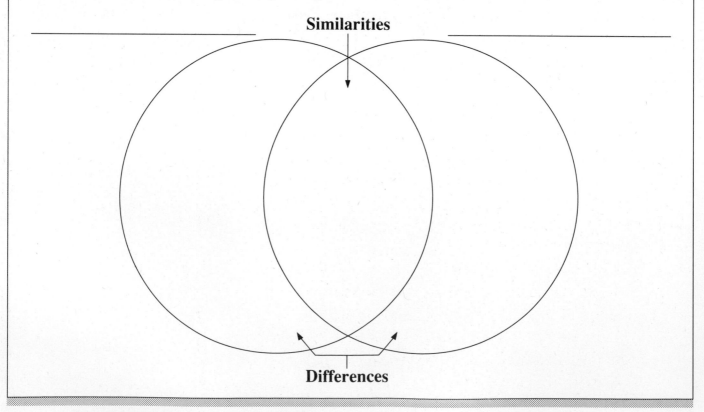

Differences

PRACTICE A
Vowel Changes I

Summing Up

To remember the spelling of a word with the schwa sound, think of a related word in which the vowel sound is more obvious.

Basic Words
1. vegetable
2. vegetation
3. strategy
4. strategic
5. stability
6. stable
7. alternative
8. alternate
9. definition
10. define

Crossed Words   Complete the word crosses with a pair of related Basic Words. The words will cross at the vowel that changes from the schwa sound to a long vowel sound.

1–2.

3–4.

5–6.

7–8.

9–10.

Synonym Switch   Write the Basic Word that has the same meaning as the underlined word or words in these ads seen on the sides of city buses.

11. Avoid highway hazards! Public transportation gives you the <u>choice</u> of not driving.

12. Are you looking for <u>security</u> in your job? Midwest Tech offers training that will guarantee lifetime employment.

13. Local programming will <u>take turns</u> with network reruns during the summer months. Watch Channel 90 for variety.

14. Help our state achieve a <u>steady</u> economy. Support local manufacturers and retailers.

11. _____

12. _____

13. _____

14. _____

Skill: Students will practice spelling pairs of related words with vowel changes.

Home Use: Help your child practice the spelling words by having him or her complete the activities on this page. Check the completed page, and have your child practice saying and spelling any misspelled words.

Basic Words
1. vegetable
2. vegetation
3. strategy
4. strategic
5. stability
6. stable
7. alternative
8. alternate
9. definition
10. define
11. remedy
12. remedial
13. immunize
14. immune
15. deprivation
16. deprive
17. indicative
18. indicate
19. infinite
20. finite

PRACTICE B
Vowel Changes I

Anagrams   The words in each equation are formed from the letters of one Basic Word. Rearrange the letters to write the Basic Word.

Example: gave + let + be   *vegetable*

1. feed + in
2. rove + tin + paid
3. deem + rail
4. dive + per
5. tie + fin
6. tics + grate

7. rent + teal + via
8. dice + vain + it
9. get + stray
10. diet + ion + fin
11. my + reed
12. nine + if + it

1. _____   7. _____

2. _____   8. _____

3. _____   9. _____

4. _____   10. _____

5. _____   11. _____

6. _____   12. _____

Puzzle Play   Write the Basic Word that fits each clue. Then write the circled letters in order. They will spell the name of a flower.

13. to vaccinate   _ _ ⃝ _ _ _ _ _

14. the state of being steady   _ _ _ ⃝ _ _ _ _ _

15. to take turns   _ _ _ _ ⃝ _ _ _ _

16. protected   ⃝ _ _ _ _ _

17. a plant used as food   _ _ ⃝ _ _ _ _ _

18. plant life   _ _ _ _ _ ⃝ _ _ _ _

19. a shelter for horses   _ _ _ _ ⃝ _

20. to point out precisely   _ _ _ ⃝ _ _ _ _

Answer: _ _ _ _ _ _ _ _

EXTRA!   Make your own anagram equations for the Basic Words *stable, alternate, vegetable,* and *vegetation.*

Skill: Students will practice spelling pairs of related words with vowel changes.

Home Use: Help your child practice the spelling words by having him or her complete the activities on this page. Check the completed page, and have your child practice saying and spelling any misspelled words.

PRACTICE C
Vowel Changes I

Sentence Scrambler **1–6.** Use the words below to write sentences about agriculture. First, list the words in separate groups according to their box numbers. Then write six statements by unscrambling each group and adding two Challenge or Vocabulary Words to complete each sentence.

<table>
<tr><td>⁴ against</td><td>⁵ in</td><td>³ tomato</td><td>¹ the</td><td>² repaired</td><td>⁶ harvest</td></tr>
<tr><td>³ university's</td><td>² and</td><td>⁵ making</td><td>⁶ you</td><td>² the</td><td>¹ Angus</td></tr>
<tr><td>⁵ cooperative</td><td>¹ year</td><td>³ new</td><td>⁴ a</td><td>¹ field</td><td>⁶ swinging</td></tr>
<tr><td>³ scientists</td><td>⁵ the</td><td>⁵ farmers'</td><td>⁶ by</td><td>² Aaron</td><td>⁴ issued</td></tr>
<tr><td>⁴ controversial</td><td>² the</td><td>⁵ the</td><td>⁶ that</td><td>³ in</td><td>² motors</td></tr>
<tr><td>⁵ procedure</td><td>² in</td><td>² the</td><td>¹ will</td><td>⁴ the</td><td>⁶ can</td></tr>
<tr><td>⁴ government</td><td>³ the</td><td>⁴ spraying</td><td>⁶ the</td><td>⁵ took</td><td>the</td></tr>
<tr><td>³ created</td><td>⁵ new</td><td>⁴ the</td><td>³ a</td><td>³ department</td><td>¹ next</td></tr>
</table>

Challenge Words

1. mandatory
2. mandate
3. initiative
4. initiate

Theme Vocabulary

5. agriculture
6. cultivate
7. pesticide
8. hybrid
9. reaper
10. scythe
11. thresher
12. fallow

1. _____

_____

2. _____

_____

3. _____

_____

4. _____

_____

5. _____

_____

6. _____

_____

Skill: Students will practice spelling pairs of related words with vowel changes and words related to the theme of agriculture.

Home Use: Help your child practice the spelling words by having him or her complete the activities on this page. Check the completed page, and have your child practice saying and spelling any misspelled words.

Unit 13 Test: Vowel Changes I

Each item below gives four possible spellings of a word. Fill in the letter beside the correct spelling.

Sample:
ⓐ harrmonious
● harmonious
ⓒ harmonoius
ⓓ harmonius

1. ⓐ allternative
   ⓑ alternative
   ⓒ alternitive
   ⓓ alternetive

2. ⓐ stratigy
   ⓑ strategy
   ⓒ strattegy
   ⓓ stratagy

3. ⓐ stabillity
   ⓑ stubility
   ⓒ stability
   ⓓ stabbility

4. ⓐ vegetable
   ⓑ vegetabal
   ⓒ vegatable
   ⓓ vegeteble

5. ⓐ stabel
   ⓑ stable
   ⓒ stabbel
   ⓓ stayble

6. ⓐ strutegic
   ⓑ strategick
   ⓒ stretegic
   ⓓ strategic

7. ⓐ deefine
   ⓑ deafine
   ⓒ define
   ⓓ defyne

8. ⓐ alternite
   ⓑ alternate
   ⓒ altarnate
   ⓓ alternitt

9. ⓐ defenition
   ⓑ deffinition
   ⓒ definnition
   ⓓ definition

10. ⓐ vegatation
    ⓑ veggetation
    ⓒ vegitation
    ⓓ vegetation

11. ⓐ deprive
    ⓑ depprive
    ⓒ diprive
    ⓓ deprrive

12. ⓐ remmedy
    ⓑ remedie
    ⓒ remedy
    ⓓ remidy

13. ⓐ indicative
    ⓑ indicitive
    ⓒ indikative
    ⓓ indickative

14. ⓐ fynite
    ⓑ finite
    ⓒ finyte
    ⓓ finit

15. ⓐ imunize
    ⓑ immunnize
    ⓒ immunize
    ⓓ imunnize

16. ⓐ infinite
    ⓑ infinit
    ⓒ innfinite
    ⓓ infinate

17. ⓐ ramedial
    ⓑ remedial
    ⓒ remeedial
    ⓓ remediel

18. ⓐ imune
    ⓑ emmune
    ⓒ immune
    ⓓ emune

19. ⓐ deprevation
    ⓑ depprivation
    ⓒ depravation
    ⓓ deprivation

20. ⓐ indicate
    ⓑ inndicate
    ⓒ indecate
    ⓓ indacate

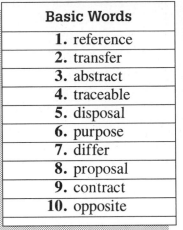

PRACTICE A
Latin Roots I

Summing Up

Three common Latin roots are *fer, pos,* and *tract.*

Basic Words
1. reference
2. transfer
3. abstract
4. traceable
5. disposal
6. purpose
7. differ
8. proposal
9. contract
10. opposite

Word Root Robots   Each robot is programmed only with words having a certain word root. On each robot, write the Basic Words that have its word root. Then match each Basic Word with its definition by writing the number of its definition next to the Basic Word.

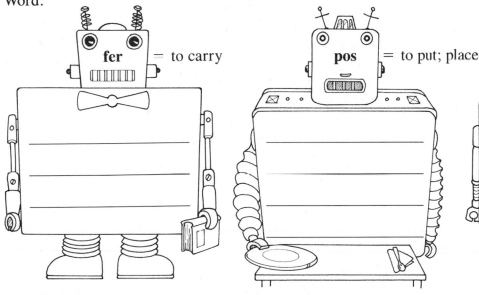

fer = to carry

pos = to put; place

tract = to draw; pull

Definitions

1. contrary in nature
2. not concrete
3. a formal agreement
4. a goal
5. a suggestion

6. able to be followed
7. to be unlike
8. the source of information
9. the act of throwing away
10. to move from one place to another

Word Search   **11–18.** Find eight Basic Words hidden in the puzzle. The words may cross each other and appear horizontally, vertically, or diagonally. Circle each word, and then write it.

```
w p h e h o g y t h c t w o n t o s w
o r r t e e p s t j a o p u r p o s e
a o s s d i s p o s a l n r k h p w a
p p r f m i h e o o d c e t i a g n x
a o t e e t f f t s a b s t r a c t s
j s t r a n s f e r i r i s a a n g r
s a b s o h e r e m o t s f m x c h o
e l c t o l i n h r a h e a e l i t a
```

11. _____
12. _____
13. _____
14. _____
15. _____
16. _____
17. _____
18. _____

Skill: Students will practice spelling words with the Latin roots *fer, pos,* and *tract.*

Home Use: Help your child practice the spelling words by having him or her complete the activities on this page. Check the completed page, and have your child practice saying and spelling any misspelled words.

Basic Words
1. reference
2. transfer
3. abstract
4. traceable
5. disposal
6. purpose
7. differ
8. proposal
9. contract
10. opposite
11. preposition
12. confer
13. distract
14. exposure
15. posture
16. inference
17. traction
18. transpose
19. fertile
20. preference

PRACTICE B
Latin Roots I

Roman Riddle Clues   Write the Basic Word that fits each group.

1. reverse, contrary, _ _ _ _ _ ◯ _ _

2. noun, adverb, _ _ _ _ _ _ _ ◯ _ _ _

3. obscure, theoretical, _ _ _ _ _ _ _ _

4. discarding, dumping, _ _ _ ◯ _ _ _ _

5. stance, carriage, _ _ ◯ _ _ _ _

6. contradict, disagree, _ _ _ _ _ _

7. fruitful, productive, _ ◯ _ _ _ _ _

8. suggestion, offer, _ _ _ _ _ _ ◯ _

9. agreement, deal, _ _ _ _ ◯ _ _

10. goal, aim, _ _ _ _ _ _ ◯

Write the circled letters in order to answer this riddle: *Why shouldn't one complain about the price of a chariot ride ticket?*

Answer: because   _ _   _ _   _ _ _ _

Proofreading   **11–20.** Find and cross out ten misspelled Basic Words in this list of directions that an ancient Roman Senator gave to his assistant. Then write each word correctly.

✓ Check the new chariot driver's refference.
✓ Buy new chariot wheels for better tracksion.
✓ Explain to the architect that the new columns should not distrack from the beauty of the house.
✓ Make sure that the building supply contract includes my wife's preferrence for marble over plaster columns.
✓ Set up a time to conferr with Senator Theta on the issue of trash disposal. Explain that I differ with him on this issue.
✓ Ask the gardener to transferr delicate plants indoors to avoid expossure to cold weather.
✓ Ask the editor of the <u>Roman Times</u> about his inferrence that I am concerned about the upcoming election. Find out if that statement is tracable to my opponent.
✓ Ask the editor to transpoze the election story on page five with the home improvement article on page one.

11. _____

12. _____

13. _____

14. _____

15. _____

16. _____

17. _____

18. _____

19. _____

20. _____

Skill: Students will practice spelling words with the Latin roots *fer, pos,* and *tract.*

Home Use: Help your child practice the spelling words by having him or her complete the activities on this page. Check the completed page, and have your child practice saying and spelling any misspelled words.

PRACTICE C
Latin Roots I

Hidden Words   Use the clues below to find little words hidden in seven Challenge or Vocabulary Words. Write each hidden word and the Challenge or Vocabulary Word in which it is found.

Example: auto   *car*   *carrel*

1. to hit lightly
2. to create music
3. a farm vehicle
4. a brim or edge
5. a wager
6. an antonym for *out*
7. a location or place

Hidden Word	Challenge/Vocabulary Word
1.	
2.	
3.	
4.	
5.	
6.	
7.	

On the back of this paper, write the definitions for the Challenge and Vocabulary Words that you wrote above.

Library Locations   Write a Vocabulary Word to complete each clue. Then identify the parts of the library on the floor plan by writing the number of each clue in the correct location.

8. Check out books at the _____ desk just east of the entrance.
9. Magazines are on the _____ shelves in the southwest corner.
10. Use microfilm readers with the _____ in the northwest corner.
11. You can study in a _____ located just north of the magazines.
12. History books are in the _____ section, east of the study area.
13. Novels are in the _____ section, located in the northeast corner.

Challenge Words	
1. composite	
2. juxtapose	
3. protractor	
4. decompose	
5. superimpose	
Theme Vocabulary	
6. index	
7. periodical	
8. alphabetical	
9. microfiche	
10. carrel	
11. circulation	
12. fiction	
13. nonfiction	

8. _____

9. _____

10. _____

11. _____

12. _____

13. _____

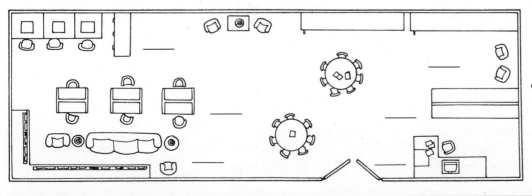

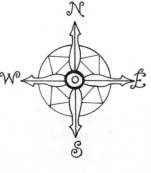

Skill: Students will practice spelling words with the Latin roots *fer, pos,* and *tract* and words related to the theme of library skills.

Home Use: Help your child practice the spelling words by having him or her complete the activities on this page. Check the completed page, and have your child practice saying and spelling any misspelled words.

Unit 14 Test: Latin Roots I

Find the correctly spelled word to complete each phrase. Fill in the letter beside the correct spelling.

Sample:
to look up in a _____
- ⓐ dictionery
- ● dictionary
- ⓒ dicshunary
- ⓓ dicshunery

1. the garbage _____
- ⓐ dissposal
- ⓑ disposal
- ⓒ disposel
- ⓓ dissposel

2. to serve a _____
- ⓐ purpose
- ⓑ perpose
- ⓒ purpess
- ⓓ purrpose

3. to request a _____
- ⓐ trannsfer
- ⓑ transferr
- ⓒ transfer
- ⓓ transffer

4. to make a _____ to
- ⓐ reference
- ⓑ referrence
- ⓒ referance
- ⓓ referrance

5. to _____ from one another
- ⓐ difer
- ⓑ differr
- ⓒ diffir
- ⓓ differ

6. signed the _____
- ⓐ contracte
- ⓑ kontract
- ⓒ contract
- ⓓ conntract

7. to accept the _____
- ⓐ proposel
- ⓑ proposal
- ⓒ proposle
- ⓓ propposal

8. a piece of _____ art
- ⓐ abstract
- ⓑ abbstract
- ⓒ abstracte
- ⓓ abbstracte

9. on the _____ side
- ⓐ oposite
- ⓑ opposite
- ⓒ opposit
- ⓓ oppossite

10. something _____ to its source
- ⓐ traseable
- ⓑ tracable
- ⓒ trasable
- ⓓ traceable

11. to have good _____
- ⓐ poschure
- ⓑ posture
- ⓒ postcher
- ⓓ posscher

12. the object of a _____
- ⓐ preposition
- ⓑ prepposition
- ⓒ prepasition
- ⓓ preposetion

13. a double _____
- ⓐ eksposure
- ⓑ ecksposure
- ⓒ expposure
- ⓓ exposure

14. to have a _____ for
- ⓐ prefference
- ⓑ preferance
- ⓒ preferrence
- ⓓ preference

15. to _____ with the others
- ⓐ confer
- ⓑ conferr
- ⓒ connfer
- ⓓ cunnfer

16. to _____ two words
- ⓐ transppose
- ⓑ trannspose
- ⓒ transpose
- ⓓ trenspose

17. to _____ one's opponent
- ⓐ distract
- ⓑ disstract
- ⓒ disteract
- ⓓ distrect

18. gaining _____ on the icy slope
- ⓐ tracction
- ⓑ traction
- ⓒ trection
- ⓓ tracton

19. the _____ soil
- ⓐ fertill
- ⓑ ferrtile
- ⓒ fertile
- ⓓ fertall

20. to make an _____
- ⓐ inferrence
- ⓑ inference
- ⓒ inferance
- ⓓ inferrance

PRACTICE A
Noun Suffixes I

Basic Words
1. nationality
2. hospitality
3. agency
4. society
5. curiosity
6. generosity
7. familiarity
8. majority
9. privacy
10. frequency

Summing Up

The suffixes -*cy*, -*ty*, and -*ity* form nouns.

Bumper Stickers   Help finish printing the bumper stickers by writing the Basic Word that fits in each blank. On the lines below each sticker, write the other Basic Words that have the same suffix as each word you wrote in the sticker.

-cy

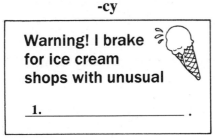

Warning! I brake for ice cream shops with unusual

1. _____ .

2. _____

3. _____

-ity

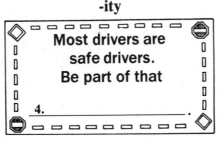

Most drivers are safe drivers. Be part of that

4. _____ .

5. _____

6. _____

7. _____

8. _____

9. _____

-ty

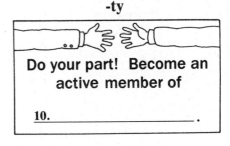

Do your part! Become an active member of

10. _____ .

Word Riddles   Write the Basic Word that answers each riddle.
11. You can find me only when you are alone.
12. Everyone is a part of me.
13. I am the number of occurrences within a given period.
14. I am characteristic of someone who likes to give.
15. I am indicated on your passport.
16. I am a business that acts for others.
17. I am what you feel when you want to know something.
18. I exist when you know someone or something well.
19. I am the greater number or part of something.
20. I am what every guest expects.

11. _____

12. _____

13. _____

14. _____

15. _____

16. _____

17. _____

18. _____

19. _____

20. _____

Skill: Students will practice spelling words with the suffixes -*cy*, -*ty*, and -*ity*.

Home Use: Help your child practice the spelling words by having him or her complete the activities on this page. Check the completed page, and have your child practice saying and spelling any misspelled words.

Basic Words
1. nationality
2. hospitality
3. agency
4. society
5. curiosity
6. generosity
7. familiarity
8. majority
9. privacy
10. frequency
11. popularity
12. accuracy
13. minority
14. urgency
15. democracy
16. emergency
17. personality
18. maturity
19. anxiety
20. humidity

PRACTICE B
Noun Suffixes I

Mystery Titles   Read these book titles and descriptions. Unscramble the Basic Words in each title to write a book title that matches each description. Capitalize each important word.

1–2. *The Saltyhipoti of a Torymini*
Only a few townspeople welcome the mysterious newcomer.

3–4. *The Yergosenit of Yetsoci*
Earthquake victims are overwhelmed by financial support.

5–6. *A Roitycusi About Alatniotiny*
While vacationing in Switzerland, Barney Bosco loses his passport and his memory. What country does he come from? Barney must know the truth.

7–8. *The Dumihity Germeency*
A mad scientist finds a way to control the moisture content of the world's air—with devastating results.

9–10. *An Ecgany of Rodymecac*
An office in the capital of Westania is opened to teach citizens about the new system of government elections.

1–2. _____

3–4. _____

5–6. _____

7–8. _____

9–10. _____

11. _____

12. _____

13. _____

14. _____

15. _____

16. _____

17. _____

18. _____

19. _____

20. _____

Sports Article   Write ten Basic Words to complete this excerpt from an article in a sports magazine.

In the __(11)__ of his room, Matt Miller talks about the crowd that will be at the tie-breaking meet. He will be mobbed, for he enjoys immense __(12)__ . With his cheerful, friendly __(13)__ and the __(14)__ of his victories, Miller has made quite a name for himself. His fans, at least the __(15)__ of them, think of him as an old friend and greet him with __(16)__ wherever he goes.

A sportswriter once called him an amateur in search of glory. There is a degree of __(17)__ in that observation—Miller has always taken his fame more seriously than his running, but he does not anymore. He has grown up and achieved __(18)__ . He still suffers __(19)__ about losing, but he no longer feels the pressure or the __(20)__ to succeed. Although he still loves to win, he now knows that there is more to sport than victory.

Skill: Students will practice spelling words with the suffixes *-cy, -ty,* and *-ity.*

Home Use: Help your child practice the spelling words by having him or her complete the activities on this page. Check the completed page, and have your child practice saying and spelling any misspelled words.

PRACTICE C
Noun Suffixes I

Word Merge Use the clues to write two words on each line. One word will be a Challenge or Vocabulary Word. The letters at the end of the first word will be the letters that also begin the second word. You may want to use a class dictionary. Circle the common letters.

Example: _c u l t u r (a l) l i a n c e_

1–2. _ _ _ _ _ _ _ _ _ _ _ _ _ _

3–4. _ _ _ _ _ _ _ _ _ _

5–6. _ _ _ _ _ _ _ _ _ _ _ _

7–8. _ _ _ _ _ _ _ _ _ _

9–10. _ _ _ _ _ _ _ _ _ _ _ _ _

11–12. _ _ _ _ _ _ _ _ _ _ _ _ _ _ _

13–14. _ _ _ _ _ _ _ _ _ _

15–16. _ _ _ _ _ _ _ _ _ _ _ _ _ _ _ _ _ _ _

Challenge Words
1. prosperity
2. anonymity
3. consistency
4. spontaneity
5. eccentricity

Theme Vocabulary
6. scholarship
7. recipient
8. abroad
9. visa
10. reciprocate
11. semester
12. cultural
13. tuition

Clues

1. a school term
2. to put an end to
3. a school fee
4. a strong-smelling vegetable
5. someone who acquires
6. to amuse
7. in foreign places
8. a barrier across a highway
9. a light for guiding ships
10. conformity
11. to give in return
12. an insect that eats wood
13. a travel permit
14. to protect
15. money awarded to a student
16. a large African river animal

Read All About It **17–21.** A wealthy citizen has secretly donated a fortune to a museum. Write five headlines about the donation, using these Challenge and Vocabulary Words: *cultural, prosperity, anonymity, spontaneity, eccentricity.*

17. _____

18. _____

19. _____

20. _____

21. _____

Skill: Students will practice spelling words with the noun suffixes *-cy, -ty,* and *-ity* and words related to the theme of student exchange programs.

Home Use: Help your child practice the spelling words by having him or her complete the activities on this page. Check the completed page, and have your child practice saying and spelling any misspelled words.

Unit **15** Test: Noun Suffixes I

Each item below gives four possible spellings of a word. Fill in the letter beside the correct spelling.

Sample:
- ⓐ varriety
- ⓑ variaty
- ● variety
- ⓓ varriaty

1. ⓐ frequency
   ⓑ frequencie
   ⓒ frequancy
   ⓓ freequency

2. ⓐ hospitalety
   ⓑ hospetality
   ⓒ hospitality
   ⓓ hospitelity

3. ⓐ sosiety
   ⓑ sociaty
   ⓒ society
   ⓓ societie

4. ⓐ familarity
   ⓑ familiarety
   ⓒ familyarity
   ⓓ familiarity

5. ⓐ majorrity
   ⓑ majority
   ⓒ majorety
   ⓓ majoritty

6. ⓐ generosity
   ⓑ gennerrosity
   ⓒ gennerosity
   ⓓ generrosity

7. ⓐ nationality
   ⓑ nationallity
   ⓒ nationnality
   ⓓ nationalety

8. ⓐ curriosity
   ⓑ curiousity
   ⓒ cureiosity
   ⓓ curiosity

9. ⓐ agency
   ⓑ agenncy
   ⓒ ajency
   ⓓ agencie

10. ⓐ privicy
    ⓑ privecy
    ⓒ privacy
    ⓓ privacie

11. ⓐ minorrity
    ⓑ minoraty
    ⓒ mynority
    ⓓ minority

12. ⓐ angsiety
    ⓑ angziety
    ⓒ anxiety
    ⓓ anxiaty

13. ⓐ machurity
    ⓑ maturity
    ⓒ muchurity
    ⓓ matureity

14. ⓐ democracy
    ⓑ democrecy
    ⓒ demacracy
    ⓓ dimocracy

15. ⓐ poppularity
    ⓑ popularity
    ⓒ populareity
    ⓓ popyularity

16. ⓐ humididy
    ⓑ humidity
    ⓒ humiddity
    ⓓ humiditey

17. ⓐ urgency
    ⓑ ergensy
    ⓒ urgensy
    ⓓ urrgency

18. ⓐ emurgency
    ⓑ emmergency
    ⓒ emergency
    ⓓ emerrgency

19. ⓐ pursonality
    ⓑ personelity
    ⓒ persunality
    ⓓ personality

20. ⓐ acuracy
    ⓑ accurracy
    ⓒ accuracy
    ⓓ accurecy

PRACTICE A
Words from French

Basic Words
1. chef
2. gourmet
3. buffet
4. saute
5. fillet
6. parfait
7. omelet
8. foyer
9. brochure
10. suite

Summing Up
Many French words have become part of the English language.

Parlez-vous Franglais?   Your French cousin wants to practice speaking English and refuses to use any French words. Underline the word or words in each of your cousin's sentences that can be replaced by a Basic Word. Then write the Basic Word.

1. The small pamphlet mentioned a special restaurant.
2. I left my series of connected rooms in the hotel to find it.
3. I called a taxi from the hotel lobby.
4. When I arrived, the manager told me that a world-famous chief cook of a large kitchen staff was in the kitchen.
5. She knew that I was a person who liked fine food.
6. The restaurant had a counter from which food was served.
7. First, I had a cheese dish of beaten eggs.
8. From where I was sitting I could watch the cooks fry lightly my main dish.
9. I had a delicious boneless piece of salmon.
10. Last, I had a superb dessert of layers of ice cream with various toppings, served in a tall glass.

1. _____   6. _____
2. _____   7. _____
3. _____   8. _____
4. _____   9. _____
5. _____   10. _____

Tongue Twisters   Write the Basic Word that completes each tongue twister. The Basic Word should begin with the same sound(s) as most of the other words in the sentence. See how quickly you can say each sentence.

11. Cheryl Chevron showed the shellfish to the shocked ____ .
12. Gorgeous Gordon Gormless is a great ____ .
13. Parsival Parsnip ate part of a ____ at a party.
14. Snarling Sonya Snapper sought to ____ the snails.
15. Freddy Farley found the fish ____ fantastic.
16. Brooding Billy brought a British ____ in his briefcase.
17. Bob Baley's band blew brass bugles at the brunch ____ .
18. Superstar Susie Swazy sweltered in her swanky Swedish ____ .

11. _____
12. _____
13. _____
14. _____
15. _____
16. _____
17. _____
18. _____

Skill: Students will practice spelling words borrowed from French.

Home Use: Help your child practice the spelling words by having him or her complete the activities on this page. Check the completed page, and have your child practice saying and spelling any misspelled words.

Basic Words
1. chef
2. gourmet
3. buffet
4. saute
5. fillet
6. parfait
7. omelet
8. foyer
9. brochure
10. suite
11. etiquette
12. mustache
13. memoir
14. souvenir
15. camouflage
16. chauffeur
17. opaque
18. intrigue
19. rendezvous
20. elite

PRACTICE B
Words from French

Word Associations Write the Basic Word associated with each situation below.

1. driving a limousine
2. introducing strangers
3. meeting a friend
4. waiting at a hotel entrance
5. remembering a vacation
6. scheming in secrecy
7. finding travel information
8. blocking out light
9. decorating a series of rooms
10. writing an autobiography
11. hiding in the jungle
12. shaving above the lip

1. _____
2. _____
3. _____
4. _____
5. _____
6. _____

7. _____
8. _____
9. _____
10. _____
11. _____
12. _____

Proofreading **13–20.** Find and cross out eight misspelled Basic Words in this newspaper advertisement. Then write each word correctly.

GRETA'S GRACIOUS GROCERY

Eggs à la Snob—Eggs for the gourmay eleet! The most exquisite eggs you'll find this side of Paris. Poach them, scramble them, or use them to make the ultimate omelett. At $50 per dozen, these are a special bargain.

◡ ◡

White Fish Superior—Buy it whole or let us fillett it for you. Bake it, sautee it, cover it with ketchup—nothing can camouflage the overpowering taste of this unforgettable fish. $67.99 per pound.

◡ ◡

Too weary to shop? Send your chauffeur round to inspect our new buffay. Our dessert section is superb, with everything from sophisticated Creme Cremoo to an ordinary parfate prepared for you by a French cheff.

---

13. _____
14. _____
15. _____
16. _____
17. _____
18. _____
19. _____
20. _____

Skill: Students will practice spelling words borrowed from French.

Home Use: Help your child practice the spelling words by having him or her complete the activities on this page. Check the completed page, and have your child practice saying and spelling any misspelled words.

PRACTICE C
Words from French

Dining Out   1–9. Five chefs are preparing to open a restaurant. Write nine Challenge and Vocabulary Words to complete the following clues. Then use the clues to help you figure out what each chef plans. Put a check mark in each correct box and an X in each incorrect box.

- One chef, who is in charge of the main courses, is planning a delicious fish __(1)__ .

- Suzanne is a __(2)__ of foreign food. Her expertise will be put to good use.

- A variety of dishes will be offered for the Sunday __(3)__ .

- One chef has designed the __(4)__ , which lists the food that the restaurant will serve. She is very satisfied with her design.

- Although he has not had much experience in making appetizers, one chef is preparing an __(5)__ of snails in puff pastry.

- One chef will plan all the Spanish and French __(6)__ .

- A male chef, whose __(7)__ skill is world-famous, is planning a buffet.

- Chef Edward is making a special trip to the local market to buy trout for Chef Henri's dish. When he returns from the market, he will begin rolling out the dough for his own dish.

- Chef Henri will give a 10 percent discount to each __(8)__ who makes a __(9)__ for dinner at the new restaurant before Tuesday.

	hors d'oeuvre	Spanish and French cuisine	menu	entree	smorgasbord
Henri					
Rosa					
Suzanne					
Edward					
Lionel					

Challenge Words
1. hors d'oeuvre
2. connoisseur
3. liaison
4. genre
5. detente

Theme Vocabulary
6. franchise
7. cuisine
8. menu
9. customer
10. entree
11. reservation
12. smorgasbord
13. culinary

1. _____

2. _____

3. _____

4. _____

5. _____

6. _____

7. _____

8. _____

9. _____

Tongue Twisters   10–14. A tongue twister is a sentence in which all or almost all the words begin with the same letter. On the back of this paper, write five tongue twisters. Use each of these Challenge and Vocabulary Words: *connoisseur, liaison, detente, franchise, genre.*

Skill: Students will practice spelling words borrowed from French and words related to the theme of restaurant management.

Home Use: Help your child practice the spelling words by having him or her complete the activities on this page. Check the completed page, and have your child practice saying and spelling any misspelled words.

Unit 16 Test: Words from French

Find the correctly spelled word to complete each phrase. Fill in the letter beside the correct spelling.

Sample:

the _____ tennis player
- ⓐ amachure
- ⓒ ammateur
- ⓑ amatuer
- ● amateur

1. a _____ cook
   - ⓐ gormet
   - ⓒ gormay
   - ⓑ gourmet
   - ⓓ gourmay

2. the head _____
   - ⓐ shef
   - ⓒ cheff
   - ⓑ sheff
   - ⓓ chef

3. a strawberry _____
   - ⓐ parfay
   - ⓒ parffait
   - ⓑ parfait
   - ⓓ parrfay

4. to _____ the onions
   - ⓐ saute
   - ⓒ sautay
   - ⓑ suate
   - ⓓ suatay

5. a slate floor in the _____
   - ⓐ foier
   - ⓒ foyer
   - ⓑ foyere
   - ⓓ foiyer

6. a mushroom _____
   - ⓐ ommelet
   - ⓒ omelett
   - ⓑ omelet
   - ⓓ omalet

7. a _____ of rooms
   - ⓐ sweete
   - ⓒ swete
   - ⓑ suitte
   - ⓓ suite

8. a _____ meal
   - ⓐ buffay
   - ⓒ buffet
   - ⓑ bufet
   - ⓓ buffett

9. a _____ of fish
   - ⓐ filett
   - ⓒ filay
   - ⓑ fillay
   - ⓓ fillet

10. a colorful _____
    - ⓐ brochure
    - ⓒ brosure
    - ⓑ broshure
    - ⓓ brochur

11. the _____ in the car
    - ⓐ chauffer
    - ⓒ chauffeur
    - ⓑ chauffuer
    - ⓓ choffeur

12. a _____ with destiny
    - ⓐ rondayvous
    - ⓒ rendezvoo
    - ⓑ rondezvous
    - ⓓ rendezvous

13. an _____ glass
    - ⓐ opake
    - ⓒ oppaque
    - ⓑ opaque
    - ⓓ opakke

14. a book on proper _____
    - ⓐ etiquette
    - ⓒ ettiquette
    - ⓑ etikette
    - ⓓ etiquete

15. the man's _____
    - ⓐ mustache
    - ⓒ mustach
    - ⓑ mustashe
    - ⓓ musstache

16. mystery and _____
    - ⓐ intreeg
    - ⓒ intrigue
    - ⓑ intreegue
    - ⓓ intregue

17. having a _____
    - ⓐ memmoir
    - ⓒ memwoir
    - ⓑ memoir
    - ⓓ memmwoir

18. a vacation _____
    - ⓐ souvenir
    - ⓒ souvenire
    - ⓑ soovenir
    - ⓓ souvennir

19. the _____ of society
    - ⓐ elitte
    - ⓒ elite
    - ⓑ ellite
    - ⓓ ellitte

20. color used as a _____
    - ⓐ camouflage
    - ⓒ cammaflage
    - ⓑ camaflage
    - ⓓ cammouflage

PRACTICE A
Words Often Misspelled I

Summing Up

Practicing words and learning more about them will help you spell them correctly.

Basic Words
1. playwright
2. tragedy
3. metaphor
4. melancholy
5. propaganda
6. subtle
7. pageant
8. unanimous
9. extraordinary
10. enthusiastic

Similar Titles   Write the Basic Word that can replace each underlined word or phrase in this bookstore sales promotion letter. Begin each word with a capital letter.

Dear Reader:

Here's an offer you can't refuse! Receive 87% off the price of your next purchase if you buy now. Choose the titles you want to order. Mail the enclosed form in the prepaid envelope.

1. *Exceptional Treasures of the Desert*
2. *Watching for Persuasive Information*
3. *Balancing Joy and Gloom*
4. *The Beginning Dramatist*
5. *Comedy and Misfortune*
6. *Dropping Elusive Hints*
7. *How to Organize a Successful Spectacle*
8. *The Eager Employee*
9. *A Figure of Speech for Success*
10. *How to Have Agreed by All Appeal*

Thank you,
Book Order Sales Department

1. _____

2. _____

3. _____

4. _____

5. _____

6. _____

7. _____

8. _____

9. _____

10. _____

Which Is It?   **11–15.** A literary critic is letting you decide which Basic Words deserve thumbs up and which deserve thumbs down. Look at each word given below. If it is a synonym for a Basic Word, write the Basic Word in the thumbs up hand. If it is an antonym, write the Basic Word in the thumbs down hand. Then draw a line to connect each given word with the correct Basic Word in each hand.

Antonym

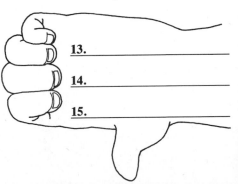

13. _____

14. _____

15. _____

Synonym

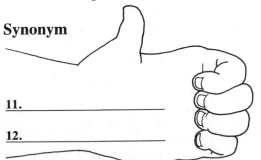

11. _____

12. _____

author

comedy

obvious

comparison

uninterested

Skill: Students will practice spelling words that are often misspelled.

Home Use: Help your child practice the spelling words by having him or her complete the activities on this page. Check the completed page, and have your child practice saying and spelling any misspelled words.

Basic Words
1. playwright
2. tragedy
3. metaphor
4. melancholy
5. propaganda
6. subtle
7. pageant
8. unanimous
9. extraordinary
10. enthusiastic
11. outrageous
12. pneumonia
13. khaki
14. adjourn
15. minuscule
16. siege
17. endeavor
18. prominent
19. wretched
20. flourish

PRACTICE B
Words Often Misspelled I

Crossword Puzzle   Complete the puzzle by writing the Basic Word that fits each clue.

Across

4. persuasive information
7. to put off until later
11. a dull tan color
12. a person who writes drama
14. conspicuous
17. to thrive
18. not obvious
19. a major effort
20. very unusual

Down

1. a spectacle
2. extremely small
3. a disastrous event
5. a lung disease
6. showing great interest
8. in complete agreement
9. a figure of speech
10. shocking
13. full of misery
15. pervasive gloom
16. the blockading of a town

Skill: Students will practice spelling words that are often misspelled.

Home Use: Help your child practice the spelling words by having him or her complete the activities on this page. Check the completed page, and have your child practice saying and spelling any misspelled words.

PRACTICE C
Words Often Misspelled I

A Puzzling Predicament   In the dark box in the puzzle, write the Vocabulary Word that is an antonym for *instructor*. Then write ten other Challenge and Vocabulary Words to complete the puzzle. Finally, write a short definition for each word used in the puzzle.

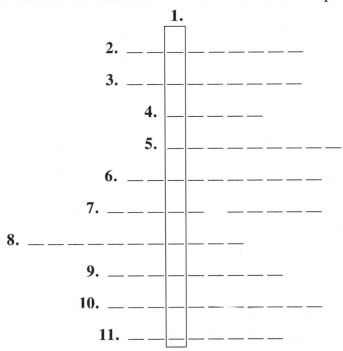

Challenge Words
1. soliloquy
2. rhetoric
3. hypocrite
4. queue
5. susceptible
Theme Vocabulary
6. dramatist
7. Elizabethan
8. sonnet
9. prose
10. blank verse
11. theatrical
12. apprentice
13. repertory

1. _____

2. _____

3. _____

4. _____

5. _____

6. _____

7. _____

8. _____

9. _____

10. _____

11. _____

Hink Pink Challenge   Write a Vocabulary or Challenge Word and another rhyming word to answer each riddle.
Example: What is concise poetry?   *terse verse*
12. What is a hat with poetry written on it?
13. What is a line to see a collection of animals?

14. What are lines of ordinary writing?
15. What is a detailed list of a collection of information?

12. _____

13. _____

14. _____

15. _____

Skill: Students will practice words that are often misspelled and words related to the theme of Shakespeare.

Home Use: Help your child practice the spelling words by having him or her complete the activities on this page. Check the completed page, and have your child practice saying and spelling any misspelled words.

Unit **17** Test: Words Often Misspelled I

Each item below gives four possible spellings of a word. Fill in the letter beside the correct spelling.

Sample:
- ⓐ campane
- ● campaign
- ⓒ campain
- ⓓ cammpaign

---

1. ⓐ propaganda
- ⓑ propiganda
- ⓒ proppaganda
- ⓓ propagganda

2. ⓐ mellancholy
- ⓑ melancholy
- ⓒ melincholy
- ⓓ melanncholy

3. ⓐ mettaphor
- ⓑ metafore
- ⓒ metafor
- ⓓ metaphor

4. ⓐ tragidy
- ⓑ traggedy
- ⓒ tragedy
- ⓓ traggidy

5. ⓐ playright
- ⓑ playrite
- ⓒ playwright
- ⓓ playwrite

6. ⓐ suptle
- ⓑ subtle
- ⓒ sutle
- ⓓ suddle

7. ⓐ unanimous
- ⓑ unannimous
- ⓒ unanimmous
- ⓓ unanimos

8. ⓐ enthussiastic
- ⓑ ennthusiastic
- ⓒ enthoosiastic
- ⓓ enthusiastic

9. ⓐ pagent
- ⓑ pagaent
- ⓒ pagient
- ⓓ pageant

10. ⓐ extrordinary
- ⓑ extraordinary
- ⓒ extrordnary
- ⓓ extrodinary

11. ⓐ flourish
- ⓑ flurrish
- ⓒ floresh
- ⓓ florrish

12. ⓐ wretched
- ⓑ wreched
- ⓒ retchid
- ⓓ reched

13. ⓐ promenent
- ⓑ promenant
- ⓒ prominent
- ⓓ prominant

14. ⓐ endevor
- ⓑ endeavor
- ⓒ endeaver
- ⓓ endaevor

15. ⓐ newmonia
- ⓑ pneumonia
- ⓒ nummonia
- ⓓ pnemonia

16. ⓐ ajourn
- ⓑ ajurne
- ⓒ adjourn
- ⓓ adjern

17. ⓐ miniscule
- ⓑ minniscule
- ⓒ minuscule
- ⓓ minnuscule

18. ⓐ outragous
- ⓑ outrageous
- ⓒ outtrageous
- ⓓ outrageus

19. ⓐ siege
- ⓑ seege
- ⓒ seige
- ⓓ seage

20. ⓐ kaki
- ⓑ kakhi
- ⓒ khaky
- ⓓ khaki

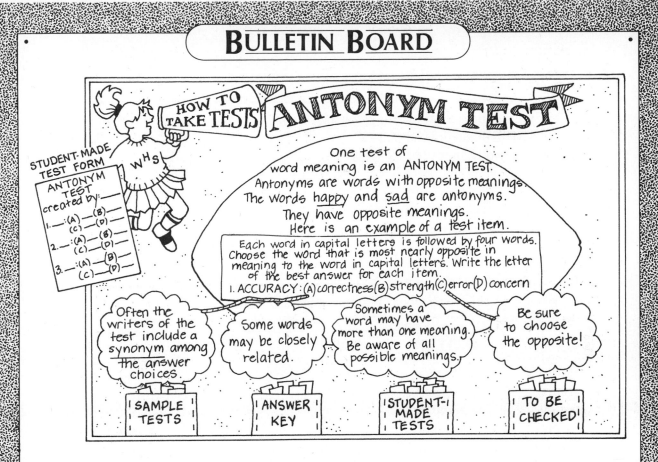

How to make: Make a bulletin-board display to highlight the importance of learning how to take tests. For these units, prepare the bulletin board for antonym tests. Cut out a large, brown paper football. On it, write a summary of the type of test and an example of a test item as shown. Cut 4 large pom-pom shapes from colored paper. (Use your school colors.) In each, write a test-taking tip. Then string a piece of yarn between the tip and any answer in the test item to which it applies.

Draw and cut out a cheerleader wearing your school colors. Put a paper megaphone with the bulletin board title on it in his or her hand. Beside the megaphone attach a card that says *ANTONYM TEST*.

Staple 4 cardboard pockets to the bottom of the board. Label them as shown. Put sample tests in the first pocket and an answer key in the second pocket. Design a form for student-made tests. (See example above.) Then have students use Basic Words to devise their own antonym tests on the forms. Duplicate these and put them in the third pocket.

How to use: Let students take the student-made tests. The completed tests should be placed in the pocket labeled *To Be Checked*. The test creator does the checking.

You may wish to use this bulletin board idea with other types of tests you wish to highlight also.

Use: For use with Units 13–15, 17.

SPELLING NEWSLETTER
for Students and Their Families

Moving Ahead

Unit 13 in your child's level of *Houghton Mifflin Spelling and Vocabulary* presents related word pairs such as *stable* and *stability*, in which a vowel sound changes but its spelling remains the same. Unit 14 focuses on words containing Latin roots, while Unit 15 studies the suffixes in words such as *agency, maturity,* and *curiosity*. Unit 16 studies words with French origins. Finally, Unit 17 discusses words that are often misspelled, such as *extraordinary* and *pneumonia*.

Word Lists

Here are some of the words your child has studied in Units 13–17.

UNIT 13	UNIT 14	UNIT 15	UNIT 16	UNIT 17
strategy	reference	agency	gourmet	playwright
strategic	abstract	society	sauté	propaganda
alternative	traceable	curiosity	parfait	pageant
alternate	proposal	privacy	omelet	unanimous
definition	opposite	frequency	foyer	extraordinary
define	confer	accuracy	etiquette	pneumonia
immunize	exposure	maturity	souvenir	khaki
immune	inference	emergency	camouflage	siege
remedy	traction	anxiety	chauffeur	endeavor
remedial	posture	humidity	intrigue	prominent

👪 Family Activity

Create Crazy Word Stairs with your child. Choose two words from the lists and cross one with the other at a common letter so that the two words appear to form a stair "step." For example, you might cross *confer* and *foyer* at the common *r*. Then have your child add a word to create another step in the stairs. Additional words will have to cross at the first and last letters, as shown. Words must read from left to right and from top to bottom. Stair steps do not have to be equal in length or depth. Start another set of steps when you or your child has difficulty adding to the first set of steps.

```
                    f r e q u e n c y
                    o
                    y
                    e
          c o n f e r
```

Boletín de noticias de ortografía
para estudiantes y para sus familias

Para continuar

Las siguientes son palabras para ejercicios de ortografía que su hijo o hija ha estado estudiando en las Unidades 13 a 17 del libro *Houghton Mifflin Spelling and Vocabulary*.

UNIDAD 13	UNIDAD 14	UNIDAD 15	UNIDAD 16	UNIDAD 17
strategy	reference	agency	gourmet	playwright
strategic	abstract	society	sauté	propaganda
alternative	traceable	curiosity	parfait	pageant
alternate	proposal	privacy	omelet	unanimous
definition	opposite	frequency	foyer	extraordinary
define	confer	accuracy	etiquette	pneumonia
immunize	exposure	maturity	souvenir	khaki
immune	inference	emergency	camouflage	siege
remedy	traction	anxiety	chauffeur	endeavor
remedial	posture	humidity	intrigue	prominent

Actividad para la familia

Formen "escaleras de palabras" con su hijo o hija. Escojan dos palabras de las listas y júntenlas en una letra común de forma que las dos palabras parezcan formar un peldaño de escalera. Por ejemplo, pueden juntar *confer* y *foyer* en la letra común *r*. Después hagan que su hijo o hija añada otra palabra para crear otro peldaño de la escalera. Las palabras que se añadan tendrán que cruzarse en la primera y última letras, como se muestra abajo. Las palabras deben poder leerse de izquierda a derecha y de arriba hacia abajo. Los peldaños de la escalera no tienen que ser iguales en longitud ni altura. Comiencen otra "escalera" cuando a ustedes o a su hijo o hija les dé trabajo añadir más palabras al primer grupo de peldaños.

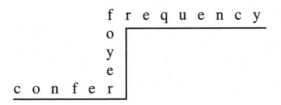

SENTENCE SENSE

Players: any number

You need: one copy of a unit's Basic Word list for each player, paper, pencils

How to play: One player thinks of a sentence that contains one of the Basic Words on the list and writes it on his or her paper. It should be a sentence in which only that Basic Word can be used if the sentence is to make sense. The sentence should not give away the definition of the word. The player reads the sentence aloud, omitting the Basic Word that is to be filled in.

The second player has one minute to look at the Basic Word list and supply the missing word. The first player keeps track of the time. If the second player cannot supply the word, he or she is out. The next player then tries to give the answer.

The player who completes the sentence correctly must think up the next incomplete sentence. None of the Basic Words may be reused. Continue play until all Basic Words have been supplied or until all players are stumped.

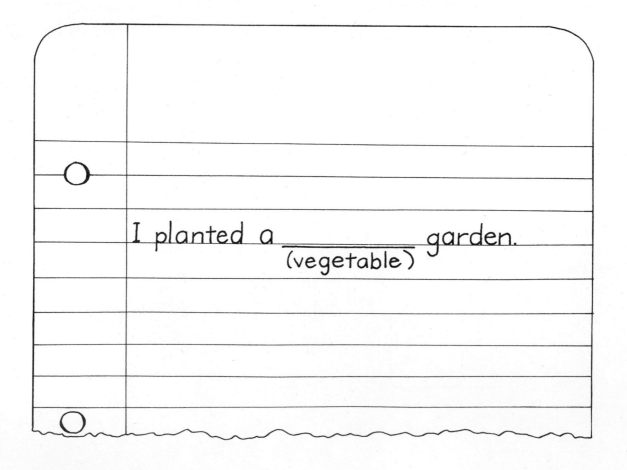

I planted a _____ garden.
(vegetable)

Use: For use with Units 13–17.

Unit **18** Review: Test A

Read the four phrases in each item. Find the underlined word that is spelled incorrectly. Fill in the letter for the phrase with the misspelled word in the answer column.

ANSWERS

Sample:
    a. the opposite direction   **c.** a parfait glass   ⓐ ● ⓒ ⓓ
    b. a holiday pagent   **d.** a clear definition

---

1. **a.** an enthusiastic reaction   **c.** a green vegetable   1. ⓐ ⓑ ⓒ ⓓ
    b. a guormet meal   **d.** a familiarity with

2. **a.** strategic planning   **c.** a job transfer   2. ⓐ ⓑ ⓒ ⓓ
    b. advertising agency   **d.** met the playright

3. **a.** a unannnimous vote   **c.** a delicious omelet   3. ⓐ ⓑ ⓒ ⓓ
    b. sparse vegetation   **d.** a reference book

4. **a.** an alternate form   **c.** the perpose of   4. ⓐ ⓑ ⓒ ⓓ
    b. her nationality   **d.** comedy or tragedy

5. **a.** a subtle hint   **c.** a stabel economy   5. ⓐ ⓑ ⓒ ⓓ
    b. her generosity in giving   **d.** to saute onions

6. **a.** a traceable clue   **c.** a defense strategy   6. ⓐ ⓑ ⓒ ⓓ
    b. her curiousity about him   **d.** a melancholy feeling

7. **a.** a vacation broshure   **c.** a majority of voters   7. ⓐ ⓑ ⓒ ⓓ
    b. a marriage proposal   **d.** a suite of rooms

8. **a.** to define the word   **c.** a binding contract   8. ⓐ ⓑ ⓒ ⓓ
    b. needing privecy   **d.** the door to the foyer

9. **a.** an extraordinary meal   **c.** the head chef   9. ⓐ ⓑ ⓒ ⓓ
    b. a mixed metaphor   **d.** an abbstract concept

10. **a.** a sociaty function   **c.** a garbage disposal   10. ⓐ ⓑ ⓒ ⓓ
    b. a feeling of stability   **d.** a fillet of fish

Unit 18 Review: Test B

Read the four phrases in each item. Find the underlined word that is spelled incorrectly. Fill in the letter for the phrase with the misspelled word in the answer column.

Sample:

a. a home remedy
b. suspense and intrigue
c. a warm personnality
d. a prominent figure

Houghton Mifflin Spelling and Vocabulary. Copyright © Houghton Mifflin Company. All rights reserved.

ANSWERS
ⓐ ⓑ ● ⓓ

1. a. a vacation sovenir
   b. hired a chauffeur
   c. to move to adjourn
   d. to be immune to
   1. ⓐ ⓑ ⓒ ⓓ

2. a. exposure to radiation
   b. a finite set
   c. an elite class
   d. attention to acuracy
   2. ⓐ ⓑ ⓒ ⓓ

3. a. an outrageous idea
   b. those in the minoraty
   c. a preference for
   d. indicative of failure
   3. ⓐ ⓑ ⓒ ⓓ

4. a. to trannspose the numbers
   b. a remedial course of study
   c. wore khaki trousers
   d. based on democracy
   4. ⓐ ⓑ ⓒ ⓓ

5. a. under siege
   b. to use a prepasition
   c. heat and humidity
   d. a wretched feeling
   5. ⓐ ⓑ ⓒ ⓓ

6. a. to indicate a change
   b. to reach maturity
   c. to conferr with them
   d. sensory deprivation
   6. ⓐ ⓑ ⓒ ⓓ

7. a. to flourish there
   b. response to an emergency
   c. an opake glass
   d. straight posture
   7. ⓐ ⓑ ⓒ ⓓ

8. a. to imunize the group
   b. sense of urgency
   c. fertile soil
   d. proper etiquette
   8. ⓐ ⓑ ⓒ ⓓ

9. a. a case of pneumonia
   b. to make an inference
   c. the man's mustache
   d. a miniscule item
   9. ⓐ ⓑ ⓒ ⓓ

10. a. used to camouflage
    b. to rendevous with him
    c. an infinite number
    d. in anxiety and dread
    10. ⓐ ⓑ ⓒ ⓓ

Unit 18 Review: Test C

Find the correctly spelled word to complete each phrase. Fill in the letter beside the correct spelling.

Sample:
known by her _____
● eccentricity   ⓒ ecsentricity
ⓑ eccentrisity   ⓓ escentricity

1. to _____ the game
   ⓐ initiate   ⓒ innitiate
   ⓑ inishiate   ⓓ inisheate

2. to _____ two photographs
   ⓐ juckstapose   ⓒ jukstapose
   ⓑ juxtapose   ⓓ juxtepose

3. that country's _____
   ⓐ prossperity   ⓒ prosperity
   ⓑ prosparity   ⓓ prossparity

4. a _____ of stews
   ⓐ connoisseur   ⓒ conoisseur
   ⓑ connoiseur   ⓓ connoissuer

5. a _____ out to the street
   ⓐ queeu   ⓒ queue
   ⓑ qeueu   ⓓ quewe

6. to be _____ to failure
   ⓐ suseptible   ⓒ susceptable
   ⓑ susceptible   ⓓ susseptible

7. to issue a _____
   ⓐ manndate   ⓒ mandait
   ⓑ mandaite   ⓓ mandate

8. a _____ sketch
   ⓐ commposite   ⓒ composite
   ⓑ composit   ⓓ compositt

9. to behave like a _____
   ⓐ hipocrite   ⓒ hyppocrite
   ⓑ hypocrit   ⓓ hypocrite

10. the book's _____
   ⓐ jenre   ⓒ genra
   ⓑ genre   ⓓ gennre

11. the _____ of the soup
   ⓐ consistancy   ⓒ concistency
   ⓑ consistency   ⓓ connsistency

12. to _____ the picture
   ⓐ superimmpose   ⓒ superempose
   ⓑ super-impose   ⓓ superimpose

13. a beautiful _____
   ⓐ solilaquy   ⓒ soliloquy
   ⓑ saliloquy   ⓓ solilloquy

14. to act as a _____
   ⓐ liaison   ⓒ laison
   ⓑ liason   ⓓ lieison

15. quest for _____
   ⓐ anonimity   ⓒ annonymity
   ⓑ anonymmity   ⓓ anonymity

16. a _____ restriction
   ⓐ mandatory   ⓒ manndatory
   ⓑ mandutory   ⓓ mandetory

17. to use a _____
   ⓐ protracter   ⓒ proteractor
   ⓑ protracktor   ⓓ protractor

18. ate an _____
   ⓐ hors d'oevre   ⓒ hor d'oeuvre
   ⓑ hors d'oeuvre   ⓓ hors d'ouevre

19. to take the _____
   ⓐ inisheative   ⓒ initiative
   ⓑ inetiative   ⓓ inishiative

20. showed real _____
   ⓐ spontaneity   ⓒ spontanity
   ⓑ spontanaity   ⓓ sponteneity

Prewriting Ideas: Story

Choosing a Topic Listed below are some topics that one student thought of for writing a story. What story ideas of your own do they make you think of?

On the lines below *My Five Ideas*, list five sad, funny, or unusual ideas for a story. Which ones do you have the most ideas about? Which ones would your readers find most entertaining? Circle the topic that you would like to write about.

Ideas for Writing

When Two Friends Competed in the Same
    Race
Athletes Who Became Friends at the
    Olympics
The Adventures of an Exchange Student
The Haunted Library
The Only Girl on the Team
The Time Machine in Murph's Back Yard
The Dream That Came True
The Strange New Neighbors Next Door

My Five Ideas

1. _____
2. _____
3. _____
4. _____
5. _____

Exploring Your Topic Use a story map to plan your story. Write the topic you chose in the top rectangle. Describe the setting, the main characters, and the plot conflict, climax, and resolution for your story in the boxes in the story map. Provide some details for each part of your story plan.

Topic

Setting	Characters

Plot

conflict
climax
resolution

Use: For use with Step 1: Prewriting on page 119.

Midyear Test

Find the word that is spelled incorrectly. Fill in the letter beside the misspelled word.

Sample:
- ● outrageus
- ⓑ emergency
- ⓒ transpose
- ⓓ astrology

---

1. ⓐ interferance
   ⓑ liable
   ⓒ emission
   ⓓ oxygen

2. ⓐ mercury
   ⓑ allude
   ⓒ definition
   ⓓ subttle

3. ⓐ chord
   ⓑ terminalogy
   ⓒ transform
   ⓓ bronco

4. ⓐ proposel
   ⓑ nationality
   ⓒ brochure
   ⓓ translate

5. ⓐ psychology
   ⓑ symptom
   ⓒ Farhenheit
   ⓓ aisle

6. ⓐ superletive
   ⓑ stampede
   ⓒ tragedy
   ⓓ emigrate

7. ⓐ communication
   ⓑ submit
   ⓒ strategic
   ⓓ traceble

8. ⓐ generocity
   ⓑ buffet
   ⓒ coyote
   ⓓ interstate

9. ⓐ enthusiastic
   ⓑ narciscus
   ⓒ immerse
   ⓓ reference

10. ⓐ intercession
    ⓑ choral
    ⓒ adverse
    ⓓ parfay

11. ⓐ society
    ⓑ stability
    ⓒ biology
    ⓓ submurge

12. ⓐ protein
    ⓑ oddysey
    ⓒ vegetable
    ⓓ opposite

13. ⓐ commit
    ⓑ assent
    ⓒ homoginized
    ⓓ submarine

14. ⓐ canvas
    ⓑ superintendant
    ⓒ immune
    ⓓ maturity

15. ⓐ khaki
    ⓑ mythology
    ⓒ omission
    ⓓ symetrical

(continued)

Midyear Test (continued)

16. ⓐ subdivide
    ⓑ Celsius
    ⓒ collapse
    ⓓ cafateria

17. ⓐ regiment
    ⓑ exposure
    ⓒ ettiquette
    ⓓ elite

18. ⓐ flourish
    ⓑ accummulate
    ⓒ transmit
    ⓓ jaguar

19. ⓐ prospective
    ⓑ imunize
    ⓒ distract
    ⓓ mustache

20. ⓐ miniscule
    ⓑ urgency
    ⓒ fertile
    ⓓ infinite

21. ⓐ recession
    ⓑ counterclockwise
    ⓒ allfalfa
    ⓓ photogenic

22. ⓐ transaction
    ⓑ tantilize
    ⓒ stationary
    ⓓ meteorology

23. ⓐ accurracy
    ⓑ rationale
    ⓒ intervention
    ⓓ dialogue

24. ⓐ appliance
    ⓑ phase
    ⓒ galvinized
    ⓓ subtitle

25. ⓐ illuminate
    ⓑ souvenir
    ⓒ geneology
    ⓓ sierra

PRACTICE A
Vowel Changes II

Houghton Mifflin Spelling and Vocabulary. Copyright © Houghton Mifflin Company. All rights reserved.

Basic Words
1. restoration
2. restore
3. original
4. origin
5. illustrate
6. illustrative
7. sequence
8. sequential
9. punctual
10. punctuality

Summing Up

To remember the spelling of a word with the schwa sound, think of a related word in which the vowel sound is more obvious.

Word Pairs   Complete each sentence by writing a pair of related Basic Words. Then underline the vowels that change from |ə| to a short vowel sound in each pair. (More than one vowel should be underlined in one pair of words.)

1–2. Betsy is always _____ about turning in her schoolwork because she knows that her teacher values _____ .

3–4. The author has used many _____ examples in the book, and the artist will _____ each one.

5–6. Once the _____ of the first painting is finished, the expert will begin to _____ the second painting.

7–8. José wrote a very _____ story about the _____ of the world.

9–10. Because the episodes in the book are not _____ , it is very difficult to understand the _____ of events.

1. _____
2. _____
3. _____
4. _____
5. _____

6. _____
7. _____
8. _____
9. _____
10. _____

Wrong Words   The wrong Basic Word has been used in each of the following sentences. Cross out the word that does not belong, and write the correct Basic Word.

11. That car is being sold by its sequential owner.
12. Edwin will illustrate the old house to its former condition.
13. We expect Jane at exactly five o'clock because she is known for her originality.
14. The airline's short film of emergency procedures was helpful and punctual, clearly showing us exactly what to do.
15. After Marina finishes her story, she will restore it in watercolors.
16. Dr. Riddle was asked to determine the sequence of the rock.
17. Do you remember the punctuality of events in that book?
18. The museum has sent several paintings out for origin.
19. Charlie bought a new watch to make sure he is original.
20. I will do those tasks in illustrative order.

11. _____
12. _____
13. _____
14. _____
15. _____
16. _____
17. _____
18. _____
19. _____
20. _____

Skill: Students will practice spelling pairs of related words with vowel changes.

Home Use: Help your child practice the spelling words by having him or her complete the activities on this page. Check the completed page, and have your child practice saying and spelling any misspelled words.

Basic Words
1. restoration
2. restore
3. original
4. origin
5. illustrate
6. illustrative
7. sequence
8. sequential
9. punctual
10. punctuality
11. symbolism
12. symbolic
13. tranquil
14. tranquility
15. syllable
16. syllabication
17. neutral
18. neutrality
19. trivial
20. triviality

PRACTICE B

Vowel Changes II

Puzzle Play   Write the Basic Word that fits each clue.

1. a part of a word   _ _ _ ◯ _ _ _ _ _

2. first   _ _ _ _ _ _ _ _

3. 1, 2, 3, 4 . . .   _ _ _ ◯ _ _ _ _

4. insignificance   ◯ _ _ _ _ _ _ _ _ _ _

5. representative   _ _ _ _ _ _ _ _ _ _

6. peaceful   ◯ _ _ _ _ _ _ _

7. impartiality   _ ◯ _ _ _ _ _ _ _

8. promptness   _ _ _ _ _ _ _ _ _ _

9. the source of something   _ _ ◯ _ _ _ _

10. the use of symbols   _ _ ◯ _ _ _ _ _

Now write the letters in the circles in order to answer this riddle:
What occurs once in every minute, twice in every moment, but not once in a thousand years?

Answer: the   _ _ _ _ _ _   _

Word Squeeze   Each group of three words contains a hidden Basic Word. To find the word, cross out one letter in each of the three words. Then squeeze the remaining letters together to write the Basic Word.
Example: tr*y* an*d* quil*t*   *tranquil*

11. spun   cat   dual
12. train   quail   city
13. are   story   nation
14. sequel   not   dial
15. syllabic   cast   iron

16. hill   must   grate
17. trim   vie   all
18. new   hut   rail
19. red   stop   are
20. ail   luster   native

11. _____

12. _____

13. _____

14. _____

15. _____

16. _____

17. _____

18. _____

19. _____

20. _____

EXTRA!   Write your own Word Squeeze activity for at least five Basic Words.

Skill: Students will practice spelling pairs of related words with vowel changes.

Home Use: Help your child practice the spelling words by having him or her complete the activities on this page. Check the completed page, and have your child practice saying and spelling any misspelled words.

PRACTICE C
Vowel Changes II

Challenge Words
1. emphasis
2. emphatic
3. economy
4. economics

Theme Vocabulary
5. fresco
6. varnish
7. deteriorate
8. expertise
9. plaster
10. pigment
11. scaffold
12. meticulous

In Other Words   Find and underline a synonym or an antonym of a Challenge or Vocabulary Word in each sentence. Write the Challenge or Vocabulary Word. Then write *S* or *A* to identify each answer as a synonym or an antonym of the underlined word.

1. Leo put a lot of significance on the main argument in his speech.
2. Gloria showed extravagance in spending her allowance.
3. Steve took an interesting finance course this semester.
4. "Stop environmental pollution!" the senator proclaimed in an impassioned voice.
5. Acid rain has caused those statues to decay over the years.
6. The careless worker's habits were widely known.
7. Melanie demonstrated her incompetence in cooking.
8. The painter stood on a platform to reach the ceiling.

1. _____   **5.** _____

2. _____   **6.** _____

3. _____   **7.** _____

4. _____   **8.** _____

Art Advice   Imagine that you are a student of the great artist Michelangelo. What advice might he give you about painting frescoes? In the speech balloons, write several suggestions that Michelangelo might have made. Use the Vocabulary Words *fresco*, *varnish*, *plaster*, *pigment*, and *scaffold*.

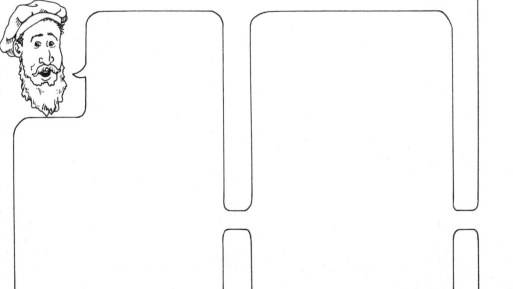

Skill: Students will practice spelling pairs of related words with vowel changes and words related to the theme of painting restoration.

Home Use: Help your child practice the spelling words by having him or her complete the activities on this page. Check the completed page, and have your child practice saying and spelling any misspelled words.

Unit **19** Test: Vowel Changes II

Find the correctly spelled word to complete each phrase. Fill in the letter beside the correct spelling.

Sample:

to _____ at sports

● excel   ⓒ excell

ⓑ exsell   ⓓ exell

1. to put in _____ order
   - ⓐ seequential
   - ⓑ sequential
   - ⓒ sequenntial
   - ⓓ sequencial

2. to _____ with an example
   - ⓐ ilustrate
   - ⓑ illusstrate
   - ⓒ illustrate
   - ⓓ illistrate

3. known for his _____
   - ⓐ punctuality
   - ⓑ puncuality
   - ⓒ punnctuality
   - ⓓ puntcuality

4. the _____ of the building
   - ⓐ restoration
   - ⓑ restorration
   - ⓒ resstoration
   - ⓓ resteration

5. the _____ of the universe
   - ⓐ orrigin
   - ⓑ origin
   - ⓒ origen
   - ⓓ orrigen

6. to be _____
   - ⓐ puntual
   - ⓑ punctal
   - ⓒ puncual
   - ⓓ punctual

7. an _____ example
   - ⓐ illustrative
   - ⓑ ilustrative
   - ⓒ ilastrative
   - ⓓ illastrative

8. to _____ to the original condition
   - ⓐ reestore
   - ⓑ reastore
   - ⓒ restorr
   - ⓓ restore

9. the _____ of events
   - ⓐ seequence
   - ⓑ sequance
   - ⓒ sequence
   - ⓓ seaquence

10. an _____ painting
    - ⓐ orriginal
    - ⓑ original
    - ⓒ originel
    - ⓓ originil

11. a position of _____
    - ⓐ nuetrality
    - ⓑ nutrality
    - ⓒ neutrallity
    - ⓓ neutrality

12. a feeling of _____
    - ⓐ trannquility
    - ⓑ tranquility
    - ⓒ tranquelity
    - ⓓ tranquilitty

13. to take a _____ position
    - ⓐ newtrel
    - ⓑ nutrel
    - ⓒ nutral
    - ⓓ neutral

14. found _____ in the poem
    - ⓐ symbollism
    - ⓑ simbolism
    - ⓒ symbolism
    - ⓓ synbolism

15. the _____ of the word
    - ⓐ sylabication
    - ⓑ sillabication
    - ⓒ syllabication
    - ⓓ sylabbication

16. a _____ piece of information
    - ⓐ trivial
    - ⓑ triveal
    - ⓒ trivvial
    - ⓓ triviall

17. a _____ gesture
    - ⓐ synbolic
    - ⓑ symbolic
    - ⓒ symbollic
    - ⓓ simbolic

18. the _____ of the event
    - ⓐ triviality
    - ⓑ trivviality
    - ⓒ triveality
    - ⓓ triviallity

19. a _____ landscape
    - ⓐ tranquil
    - ⓑ tranquel
    - ⓒ tranquill
    - ⓓ trainquil

20. stress on the third _____
    - ⓐ sylable
    - ⓑ syllable
    - ⓒ sylabble
    - ⓓ sillable

PRACTICE A
Latin Roots II

Basic Words
1. conspiracy
2. diversion
3. transpire
4. convert
5. expire
6. advertisement
7. universal
8. reverse
9. perspiration
10. extrovert

Summing Up
Many English words contain the Latin roots *ver* and *spir*.

Root Tick-Tack-Toe Add the correct Latin root to form a Basic Word in the tick-tack-toe grid. Draw a line through the boxes that make tick-tack-toe, and write those Basic Words on lines 1–3.

re _____ se	con _____ acy	ad _____ tisement
tran _____ e	di _____ sion	uni _____ sal
con _____ t	extro _____ t	per _____ ation

1. _____   2. _____   3. _____

Now write each of the ten Basic Words under the correct word root below.

ver = to turn   **spir** = to breathe

4. _____   10. _____

5. _____   11. _____

6. _____   12. _____

7. _____   13. _____

8. _____

9. _____

Silly Book Titles Write the Basic Word that completes each silly title. Remember to capitalize each word.
14. *An ____ Tells How to Make Friends* by I. M. Outgoing
15. *A ____ Revealed* by Kip No Secrets
16. *A Distracting ____* by N. Tertainment
17. *The ____ Need for Sleep: A Worldwide Study* by I. M. Tired
18. *How to ____ Your Roof into a Sun Deck* by Sonny Bathe

14. _____

15. _____

16. _____

17. _____

18. _____

Skill: Students will practice spelling words with the Latin roots *ver* and *spir*.

Home Use: Help your child practice the spelling words by having him or her complete the activities on this page. Check the completed page, and have your child practice saying and spelling any misspelled words.

Basic Words

1. conspiracy
2. diversion
3. transpire
4. convert
5. expire
6. advertisement
7. universal
8. reverse
9. perspiration
10. extrovert
11. diverse
12. respiration
13. vertical
14. controversy
15. versus
16. anniversary
17. aspire
18. versatile
19. introvert
20. invert

PRACTICE B
Latin Roots II

Crossword Puzzle   Complete the puzzle by writing the Basic Word that fits each clue.

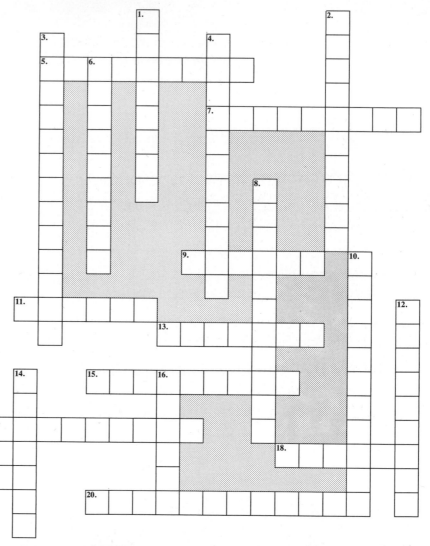

Across

5. recreation
7. to happen
9. to desire strongly
11. to turn upside down
13. different in kind
15. worldwide
17. an inward-looking person
18. to terminate
19. the opposite of something
20. sweat

Down

1. directly upright
2. a secret plan
3. a public notice
4. argument
6. able to do many things
8. a date's yearly return
10. breathing
12. an outgoing person
14. to change
16. against

Skill: Students will practice spelling words with the Latin roots *ver* and *spir*.

Home Use: Help your child practice the spelling words by having him or her complete the activities on this page. Check the completed page, and have your child practice saying and spelling any misspelled words.

PRACTICE C
Latin Roots II

Synonym Search   1–16. Find eight Challenge and Vocabulary Words hidden in the puzzle. The words may appear horizontally, vertically, or diagonally. Circle each word, and then write it. Then find and circle a synonym for each word you wrote. Write the synonym next to the matching Challenge or Vocabulary Word.

```
s e p l t i n v e r s e e r o q e
i u l a d i v u l g e n g e p z s
n r r d i n d a t i u v a t i l p
c e n v b e o i d u x v e u s b i
o v a e e f g p g i s n e r o j o
g e l r t i n v p r s e m n t p n
n a w s b t l s i o u g b o t k a
i l h a s c r l p e n g u p u b g
t v e r t e b r a y p e r i t o e
o s w y b q s i e n i e n t s n o
o p p o s i t e g t c n r t s e v
o b s e r v a t i o n e g u v l d
```

<table>
<tr><td colspan="2">**Challenge Words**</td></tr>
<tr><td>**1.**</td><td>adversary</td></tr>
<tr><td>**2.**</td><td>revert</td></tr>
<tr><td>**3.**</td><td>vice versa</td></tr>
<tr><td>**4.**</td><td>inverse</td></tr>
<tr><td>**5.**</td><td>vertebra</td></tr>
<tr><td colspan="2">**Theme Vocabulary**</td></tr>
<tr><td>**6.**</td><td>espionage</td></tr>
<tr><td>**7.**</td><td>divulge</td></tr>
<tr><td>**8.**</td><td>incognito</td></tr>
<tr><td>**9.**</td><td>dossier</td></tr>
<tr><td>**10.**</td><td>microfilm</td></tr>
<tr><td>**11.**</td><td>clearance</td></tr>
<tr><td>**12.**</td><td>surveillance</td></tr>
<tr><td>**13.**</td><td>Interpol</td></tr>
</table>

Challenge/ Vocabulary Word	**Synonym**
1–2. _____	_____
3–4. _____	_____
5–6. _____	_____
7–8. _____	_____
9–10. _____	_____
11–12. _____	_____
13–14. _____	_____
15–16. _____	_____

Telegram Espionage   On the back of this paper, write a telegram to Interpol, giving information concerning the activities of Master X, a famous spy. Include these Challenge and Vocabulary Words in your telegram: *clearance, vice versa, incognito, dossier, microfilm, Interpol.*

Skill: Students will practice spelling words with the Latin roots *ver* and *spir* and words related to the theme of spy novels.

Home Use: Help your child practice the spelling words by having him or her complete the activities on this page. Check the completed page, and have your child practice saying and spelling any misspelled words.

Unit **20** Test: Latin Roots II

Each item below gives four possible spellings of a word. Fill in the letter beside the correct spelling.

Sample:
- ⓐ insperation
- ⓑ insperassion
- ⓒ insperration
- ● inspiration

---

1. ⓐ transpire
   ⓑ transpier
   ⓒ trannspire
   ⓓ transspire

2. ⓐ conspirecy
   ⓑ conspiracy
   ⓒ consperecy
   ⓓ consperacy

3. ⓐ revirce
   ⓑ reverse
   ⓒ riverse
   ⓓ reverce

4. ⓐ exspire
   ⓑ expier
   ⓒ expire
   ⓓ excpire

5. ⓐ divursion
   ⓑ diversion
   ⓒ deversion
   ⓓ diverrsion

6. ⓐ converte
   ⓑ convurt
   ⓒ convert
   ⓓ convirt

7. ⓐ addvertisement
   ⓑ adverrtisement
   ⓒ advertisement
   ⓓ advurtisement

8. ⓐ pirspiration
   ⓑ pirspration
   ⓒ persperation
   ⓓ perspiration

9. ⓐ universal
   ⓑ unerversal
   ⓒ unaversle
   ⓓ unaversal

10. ⓐ extrovert
    ⓑ extrovurt
    ⓒ extrovirt
    ⓓ extravert

11. ⓐ inverte
    ⓑ invertt
    ⓒ innvert
    ⓓ invert

12. ⓐ contraversy
    ⓑ contraversey
    ⓒ controversey
    ⓓ controversy

13. ⓐ introvert
    ⓑ introverte
    ⓒ intravert
    ⓓ inntrovert

14. ⓐ vurtacal
    ⓑ vertical
    ⓒ verticle
    ⓓ virtical

15. ⓐ resperation
    ⓑ resspiration
    ⓒ resparration
    ⓓ respiration

16. ⓐ virsatile
    ⓑ verrsatile
    ⓒ versatile
    ⓓ versitile

17. ⓐ anniversery
    ⓑ anniversary
    ⓒ aniversary
    ⓓ aniversery

18. ⓐ verssus
    ⓑ verrsus
    ⓒ verrses
    ⓓ versus

19. ⓐ deverse
    ⓑ diverse
    ⓒ divurse
    ⓓ divirse

20. ⓐ aspire
    ⓑ aspier
    ⓒ aspiere
    ⓓ ascpier

PRACTICE A
Noun Suffixes II

Summing Up

The endings *-ian*, *-ist*, and *-ism* are noun suffixes.

Basic Words
1. historian
2. politician
3. comedian
4. pianist
5. librarian
6. novelist
7. pharmacist
8. custodian
9. criticism
10. idealism

Suffix Puzzle   1–10. Find and circle ten words that can be combined with the suffixes *-ian*, *-ist*, and *-ism* to form the Basic Words. Then write the Basic Words.

```
a b n a n o v a r c t u v w
d e p o v r w c c n o b c l
e t h w v i c a i w v n m i
w a p c b e p u m z t c d s
p o i d s a l n s b i o j h
p h a r m a c y a t o m z s
p i n a f l r h s g o e h i
a s o g e w i g h t o d p w
b t t m o n t b e c a y y m
p o t i m y i g r h k a l c
r r t i y t c h k a e n w z
a y d e m l i b m b r v c x
a i d e a l v m o q e y p t
q n w b r t m r w o i e q t
p t e i p o l i t i c x b n
```

1. _____

2. _____

3. _____

4. _____

5. _____

6. _____

7. _____

8. _____

9. _____

10. _____

Tongue Twisters   Write the Basic Word that best completes each tongue twister. The word should begin with the same sound that begins most of the other words in the sentence. See how quickly you can say each sentence.

11. Carrie coaxed the colorful _____ into coming to the countryside for a crazy comic convention.

12. Patty painted a perfect picture of her pal Peter, the _____ who also plays percussion.

13. Lorna listened to the _____ lecture on literature.

14. Please pay the _____ for the pamphlet on his party's previous campaign pledges.

15. Perhaps Phil's _____ can fly to Philadelphia to find a physician.

16. Henry hired the _____ to help him with his history homework.

17. Cathy's casual _____ of Curt's cat's conduct caused a considerable catastrophe.

18. The cathedral's conscientious _____ carefully cleaned up the choir chambers.

11. _____

12. _____

13. _____

14. _____

15. _____

16. _____

17. _____

18. _____

Skill: Students will practice spelling words with the noun suffixes *-ian*, *-ist*, and *-ism*.

Home Use: Help your child practice the spelling words by having him or her complete the activities on this page. Check the completed page, and have your child practice saying and spelling any misspelled words.

Basic Words
1. historian
2. politician
3. comedian
4. pianist
5. librarian
6. novelist
7. pharmacist
8. custodian
9. criticism
10. idealism
11. guitarist
12. soloist
13. realism
14. civilian
15. conformist
16. perfectionist
17. mannerism
18. pedestrian
19. guardian
20. individualist

PRACTICE B
Noun Suffixes II

Analogies Write the Basic Word that completes each analogy.
1. hospital : doctor :: drugstore : _____
2. present : reporter :: past : _____
3. script : playwright :: manuscript : _____
4. race : runner :: campaign : _____
5. reed : clarinetist :: strings : _____
6. knowledge : teacher :: protection : _____
7. information : professor :: joke : _____
8. money : banker :: books : _____
9. sew : tailor :: clean : _____
10. drive : motorist :: walk : _____

1. _____   6. _____
2. _____   7. _____
3. _____   8. _____
4. _____   9. _____
5. _____   10. _____

Proofreading **11–20.** Find and cross out ten misspelled Basic Words in this letter. Then write each word correctly.

Dear Sophie,

I'm really enjoying college! I love my literary critisism class. The professor, Dr. Sterne, is a perrfectionist. He keeps us on our toes. He has a startling manerism, a sharp cough. I jump every time I hear it! Dr. Sterne was once a military man and has carried a sense of discipline into his civillian life.

My roommate Charmaine is a pianoist and a soloiste in the choir. She is a real indevidualist. It is nice to see someone so unique when it is easier to be a cunformist.

The ideelism I'd had about college life is not too far off the mark. It is a charmed existence. Father tells me to enjoy it while it lasts because I'll have to approach life with raelism soon enough. I think I'll take his advice. I still have time to decide whether I want to be a pharmacist or a librarian. Write soon!

Your sister,
Alexa

11. _____
12. _____
13. _____
14. _____
15. _____
16. _____
17. _____
18. _____
19. _____
20. _____

Skill: Students will practice spelling words with the noun suffixes -ian, -ist, and -ism.

Home Use: Help your child practice the spelling words by having him or her complete the activities on this page. Check the completed page, and have your child practice saying and spelling any misspelled words.

PRACTICE C
Noun Suffixes II

Overachievers Anton, Roberto, Laureen, Mamie, and Willard each have two careers. Read the clues. Then complete the chart. Put a check mark in each correct box and an X in each incorrect box.

- Mamie, whose brother is a linguist, dislikes animals.
- Willard uses lenses in both of his occupations.
- Anton's area of expertise is modern art.
- Roberto, who works on Wall Street, failed French in college.
- The chiropractor asked her stockbroker to invest some of her money. She also asked Mamie to install a chandelier in her dining room.
- The stockbroker has developed a new hors d'oeuvre recipe.
- At lunch yesterday, the equestrian, the cartographer, and the optometrist discussed the stock market.

    "My stockbroker predicts that the market will make enormous gains this year," said the equestrian. "I agree with him."
    "I'm not sure about that," said the optometrist.
    "A worldwide depression is coming," the cartographer said. "My brother works as a translator for foreign businesspeople, who are all predicting the worst. He agrees with them."

Challenge Words
1. linguist
2. equestrian
3. optimism
4. pessimism
5. skepticism
Theme Vocabulary
6. electrician
7. curator
8. photographer
9. stockbroker
10. optometrist
11. caterer
12. chiropractor
13. cartographer

	cartographer	caterer	chiropractor	curator	electrician	equestrian	linguist	optometrist	photographer	stockbroker
Anton										
Roberto										
Laureen										
Mamie										
Willard										

Now write the Challenge and Vocabulary Words that name each person's careers. Then write the Challenge Word that best describes his or her attitude toward the stock market.

	Career	Career	Attitude
1–3. Anton	_____	_____	_____
4–6. Roberto	_____	_____	_____
7–9. Laureen	_____	_____	_____
10–12. Mamie	_____	_____	_____
13–15. Willard	_____	_____	_____

Skill: Students will practice spelling words with the noun suffixes *-ian, -ist,* and *-ism* and words related to the theme of careers.

Home Use: Help your child practice the spelling words by having him or her complete the activities on this page. Check the completed page, and have your child practice saying and spelling any misspelled words.

Unit **21** Test: Noun Suffixes II

Find the correctly spelled word to complete each phrase. Fill in the letter beside the correct spelling.

Sample:

a newspaper _____
- ⓐ repportor
- ⓑ riporter
- ⓒ reportor
- ● reporter

1. to ask the _____
   - ⓐ farmacist
   - ⓑ pharmacist
   - ⓒ pharmmacist
   - ⓓ pharmasist

2. the _____ of the building
   - ⓐ custodian
   - ⓑ custodiane
   - ⓒ custodan
   - ⓓ custodain

3. a talented _____
   - ⓐ peanist
   - ⓑ pianist
   - ⓒ piannist
   - ⓓ pianiste

4. constructive _____
   - ⓐ critticism
   - ⓑ critisism
   - ⓒ criticism
   - ⓓ critticism

5. a sense of _____
   - ⓐ ideelism
   - ⓑ idaelism
   - ⓒ iddealism
   - ⓓ idealism

6. the school _____
   - ⓐ librarian
   - ⓑ libbrarian
   - ⓒ librarien
   - ⓓ librairian

7. the family _____
   - ⓐ historyian
   - ⓑ histroyan
   - ⓒ histrian
   - ⓓ historian

8. a _____ running for office
   - ⓐ pollitician
   - ⓑ politician
   - ⓒ politisian
   - ⓓ polatician

9. a famous _____
   - ⓐ novellist
   - ⓑ novalist
   - ⓒ novelist
   - ⓓ novilist

10. a stand-up _____
    - ⓐ comediane
    - ⓑ comedian
    - ⓒ comedien
    - ⓓ comedan

11. an outlook of _____
    - ⓐ realism
    - ⓑ raelism
    - ⓒ reelism
    - ⓓ realisme

12. wearing _____ clothing
    - ⓐ civillian
    - ⓑ civelian
    - ⓒ civilien
    - ⓓ civilian

13. an interesting _____
    - ⓐ inndividualist
    - ⓑ indivijualist
    - ⓒ individualist
    - ⓓ inndivijualist

14. being a _____
    - ⓐ connformist
    - ⓑ conforrmist
    - ⓒ conformist
    - ⓓ cunformist

15. to be a _____
    - ⓐ perrfectionist
    - ⓑ perfectionist
    - ⓒ perffectionist
    - ⓓ purfectionist

16. a famous _____
    - ⓐ guitarist
    - ⓑ gitarist
    - ⓒ gittarist
    - ⓓ guittarist

17. a strange _____
    - ⓐ manerism
    - ⓑ manirism
    - ⓒ mannirism
    - ⓓ mannerism

18. reserved for _____ traffic only
    - ⓐ pedstrian
    - ⓑ peddestrian
    - ⓒ pedestrien
    - ⓓ pedestrian

19. a song by the _____
    - ⓐ solloist
    - ⓑ soloist
    - ⓒ soloiste
    - ⓓ soleoist

20. parent or _____
    - ⓐ guardian
    - ⓑ gardian
    - ⓒ ghardian
    - ⓓ guardien

PRACTICE A
Words from Other Languages

Basic Words
1. villa
2. pizza
3. spaghetti
4. gondola
5. accordion
6. balcony
7. opera
8. waltz
9. macaroni
10. tycoon

> ### Summing Up
> English has borrowed words from many languages.

Crossword Puzzle   Complete the puzzle by writing the Basic Word that fits each clue.

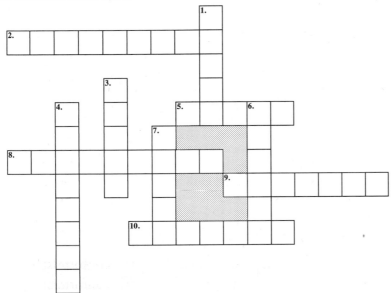

Across

2. an Italian word for a stringy pasta
5. a word taken from a German word for *dance*
8. a German word for a hand-held reed organ
9. an Italian word for a long, narrow boat
10. an Italian word for a projecting platform

Down

1. an Italian word for a country house
3. an Italian word for a play sung to music
4. an Italian word for a tube-shaped pasta
6. a Japanese word for a great lord
7. an Italian word for a pielike dish

Word Riddles   Write the Basic Word that answers each riddle.
11. I can be found on a Venetian canal.
12. I am full of graceful movement.
13. I am squeezed but never hugged.
14. I am full of song.
15. I am tasty but a little flat.
16. I am a house that is always out of town.

13. _____
14. _____
15. _____

11. _____   12. _____   16. _____

Skill: Students will practice spelling words borrowed from other languages.

Home Use: Help your child practice the spelling words by having him or her complete the activities on this page. Check the completed page, and have your child practice saying and spelling any misspelled words.

103

Basic Words
1. villa
2. pizza
3. spaghetti
4. gondola
5. accordion
6. balcony
7. opera
8. waltz
9. macaroni
10. tycoon
11. finale
12. violin
13. confetti
14. pretzel
15. kindergarten
16. kimono
17. influenza
18. umbrella
19. sauerkraut
20. graffiti

PRACTICE B
Words from Other Languages

Rhyming Pairs   Write the Basic Word that rhymes with the given word to answer each riddle.
1. What is a country house for apes?   gorilla ____
2. What is tube pasta for small horses?   pony ____
3. What is a conclusion in a canyon?   valley ____
4. What is the name of a parasol carried by a fairy tale character in glass slippers?   Cinderella ____
5. What is a bulky, tangy cabbage?   stout ____
6. What is trivial, stringy pasta?   petty ____
7. What is a robe from the island of Nakono?   Nakono ____
8. What is a large, wealthy monkey?   baboon ____

1. _____   5. _____

2. _____   6. _____

3. _____   7. _____

4. _____   8. _____

Proofreading   **9–20.** Find and cross out twelve misspelled Basic Words in this travel itinerary. Then write each word correctly.

9. _____

10. _____

11. _____

12. _____

13. _____

14. _____

15. _____

16. _____

17. _____

18. _____

19. _____

20. _____

Saturday: Arrive in Verona, Italy. Transfer by motor coach to our private villa on the Adige River. After a quick visit to the main points of interest in town, we will dine on spaghetti and walse to vialin and accordian music. After dinner, join us in our balconie seats at the opara.

Sunday: Leave for Venice at 4:00 A.M. Check into the hotel before our day of sightseeing. Our leisurely stroll through the city will include a ten-second visit to St. Mark's Cathedral and a five-second gondolla ride. We will also visit an exhibition of kindergarden grafiti art and a medieval pretsel factory.

Monday: After visiting a few Renaissance palaces, we will be ready for the highlight of our tour—a six-hour visit to a paper factory to study how confeti is made. Then join us for our farewell dinner of tiny slices of peetza and delicious bottled water. Leave the city at 11:00 P.M. for the flight home.

Precautions: Due to a recent outbreak of influensa, all travelers are advised to receive vaccinations before departure.

Skill: Students will practice spelling words borrowed from other languages.

104

Home Use: Help your child practice the spelling words by having him or her complete the activities on this page. Check the completed page, and have your child practice saying and spelling any misspelled words.

PRACTICE C
Words from Other Languages

Happy Endings   Each short story description below includes a clue to a Challenge or Vocabulary Word. On another sheet of paper, write a sentence that might conclude each story, using the Challenge or Vocabulary Word suggested by each description.

Example: A young couple marry in a magnificent church.
   The last of the confetti gusted across the cathedral steps.

1. Nigel Newport enters his yacht in the boat race.
2. A famous actor inherits a nut plantation.
3. Giselle Ferrez creates a fantastic costume for the festival.
4. A Japanese family buys a new stove.
5. A Bavarian schoolboy is overcome with the urge to travel.
6. Archaeologists discover the remains of a public square.
7. Artist Bernard Brush's new painting brings him sudden fame.
8. Leonora Borgia wins first prize in a macaroni competition.
9. Explorers uncover the burial place of an Egyptian pharaoh.
10. Kyle Kluss opens a store selling salads and cooked meats.

Challenge Words
1. pistachio
2. tempera
3. wanderlust
4. hibachi
5. delicatessen

Theme Vocabulary
6. pasta
7. cathedral
8. tomb
9. cafe
10. forum
11. catacombs
12. carnival
13. regatta

Souvenirs of Italy   The Bernini family has returned from a vacation in Italy with eight souvenirs. Figure out the code to write the descriptions of their souvenirs. Each description includes one Vocabulary Word. Write the letters for the code in the code box.

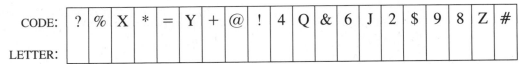

CODE:	?	%	X	*	=	Y	+	@	!	4	Q	&	6	J	2	$	9	8	Z	#
LETTER:																				

11. <u>2 J 9 8</u> <u>X ? $ *</u> <u>J Y</u> <u>?</u> <u>Y J $ Z &</u>

12. <u>X J J 4 % J J 4</u> <u>J Y</u> <u>2 ? 9 8 ?</u> <u>$ = X ! 2 = 9</u>

13. <u>& ? 8 X @ % J J 4</u> <u>Y $ J &</u> <u>?</u> <u>X ? Y =</u>

14. <u>& ? 2</u> <u>J Y</u> <u>8 @ =</u> <u>X ? 8 ? X J & % 9</u>

15. <u>2 ! X 8 Z $ = 9</u> <u>J Y</u> <u>8 @ =</u> <u>X ? 8 @ = * $? Q</u>

16. <u>X ? $ 6 ! # ? Q</u> <u>& ? 9 4 9</u>

17. <u>2 @ J 8 J</u> <u>J Y</u> <u>8 @ =</u> <u>$ = + ? 8 8 ?</u>

Skill: Students will practice spelling words borrowed from other languages and words related to the theme of Italy.

Home Use: Help your child practice the spelling words by having him or her complete the activities on this page. Check the completed page, and have your child practice saying and spelling any misspelled words.

Unit 22 Test: Words from Other Languages

Each item below gives four possible spellings of a word. Fill in the letter beside the correct spelling.

Sample:
- (a) mammath
- ● mammoth
- (c) mamoth
- (d) mammathe

1. (a) opera
   (b) oppra
   (c) opra
   (d) opara

2. (a) maccaroni
   (b) macceroni
   (c) macarroni
   (d) macaroni

3. (a) vila
   (b) villa
   (c) villah
   (d) vilah

4. (a) balcuny
   (b) ballcony
   (c) balcony
   (d) ballcuny

5. (a) gonndola
   (b) gawndola
   (c) gondolla
   (d) gondola

6. (a) tycoon
   (b) ticune
   (c) tycune
   (d) ticoon

7. (a) waltse
   (b) waltze
   (c) waltz
   (d) walze

8. (a) acordion
   (b) accordian
   (c) accordion
   (d) acordian

9. (a) spagetti
   (b) spaghetti
   (c) spagheti
   (d) spageti

10. (a) piza
    (b) pizza
    (c) pitza
    (d) peetza

11. (a) kimmono
    (b) kimino
    (c) kimono
    (d) kamono

12. (a) graffiti
    (b) grafitti
    (c) graffitti
    (d) grafiti

13. (a) vialin
    (b) violin
    (c) violinn
    (d) viulin

14. (a) umbrella
    (b) ummbrella
    (c) umbrela
    (d) ummbrela

15. (a) finalee
    (b) finale
    (c) finnale
    (d) finallee

16. (a) pretzle
    (b) pretzell
    (c) prettzel
    (d) pretzel

17. (a) confetti
    (b) confeti
    (c) confetty
    (d) confety

18. (a) innfluenza
    (b) inflooenza
    (c) influenza
    (d) influennza

19. (a) sourkraut
    (b) saurkraut
    (c) saeurkraut
    (d) sauerkraut

20. (a) kindergarden
    (b) kintergarden
    (c) kindergarten
    (d) kintergarten

PRACTICE A
Words Often Misspelled II

Summing Up

The more you learn about words, the easier it is to remember how to spell them.

Basic Words
1. mortgage
2. acreage
3. vacancy
4. license
5. pamphlet
6. acquaintance
7. drought
8. conscientious
9. miscellaneous
10. exquisite

Mother Goose Times   Write the Basic Words to complete these headlines. Capitalize the words except for those used in direct quotations.

Mother Goose Times

Queen of Hearts Makes ___(1)___ Apple Tarts and ___(2)___ Other Desserts for Mother Hubbard's Bake Sale

Mary Lacks ___(3)___ to Raise Sheep; Switches to Raising Hamsters

Little Ms. Muffet Refuses to Make ___(4)___ of Spider

New Scientific ___(5)___ Contains Information on Little Star and Explains Why It Twinkles

Mrs. Jack Sprat Lowers Cholesterol! "She is very ___(6)___ about sticking to her diet," says Jack.

Yankee Doodle Arrested! Rider's ___(7)___ Revoked

As ___(8)___ Continues, Jack and Jill Forced to Fetch Water from Hill

Old Woman Leaves House to Live in Shoe! "I couldn't pay my ___(9)___," says Old Woman, "and there was no ___(10)___ at the Goose Hotel."

1. _____
2. _____
3. _____
4. _____
5. _____
6. _____
7. _____
8. _____
9. _____
10. _____

Word Groups   Write the Basic Word that fits each group.
11. friend, associate, neighbor, _____
12. flier, leaflet, brochure, _____
13. delicate, beautiful, delightful, _____
14. yardage, footage, mileage, _____
15. thoughtful, serious, careful, _____

11. _____
12. _____
13. _____
14. _____
15. _____

Skill: Students will practice spelling words that are often misspelled.

Home Use: Help your child practice the spelling words by having him or her complete the activities on this page. Check the completed page, and have your child practice saying and spelling any misspelled words.

107

Basic Words
1. mortgage
2. acreage
3. vacancy
4. license
5. pamphlet
6. acquaintance
7. drought
8. conscientious
9. miscellaneous
10. exquisite
11. aerial
12. catastrophe
13. inevitable
14. forfeit
15. lieutenant
16. abundant
17. colossal
18. quarantine
19. succumb
20. anxious

PRACTICE B
Words Often Misspelled II

Synonym / Antonym Switch   Each sentence below contains a synonym or an antonym of a Basic Word. Cross out each synonym or antonym, and write a Basic Word to replace it. Write *A* (for *antonym*) or *S* (for *synonym*) to show the words' relationship.

1. Aunt Vinnie knew that I would resist and turn on the radio.
2. The company made an effort to reward dutiful employees.
3. Thomas Paine wrote a famous brochure titled "Common Sense."
4. The crops were ruined by the previous summer's flood.
5. The mountain climbers' meager supply of food lasted weeks.
6. We found some books and various antiques in the attic.
7. The tiny statue stood at the harbor of ancient Rhodes.
8. The captain was relaxed after hearing the storm warning.

1. _____   5. _____

2. _____   6. _____

3. _____   7. _____

4. _____   8. _____

Hidden Words   9–20.   Read from left to right to find twelve Basic Words in this puzzle. Circle the letters in each Basic Word. Then write the words in the order they appear in the puzzle.

Example: t n Ⓢ Ⓤ Ⓒ Ⓒ Ⓤ   *succumb*
　　　　　　　　Ⓜ Ⓑ t y o l t

```
s t c a t a s t r o p h e l i
  e u t e n a n t r a i m o
  r t g a g e e x q u i
  s i t e t o i n e
      v i t a b l e
      a c r e a
      g e q u a
      r a n t i n e
    f m a e r i a l v
  a c a n c y a g l i c
e n s e e l a c q u a i n
t a n c e l a f o r f e i t n
```

Write the remaining letters in order to spell the body of water that separates the tip of South America from Tierra del Fuego.

Answer: __ __ __ __ __ __ __ __ __ __ __ __ __ __ __ __

9. _____

10. _____

11. _____

12. _____

13. _____

14. _____

15. _____

16. _____

17. _____

18. _____

19. _____

20. _____

Skill: Students will practice spelling words that are often misspelled.

Home Use: Help your child practice the spelling words by having him or her complete the activities on this page. Check the completed page, and have your child practice saying and spelling any misspelled words.

PRACTICE C
Words Often Misspelled II

Two-Step Crosswords   Fill in all the Challenge and Vocabulary Words in the puzzle. (There is only one way to arrange them.) Then write a short clue for each word.

Challenge Words
1. aesthetic
2. bureaucrat
3. continuum
4. disheveled
5. bouillon
Theme Vocabulary
6. Realtor
7. appraisal
8. zoning
9. surveyor
10. negotiate
11. deed
12. evict
13. tenant

Across	**Down**
2. _____	**1.** _____
5. _____	**3.** _____
9. _____	**4.** _____
10. _____	**6.** _____
11. _____	**7.** _____
12. _____	**8.** _____
13. _____	

EXTRA!   Create your own crossword puzzle. Draw a puzzle shape that includes all of the Challenge and Vocabulary Words. Trade puzzles with a classmate, and complete each other's puzzles.

Skill: Students will practice spelling words that are often misspelled and words related to the theme of real estate.

Home Use: Help your child practice the spelling words by having him or her complete the activities on this page. Check the completed page, and have your child practice saying and spelling any misspelled words.

Unit 23 Test: Words Often Misspelled II

Find the correctly spelled word to complete each phrase. Fill in the letter beside the correct spelling.

Sample:

a _____ of quality
- (a) garantee
- (b) guarentee
- (c) garentee
- ● guarantee

1. a box of _____ items
   - (a) misellaneous
   - (b) miscelaneous
   - (c) misselaneous
   - (d) miscellaneous

2. a _____ worker
   - (a) consientious
   - (b) conshientious
   - (c) conscientius
   - (d) conscientious

3. either flood or _____
   - (a) drought
   - (b) drout
   - (c) drowt
   - (d) droutt

4. a driver's _____
   - (a) lisense
   - (b) license
   - (c) licence
   - (d) liscense

5. to have _____ taste
   - (a) exwisite
   - (b) exquisit
   - (c) exquisite
   - (d) exquisitt

6. a four-page _____
   - (a) pamflet
   - (b) pamphlet
   - (c) pamphlett
   - (d) pamflett

7. through an _____
   - (a) aquaintance
   - (b) aquaintence
   - (c) acquaintence
   - (d) acquaintance

8. no _____
   - (a) vacancy
   - (b) vacency
   - (c) vacansy
   - (d) vacensy

9. plenty of _____
   - (a) acreage
   - (b) acrage
   - (c) acredge
   - (d) acrege

10. a _____ on the house
    - (a) morgage
    - (b) mortgage
    - (c) morgege
    - (d) mortgige

11. a _____ error
    - (a) collossal
    - (b) collosal
    - (c) colossel
    - (d) colossal

12. to have _____ resources
    - (a) abundent
    - (b) abundint
    - (c) abundant
    - (d) abbundant

13. a _____ in the army
    - (a) leutenant
    - (b) lieutenant
    - (c) lieutenent
    - (d) leutenent

14. to feel _____
    - (a) anxius
    - (b) anxous
    - (c) anxious
    - (d) anxios

15. to _____ the prize
    - (a) forfeit
    - (b) forfet
    - (c) forfit
    - (d) forfiet

16. to be _____
    - (a) inevitabel
    - (b) inevatable
    - (c) inevitible
    - (d) inevitable

17. to avoid _____
    - (a) catastrophy
    - (b) catastraphy
    - (c) catastrophe
    - (d) catastrophie

18. an _____ view
    - (a) areal
    - (b) aireal
    - (c) aerial
    - (d) arial

19. to put into _____
    - (a) quarentine
    - (b) quarantine
    - (c) quaranteen
    - (d) quarentene

20. to _____ to an attack
    - (a) succumb
    - (b) sucumb
    - (c) sucumn
    - (d) succumnb

BULLETIN BOARD

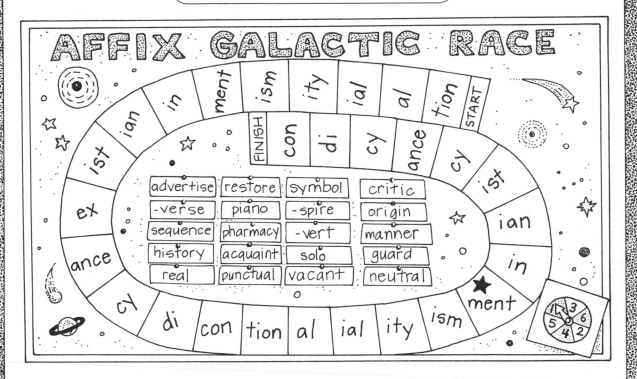

AFFIX GALACTIC RACE

How to make: Use a piece of bulletin board paper to make a large spiral galaxy like the one shown above. Write a prefix or a suffix in each space as shown. Then write a base word or word root for Basic Words containing the affixes on each of 20 index cards. Staple the galaxy and the title "Affix Galactic Race" to the bulletin board. Pin the word cards in the center of the galaxy. Use thumbtacked cardboard stars for markers. Make a spinner by dividing a cardboard square into six spaces that radiate from the center of the square. Number the spaces 1–6 and color each one a different color. In the center of the square, secure an arrow-shaped piece of cardboard with a brad. Attach the arrow loosely enough to be spun around.

How to use: Students will need a pencil and a piece of paper. A student spins the arrow and moves that many spaces. The student then reads the affix on the space where he or she has landed. Have the student remove from the center of the galaxy the base word or word root that can be combined with his or her affix to make a Basic Word and write the word on the paper.

Remind students that adding certain affixes will cause the spelling of the base word or word root to change. Have students check one another's spellings. If the spelling is correct, the student will stay in that space until his or her next turn. If the spelling is wrong, the student will go back to his or her original space and return the card to the center of the galaxy. The first person to finish wins the game.

Use: For use with Units 19–21, 23.

SPELLING NEWSLETTER
for Students and Their Families

Moving Ahead

Unit 19 of your child's level of *Houghton Mifflin Spelling and Vocabulary* studies related word pairs such as *origin* and *original,* in which a vowel sound changes but its spelling remains the same. Unit 20 studies words with Latin roots, while Unit 21 focuses on words with the suffixes *-ian, -ist,* and *-ism.* Unit 22 focuses on words from other languages, such as *waltz,* from German. Finally, Unit 23 studies words that are often misspelled.

Word Lists

Here are some of the words your child has studied in Units 19–23.

UNIT 19	UNIT 20	UNIT 21	UNIT 22	UNIT 23
illustrate	conspiracy	politician	spaghetti	mortgage
illustrative	diversion	comedian	accordion	license
sequence	transpire	pianist	balcony	drought
sequential	advertisement	pharmacist	waltz	conscientious
original	extrovert	criticism	tycoon	miscellaneous
origin	respiration	perfectionist	sauerkraut	colossal
symbolism	versatile	guardian	kindergarten	aerial
symbolic	diverse	mannerism	graffiti	succumb
syllable	controversy	pedestrian	kimono	lieutenant
syllabication	aspire	individualist	finale	quarantine

👪 Family Activity

Take turns with your child combining two words from the lists above and giving a description that will identify the words. Then identify each other's words from the description. Have your child spell the words correctly.

Examples:
a very large group of young children in school (*colossal kindergarten*)
a person who does many things exactly right (*versatile perfectionist*)

List words can be used more than once in descriptions.

Boletín de noticias de ortografía
para estudiantes y para sus familias

Para continuar

Las siguientes son palabras para ejercicios de ortografía que su hijo o hija ha estado estudiando en las Unidades 19 a 23 del libro *Houghton Mifflin Spelling and Vocabulary*.

UNIDAD 19	UNIDAD 20	UNIDAD 21	UNIDAD 22	UNIDAD 23
illustrate	conspiracy	politician	spaghetti	mortgage
illustrative	diversion	comedian	accordion	license
sequence	transpire	pianist	balcony	drought
sequential	advertisement	pharmacist	waltz	conscientious
original	extrovert	criticism	tycoon	miscellaneous
origin	respiration	perfectionist	sauerkraut	colossal
symbolism	versatile	guardian	kindergarten	aerial
symbolic	diverse	mannerism	graffiti	succumb
syllable	controversy	pedestrian	kimono	lieutenant
syllabication	aspire	individualist	finale	quarantine

Actividad para la familia

Túrnense con su hijo o hija para combinar dos palabras de las listas presentadas arriba y para dar una descripción que identifique las palabras. Luego identifiquen las palabras de las otras personas a partir de la descripción. Hagan que su hijo o hija deletree las palabras correctamente.

Ejemplos:
un grupo enorme de niños pequeños en la escuela (*colossal kindergarten*)
una persona que hace muchas cosas de la mejor manera posible (*versatile perfectionist*)

Las palabras de las listas pueden usarse más de una vez en las descripciones.

THEME CROSSWORD PUZZLES

 Players: any number

You need: pencil, spelling book, two sheets of graph paper for each player

How to play: Choose a Basic Word that either names or suggests a category. For example, the Basic Word *advertisement* from Unit 20 suggests the category advertising. Build a crossword puzzle around the category name. Draft your puzzle on one sheet of graph paper.

Write the name of the category across or down in the puzzle squares. Work lightly in pencil. Include as many Basic Words and other words that fit the same category as possible. Words such as *advertisement, newspaper,* and *display* would fit the category advertising, for example. Write these words across or down in your puzzle, making sure that the words that cross have at least one letter in common.

When you have created as complete a puzzle as possible, number the words and write definitions for them under the heads **Across** and **Down.** Match the **Across** and **Down** numerals carefully so that whoever works your puzzle will not become confused.

When you have finished, copy the numerals and definitions on the clean sheet of graph paper. Outline your puzzle with a ruled box. Darken all the squares that are not to be filled in.

Exchange puzzles and try to complete them.

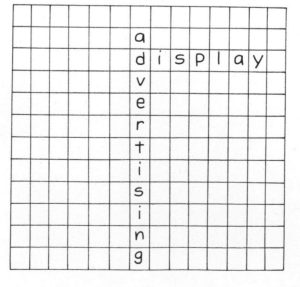

THEME CROSSWORD PUZZLE

Unit **24** Review: Test A

Find the word that is spelled incorrectly. Fill in the letter beside the misspelled word.

Sample:
- ⓐ punctuality
- ⓑ convert
- ● critisism
- ⓓ gondola

1.
- ⓐ exquisite
- ⓑ ideelism
- ⓒ universal
- ⓓ punctual

2.
- ⓐ conspiracy
- ⓑ historian
- ⓒ accordian
- ⓓ mortgage

3.
- ⓐ restoration
- ⓑ extravert
- ⓒ comedian
- ⓓ acreage

4.
- ⓐ miscelaneous
- ⓑ tycoon
- ⓒ sequence
- ⓓ reverse

5.
- ⓐ opera
- ⓑ pharmacist
- ⓒ origin
- ⓓ conscientius

6.
- ⓐ drought
- ⓑ advertisment
- ⓒ restore
- ⓓ villa

7.
- ⓐ sequentiel
- ⓑ perspiration
- ⓒ librarian
- ⓓ waltz

8.
- ⓐ original
- ⓑ transpire
- ⓒ politician
- ⓓ macarroni

9.
- ⓐ vacancy
- ⓑ pizza
- ⓒ custodien
- ⓓ illustrate

10.
- ⓐ balcony
- ⓑ diversion
- ⓒ novilist
- ⓓ license

Unit **24** Review: Test B

Find the word that is spelled incorrectly. Fill in the letter beside the misspelled word.

Sample:
- ⓐ anniversary
- ⓑ realism
- ● kindergarden
- ⓓ abundant

1. ⓐ symbolic
   ⓑ versus
   ⓒ individualist
   ⓓ grafitti

2. ⓐ liuetenant
   ⓑ umbrella
   ⓒ guitarist
   ⓓ triviality

3. ⓐ diverse
   ⓑ aerial
   ⓒ triviel
   ⓓ mannerism

4. ⓐ tranquil
   ⓑ anxious
   ⓒ kimono
   ⓓ intravert

5. ⓐ nuetrality
   ⓑ vertical
   ⓒ civilian
   ⓓ finale

6. ⓐ catastrophe
   ⓑ pretzel
   ⓒ guardien
   ⓓ aspire

7. ⓐ forfeit
   ⓑ contraversy
   ⓒ perfectionist
   ⓓ influenza

8. ⓐ collosal
   ⓑ syllable
   ⓒ pedestrian
   ⓓ invert

9. ⓐ tranquility
   ⓑ resperation
   ⓒ soloist
   ⓓ inevitable

10. ⓐ quarantine
    ⓑ neutral
    ⓒ sauerkraut
    ⓓ connfetti

Unit 24 Review: Test C

Each item below gives four possible spellings of a word. Fill in the letter beside the correct spelling.

Sample:
- ⓐ continuem
- ● continuum
- ⓒ continuam
- ⓓ continum

1. ⓐ pesimism
   ⓑ pessimism
   ⓒ pessamism
   ⓓ pessemism

2. ⓐ emfasis
   ⓑ emmphasis
   ⓒ emphasis
   ⓓ emphesis

3. ⓐ pestachio
   ⓑ pistacchio
   ⓒ pistachioe
   ⓓ pistachio

4. ⓐ diseveled
   ⓑ dishevelled
   ⓒ disheveled
   ⓓ dishevled

5. ⓐ vice versa
   ⓑ viceversa
   ⓒ vice-versa
   ⓓ vice vursa

6. ⓐ ecanomics
   ⓑ economics
   ⓒ econnomics
   ⓓ econommics

7. ⓐ equestrien
   ⓑ equestriene
   ⓒ equesstrian
   ⓓ equestrian

8. ⓐ hibbachi
   ⓑ habachi
   ⓒ hibachi
   ⓓ hibacchi

9. ⓐ asthetic
   ⓑ esthetic
   ⓒ easthetic
   ⓓ aesthetic

10. ⓐ optimism
    ⓑ optemism
    ⓒ optamism
    ⓓ opptimism

11. ⓐ addversary
    ⓑ adversery
    ⓒ adverrsary
    ⓓ adversary

12. ⓐ emmphatic
    ⓑ emphatic
    ⓒ emphattic
    ⓓ emfatic

13. ⓐ vertebra
    ⓑ vertabra
    ⓒ vertebre
    ⓓ verrtebra

14. ⓐ linnguist
    ⓑ linguist
    ⓒ lingwist
    ⓓ linguest

15. ⓐ wanderlust
    ⓑ wonderlust
    ⓒ wanderluste
    ⓓ wanderrlust

16. ⓐ bureaucrat
    ⓑ bureucrat
    ⓒ buraucrat
    ⓓ bureacrat

17. ⓐ delicatesen
    ⓑ delicatesan
    ⓒ dellicatessan
    ⓓ delicatessen

18. ⓐ econnomy
    ⓑ econommy
    ⓒ economy
    ⓓ economie

19. ⓐ boullon
    ⓑ bouillion
    ⓒ bouillon
    ⓓ boillion

20. ⓐ inverse
    ⓑ innverse
    ⓒ invurse
    ⓓ innvurse

Prewriting Ideas: Description

Choosing a Topic   Listed below are some topics that one student thought of for writing a description. What places, people, things, or experiences of your own could you describe?

On the lines below *My Five Ideas*, list five topics that appeal to the senses. Which ones can you remember clearly? Which ones can you describe vividly? Circle the topic that you would like to write about.

Ideas for Writing	**My Five Ideas**
A foggy night	1. _____
Flying through clouds	
A painting	2. _____
A meal of Italian food	3. _____
An attic or a basement	
The beach during a storm	4. _____
The most valuable thing in my bedroom	
My favorite relative	5. _____

Exploring Your Topic   Make up three riddles to describe your topic to a classmate. Fill in the ovals below with questions containing exact words, a simile, and a metaphor that describe your topic. Fold back the top part of this paper before you give your riddles to a classmate to figure out. If your classmate cannot name your topic on the line provided, write additional details on the line at the bottom.

Topic Riddles

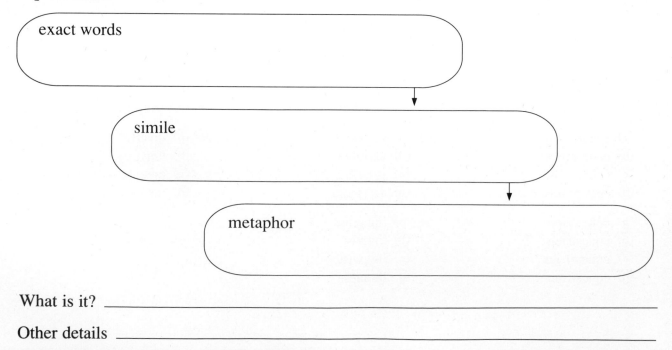

exact words

simile

metaphor

What is it? _____

Other details _____

Houghton Mifflin Spelling and Vocabulary. Copyright © Houghton Mifflin Company. All rights reserved.

PRACTICE A
Vowel Changes III

Summing Up

Learning how the vowels change in one word pair may help
you predict changes in other pairs with the same root.

Basic Words
1. produce
2. production
3. consume
4. consumption
5. reduce
6. reduction
7. retain
8. retention
9. detain
10. detention

Word Equations   Write the Basic Word that completes each
equation. Keep in mind that the addition or subtraction of *tion* may
involve additional spelling changes in each Basic Word.

1. retain + tion =
2. produce + tion =
3. consumption − tion =
4. detention − tion =
5. consume + tion =
6. production − tion =
7. reduce + tion =
8. retention − tion =
9. detain + tion =
10. reduction − tion =

1. _____
2. _____
3. _____
4. _____
5. _____
6. _____
7. _____
8. _____
9. _____
10. _____

News Clues   Write the pair of Basic Words that completes each
pair of headlines. Capitalize each word.

Dromian Parliament Will __(11)__ the Price of Grain
Ministers Say Price __(12)__ Will Help the Economy

Police __(13)__ "Spudsy" Harrison for Questioning
Spudsy's Lawyers Vow to End His __(14)__

Envian Empire Agrees to Return Batland but Will __(15)__ Dravia
World Leaders Say __(16)__ of Dravian Territory Is Illegal

Morcar Motors Will __(17)__ Smaller, Cleaner Car by Spring
Company Hopes That __(18)__ Will Meet Demand

Study Shows Families __(19)__ Less Fat Than Ten Years Ago
Report Credits Health Education Campaign for Decline in __(20)__

11. _____
12. _____
13. _____
14. _____
15. _____
16. _____
17. _____
18. _____
19. _____
20. _____

Skill: Students will practice spelling pairs of related words with vowel changes.

Home Use: Help your child practice the spelling words by having him or her complete the activities on this page. Check the completed page, and have your child practice saying and spelling any misspelled words.

Basic Words
1. produce
2. production
3. consume
4. consumption
5. reduce
6. reduction
7. retain
8. retention
9. detain
10. detention
11. introduce
12. introduction
13. resume
14. resumption
15. induce
16. induction
17. abstain
18. abstention
19. presume
20. presumption

PRACTICE B
Vowel Changes III

Tongue Twisters   Write the Basic Word that completes each tongue twister. The Basic Word should begin with the same sound as most of the other words in the sentence. See how quickly you can say each sentence.

1. The ranchers will rapidly _____ rebuilding the railroad.
2. Carole could quickly _____ Curt's carrot cake.
3. Representatives wished to _____ the rate of redevelopment.
4. Paul's _____ that Polly had painted the parlor was premature.
5. The divers will _____ the dolphin to diagnose its disease.
6. Richard was relieved at the _____ in rehearsal hours.
7. It was easy indeed to _____ Ingrid to inspect the insects.
8. Patty promised to _____ a priceless painting on porcelain.
9. The innkeeper included an _____ written in India ink.
10. Ruby reassured Ruth that Rick will _____ Robert's respect.

1. _____   6. _____

2. _____   7. _____

3. _____   8. _____

4. _____   9. _____

5. _____   10. _____

Telephone Code   Ten Basic Words are written in code, based on the numbers of a telephone keypad. Use the following number key to figure out each word. The vowels are underlined. Write the decoded words correctly.

Example: 7 3̲ 7 8̲ 6 3̲   *resume*

11. 7 7 6̲ 3̲ 8̲ 2 8̲ 4̲ 6 6
12. 7 7 3̲ 7 8̲ 6 3̲
13. 3̲ 3̲ 8̲ 3̲ 6 8̲ 4̲ 6 6
14. 7 3̲ 8̲ 3̲ 6 8̲ 4̲ 6 6
15. 2̲ 2 7 8̲ 3̲ 6 8̲ 4̲ 6 6
16. 4̲ 6 8̲ 7 6̲ 3̲ 8̲ 2̲ 3̲
17. 7̲ 3̲ 7 8̲ 6̲ 7 8̲ 4̲ 6 6
18. 2̲ 2 7 8̲ 2̲ 4̲ 6
19. 4̲ 6 3̲ 8̲ 2 8̲ 4̲ 6 6
20. 2̲ 6 6 7 8̲ 6 7 8̲ 4̲ 6 6

	a b c	d e f
1	2	3
g h i	j k l	m n o
4	5	6
p r s	t u v	w x y
7	8	9
*	0	#

11. _____

12. _____

13. _____

14. _____

15. _____

16. _____

17. _____

18. _____

19. _____

20. _____

Skill: Students will practice spelling pairs of related words with vowel changes.

Home Use: Help your child practice the spelling words by having him or her complete the activities on this page. Check the completed page, and have your child practice saying and spelling any misspelled words.

PRACTICE C
Vowel Changes III

Business News   **1–5.** Read these summaries of five news articles. Write a headline for each article. Use each Vocabulary Word at least once in your headlines.

VOL. 407 NO. 21	**BUSINESS EXTRA**	45 CENTS

1. _____

Across the state, more than 50,000 people are out of work. Economists blame the closing of many high-tech industries.

2. _____

The Pandora Department of Commerce reports that the average income last year for each resident of Pandora was $16,444, up from $15,482 the previous year.

3. _____

Retail prices made a steep jump last month. The Consumer Price Index rose 1.3 percent.

4. _____

Officials say that oil reserves fell during the recent cold snap but that coal stockpiles increased.

5. _____

RayMel Corporation reported sales of $14 million for the year just ended. This is an increase of $2.1 million from the previous year. RayMel executive Abel Shirm also reported that after al-

lowing for expenses the company will realize a profit of $1.3 million. Shirm announced that a large part of these profits will be shared with company employees.

Challenge Words
1. atrocious
2. atrocity
3. ferocious
4. ferocity
Theme Vocabulary
5. income
6. gross
7. net
8. per capita
9. scarcity
10. surplus
11. inflation
12. unemployment

The Front Page   Complete each headline by writing the correct Challenge Word. Capitalize each word.

> **Islands Buffeted by __(6)__ Winds**
> *Storm's __(7)__ Catches Residents Unprepared*

> **Governor Calls False Accusation an __(8)__**
> *"This __(9)__ Behavior Must Stop!"*

On the back of this paper, write the lead for a news story to go with each headline you completed. Answer the questions *Who? What? When? Where?* and *Why?* in your leads.

6. _____

7. _____

8. _____

9. _____

Skill: Students will practice spelling word pairs with vowel changes and words related to the theme of economics.

Home Use: Help your child practice the spelling words by having him or her complete the activities on this page. Check the completed page, and have your child practice saying and spelling any misspelled words.

121

Unit 25 Test: Vowel Changes III

Each item below gives four possible spellings of a word. Fill in the letter beside the correct spelling.

Sample:
- ● grateful
- ⓑ greatful
- ⓒ gratfull
- ⓓ gradefull

1. ⓐ prodution
   ⓑ production
   ⓒ producsion
   ⓓ produssion

2. ⓐ ditain
   ⓑ detane
   ⓒ detain
   ⓓ ditane

3. ⓐ retain
   ⓑ ritain
   ⓒ retane
   ⓓ ritane

4. ⓐ consoom
   ⓑ consoume
   ⓒ consum
   ⓓ consume

5. ⓐ consmption
   ⓑ consumption
   ⓒ consumtion
   ⓓ consoumtion

6. ⓐ produss
   ⓑ produse
   ⓒ produce
   ⓓ produsse

7. ⓐ detantion
   ⓑ ditention
   ⓒ detention
   ⓓ detaintion

8. ⓐ retention
   ⓑ reatention
   ⓒ retenntion
   ⓓ ritention

9. ⓐ redusce
   ⓑ reduce
   ⓒ reduss
   ⓓ reduse

10. ⓐ redussion
    ⓑ reducsion
    ⓒ reduktion
    ⓓ reduction

11. ⓐ presumption
    ⓑ persumption
    ⓒ presemption
    ⓓ presummtion

12. ⓐ abstaintion
    ⓑ abstenntion
    ⓒ abstination
    ⓓ abstention

13. ⓐ resumtionm
    ⓑ resumption
    ⓒ resumbtion
    ⓓ resummtion

14. ⓐ intreduse
    ⓑ introduce
    ⓒ interduce
    ⓓ intraduse

15. ⓐ induse
    ⓑ innduce
    ⓒ indoose
    ⓓ induce

16. ⓐ introdution
    ⓑ intraduction
    ⓒ introduction
    ⓓ interducsion

17. ⓐ presume
    ⓑ persume
    ⓒ presum
    ⓓ presumme

18. ⓐ resume
    ⓑ resoume
    ⓒ resum
    ⓓ resoom

19. ⓐ abbstain
    ⓑ abstane
    ⓒ abstain
    ⓓ abstaine

20. ⓐ induktion
    ⓑ induction
    ⓒ innduction
    ⓓ inducsion

PRACTICE A
Latin Roots III

Summing Up
Many words contain the Latin roots *plic, sens,* and *struct.*

Basic Words
1. structure
2. complexity
3. reconstruct
4. complication
5. sensible
6. obstruct
7. imply
8. pliers
9. sentry
10. sensation

Root Clues   Complete each sentence by writing a Basic Word that makes sense in the sentence and that has the same Latin root as the underlined word. Then underline another word in each sentence that is a clue to the meaning of the Latin root.

Example: A builder will ____ the fort at a low construction cost.
      A builder will *reconstruct* the fort at a low construction cost.

1. Sam and Kay are looking for a sensitive, yet ____ , person who feels able to care for their three young children.
2. I felt a warm ____ as I touched the overheated sensor.
3. These instructions show how to build the entire ____ .
4. The ____ of the map's folds made it complicated to close.
5. Is the plastic pliable enough to fold with a pair of ____ ?
6. We felt that it was senseless to visit the old ____ post.
7. The fence the construction workers are building will not ____ traffic.

5. _____

1. _____   3. _____   6. _____

2. _____   4. _____   7. _____

Book Review   Write seven Basic Words to complete this review.

Build That House by Dee Construct is full of sound and __(8)__ advice for the first-time builder. The author is knowledgeable about every kind of __(9)__ , from the simple garden shed to the suburban house. The book will help you through every frustrating __(10)__ in your project.

   One chapter addresses the difficulty and __(11)__ of some printed instructions. "Throw them away," says the author. "They don't help with small projects. Instead, they just __(12)__ one's progress." The author concedes, however, that there are certain projects that do require careful attention to instructions. "I do not mean to __(13)__ that they never come in handy," admits Dee. "I used them in my most recent effort to __(14)__ a Victorian porch."

8. _____

9. _____

10. _____

11. _____

12. _____

13. _____

14. _____

Skill: Students will practice spelling words with the Latin roots *plic, sens,* and *struct.*

Home Use: Help your child practice the spelling words by having him or her complete the activities on this page. Check the completed page, and have your child practice saying and spelling any misspelled words.

Basic Words
1. structure
2. complexity
3. reconstruct
4. complication
5. sensible
6. obstruct
7. imply
8. pliers
9. sentry
10. sensation
11. accomplice
12. destruction
13. resent
14. sentimental
15. applicable
16. sensor
17. perplex
18. multiplication
19. instructor
20. sensitivity

PRACTICE B

Latin Roots III

Roman Ruins   On the stones of the Roman ruin, write the Basic Word that fits each clue.

1. to block
2. a sensing device
3. to suggest
4. to feel angry about
5. a tool
6. reasonable
7. to restore
8. appropriate
9. a teacher
10. emotional
11. a criminal partner
12. 4 × 4

Proofreading   **13–20.** Find and cross out eight misspelled Basic Words in this account of an ancient Roman archaeological site. Then write each word correctly.

It was easy to reconstruct the city mentally, despite the complixity of the site and the extensive destrucktion. My study proceeded without much complacation. The first struchur I noticed was the city gate, where a senntry had once stood. I recognized the temples, the baths, and the shops with a sensaytion of familiarity. Indeed, I was so well acquainted with Roman city planning that there was little here to perplecs me. The Romans were a sensible people who built with great sensetivity. There is still much we can learn from them.

13. _____

14. _____

15. _____

16. _____

17. _____

18. _____

19. _____

20. _____

Skill: Students will practice spelling words with the Latin roots *plic, sens,* and *struct.*

Home Use: Help your child practice the spelling words by having him or her complete the activities on this page. Check the completed page, and have your child practice saying and spelling any misspelled words.

PRACTICE C
Latin Roots III

Synonym Search   One word in each sentence is a synonym for a Challenge or Vocabulary Word. Underline the synonym. Then write the Challenge or Vocabulary Word that can replace it.

1. Karen and Alice took several months to remodel the kitchen.
2. The building had a marble front.
3. The architect reinforced the wall with a support.
4. We found an old plan of the house in the attic.
5. The writer's opinion of pollution is implied in her work.
6. The carpenter built a reproduction of the old gazebo.
7. That lump of modeling clay is very soft.
8. The group stopped arguing and reached a general agreement.
9. The king had a little tower added to the castle wall.
10. The vacuum cleaner came with precise directions.

1. _____   6. _____
2. _____   7. _____
3. _____   8. _____
4. _____   9. _____
5. _____   10. _____

Challenge Words
1. replica
2. consensus
3. explicit
4. implicit
5. pliable

Theme Vocabulary
6. blueprint
7. renovate
8. colonnade
9. facade
10. pilaster
11. atrium
12. turret
13. buttress

Word Building   11–16. Write a Vocabulary Word to identify each architectural feature of this design.

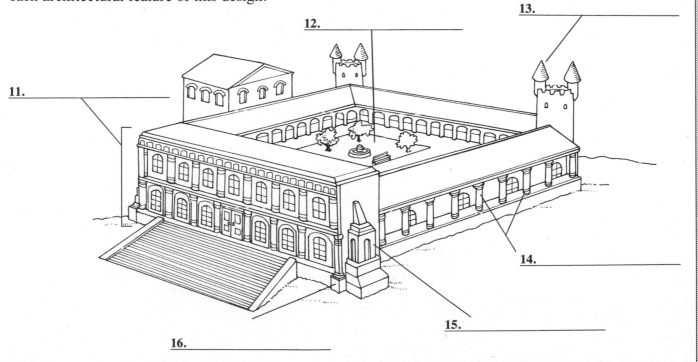

Skill: Students will practice spelling words with the Latin roots *plic, sens,* and *struct* and words related to the theme of architecture.

Home Use: Help your child practice the spelling words by having him or her complete the activities on this page. Check the completed page, and have your child practice saying and spelling any misspelled words.

Unit **26** Test: Latin Roots III

Find the correctly spelled word to complete each phrase. Fill in the letter beside the correct spelling.

Sample:

a marble _____
- ⓐ calumn
- ⬤ column
- ⓒ collum
- ⓓ collumn

1. to have a _____ thought
   - ⓐ sensible
   - ⓑ senseable
   - ⓒ sensable
   - ⓓ senseible

2. a sturdy _____
   - ⓐ structiur
   - ⓑ structure
   - ⓒ structier
   - ⓓ structer

3. the _____ of the design
   - ⓐ commplexity
   - ⓑ cumplexity
   - ⓒ complecsity
   - ⓓ complexity

4. a _____ standing watch
   - ⓐ sentrey
   - ⓑ sentery
   - ⓒ sentrie
   - ⓓ sentry

5. to run into a _____
   - ⓐ commplication
   - ⓑ complication
   - ⓒ complecation
   - ⓓ compelication

6. to _____ the building
   - ⓐ reconstrouct
   - ⓑ reconstruct
   - ⓒ recconstruct
   - ⓓ reconstruck

7. to use _____
   - ⓐ pliurs
   - ⓑ plyers
   - ⓒ pliers
   - ⓓ plierse

8. an unusual _____
   - ⓐ sennsation
   - ⓑ sensetion
   - ⓒ senscation
   - ⓓ sensation

9. to _____ the view
   - ⓐ obstruct
   - ⓑ ubstruct
   - ⓒ obbstruct
   - ⓓ obsteruct

10. to _____ something else
    - ⓐ immply
    - ⓑ emply
    - ⓒ imply
    - ⓓ implie

11. a heat _____
    - ⓐ sensorr
    - ⓑ sensor
    - ⓒ sencor
    - ⓓ sencer

12. an _____ to the crime
    - ⓐ accomplice
    - ⓑ accomplise
    - ⓒ acompliss
    - ⓓ acomplice

13. to confuse and _____
    - ⓐ perrplex
    - ⓑ perplecs
    - ⓒ perplex
    - ⓓ purplex

14. warmth and _____
    - ⓐ sensetivity
    - ⓑ sensitivity
    - ⓒ sensativity
    - ⓓ senssativity

15. the _____ of the warehouse
    - ⓐ distruction
    - ⓑ disstruction
    - ⓒ destruction
    - ⓓ desstruction

16. to be _____ to everyday life
    - ⓐ applicable
    - ⓑ aplicable
    - ⓒ applicible
    - ⓓ applacable

17. a good _____
    - ⓐ instructer
    - ⓑ enstructer
    - ⓒ instructor
    - ⓓ instructre

18. to _____ the intrusion
    - ⓐ resent
    - ⓑ rasent
    - ⓒ rissent
    - ⓓ resente

19. to learn the _____ tables
    - ⓐ multiplacation
    - ⓑ multeplication
    - ⓒ multiplication
    - ⓓ mulltiplication

20. a _____ feeling
    - ⓐ sentamental
    - ⓑ sentimental
    - ⓒ sentimentle
    - ⓓ sentimentel

PRACTICE A
Adjective Suffixes

Summing Up

Three common adjective suffixes are *-al, -ile,* and *-ous*.

Basic Words
1. mountainous
2. gradual
3. agile
4. cautious
5. strenuous
6. crucial
7. mobile
8. horizontal
9. disastrous
10. tremendous

Related Words   Complete each sentence by writing the Basic Word that is a form of the underlined noun. Then underline the adjective suffix in the Basic Word.

1. From the top of the <u>mountain</u>, we could see a region even more ____ than the one we were in.
2. I have lived through many natural <u>disasters</u>, but this flood is the most ____ of all.
3. The steep <u>grade</u> of the road soon became a more ____ incline.
4. We used considerable <u>caution</u> as we approached the bear cub, which was clearly as ____ as we were.
5. It was a <u>strain</u> to participate in such ____ exercise.
6. Jo's <u>agility</u> enabled her to outshine the less ____ athletes.
7. The ships on the <u>horizon</u> had ____ stripes on their flags.
8. The Carrolls wanted more <u>mobility</u> on their vacation, so they towed their car behind their ____ home.

1. _____   4. _____   7. _____

2. _____   5. _____   8. _____

3. _____   6. _____

Word Search   **9–18.** Find and circle the ten Basic Words hidden in the puzzle. The words may appear horizontally, vertically, or diagonally. Write the words.

```
        a b g r a d u a l c c f
        v m h n m r e g o m a x
        a s o o b i w i g s u h
      w t t s u r m u l g d t l i
      z f m r r w n i b e c c i c o p
    v s e o e e u k t z w o e o r c j l
  t y b n b n y m r f a o q i u u x r i l
    e t a i u u t e x w i n c s c d n e
    u h l o o p t n i o n t y i c m
      u e u i p s s d d e o a a r
        t s e n e y b o k m u l
        q w a r t c v e u n a s
        d i s a s t r o u s y t
```

9. _____

10. _____

11. _____

12. _____

13. _____

14. _____

15. _____

16. _____

17. _____

18. _____

Skill: Students will practice spelling words with the adjective suffixes *-al, -ile,* and *-ous.*

Home Use: Help your child practice the spelling words by having him or her complete the activities on this page. Check the completed page, and have your child practice saying and spelling any misspelled words.

Basic Words
1. mountainous
2. gradual
3. agile
4. cautious
5. strenuous
6. crucial
7. mobile
8. horizontal
9. disastrous
10. tremendous
11. occasional
12. artificial
13. fragile
14. precious
15. juvenile
16. ridiculous
17. impartial
18. social
19. hysterical
20. contagious

PRACTICE B
Adjective Suffixes

Antonym Crossword   Complete the puzzle by writing the Basic Word that is the antonym of each clue.

Across
3. worthless
6. real
8. sturdy
10. calm
12. sudden
13. clumsy
14. motionless

Down
1. mature
2. unfriendly
4. vertical
5. sensible
7. prejudiced
9. easy
11. careless

Proofreading   15–20. Find and cross out six misspelled Basic Words in this notice to campers. Then write each word correctly.

ATTENTION CAMPERS! We have captured a sick bear in the mountanous area of the park. This is not a tremendus problem! The bear is not contagius. However, please be cautious.

An occasonal bear near the campsite does not present a crucal problem. Park rangers have completed strenuous training classes that enable them to deal with such problems.

Our mobile units will patrol the park, though we do not expect to find anything disastrus. Please enjoy your stay here!

15. _____

16. _____

17. _____

18. _____

19. _____

20. _____

128

Skill: Students will practice spelling words with the adjective suffixes *-al, -ile,* and *-ous.*

Home Use: Help your child practice the spelling words by having him or her complete the activities on this page. Check the completed page, and have your child practice saying and spelling any misspelled words.

PRACTICE C
Adjective Suffixes

Scaling New Heights   1–3. The director of the Mount Majestic School of Mountaineering has hired you to write a flier describing courses at her school. Write titles and brief descriptions of three courses that the school offers, using all of the Vocabulary Words.

Challenge Words
1. notorious
2. simultaneous
3. volatile
4. ambiguous
5. intellectual
Theme Vocabulary
6. scale
7. rappel
8. summit
9. crevice
10. avalanche
11. piton
12. crampons
13. hypothermia

Mount Majestic School of Mountaineering

1. _____

_____

_____

2. _____

_____

_____

3. _____

_____

_____

Word Relatives   In each pair of sentences, write the Challenge Word that completes the first sentence. Then write a word that is related in spelling and meaning to the Challenge Word to complete the second sentence. You may want to use a class dictionary.

A. A stable leader would not exhibit __(4)__ behavior. Many citizens were shocked by the prime minister's __(5)__ .

B. The exam tested the students' creative and __(6)__ abilities. Every student was able to use his or her __(7)__ .

C. The __(8)__ ringing of the telephone and knocking at the door caused Deng to jump. He tried to answer both __(9)__ .

D. Maggie was __(10)__ for borrowing money and not returning it. She never seemed to understand the cause of her __(11)__ .

E. I cannot figure out what Reggie meant by that __(12)__ statement. His arguments are usually quite free of __(13)__ .

4. _____

5. _____

6. _____

7. _____

8. _____

9. _____

10. _____

11. _____

12. _____

13. _____

Skill: Students will practice spelling words with the adjective suffixes *-al, -ile,* and *-ous* and words related to the theme of mountain climbing.

Home Use: Help your child practice the spelling words by having him or her complete the activities on this page. Check the completed page, and have your child practice saying and spelling any misspelled words.

Unit 27 Test: Adjective Suffixes

Each item below gives four possible spellings of a word. Fill in the letter beside the correct spelling.

Sample:
- (a) abnormle
- (b) abbnormal
- (c) abnormall
- ● abnormal

1.
- (a) mobbile
- (b) mobile
- (c) mobill
- (d) mobille

2.
- (a) aggile
- (b) agile
- (c) ajile
- (d) agyle

3.
- (a) strennuous
- (b) sterenuous
- (c) strenuous
- (d) strenous

4.
- (a) mountainous
- (b) mountenous
- (c) montainous
- (d) mountainious

5.
- (a) cruecial
- (b) crucial
- (c) crusial
- (d) cruciel

6.
- (a) cotious
- (b) causious
- (c) causias
- (d) cautious

7.
- (a) tremindous
- (b) tremmendous
- (c) tremendous
- (d) tremendious

8.
- (a) horrizontal
- (b) horizontal
- (c) horizontle
- (d) horizontel

9.
- (a) dissastrous
- (b) disastriss
- (c) disasstrous
- (d) disastrous

10.
- (a) gradeual
- (b) graduall
- (c) graddual
- (d) gradual

11.
- (a) ridiculous
- (b) riddiculous
- (c) rediculous
- (d) rideculous

12.
- (a) ocasional
- (b) ocassional
- (c) occasional
- (d) occasionel

13.
- (a) impartial
- (b) immpartial
- (c) impartiel
- (d) immpartiel

14.
- (a) conntagious
- (b) contagious
- (c) contagous
- (d) contageous

15.
- (a) fragale
- (b) fragil
- (c) fragile
- (d) fragel

16.
- (a) hysterical
- (b) hystarical
- (c) histerical
- (d) hystericel

17.
- (a) artifisial
- (b) artificial
- (c) artifical
- (d) artifishel

18.
- (a) pretious
- (b) presious
- (c) precious
- (d) pressous

19.
- (a) juvinel
- (b) juvinal
- (c) juvenal
- (d) juvenile

20.
- (a) social
- (b) soshal
- (c) socal
- (d) sosial

PRACTICE A
Words from Places

Summing Up

Many English words come from the names of places.

Basic Words
1. denim
2. jersey
3. satin
4. suede
5. cashmere
6. gauze
7. calico
8. turquoise
9. dungarees
10. italics

Word Histories   Write the Basic Word that fits each word history.

This word comes from

1. Old French words meaning "Turkish stone," because this stone was first found in Turkestan.
2. the French phrase *gants de suède*, meaning "gloves of Sweden," from *Suède* (Sweden).
3. the name for a woolen sweater peculiar to the fishermen of the British isle of Jersey.
4. the French phrase *serge de Nîmes* that refers to a coarse cloth manufactured in the French town of Nîmes.
5. Zaytūn (Arabic for Tseutung), a city in southern China where this cloth was probably first exported.
6. Kashmir, a territory north of India where mountain goats with this soft wool are found.
7. Gaza, where this cloth was supposed to be made.
8. Calicut, a city in India, from which this cloth was first exported.
9. Dungrī, a section of Bombay where fabric for these trousers originated.
10. Venice, Italy, where this style of type was introduced in 1501.

1. _____   4. _____   7. _____
2. _____   5. _____   8. _____
3. _____   6. _____   9. _____
                                          10. _____

Rhyming Pairs   Write the Basic Word that rhymes with the given word to complete the answer to each riddle.

11. What is a reason to use a loosely woven cloth often made into bandages? _____ cause
12. What are models of ducks that are all painted a bluish-green color? _____ decoys
13. What is a patterned cotton cloth that is a rich, brown color? cocoa _____
14. What is a 365-day time period during which only a soft, fine wool is worn? _____ year
15. What is a pair of trousers made of a coarse, heavy, cotton fabric worn by an insect? flea's _____
16. What is a smooth and glossy ancient Roman fabric? Latin _____

11. _____
12. _____
13. _____
14. _____
15. _____
16. _____

Skill: Students will practice spelling words that come from the names of places.

Home Use: Help your child practice the spelling words by having him or her complete the activities on this page. Check the completed page, and have your child practice saying and spelling any misspelled words.

Basic Words
1. denim
2. jersey
3. satin
4. suede
5. cashmere
6. gauze
7. calico
8. turquoise
9. dungarees
10. italics
11. tuxedo
12. muslin
13. rhinestone
14. magenta
15. damask
16. duffel
17. limousine
18. spa
19. Rugby
20. geyser

PRACTICE B
Words from Places

Categories 1–10 Find and circle ten Basic Words in the puzzle. They may appear across, down, or diagonally. Then write each Basic Word you circled under the correct category heading.

```
b n c l g n m u s l i n c l a t
a l o i e n e u a t j p x y
  i k r m y d e b a c l l
    t s p o s d c l u a
      u a c u e c i q
      s a d t g s r c r o
    f i m e l i a i s p a s
  d c a l i c o n u n b z s v
a d e n i m c g a u z e p p e y
```

Location

1. _____

Transportation

2. _____

Print

3. _____

Nature

4. _____

Fabric

5. _____

6. _____

7. _____

8. _____

9. _____

10. _____

Proofreading 11–20. Find and cross out ten misspelled Basic Words in this fashion script. Then write each word correctly.

If you want to say fashion, say it in mujenta! This season's garments are all a tribute to that stunning shade.

Here's Carol, wearing a soft, knee-length jersy dress. Notice how her simple accessories complete the outfit.

Chloe wears a cotton dammask jacket and matching trousers. What a smashing outfit for work or for play!

And here comes Jacqueline in a pair of dungerees with suede trim. We've teamed them with an oversized Rugbey shirt. Jacqueline's denim duffle bag has rinestone accents.

Finally, Neal and Sandra are dressed for a night on the town. Neal's tuxedoe is complemented by a bright satin bow tie and sash combination—a lively alternative to basic black. Sandra steals the show in her cashemere gown and turcquoise cape. Please call a limousine! They're ready!

11. _____

12. _____

13. _____

14. _____

15. _____

16. _____

17. _____

18. _____

19. _____

20. _____

Skill: Students will practice spelling words that come from the names of places.

Home Use: Help your child practice the spelling words by having him or her complete the activities on this page. Check the completed page, and have your child practice saying and spelling any misspelled words.

PRACTICE C
Words from Places

Overlapping Words   Write three words to fit the clues in each item. One word will be a Vocabulary Word. Write the letters in the squares shown for each clue. The words will overlap. You may want to use a class dictionary.

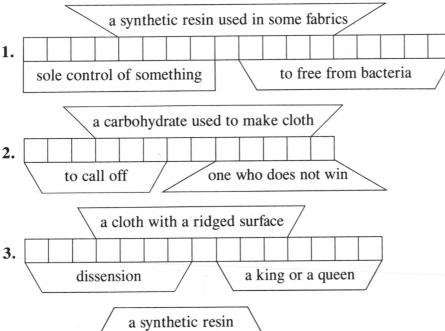

1. a synthetic resin used in some fabrics
   sole control of something / to free from bacteria

2. a carbohydrate used to make cloth
   to call off / one who does not win

3. a cloth with a ridged surface
   dissension / a king or a queen

4. a synthetic resin
   a shrub with white or purple flowers / legal permission to do something

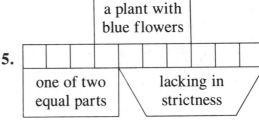

5. a plant with blue flowers
   one of two equal parts / lacking in strictness

Challenge Words
1. jodhpurs
2. laconic
3. serendipity
4. frieze
5. sardonic

Theme Vocabulary
6. textile
7. polyester
8. acrylic
9. corduroy
10. flax
11. cellulose
12. dyeing
13. apparel

Out of the Past   Write the Challenge or Vocabulary Word that fits each word history below. You may want to use your Spelling Dictionary and a class dictionary.

This word comes from

6. Laconia, a region in Greece inhabited by the Spartans, who were noted for their brief, pithy manner of speech.
7. the name of a city in India.
8. characters in the story *The Three Princes of Serendip*, who were always making discoveries by accident.
9. Phrygia, a place noted for its embroidery.
10. Latin words meaning "Sardinian herb," a poisonous plant supposed to distort the face of the eater.
11. the Latin word *textilis*, meaning "woven."
12. the Old English word *dēah*, meaning "hue."
13. the Latin word *apparāre*, meaning "to make ready."

6. _____
7. _____
8. _____
9. _____
10. _____
11. _____
12. _____
13. _____

Skill: Students will practice spelling words that come from the names of places and words related to the theme of textiles.

Home Use: Help your child practice the spelling words by having him or her complete the activities on this page. Check the completed page, and have your child practice saying and spelling any misspelled words.

Unit **28** Test: Words from Places

Find the correctly spelled word to complete each phrase. Fill in the letter beside the correct spelling.

Sample:
    a bottle of _____
    ⓐ collogne   © colone
    ⓑ cologn   ● cologne

1. words in _____
    ⓐ italics   © itallics
    ⓑ ittalics   ⓓ italecs

2. a football _____
    ⓐ jerrsey   © jersey
    ⓑ jerzey   ⓓ jerrsy

3. a pair of _____ shoes
    ⓐ swade   © suede
    ⓑ suade   ⓓ swaid

4. a _____ pin
    ⓐ terquoise   © turrquoise
    ⓑ turquoise   ⓓ terrquoise

5. a _____ sweater
    ⓐ casmere   © cashmear
    ⓑ cazhmere   ⓓ cashmere

6. a dress made of _____
    ⓐ calico   © calliko
    ⓑ callico   ⓓ caleco

7. a _____ jacket
    ⓐ denim   © dennimm
    ⓑ dennim   ⓓ dennem

8. sheer _____ fabric
    ⓐ gawze   © gauz
    ⓑ guaze   ⓓ gauze

9. a _____ gown
    ⓐ satin   © satinn
    ⓑ sattin   ⓓ satine

10. an old pair of _____
    ⓐ dungares   © dungarees
    ⓑ dungarres ⓓ dungurees

11. a pair of _____ earrings
    ⓐ rinestone   © rhineston
    ⓑ rienstone   ⓓ rhinestone

12. a _____ match
    ⓐ Rugbee   © Rugby
    ⓑ Ruggby   ⓓ Ruggbe

13. the health _____
    ⓐ spah   © spaa
    ⓑ spa   ⓓ spaw

14. a tablecloth of _____
    ⓐ damask   © damesk
    ⓑ dammask   ⓓ damusk

15. a _____ for the bridegroom
    ⓐ tucsedo   © tuxedoe
    ⓑ tuxedo   ⓓ tuxsedo

16. steam from the _____
    ⓐ giser   © geyzer
    ⓑ geyser   ⓓ gizer

17. a _____ blouse
    ⓐ magenta   © mugenta
    ⓑ majenta   ⓓ maggenta

18. in a _____ bag
    ⓐ dufal   © duffel
    ⓑ dufel   ⓓ duffle

19. rented a _____
    ⓐ limosine   © limozine
    ⓑ limmousine ⓓ limousine

20. cloth made of _____
    ⓐ muzlin   © muslin
    ⓑ muzzlin   ⓓ muslinn

PRACTICE A
Single or Double Consonants

Summing Up

Knowing why double consonants occur can help your spelling.

Basic Words
1. personnel
2. applicant
3. referral
4. occupation
5. recommend
6. occurrence
7. committee
8. essential
9. broccoli
10. summary

Word Factory   1–10. Help the factory workers dispense consonants to complete each Basic Word on the conveyor belt. Write a single consonant or double consonants in each blank. Then write the Basic Words in the order they appear on the conveyor belt.

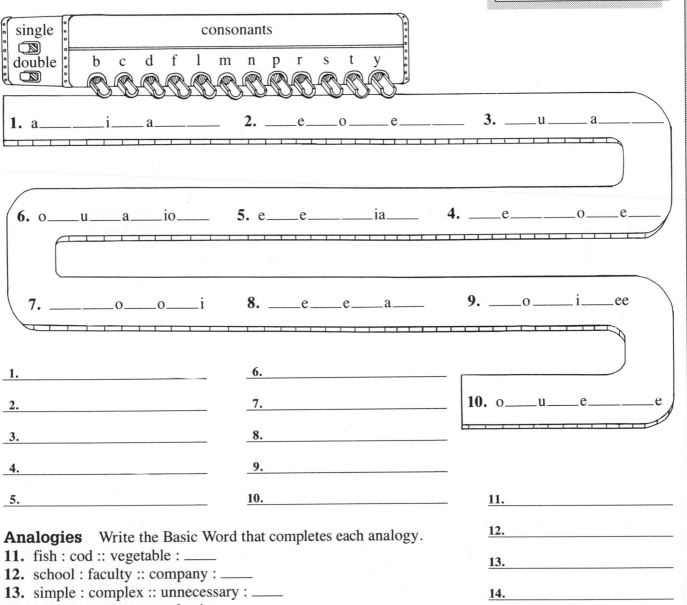

single   double

consonants

b c d f l m n p r s t y

1. a___ ___i___a___ ___   2. ___e___ ___o ___ ___e___ ___   3. ___u___ ___a___ ___

6. o___ ___u___ ___a___ ___io___ ___   5. e___e___ ___ ___ia___ ___   4. ___ ___e___ ___o___ ___e___

7. ___ ___ ___o___ ___o___i   8. ___ ___e___ ___e___a___ ___   9. ___ ___o___ ___ ___i___ee

10. o___ ___u___ ___e___ ___ ___ ___e

1. _____   6. _____   11. _____

2. _____   7. _____   12. _____

3. _____   8. _____   13. _____

4. _____   9. _____   14. _____

5. _____   10. _____   15. _____

Analogies   Write the Basic Word that completes each analogy.

11. fish : cod :: vegetable : _____

12. school : faculty :: company : _____

13. simple : complex :: unnecessary : _____

14. hobby : pastime :: profession : _____

15. presidency : candidate :: job : _____

Skill: Students will practice spelling words with single or double consonants.

Home Use: Help your child practice the spelling words by having him or her complete the activities on this page. Check the completed page, and have your child practice saying and spelling any misspelled words.

135

Basic Words
1. personnel
2. applicant
3. referral
4. occupation
5. recommend
6. occurrence
7. committee
8. essential
9. broccoli
10. summary
11. tariff
12. trespass
13. possession
14. opossum
15. accommodate
16. embarrass
17. paraffin
18. affectionate
19. shrubbery
20. harass

PRACTICE B
Single or Double Consonants

Job Descriptions   Write the Basic Words to complete this newspaper feature story.

Jobs Around Town

Keiko is a zoo keeper. The unusual is an everyday __(1)__ for her. Yesterday, for example, she found a stray __(2)__ nibbling food as it hung from her office lamp. Keiko's job demands patience with both animals and the public. Once she found some students who had wandered into the zoo workshop where employees were using hot __(3)__ to make animal models for a new exhibit. Keiko did not want to humiliate or __(4)__ the curious students, yet she had to warn them not to __(5)__ in restricted areas.

Diego works in a day-care center because he likes working with children. His job requires him to be both firm and __(6)__ . One of his most difficult tasks involves helping each child share his or her favorite __(7)__ . Diego thinks that it is also very important to teach children to show consideration for others. He tells them that sometimes this means slowing down their walking pace to __(8)__ a slower partner. Diego teaches children to be gentle and patient so that they will not annoy or __(9)__ others.

His job also requires some administrative work. He is a member of the __(10)__ that makes decisions about hiring new __(11)__ . Recently, he made a __(12)__ for an __(13)__ whom he could not hire but who had done good work as a volunteer. Diego told us, "I knew it was __(14)__ for this person to find a good job, so I wrote a brief __(15)__ of her volunteer work and sent it to another day-care facility."

Elaine has an enjoyable __(16)__—she works in a plant nursery. Her job requires her to care for flowers, trees, and __(17)__ . Customers have many questions and often ask her to __(18)__ the best fertilizers for growing vegetables such as carrots and __(19)__ . Elaine is also learning about the financial aspects of running such a business. "There are many expenses incurred when plants are imported," Elaine told us. "For example, a tax or __(20)__ can really add to the cost of a tree imported from South America or Asia. I'm always learning something new about cutting costs while maintaining a high-quality supply of plants."

1. _____
2. _____
3. _____
4. _____
5. _____
6. _____
7. _____
8. _____
9. _____
10. _____
11. _____
12. _____
13. _____
14. _____

15. _____
16. _____
17. _____

18. _____
19. _____
20. _____

Skill: Students will practice spelling words with single or double consonants.

Home Use: Help your child practice the spelling words by having him or her complete the activities on this page. Check the completed page, and have your child practice saying and spelling any misspelled words.

PRACTICE C
Single or Double Consonants

It's Business   Use the words below to write eight statements that might be found in an employee handbook. First, list the words in separate groups according to their box numbers. Then write a statement by unscrambling each group and adding the correct Vocabulary Word that completes each sentence.

³ based	⁸ remain	² attend	⁸ employee	³ be	¹ from
⁶ employee	⁸ records	³ reasons	⁷ our	² must	³ specific
⁴ message	⁶ an	⁷ health	⁷ company	¹ workers	² employees
⁵ displeased	¹ laws	⁶ a	⁵ file	⁴ an	⁴ by
⁸ all	⁷ offers	³ on	² sessions	⁶ bonus	³ a
³ must	⁴ a	⁴ conveyed	⁵ a	² new	⁴ is
⁶ is	⁴ office	⁵ a	¹ protect	⁵ employee	⁵ should

Challenge Words

1. succinct
2. renaissance
3. irrevocable
4. collateral
5. reconnaissance

Theme Vocabulary

6. orientation
7. dismissal
8. memorandum
9. discrimination
10. insurance
11. incentive
12. grievance
13. confidential

1. _____

2. _____

3. _____

4. _____

5. _____

6. _____

7. _____

8. _____

Word Categories   Cross out the word that does not belong in each group. Then write a Challenge Word that belongs with each group. You may want to use a class dictionary.

9. concise, verbose, condensed, brief

10. inevitable, unavoidable, reversible, unalterable

11. rebirth, revival, renewal, ruin

12. exploration, survey, reconciliation, inspection

13. pledge, subordinate, guarantee, deposit

9. _____

10. _____

11. _____

12. _____

13. _____

Skill: Students will practice spelling words with single or double consonants and words related to the theme of personnel management.

Home Use: Help your child practice the spelling words by having him or her complete the activities on this page. Check the completed page, and have your child practice saying and spelling any misspelled words.

137

Unit 29 Test: Single or Double Consonants

Each item below gives four possible spellings of a word. Fill in the letter beside the correct spelling.

Sample:
  ⓐ nesecary
  ⓑ necesary
  ● necessary
  ⓓ nessecary

1. ⓐ recommend
   ⓑ recomend
   ⓒ reccomend
   ⓓ reccommend

2. ⓐ ocupation
   ⓑ occupation
   ⓒ occuppation
   ⓓ ocuppation

3. ⓐ referal
   ⓑ refferel
   ⓒ referel
   ⓓ referral

4. ⓐ aplicant
   ⓑ aplecant
   ⓒ applicant
   ⓓ applecant

5. ⓐ personel
   ⓑ personnell
   ⓒ personnel
   ⓓ personell

6. ⓐ ocurence
   ⓑ occurence
   ⓒ ocurrence
   ⓓ occurrence

7. ⓐ essential
   ⓑ issential
   ⓒ isential
   ⓓ esential

8. ⓐ sumary
   ⓑ sumery
   ⓒ sumerry
   ⓓ summary

9. ⓐ committe
   ⓑ comitte
   ⓒ comitee
   ⓓ committee

10. ⓐ broccolli
    ⓑ broccoli
    ⓒ brocoli
    ⓓ brocolli

11. ⓐ harass
    ⓑ harrass
    ⓒ harras
    ⓓ haress

12. ⓐ shrubbery
    ⓑ shruberry
    ⓒ shrubery
    ⓓ shrubberry

13. ⓐ afectionate
    ⓑ affectionet
    ⓒ affectionate
    ⓓ afectionet

14. ⓐ parafin
    ⓑ paraffin
    ⓒ parrafin
    ⓓ pareffin

15. ⓐ tarriff
    ⓑ tarif
    ⓒ tariff
    ⓓ tarrif

16. ⓐ tresspass
    ⓑ trespass
    ⓒ trespas
    ⓓ tresspas

17. ⓐ posesion
    ⓑ possesion
    ⓒ posession
    ⓓ possession

18. ⓐ oppossum
    ⓑ oposum
    ⓒ opossum
    ⓓ opposum

19. ⓐ acomodate
    ⓑ accomodate
    ⓒ accommodate
    ⓓ acommodate

20. ⓐ embarrass
    ⓑ enbarrass
    ⓒ embaras
    ⓓ embarass

BULLETIN BOARD

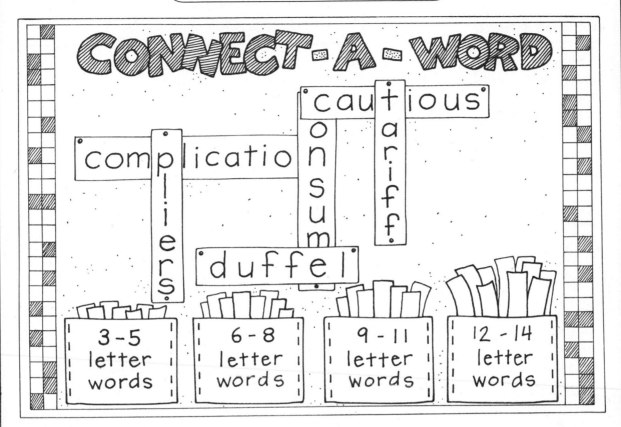

How to make: Title the bulletin board "Connect-A-Word." Provide word cards for all of the Basic Words in Units 25–29. Have students separate the words into groups by number of letters (3–14 letters in words). Then divide the word cards into 4 manila envelopes, labeled as shown, and staple the envelopes to the bulletin board. Also provide long, blank cards and pencils for students to write the words they have drawn from the envelopes.

How to use: Select a long word to begin the bulletin board activity. Print the word on a blank card and tack it to the center of the board. Students should take turns selecting a word of any length they choose and printing it on a blank word card horizontally or vertically as needed to overlap words already on the board. Letters should be equally spaced so that crossed words can be formed. At least one letter of each new word must overlap a letter in a word already on the board. As students add words, they build a crossword puzzle.

Students score 1 point for each 3-letter word they tack up, 2 points for each 4-letter word, and so on. One student acts as the scorekeeper and tallies students' points on a sheet tacked to the bulletin board. Students continue adding words in this manner until either they select a word that does not fit the crossword puzzle or they run out of space.

Use: For use with Units 25–29.

SPELLING NEWSLETTER
for Students and Their Families

Moving Ahead

Unit 25 of your child's level of *Houghton Mifflin Spelling and Vocabulary* studies related word pairs such as *consume* and *consumption,* in which a vowel sound changes but its spelling remains the same. Unit 26 focuses on words with Latin roots, while Unit 27 focuses on words with the suffixes *-al, -ile,* and *-ous.* Unit 28 studies words derived from the names of places. Finally, Unit 29 studies words such as *recommend* and *embarrass,* in which certain consonant sounds are spelled with a double consonant.

Word Lists

Here are some of the words your child has studied in Units 25–29.

UNIT 25	UNIT 26	UNIT 27	UNIT 28	UNIT 29
consume	structure	agile	suede	personnel
consumption	complication	strenuous	cashmere	recommend
reduce	obstruct	crucial	calico	occurrence
reduction	pliers	horizontal	turquoise	broccoli
detain	sensible	disastrous	italics	summary
detention	accomplice	juvenile	duffel	affectionate
induce	sentimental	contagious	rhinestone	embarrass
induction	instructor	impartial	geyser	accommodate
presume	perplex	ridiculous	limousine	trespass
presumption	sensitivity	occasional	magenta	opossum

Family Activity

Play Spell-a-House with your child. Take turns dictating a word from the lists above for each other to spell. If the word is spelled correctly, the speller draws one line of a house made up of twelve lines in all. The first person to correctly spell twelve words and to complete the twelve parts of the house wins that game. Make the house by drawing a four-sided box and then adding two sloping lines for the roof. Add three lines for a chimney and then three lines for a door, for a total of twelve lines.

Boletín de noticias de ortografía
para estudiantes y para sus familias

Para continuar

Las siguientes son palabras para ejercicios de ortografía que su hijo o hija ha estado estudiando en las Unidades 25 a 29 del libro *Houghton Mifflin Spelling and Vocabulary*.

UNIDAD 25	UNIDAD 26	UNIDAD 27	UNIDAD 28	UNIDAD 29
consume	structure	agile	suede	personnel
consumption	complication	strenuous	cashmere	recommend
reduce	obstruct	crucial	calico	occurrence
reduction	pliers	horizontal	turquoise	broccoli
detain	sensible	disastrous	italics	summary
detention	accomplice	juvenile	duffel	affectionate
induce	sentimental	contagious	rhinestone	embarrass
induction	instructor	impartial	geyser	accommodate
presume	perplex	ridiculous	limousine	trespass
presumption	sensitivity	occasional	magenta	opossum

Actividad para la familia

Jueguen con su hijo o hija a deletrear hasta formar una casa. Túrnense para dictar una palabra de las listas de arriba para que la otra persona la deletree. Si deletrea la palabra correctamente, esa persona traza una línea de una casa que se compone de doce líneas en total. Gana la primera persona que deletree doce palabras correctamente y complete las doce líneas que forman la casa. Hagan la casa dibujando una caja de cuatro lados y después añadan dos líneas inclinadas para representar el techo. Añadan tres líneas que representen una chimenea y después tres líneas para formar una puerta, alcanzando así un total de doce líneas.

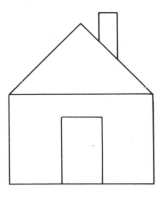

A SPELLING STORY

SPELLING GAME

Players: 2 or more

You need: 20 Basic Word cards from a single unit or from several units combined, a box, tape recorder (if available)

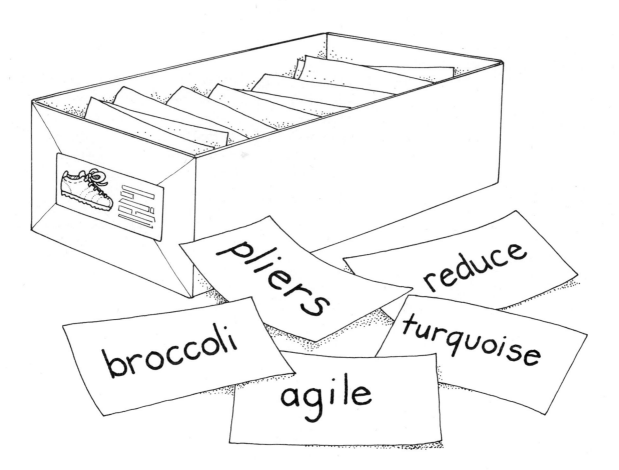

How to play: Put the word cards into the box. Choose a leader who will pick out the cards one by one, calling out the Basic Word that is written on each. The first player must use the first word in a sentence. This sentence should begin a story. The next player must continue the story with a sentence that uses the next word. Make the story as exciting as possible. Continue playing until every Basic Word has been used.

Since each sentence must contain the word called out and keep the story going as well, some sentences may be long and rambling. The player who has the last word must try to make up some kind of ending for the story. If a tape recorder is available, record the story as it develops, and play it back later.

Use: For use with Units 25–29.

Unit **30** Review: Test A

Read the four phrases in each item. Find the underlined word that is spelled incorrectly. Fill in the letter for the phrase with the misspelled word in the answer column.

ANSWERS

Sample:
- **a.** a crucial moment
- **b.** formed a comittee
- **c.** football jersey
- **d.** to retain the meaning

ⓐ ● ⓒ ⓓ

1. **a.** rate of consumption **b.** strenous activity **c.** a sensible solution **d.** a cashmere sweater — 1. ⓐ ⓑ ⓒ ⓓ

2. **a.** book summary **b.** a mountainous region **c.** a brief detenntion **d.** to obstruct the view — 2. ⓐ ⓑ ⓒ ⓓ

3. **a.** primary occupation **b.** increased production **c.** a terquoise stone **d.** used pliers — 3. ⓐ ⓑ ⓒ ⓓ

4. **a.** a tremendous help **b.** an agile cat **c.** unpleasant sensation **d.** a guaze bandage — 4. ⓐ ⓑ ⓒ ⓓ

5. **a.** faded dungarrees **b.** price reduction **c.** plate of broccoli **d.** a gradual increase — 5. ⓐ ⓑ ⓒ ⓓ

6. **a.** major complecation **b.** to produce goods **c.** a personnel manager **d.** words in italics — 6. ⓐ ⓑ ⓒ ⓓ

7. **a.** a denim jacket **b.** to detaine the speaker **c.** to recommend the dish **d.** to imply otherwise — 7. ⓐ ⓑ ⓒ ⓓ

8. **a.** a horizontal line **b.** received a referrel **c.** suede gloves **d.** to consume goods — 8. ⓐ ⓑ ⓒ ⓓ

9. **a.** job applicant **b.** disastrious situation **c.** to stand sentry **d.** a calico dress — 9. ⓐ ⓑ ⓒ ⓓ

10. **a.** strange occurrence **b.** huge structure **c.** cautius behavior **d.** to reduce in number — 10. ⓐ ⓑ ⓒ ⓓ

Unit 30 Review: Test B

Read the four phrases in each item. Find the underlined word that is spelled incorrectly. Fill in the letter for the phrase with the misspelled word in the answer column.

ANSWERS

Sample:
a. a social event
b. to harrass the witness
c. a Rugby match
d. to resent the remark

ⓐ ● ⓒ ⓓ

---

1. a. green shrubery
   b. hysterical laughter
   c. a magenta cloak
   d. sensitivity to others

   1. ⓐ ⓑ ⓒ ⓓ

2. a. a resumption of activity
   b. artificial flowers
   c. an acomplice in crime
   d. an import tariff

   2. ⓐ ⓑ ⓒ ⓓ

3. a. in possession of
   b. multiplication tables
   c. an induction ceremony
   d. juvinile behavior

   3. ⓐ ⓑ ⓒ ⓓ

4. a. stretch limuosine
   b. abstention from voting
   c. paraffin wax
   d. sentimental reasons

   4. ⓐ ⓑ ⓒ ⓓ

5. a. an occasional visit
   b. to acommodate guests
   c. a rhinestone necklace
   d. made the introduction

   5. ⓐ ⓑ ⓒ ⓓ

6. a. swimming instructor
   b. steam from a gyeser
   c. precious stones
   d. affectionate feelings

   6. ⓐ ⓑ ⓒ ⓓ

7. a. to make a presumption
   b. an impartial jury
   c. light sensor
   d. dammask draperies

   7. ⓐ ⓑ ⓒ ⓓ

8. a. to abstain from
   b. contagious laughter
   c. only where aplicable
   d. black tuxedo

   8. ⓐ ⓑ ⓒ ⓓ

9. a. to presoom innocence
   b. a health spa
   c. did embarrass them
   d. fragile crystal

   9. ⓐ ⓑ ⓒ ⓓ

10. a. to resume work
    b. a baby opossum
    c. complete destruction
    d. a duffell bag

    10. ⓐ ⓑ ⓒ ⓓ

Unit 30 Review: Test C

Find the correctly spelled word to complete each phrase. Fill in the letter beside the correct spelling.

Sample:
a _____ smile
● sardonic   ⓒ sarrdonic
ⓑ sardonnic   ⓓ sardunic

---

1. the _____ lion
   ⓐ ferrocious   ⓒ ferocius
   ⓑ feroshious   ⓓ ferocious

2. the _____ substance
   ⓐ pliable   ⓒ plyable
   ⓑ pliabel   ⓓ plyabel

3. an _____ response
   ⓐ ambigous   ⓒ ammbiguous
   ⓑ ambiguous   ⓓ ambiguois

4. a _____ man
   ⓐ renassance   ⓒ renaissance
   ⓑ rennaisance   ⓓ renaissence

5. the wind's _____
   ⓐ ferosity   ⓒ ferrocity
   ⓑ ferocity   ⓓ ferocety

6. the general _____
   ⓐ consensus   ⓒ concensus
   ⓑ consencus   ⓓ conscensus

7. a _____ criminal
   ⓐ notorrious   ⓒ notoreous
   ⓑ notorreous   ⓓ notorious

8. a _____ message
   ⓐ lackonic   ⓒ lakonic
   ⓑ laconic   ⓓ laconnic

9. an _____ contract
   ⓐ irevocable   ⓒ irrevocable
   ⓑ irrevacable   ⓓ irrevicable

10. stylish _____
    ⓐ jodpurs   ⓒ joddpurs
    ⓑ jodhpurs   ⓓ johdpurs

11. to exhibit _____ behavior
    ⓐ atrocious   ⓒ atroceous
    ⓑ attrocious   ⓓ atrotious

12. an exact _____
    ⓐ repplica   ⓒ replika
    ⓑ repplika   ⓓ replica

13. a _____ gas
    ⓐ volatile   ⓒ vollatile
    ⓑ volatil   ⓓ voletile

14. a _____ mission
    ⓐ recconnaissance   ⓒ reconaissance
    ⓑ reconnaissance   ⓓ reconaissence

15. an act of _____
    ⓐ atrosity   ⓒ attrocity
    ⓑ attrosity   ⓓ atrocity

16. an _____ direction
    ⓐ explisit   ⓒ explicit
    ⓑ explisitt   ⓓ explicitt

17. an _____ question
    ⓐ intellectual   ⓒ intelectual
    ⓑ inntelectual   ⓓ inntellectual

18. the colorful _____
    ⓐ freize   ⓒ friez
    ⓑ frieze   ⓓ freise

19. terse and _____
    ⓐ sucinct   ⓒ succinct
    ⓑ sucsinct   ⓓ suscinct

20. found through _____
    ⓐ sarendipity   ⓒ serendipidy
    ⓑ serandipity   ⓓ serendipity

Prewriting Ideas: Persuasive Letter

Choosing a Topic   Listed below are some topics that one student thought of for writing a persuasive letter. What opinions do you feel strongly about?

On the lines below *My Five Ideas*, list five good topics for a persuasive letter. Which issues really matter to you? Which ones can you support with strong reasons? Circle the topic that you would like to write about.

Ideas for Writing

To the dean of a drama school, about getting a scholarship

To the director of a theater company, about performing in your town

To your parents, about letting you go to camp

To the mayor, about helping the homeless

To your principal, about a 4-day school week

To a celebrity, about speaking at your school

My Five Ideas

1. _____

2. _____

3. _____

4. _____

5. _____

Exploring Your Topic   On another sheet of paper, copy the map below large enough to write in, and use it to plan your letter. Write the name of your audience and your opinion in the boxes with those labels.

Fill in each box with a reason that uses each persuasive strategy listed. Give an example of a similar situation that has already occurred. Give an example why something is fair or unfair. Answer a possible objection. List a few possible consequences of your argument. Finally, summarize your argument with a strong statement in the box at the bottom.

Audience	Reasons and Persuasive Strategies	Opinion

precedent	appeal to fairness	response to possible objection	possible consequences

Argument Summary

PRACTICE A
Vowel Changes IV

Summing Up

Learning how the vowels change in one pair of related words can help you predict changes in other pairs with the same root.

Basic Words
1. proclaim
2. proclamation
3. deceive
4. deception
5. acclaim
6. acclamation
7. pertain
8. pertinent
9. maintain
10. maintenance

Changing Vowels **1–10.** Complete each equation by writing the pair of Basic Words that duplicate the vowel changes shown in each example.

perc**ei**ve + tion = perc**e**ption

1. _____ + tion = **2.** _____

abst**ai**n + ent = abst**i**nent

3. _____ + ent = **4.** _____

sust**ai**n + ance = sust**e**nance

5. _____ + ance = **6.** _____

recl**ai**m + tion = recl**a**mation

7. _____ + tion = **8.** _____

9. _____ + tion = **10.** _____

Adverbial Connections Write the Basic Word that completes each sentence. The way each character says something is a clue to the missing word in each sentence.

Example: "The judge issued this _____ ," said Vera **officially.**
        proclamation

11. "How did the suspect _____ you?" asked Sue **trickily.**

12. "The witness has made quite a _____ comment," Jenny said **relevantly.**

13. "I continue to _____ my innocence," said Steve **truthfully.**

14. "The man is a master of _____ !" said Mary **misleadingly.**

15. "Other criminals will _____ his talents," said Doug **approvingly.**

16. "I _____ your guilt to all!" said Betty **publicly.**

11. _____   **14.** _____

12. _____   **15.** _____

13. _____   **16.** _____

Skill: Students will practice spelling pairs of related words with vowel changes.

Home Use: Help your child practice the spelling words by having him or her complete the activities on this page. Check the completed page, and have your child practice saying and spelling any misspelled words.

147

Basic Words
1. proclaim
2. proclamation
3. deceive
4. deception
5. acclaim
6. acclamation
7. pertain
8. pertinent
9. maintain
10. maintenance
11. exclaim
12. exclamation
13. perceive
14. perception
15. conceive
16. conception
17. prevail
18. prevalent
19. sustain
20. sustenance

PRACTICE B
Vowel Changes IV

Proofreading **1–8.** Find and cross out eight misspelled Basic Words in this letter. Then write each word correctly.

Dear Mom and Dad,

Have the newspapers given you all the pertainent facts about your son's victory? You should see the crowds that acclaim me!

I ate a big breakfast to sustain myself on the morning of the race. A head of lettuce gave me sustainence.

All through the race, I knew I would preval. After a slow start, I tried to mantane my speed; but I fell so far behind that Hare, confident of winning, fell asleep.

Hare was awakened by the crowd's aclaimation as the judges began to proclam my victory. Without using deception, I have destroyed the conseption that tortoises never win. Now perhaps tortoises everywhere will come out of their shells!

Love,
Tommy

1. _____

2. _____

3. _____

4. _____

5. _____

6. _____

7. _____

8. _____

Syllable Maze **9–20.** Trace a path through the maze. Find twelve Basic Words by connecting syllables in order. Move up, down, forward, backward, or diagonally, but use each block only once. Some blocks will not be used. The first word is shown.

START	ac	sus	per	main	tion	ceive	cla	ma
	ma	claim	as	cep	lent	sus	ex	tion
	a	ance	ten	main	a	tain	as	con
	proc	pre	cep	a	tain	cla	ceive	as
	la	tion	lent	ceive	a	per	claim	cep
	ma	sus	per	prev	lent	ex	de	ceive	END

Now write the Basic Words in the order that you connected them.

9. _____

10. _____

11. _____

12. _____

13. _____

14. _____

15. _____

16. _____

17. _____

18. _____

19. _____

20. _____

148

Skill: Students will practice spelling pairs of related words with vowel changes.

Home Use: Help your child practice the spelling words by having him or her complete the activities on this page. Check the completed page, and have your child practice saying and spelling any misspelled words.

PRACTICE C
Vowel Changes IV

Proper Propaganda   **1–6.** Write the Challenge or Vocabulary Word that completes each ad. Then write *generalization, testimonial,* or *exaggeration* to identify the propaganda technique used in each ad.

Challenge Words
1. pronounce
2. pronunciation
3. denounce
4. denunciation

Theme Vocabulary
5. generalization
6. persuasive
7. distort
8. exaggeration
9. contradiction
10. substantiate
11. testimonial
12. verification

Hi, I'm cover girl Hannah Hairdo. Are you confused about hair sprays? Try Iron-head Hair Spray. With Iron-head Hair Spray I can make my waist-length hair stand up like an iron beam. Scientists have proved that Ironhead Hair Spray sets like concrete. What other __(1)__ of its effectiveness do you need?

People are talking their way to success! Are you ashamed of the way you speak? Sign up for a Speak Up workshop to improve your expression and __(3)__ . Join all the Speak Up graduates who are no longer afraid to open their mouths. Register today!

1. _____

2. _____

3. _____

4. _____

Are you tired of glue that does not hold? Try Glory Glue. Glory Glue bonds within seconds and can hold objects together for several thousand years. Glory Glue has been used to glue mountains and skyscrapers back together. Anyone who has ever bought a tube of Glory Glue will be able to __(5)__ these claims. Buy Glory Glue today!

5. _____

6. _____

Prefix Play   Read each pair of definitions. Write the Challenge or Vocabulary Word that fits the first definition. Then substitute one of the prefixes below to write another word that fits the second definition. You may want to use a class dictionary.

pre   dis   con   re   e   an

   7–8. to articulate a sound; to make known publicly
 9–10. the act of disagreeing; the act of foretelling
11–12. having the power to convince; having the power to discourage from a course of action
13–14. to express strong disapproval of; to reject
15–16. to give a false account of; to twist out of shape
17–18. the act of condemning; how a person pronounces words

11. _____

12. _____

13. _____

14. _____

15. _____

16. _____

7. _____

8. _____

9. _____

10. _____

17. _____

18. _____

Skill: Students will practice spelling pairs of related words with vowel changes and words related to the theme of propaganda.

Home Use: Help your child practice the spelling words by having him or her complete the activities on this page. Check the completed page, and have your child practice saying and spelling any misspelled words.

Unit **31** Test: Vowel Changes IV

Find the correctly spelled word to complete each phrase. Fill in the letter beside the correct spelling.

Sample:

at the _____ moment
- ⓐ percise
- ● precise
- ⓒ procise
- ⓓ persice

---

1. some _____ information
- ⓐ perttinent
- ⓑ pertinent
- ⓒ perrtinent
- ⓓ pertinant

2. to receive wide _____
- ⓐ aclaim
- ⓑ acclame
- ⓒ acclaim
- ⓓ acklaim

3. a shout of _____
- ⓐ acclamation
- ⓑ aclamation
- ⓒ acclammation
- ⓓ aclammation

4. to _____ the event
- ⓐ proclaim
- ⓑ proclame
- ⓒ proclaem
- ⓓ proclaime

5. tricked by _____
- ⓐ desieption
- ⓑ deception
- ⓒ deceiption
- ⓓ deseption

6. an effort to _____ peace
- ⓐ manetain
- ⓑ maintane
- ⓒ mantain
- ⓓ maintain

7. routine _____
- ⓐ maintenance
- ⓑ manetenance
- ⓒ manetnance
- ⓓ maintenence

8. a royal _____
- ⓐ proclammation
- ⓑ procclamation
- ⓒ proclomation
- ⓓ proclamation

9. to _____ to the subject
- ⓐ pertane
- ⓑ pertain
- ⓒ perrtain
- ⓓ perrtane

10. did not _____ anyone
- ⓐ deseeve
- ⓑ deceive
- ⓒ decieve
- ⓓ desieve

11. to be _____ in that region
- ⓐ prevelant
- ⓑ prevalant
- ⓒ prevelent
- ⓓ prevalent

12. his _____ of the matter
- ⓐ preception
- ⓑ perception
- ⓒ preceiption
- ⓓ percepsion

13. to _____ against the wind
- ⓐ prevaile
- ⓑ prevale
- ⓒ pervail
- ⓓ prevail

14. to _____ with surprise
- ⓐ exlaim
- ⓑ exklaim
- ⓒ exclaim
- ⓓ exlame

15. the _____ of the plan
- ⓐ connception
- ⓑ conseption
- ⓒ conception
- ⓓ connseption

16. to _____ a high note
- ⓐ sustain
- ⓑ susstaine
- ⓒ susstain
- ⓓ sustane

17. an _____ mark
- ⓐ exclammation
- ⓑ exclamation
- ⓒ exlamation
- ⓓ exlammation

18. to provide _____
- ⓐ sustenance
- ⓑ sustenence
- ⓒ sustenense
- ⓓ susstenance

19. to _____ the matter
- ⓐ perceive
- ⓑ preceive
- ⓒ percieve
- ⓓ perceeve

20. to _____ of a similar situation
- ⓐ concieve
- ⓑ conceive
- ⓒ conncieve
- ⓓ conceeve

PRACTICE A
Latin Roots IV

Summing Up

Three common Latin roots are *fac, man,* and *ven.*

Basic Words
1. manufacture
2. factory
3. management
4. efficient
5. manual
6. profit
7. convenient
8. benefit
9. defect
10. inventive

Latin Root Match   **1–11.** Each Latin root factory produces words with only that root. On the lines inside each factory below, write the Basic Words that contain that root. (One Basic Word will be written under two Latin roots.) Underline the roots.

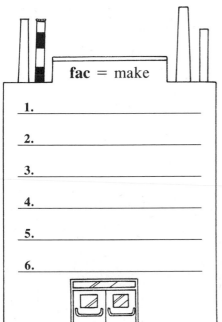

fac = make

1. _____
2. _____
3. _____
4. _____
5. _____
6. _____

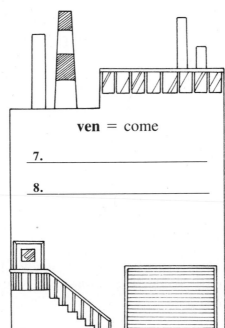

ven = come

7. _____
8. _____

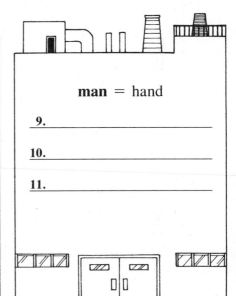

man = hand

9. _____
10. _____
11. _____

Exact Words   Write a Basic Word to replace the underlined words in each sentence.

12. The <u>book of instructions</u> clearly explains how to operate the machinery.
13. The managers must be more <u>original and creative</u> in solving these problems.
14. All employees must be <u>effectively productive</u>.
15. The directors find it <u>suited to their purpose</u> to hold the meeting in the boardroom.
16. Beginning in January, Toyco will <u>process with the use of industrial machines</u> its games in its Columbus factory.
17. Highgear Industries will open a new <u>building in which goods are made</u> in October.
18. Send a report on the machine's <u>lack of something necessary for perfection</u> to the repair service immediately.

12. _____
13. _____
14. _____
15. _____
16. _____
17. _____
18. _____

Skill: Students will practice spelling words with the Latin roots *fac, man,* and *ven.*

Home Use: Help your child practice the spelling words by having him or her complete the activities on this page. Check the completed page, and have your child practice saying and spelling any misspelled words.

Basic Words
1. manufacture
2. factory
3. management
4. efficient
5. manual
6. profit
7. convenient
8. benefit
9. defect
10. inventive
11. effect
12. manipulate
13. factor
14. convention
15. eventually
16. maneuver
17. feat
18. sacrifice
19. manicure
20. preventive

PRACTICE B
Latin Roots IV

Scrambled Memo   1–6. Unscramble the underlined Basic Words to complete this company memo. Write the six Basic Words.

MEMO

TO: All gnemmantae personnel
RE: Increasing fotpir margin

   To increase our income, we must improve the way we freumautnac our product. Sloppy work will produce a product with a cedtef. Encourage your employees to work in a careful, feintecif manner so that our consumers will continue to recognize our high standards.

   When viotnecenn, please list ways to improve production methods.

1. _____   4. _____

2. _____   5. _____

3. _____   6. _____

Word Search   7–20. Find and circle fourteen Basic Words hidden in the puzzle. The words may appear horizontally, vertically, or diagonally.

```
p a w e c a l k f s n f d r o u o h e
m r f s b f r u a e a a a s d n i a v
a t e e e f f e c t i c a m m d t o e
n h a v n d c e t s r t r w a k e a n
e a t t e e j i o t i o f i h n s i t
u l l a f n d u r i w r s h f c u r u
v e m n i c t l y o w r e n a i m a a
c w y i t t h i n v e n t i v e c c l
r m g n a c o n v e n t i o n h a e l
m a n i p u l a t e m a n i c u r e y
```

Now write the Basic Words you circled in alphabetical order.

7. _____

8. _____

9. _____

10. _____

11. _____

12. _____

13. _____

14. _____

15. _____

16. _____

17. _____

18. _____

19. _____

20. _____

Skill: Students will practice spelling words with the Latin roots *fac, man,* and *ven.*

Home Use: Help your child practice the spelling words by having him or her complete the activities on this page. Check the completed page, and have your child practice saying and spelling any misspelled words.

PRACTICE C
Latin Roots IV

Word Merge Use the clues to write two words on each line. One word will be a Challenge or Vocabulary Word. Letters at the end of the first word will also begin the second word. Circle the common letters. You may want to use a class dictionary.

Example: p a t e(n t)r a n c e

1–2. _ _ _ _ _ _ _ _ _ _

3–4. _ _ _ _ _ _ _ _ _ _ _ _

5–6. _ _ _ _ _ _ _ _ _

7–8. _ _ _ _ _ _ _ _ _ _ _ _

9–10. _ _ _ _ _ _ _ _ _

11–12. _ _ _ _ _ _ _ _ _ _ _ _

13–14. _ _ _ _ _ _ _ _ _ _ _

15–16. _ _ _ _ _ _ _ _ _ _

17–18. _ _ _ _ _ _ _ _ _

19–20. _ _ _ _ _ _ _ _ _ _ _

21–22. _ _ _ _ _ _ _ _ _ _ _ _

23–24. _ _ _ _ _ _ _ _ _ _ _

25–26. _ _ _ _ _ _ _ _ _ _ _ _ _ _

Challenge Words
1. deficit
2. manifest
3. circumvent
4. facsimile
5. artifact
Theme Vocabulary
6. automation
7. assembly
8. inventory
9. specifications
10. prototype
11. uniformity
12. component
13. patent

Clues

1. a shortage
2. a court summons
3. to avoid
4. to air out
5. obvious
6. a celebration
7. a reproduction
8. an important event
9. intelligent
10. a relic
11. elevated, flat land
12. automatic control
13. to daze

14. sameness
15. to scatter
16. an exclusive right to produce something
17. the supply of goods on hand
18. a type of grass used to make flour
19. putting together parts to make a whole
20. the words of a song
21. the first full-scale model of a new item
22. a machine that prints letters
23. a part of the whole
24. to beg
25. statements that describe a product exactly
26. a violent attack

Skill: Students will practice spelling words with the Latin roots *fac, man,* and *ven* and words related to the theme of manufacturing.

Home Use: Help your child practice the spelling words by having him or her complete the activities on this page. Check the completed page, and have your child practice saying and spelling any misspelled words.

Unit **32** Test: Latin Roots IV

Each item below gives four possible spellings of a word. Fill in the letter beside the correct spelling.

Sample:
- (a) magnifician
- (b) magnificient
- ● magnificent
- (d) magnificant

---

1. (a) factery
   (b) factory
   (c) factorry
   (d) factury

2. (a) deefect
   (b) deafect
   (c) defect
   (d) defecte

3. (a) convenient
   (b) cunvenient
   (c) connvenient
   (d) convenyent

4. (a) manigement
   (b) managmnt
   (c) manegement
   (d) management

5. (a) eficient
   (b) efficient
   (c) effecient
   (d) efficeint

6. (a) mannufacture
   (b) manafacture
   (c) manufacture
   (d) manufacure

7. (a) innventive
   (b) invenntive
   (c) inventive
   (d) inventiv

8. (a) benefit
   (b) benifit
   (c) bennifit
   (d) bennefit

9. (a) manuel
   (b) manual
   (c) manuell
   (d) manuall

10. (a) proffit
    (b) profitt
    (c) proffitt
    (d) profit

11. (a) preventive
    (b) preeventive
    (c) preaventive
    (d) prevenntive

12. (a) manuver
    (b) maneuver
    (c) manuever
    (d) manneuver

13. (a) feate
    (b) feete
    (c) feat
    (d) faet

14. (a) factor
    (b) facter
    (c) facktor
    (d) factorr

15. (a) manicure
    (b) mannicure
    (c) mannecure
    (d) mannacure

16. (a) mannipulate
    (b) manepulate
    (c) manipulate
    (d) manipyulate

17. (a) evenntually
    (b) eventally
    (c) eventualy
    (d) eventually

18. (a) sackrifice
    (b) sacrifice
    (c) sacrifise
    (d) sacrafice

19. (a) connvention
    (b) convention
    (c) convenntion
    (d) cunvention

20. (a) effect
    (b) efect
    (c) efecte
    (d) effecte

PRACTICE A
Number Prefixes

Basic Words
1. monarch
2. duel
3. dilemma
4. century
5. monk
6. decade
7. monopoly
8. decimal
9. monotone
10. duet

Summing Up

The prefixes *mon-, di-, du-, dec-,* and *cent-* are number prefixes.

Number Network Complete each sentence by writing a Basic Word that makes sense in the sentence and that contains a number prefix that has the same meaning as the underlined word. Then underline the prefix in the Basic Word.

1. One _____ after another was forced to give up the throne.
2. Under the castle walls, the two knights engaged in a _____ .
3. The previous ten years had been a _____ of prosperity.
4. The lecturer spoke in a _____ that put more than one person in the audience to sleep.
5. Those two singers performed a beautiful _____ .
6. One _____ continued to live in the deserted monastery.
7. After one hundred years of war, there came a _____ of peace.
8. Having to choose between the two colors was a real _____ .
9. One company will no longer have a _____ on the market.
10. After finding ten mistakes, the proofreader checked every _____ in the calculations.

1. _____   5. _____   9. _____

2. _____   6. _____   10. _____

3. _____   7. _____

4. _____   8. _____

Hink Pinks Answer each riddle by writing a Basic Word and a rhyming word from the box below.

rule   saxophone   minimal   bunk   cassette

11. What is a bed in a monastery?
12. What is a regulation governing combat between two people?
13. What is a tape recording of a song sung by two people?
14. What is a wind instrument that emits only one sound?
15. What is the smallest number based on 10?

11. _____   14. _____

12. _____   15. _____

13. _____

Skill: Students will practice spelling words with number prefixes.

Home Use: Help your child practice the spelling words by having him or her complete the activities on this page. Check the completed page, and have your child practice saying and spelling any misspelled words.

Basic Words
1. monarch
2. duel
3. dilemma
4. century
5. monk
6. decade
7. monopoly
8. decimal
9. monotone
10. duet
11. monotonous
12. diploma
13. decathlon
14. monologue
15. dual
16. centigrade
17. monogram
18. monorail
19. duplex
20. centennial

PRACTICE B
Number Prefixes

Word Riddles   Write the Basic Word that answers each clue.
1. I am one hundred years old.
2. I am very boring.
3. I can force you to make a difficult choice.
4. I am sought by those who want control.
5. I determine an all-around track and field champion.
6. I am very religious.
7. I have taken place when honor is at stake.
8. I can be found in calculations.
9. I do not participate in conversations.
10. I have a double personality.

1. _____   6. _____

2. _____   7. _____

3. _____   8. _____

4. _____   9. _____

5. _____   10. _____

Proofreading   **11–20.** Find and cross out ten misspelled Basic Words in these classified ads. Then write each word correctly.

Photographer for hire. During the past deccade I have photographed everything from a monark to a monarail. Call Fred Photo at 555-4777.

Do you speak in a moanotone? Do you give long, monotonous speeches that put people to sleep? Spectacular Speech School can help. Call us today at 555-5555, and ask about our daploma course.

Researchers needed to study temperatures over the course of the next century. Must be able to live to old age. The ability to convert temperatures from Fahrenheit to centagrade would also be a help. Call Professor Berry at 555-3567.

Friday, March 16: Auction at the dupelex of two local antique collectors, 58 Magpie Road. Items include a rare 1900 recording of a famous dooet between Lizzy Heartbreak and Matthew Crooner, a ring with the monagram of the Czar of Russia, and a flag made for the 1876 sentennial celebration.

11. _____

12. _____

13. _____

14. _____

15. _____

16. _____

17. _____

18. _____

19. _____

20. _____

Skill: Students will practice spelling words with number prefixes.

Home Use: Help your child practice the spelling words by having him or her complete the activities on this page. Check the completed page, and have your child practice saying and spelling any misspelled words.

PRACTICE C
Number Prefixes

Rhyming Pairs   Write a Challenge Word and another rhyming word to answer each riddle.
Example: What was a disturbance in the Middle Ages?
          medieval upheaval
1. What is a sudden rush of wormlike, many-legged animals?
2. What is a house painted in different shades of one color?
3. What is a snapshot of a pair of letters with one sound?
4. What is a unit expressing the loudness of sounds that cannot be tolerated?
5. What is a short musical composition meant for singing words with *oy*?

1. _____

2. _____

3. _____

4. _____

5. _____

Challenge Words
1. decibel
2. centipede
3. digraph
4. diphthong
5. monochrome

Theme Vocabulary
6. medieval
7. chronicle
8. chivalry
9. usurp
10. betrayal
11. sovereign
12. valor
13. conquest

Legendary Figures   Think of a plot for a story set in the Middle Ages that includes the characters pictured on this page. Write a title for the story. Then write a brief description of each character and his or her role in the story. Use all of the Vocabulary Words in your title and descriptions. Use the back of this paper also, if necessary.

Title: _____

King Aethelgird _____

_____

_____

Prince Segovia _____

_____

_____

Blasé the Fair _____

_____

_____

King Aethelgird

Prince Segovia

Blasé the Fair

Skill: Students will practice spelling words with number prefixes and words related to the theme of the legends of King Arthur.

Home Use: Help your child practice the spelling words by having him or her complete the activities on this page. Check the completed page, and have your child practice saying and spelling any misspelled words.

Unit **33** Test: Number Prefixes

Find the correctly spelled word to complete each phrase. Fill in the letter beside the correct spelling.

Sample:

reading great _____
- ⓐ literture
- ● literature
- ⓒ litrature
- ⓓ literiture

---

1. half a _____ ago
   - ⓐ century
   - ⓑ cenntury
   - ⓒ centurey
   - ⓓ centurry

2. the last _____
   - ⓐ deckade
   - ⓑ decaid
   - ⓒ decade
   - ⓓ decaide

3. to sing a _____
   - ⓐ duet
   - ⓑ dooet
   - ⓒ duete
   - ⓓ duett

4. a regal _____
   - ⓐ monarck
   - ⓑ monarch
   - ⓒ monnarch
   - ⓓ monnarck

5. the _____ point
   - ⓐ decimal
   - ⓑ desimal
   - ⓒ decimel
   - ⓓ desimel

6. written by a _____
   - ⓐ munk
   - ⓑ monnk
   - ⓒ munck
   - ⓓ monk

7. to fight a _____
   - ⓐ deul
   - ⓑ dool
   - ⓒ duel
   - ⓓ duele

8. bothered by a _____
   - ⓐ dillemma
   - ⓑ dilemma
   - ⓒ dilema
   - ⓓ dillema

9. to gain a _____
   - ⓐ minopoly
   - ⓑ monopaly
   - ⓒ monoply
   - ⓓ monopoly

10. a _____ voice
    - ⓐ monoton
    - ⓑ monatone
    - ⓒ monnotone
    - ⓓ monotone

11. the town's _____
    - ⓐ centenial
    - ⓑ centennial
    - ⓒ cenntennial
    - ⓓ centenniel

12. to recite the _____
    - ⓐ monolog
    - ⓑ monnologue
    - ⓒ monologue
    - ⓓ monalogue

13. to live in a _____
    - ⓐ duplecs
    - ⓑ duplex
    - ⓒ duplecks
    - ⓓ duplexe

14. to have a _____ purpose
    - ⓐ dule
    - ⓑ dool
    - ⓒ dual
    - ⓓ doole

15. to ride the _____
    - ⓐ monorail
    - ⓑ monorale
    - ⓒ monarail
    - ⓓ monarale

16. received his _____
    - ⓐ dipploma
    - ⓑ diplomma
    - ⓒ daploma
    - ⓓ diploma

17. completed the _____
    - ⓐ decathalon
    - ⓑ dekathlon
    - ⓒ decathelon
    - ⓓ decathlon

18. the _____ on her sweater
    - ⓐ monogram
    - ⓑ monogramm
    - ⓒ monagram
    - ⓓ monigram

19. a _____ task
    - ⓐ monnotonous
    - ⓑ monotonous
    - ⓒ monotanous
    - ⓓ monotinus

20. forty degrees _____
    - ⓐ centagrade
    - ⓑ centigraid
    - ⓒ centigrade
    - ⓓ centigrad

PRACTICE A
Words New to English

Basic Words
1. software
2. word processor
3. diskette
4. robotics
5. android
6. digital
7. transistor
8. photocopy
9. smog
10. antibiotic

Summing Up

New words are often created by combining word parts or by forming **compound words**, **blends**, or **acronyms**.

Word Puzzle Write the Basic Word that fits each clue in the numbered rows. The letters in the dark box will spell a word new to English that names a computer language.

1. a compound word meaning "data essential for operating computers"
2. a combination of a word part meaning "a round flat object for storing computer data" and a suffix meaning "small"
3. a combination of word parts meaning "light" and "to reproduce"
4. a blend of *smoke* and *fog*
5. a combination of a word meaning "a machine that works automatically" and a suffix meaning "study of"
6. a combination of a word part meaning "manlike" and a suffix meaning "form"
7. a combination of a word part meaning "finger" and a suffix meaning "characterized by"
8. a blend of *transfer* and *resistor*
9. a combination of word parts meaning "effectiveness against" and "made of life"

Analogies Write the Basic Word that completes each analogy.
10. calculator : computer :: typewriter : _____
11. film : photograph :: paper : _____
12. tapedeck : cassette :: computer : _____
13. real : human :: fake : _____
14. land : litter :: air : _____
15. iron : mineral :: penicillin : _____

10. _____

11. _____

12. _____

13. _____

14. _____

15. _____

Skill: Students will practice spelling words that are new to English.

Home Use: Help your child practice the spelling words by having him or her complete the activities on this page. Check the completed page, and have your child practice saying and spelling any misspelled words.

Basic Words
1. software
2. word processor
3. diskette
4. robotics
5. android
6. digital
7. transistor
8. photocopy
9. smog
10. antibiotic
11. laser
12. calculator
13. space shuttle
14. sonar
15. discotheque
16. microwave
17. amplifier
18. brunch
19. supersonic
20. scuba

PRACTICE B
Words New to English

Word Origins   Write the Basic Word that fits each clue. Use your Spelling Dictionary.

This word comes from
1. the words *sound, navigation,* and *ranging.*
2. the Latin word *calculus,* meaning "small stone."
3. the words *self, contained, underwater, breathing,* and *apparatus.*
4. the words *breakfast* and *lunch.*
5. the Latin words meaning "over" and "sound" and an adjective suffix.
6. the combination of two English words, one of which means "that which processes."
7. the words *light, amplification, stimulated, emission,* and *radiation.*
8. the combination of a Greek word that means "small" and an English word.

1. _____ 5. _____

2. _____ 6. _____

3. _____ 7. _____

4. _____ 8. _____

9. _____
10. _____
11. _____
12. _____
13. _____
14. _____
15. _____
16. _____
17. _____
18. _____
19. _____
20. _____

Tongue Twisters   Complete each tongue twister with a Basic Word. The Basic Word should begin with the same sound as most of the other words in the sentence. Then see how quickly you can say each one.

9. Sadie sold Sophie some special ____ to solve her schoolwork assignments.
10. An animated ____ attempted an answer in algebra class.
11. Troy and Tracey tried to trade their ____ for a tricycle.
12. Sue says someday she'll spend several semesters studying on a sleek, silver ____ .
13. Anton asked the attendant to administer an ____ to the African antelope.
14. Phyllis finally found Floyd's ____ of Frank's footnotes.
15. Dalinda drew a diagram of the ____ device Donald had described.
16. Dylan's dad discovered a damaged document on Dixie's ____ .
17. Robert wrote a research report on ____ for Dr. Riggs Riley.
18. Summer ____ smells somewhat like smoke.
19. David and Doris danced at the ____ during the dark, dreary days of December.
20. The alarmed Austrian ambassador was awakened by the ____ .

Skill: Students will practice spelling words that are new to English.

Home Use: Help your child practice the spelling words by having him or her complete the activities on this page. Check the completed page, and have your child practice saying and spelling any misspelled words.

PRACTICE C
Words New to English

Hidden Words   Write the word that matches each clue below.
Then write the Challenge or Vocabulary Word that contains the
word that matches the clue.
Example: armed conflict   *war*   *hardware*
1–2. a unit of weight   **5–6.** a step made in walking
3–4. to lead   **7–8.** the past tense of *light*

1–2. _____   _____

3–4. _____   _____

5–6. _____   _____

7–8. _____   _____

Now write a definition for each Challenge or Vocabulary Word you
wrote above. Use the back of this paper.

What's My Job?   Write the Challenge and Vocabulary Words
that complete the job descriptions. Then identify each person's job
on the chart. Put a check mark in each correct box.

   9. Dan creates unusual melodies using his _____ .

  10. Judy studies figures on a _____ in order to advise her company
on its finances.

  11. Cathy helps hire new employees for her company. At the
moment she is compiling a _____ of all employees' names
and addresses.

12–13. Rosa uses many different _____ programs to train airline pilots
to handle emergency procedures. One program includes a
_____ of a plane with malfunctioning engines.

14–15. Al's fingers fly over the _____ of his computer when he is
entering information for a project's _____ .

16–17. Before studying computer science, Rod repaired radios in an
_____ repair shop. Now he repairs computer _____ .

Challenge Words
1. semiconductor
2. simulation
3. synthesizer
4. aerospace
5. hologram

Theme Vocabulary
6. electronics
7. hardware
8. database
9. spreadsheet
10. directory
11. tutorial
12. utility
13. keyboard

9. _____

10. _____

11. _____

12. _____

13. _____

14. _____

15. _____

16. _____

17. _____

	Cathy	Dan	Rod	Rosa	Judy	Al
financial analyst						
word processing specialist						
personnel assistant						
musician						
computer technician						
instructor						

Skill: Students will practice spelling words that are new to English and words related to the theme of computers.

Home Use: Help your child practice the spelling words by having him or her complete the activities on this page. Check the completed page, and have your child practice saying and spelling any misspelled words.

Unit **34** Test: Words New to English

Each item below gives four possible spellings of a word. Fill in the letter beside the correct spelling.

Sample:
- ⓐ airobics
- ⓑ arobics
- ● aerobics
- ⓓ aerabics

---

1. ⓐ robotics
ⓑ robbotics
ⓒ robottics
ⓓ robutics

2. ⓐ anti-biotic
ⓑ antibiotic
ⓒ antebiotic
ⓓ antibiatic

3. ⓐ diskette
ⓑ disket
ⓒ diskett
ⓓ discette

4. ⓐ photo-copy
ⓑ photocopy
ⓒ fotocopy
ⓓ photocoppy

5. ⓐ smogg
ⓑ smoug
ⓒ smog
ⓓ smoeg

6. ⓐ tranzistor
ⓑ transistcr
ⓒ tranzizter
ⓓ transistor

7. ⓐ software
ⓑ soft-ware
ⓒ soft ware
ⓓ softwere

8. ⓐ wordprocessor
ⓑ word-processor
ⓒ word processor
ⓓ word processer

9. ⓐ digital
ⓑ digitel
ⓒ digitle
ⓓ digittal

10. ⓐ androyd
ⓑ android
ⓒ androide
ⓓ anndroid

11. ⓐ micrawave
ⓑ microwave
ⓒ micro-wave
ⓓ microwaive

12. ⓐ supersonic
ⓑ supersonnic
ⓒ super-sonic
ⓓ super-sonnic

13. ⓐ amplifire
ⓑ amplifier
ⓒ amplifiar
ⓓ amplifyer

14. ⓐ space shuttle
ⓑ space-shuttle
ⓒ spaceshuttle
ⓓ space shuttel

15. ⓐ brunsch
ⓑ berunch
ⓒ brunch
ⓓ bruntch

16. ⓐ calculator
ⓑ calculater
ⓒ calculatar
ⓓ calcullator

17. ⓐ skooba
ⓑ scooba
ⓒ skuba
ⓓ scuba

18. ⓐ sonnar
ⓑ soanar
ⓒ sonarr
ⓓ sonar

19. ⓐ laser
ⓑ lazer
ⓒ laiser
ⓓ laizer

20. ⓐ discoteque
ⓑ discotheque
ⓒ diskotheque
ⓓ discotheqe

PRACTICE A
Words Often Mispronounced

Summing Up

Pronouncing words correctly will help you spell them correctly.

Basic Words
1. algebra
2. mathematics
3. probably
4. nuclear
5. identity
6. liberal
7. recognition
8. laboratory
9. mischievous
10. temperamental

Campaign Promises   Read these campaign statements made by ten candidates for student council president. Cross out the incorrect pronunciation in each statement. Then write the matching Basic Word. Use your Spelling Dictionary. Last, put a check mark next to the statement that would win your vote.

1. I'm looking for an opportunity to serve you, not just for personal (|rĕk′ əg **nĭsh**′ən|, |rĕk′ĭg **nĭsh**′ən|.)

2. I may not be running on (|**nōo**′klēr|, |**nōo**′klē ər|) power, but I have the energy needed for the job!

3. You will (|**prŏb**′lē|, |**prŏb**′ə blē|) never find a more dedicated person to serve as your president!

4. As president, I will not be (|tĕm′prə **mĕn**′tl|, |tĕm pər **mĕn**′tl|), but calm and reliable.

5. Of all the candidates, I can give the school the strongest sense of (|ī **dĕn**′tĭ tē|, |ī **dĕn**′ĭ tē|).

6. You do not need to be good at (|**ăl**′jə brə|, |**ăl**′jă brə|) to figure out that I am going to win!

7. My political beliefs are both conservative and (|**lĭb**′ă rəl|, |**lĭb**′ər əl|).

8. When I am elected president, I will work to provide better courses in (|măth′**măt**′ĭks|, |măth′ə **măt**′ĭks|).

9. My goal will be to rid our school of (|**mĭs**′chēv ē əs|, |**mĭs**′chə vəs|) behavior.

10. As president, I will make sure that a new science (|**lăb**′ôr ə tôr′ē|, |**lăb**′rə tôr′ē|) is built by next year!

1. _____

2. _____

3. _____

4. _____

5. _____

6. _____

7. _____

8. _____

9. _____

10. _____

Classifying   Write the Basic Word that fits each group.

11. electric, geothermal, solar, ____
12. studio, workshop, factory, ____
13. naughty, unruly, disobedient, ____
14. discovery, acknowledgment, notice, ____
15. possibly, certainly, supposedly, ____
16. plentiful, ample, abundant, ____
17. name, title, personality, ____
18. moody, sensitive, changeable, ____

11. _____   13. _____   17. _____

12. _____   14. _____   18. _____

15. _____

16. _____

Skill: Students will practice spelling words that are often mispronounced.

Home Use: Help your child practice the spelling words by having him or her complete the activities on this page. Check the completed page, and have your child practice saying and spelling any misspelled words.

Basic Words
1. algebra
2. mathematics
3. probably
4. nuclear
5. identity
6. liberal
7. recognition
8. laboratory
9. mischievous
10. temperamental
11. candidate
12. dinghy
13. hindrance
14. privilege
15. monstrous
16. grievous
17. preferable
18. arctic
19. similarly
20. sophomore

PRACTICE B
Words Often Mispronounced

Crossword Puzzle Complete the puzzle by writing the Basic Word that fits each clue.

Across

2. a second-year student
7. alike but not the same
9. the study of numbers
11. a branch of mathematics
12. a room for research
16. naughty
17. excessively sensitive
18. an obstacle
19. generous in amount
20. individuality

Down

1. more desirable
3. shocking
4. extremely cold
5. having to do with a nucleus
6. a special right
8. causing grief
10. a person who seeks office
13. the act of recognizing
14. most likely
15. a rowboat

Skill: Students will practice spelling words that are often mispronounced.

Home Use: Help your child practice the spelling words by having him or her complete the activities on this page. Check the completed page, and have your child practice saying and spelling any misspelled words.

PRACTICE C
Words Often Mispronounced

Algebra Works   Write the Vocabulary Word that describes the underlined symbol(s) in each item.

1. $\underline{-}54.2$
4. $5\underline{x} + 7$
7. $x + 2 = 6$

2. $4x \underline{<} 2y$
5. $\sqrt[3]{2}$
8. $37{,}037 \times 18 = \underline{666{,}666}$

3. $3\underline{(}x + 7\underline{)}$
6. $7^{\underline{2}}$

1. _____
5. _____

2. _____
6. _____

3. _____
7. _____

4. _____
8. _____

Word Change   Follow the directions below to change Challenge or Vocabulary Words to other words. You may want to use a class dictionary.

9–10. Write the Challenge Word that names a star-shaped symbol. Then drop three letters to write the name of a flower.

11–12. Write the Vocabulary Word that names a symbol used to multiply a quantity by itself. Then change the prefix to write a word that means "someone who supports something."

13–14. Write the Challenge Word that means "specialty." Then change one letter to write a word that names a number.

15–16. Write the Challenge Word that means "after death." Then drop the prefix and one other vowel to write a word that names a dark-colored soil.

17–18. Write the Vocabulary Word that is a synonym for *answer*. Then add a prefix to write another word that has the same meaning.

19–20. Write the Vocabulary Word that names a mathematical root. Then replace the last three letters with two letters to write a word that names a kind of line segment.

21–22. Write the Challenge Word that means "necessary." Then replace the two prefixes with another prefix to write a word that means "of special beauty."

23–24. Write the Challenge Word that means "the equipment used in some activity." Then combine the prefix with a base word meaning "a meaningful sequence of words" to write a word that means "to restate in other words."

9. _____
11. _____

10. _____
12. _____

Challenge Words
1. prerequisite
2. asterisk
3. paraphernalia
4. forte
5. posthumous

Theme Vocabulary
6. equation
7. solution
8. radical
9. negative
10. variable
11. exponent
12. inequality
13. parentheses

13. _____
14. _____
15. _____
16. _____
17. _____
18. _____
19. _____
20. _____
21. _____
22. _____
23. _____
24. _____

Unit **35** Test: Words Often Mispronounced

Find the correctly spelled word to complete each phrase. Fill in the letter beside the correct spelling.

Sample:

a healthy _____

● environment   ⓒ envirment

ⓑ enviermment   ⓓ envirnment

---

1. the _____ child

ⓐ mischievous   ⓒ mischevous

ⓑ mishievous   ⓓ mischievus

2. a mistaken _____

ⓐ idenity   ⓒ idenntity

ⓑ idenitty   ⓓ identity

3. is _____ the best choice

ⓐ probaly   ⓒ probably

ⓑ probbly   ⓓ probly

4. the _____ football coach

ⓐ tempramental   ⓒ temperimental

ⓑ temprimantal   ⓓ temperamental

5. a look of _____

ⓐ reconition   ⓒ recunition

ⓑ recognition   ⓓ recugnition

6. experiments in the _____

ⓐ labratory   ⓒ laboratory

ⓑ laberatory   ⓓ labratorry

7. to study _____ physics

ⓐ nuclear   ⓒ nucular

ⓑ nuculer   ⓓ nuclaer

8. a _____ donation

ⓐ libberal   ⓒ liberel

ⓑ liberal   ⓓ libral

9. taking an _____ course

ⓐ algibra   ⓒ allgebra

ⓑ aljebra   ⓓ algebra

10. in _____ class

ⓐ mathematics   ⓒ mathmatics

ⓑ mathamatics   ⓓ mathimatics

11. a _____ sight

ⓐ monstrous   ⓒ monsterous

ⓑ monsteros   ⓓ monstros

12. a college _____

ⓐ sophmore   ⓒ sophomore

ⓑ sofomore   ⓓ sophamore

13. right or _____

ⓐ privilege   ⓒ privlege

ⓑ privlidge   ⓓ privelege

14. a _____ to progress

ⓐ hindrince   ⓒ hindrinse

ⓑ hindrance   ⓓ hinderance

15. an _____ region

ⓐ artic   ⓒ arctic

ⓑ arktic   ⓓ arctick

16. to row in a _____

ⓐ dinghy   ⓒ dinhgy

ⓑ dinngy   ⓓ dinghie

17. a _____ for office

ⓐ candidit   ⓒ candidite

ⓑ candadate   ⓓ candidate

18. to be _____ to

ⓐ preferible   ⓒ prefferable

ⓑ preferable   ⓓ prefurable

19. to be _____ dressed

ⓐ similiarly   ⓒ simmilarly

ⓑ similarily   ⓓ similarly

20. a _____ error

ⓐ greevous   ⓒ grievous

ⓑ greivous   ⓓ grievus

How to make: Title the bulletin board "Word Guess." Write all the Basic Words from Units 31–35 on individual cards. Place the cards in a manila envelope labeled *Basic Words* and staple it to the bulletin board. Have each student cut 20 2″×2″ blank cards for his or her own use.

How to use: One student goes to the bulletin board with a pen and the blank cards. He or she then selects a word from the envelope and tacks as many blank cards to the bulletin board as there are letters in the word. If the word he or she has selected is actually two words, the student should provide an obvious gap between the words.

Students call out letters in order to guess the word. If the letters called out are in the word, the student at the board prints them on the blank cards in the appropriate places on the board. If a letter not in the word is guessed, the student at the board prints the letter on a separate card and tacks it to a corner of the board as a reminder. The first student to call out the word correctly will be the next one to go to the board.

Use: For use with Units 31–35.

SPELLING NEWSLETTER
for Students and Their Families

Wrapping Up

Unit 31 of your child's level of *Houghton Mifflin Spelling and Vocabulary* presents related word pairs such as *prevail* and *prevalent*, in which there is a change in vowel spelling. Unit 32 focuses on words with Latin roots, while Unit 33 discusses words with number prefixes, such as *mon-*, *di-*, *dec-*, and *cent-*. Unit 34 studies words that are relatively new to the English language. Finally, Unit 35 studies words that are frequently mispronounced and, as a result, frequently misspelled.

Word Lists

Here are some of the words your child has studied in Units 31–35.

UNIT 31	UNIT 32	UNIT 33	UNIT 34	UNIT 35
deceive	manufacture	monarch	word processor	laboratory
deception	management	duel	robotics	mathematics
acclaim	efficient	dilemma	diskette	nuclear
acclamation	convenient	century	digital	recognition
pertain	inventive	decimal	transistor	mischievous
pertinent	manicure	monotonous	calculator	similarly
prevail	eventually	dual	microwave	candidate
prevalent	maneuver	monologue	laser	arctic
sustain	feat	decathlon	sonar	privilege
sustenance	sacrifice	centennial	discotheque	sophomore

Family Activity

Take turns with your child making up sentences containing at least three of the words from the lists above. The words must be used correctly, and the sentences must make some kind of sense. Set a time limit for coming up with a sentence. Score one point for each sentence composed within the time limit.

Boletín de noticias de ortografía
para estudiantes y para sus familias

Para terminar

Las siguientes son palabras para ejercicios de ortografía que su hijo o hija ha estado estudiando en las Unidades 31 a 35 del libro *Houghton Mifflin Spelling and Vocabulary*.

UNIDAD 31	UNIDAD 32	UNIDAD 33	UNIDAD 34	UNIDAD 35
deceive	manufacture	monarch	word processor	laboratory
deception	management	duel	robotics	mathematics
acclaim	efficient	dilemma	diskette	nuclear
acclamation	convenient	century	digital	recognition
pertain	inventive	decimal	transistor	mischievous
pertinent	manicure	monotonous	calculator	similarly
prevail	eventually	dual	microwave	candidate
prevalent	maneuver	monologue	laser	arctic
sustain	feat	decathlon	sonar	privilege
sustenance	sacrifice	centennial	discotheque	sophomore

👪 Actividad para la familia

Túrnense con su hijo o hija para hacer oraciones que tengan por lo menos tres de las palabras de las listas presentadas arriba. Las palabras deben usarse correctamente y las oraciones deben tener algún sentido. Establezcan un plazo fijo de tiempo para inventar una oración. Den un punto por cada oración inventada dentro del plazo.

INITIALS

SPELLING
GAME

Players: any number

You need: paper, pencils

How to play: Select two Basic Words of equal length from a unit spelling list. Each player should print the words next to each other in two vertical columns on a sheet of paper, as shown in the example. The two words form pairs of letters. Players pretend that these pairs of letters are the initials of famous people. (Classmates' names may be included.) The first player to complete a set of names to match the initials is the winner.

L	S	Leon Spinks	(sports figure)
A	O	Annie Oakley	(historical figure)
S	N	Sara Nelson	(classmate)
E	A	Ethan Allen	(historical figure)
R	R	Ronald Reagan	(former President)

Other ways to play this game: Instead of people's names, use two-word object names or phrases.

Unit 36 Review: Test A

Find the word that is spelled incorrectly. Fill in the letter beside the misspelled word.

___

Sample:
- (a) laboratory
- ● antebiotic
- (c) manual
- (d) deception

___

1.
- (a) maintenance
- (b) benefit
- (c) dillema
- (d) android

2.
- (a) nuclear
- (b) pertain
- (c) managment
- (d) monopoly

3.
- (a) software
- (b) liberel
- (c) monotone
- (d) profit

4.
- (a) acclaim
- (b) manufacture
- (c) transister
- (d) mathematics

5.
- (a) proclaim
- (b) monk
- (c) diskette
- (d) mischeivous

6.
- (a) factory
- (b) pertinant
- (c) duet
- (d) photocopy

7.
- (a) algebra
- (b) maintain
- (c) efficient
- (d) monarck

8.
- (a) probebly
- (b) robotics
- (c) decimal
- (d) defect

9.
- (a) smog
- (b) decieve
- (c) inventive
- (d) recognition

10.
- (a) temperamental
- (b) digital
- (c) duel
- (d) acclammation

Unit 36 Review: Test B

Find the word that is spelled incorrectly. Fill in the letter beside the misspelled word.

Sample:
- ⓐ microwave
- ● cenntennial
- ⓒ convention
- ⓓ perception

1. ⓐ sustain
   ⓑ manuever
   ⓒ duplex
   ⓓ laser

2. ⓐ monstrous
   ⓑ sonar
   ⓒ monalogue
   ⓓ factor

3. ⓐ concieve
   ⓑ preventive
   ⓒ dual
   ⓓ calculator

4. ⓐ scuba
   ⓑ privelege
   ⓒ prevail
   ⓓ manicure

5. ⓐ arctic
   ⓑ centigrade
   ⓒ sustenence
   ⓓ effect

6. ⓐ candidate
   ⓑ brunch
   ⓒ monarail
   ⓓ exclaim

7. ⓐ discoteque
   ⓑ dinghy
   ⓒ diploma
   ⓓ sacrifice

8. ⓐ conception
   ⓑ feat
   ⓒ monogram
   ⓓ greivous

9. ⓐ prevalant
   ⓑ amplifier
   ⓒ sophomore
   ⓓ decathlon

10. ⓐ perceive
    ⓑ eventually
    ⓒ supersonic
    ⓓ hindrence

Unit **36** Review: Test C

Each item below gives four possible spellings of a word. Fill in the letter beside the correct spelling.

Sample:

● manifest
ⓑ mannifest
ⓒ manefest
ⓓ manafest

1. ⓐ artefact
   ⓑ arrtifact
   ⓒ arrtefact
   ⓓ artifact

2. ⓐ denounce
   ⓑ deenounce
   ⓒ denownce
   ⓓ denounse

3. ⓐ centepede
   ⓑ centepeed
   ⓒ centipeed
   ⓓ centipede

4. ⓐ hologram
   ⓑ holagram
   ⓒ hollagram
   ⓓ hollogram

5. ⓐ prerequisit
   ⓑ perequisite
   ⓒ prerequisite
   ⓓ prerecwisite

6. ⓐ sinthesiser
   ⓑ synthasiser
   ⓒ synthesizer
   ⓓ synthesiser

7. ⓐ pranounce
   ⓑ pronounce
   ⓒ pronownce
   ⓓ pronownse

8. ⓐ deficit
   ⓑ defficit
   ⓒ defisit
   ⓓ deficitt

9. ⓐ dipthong
   ⓑ diphthung
   ⓒ diphthong
   ⓓ diphtong

10. ⓐ asteriks
    ⓑ asterisk
    ⓒ asterrisk
    ⓓ asterisck

11. ⓐ airospace
    ⓑ arospace
    ⓒ aroespace
    ⓓ aerospace

12. ⓐ decible
    ⓑ decibel
    ⓒ decibell
    ⓓ desibel

13. ⓐ circumvent
    ⓑ cirrcumvent
    ⓒ circkumvent
    ⓓ circummvent

14. ⓐ pronounciation
    ⓑ pronnunciation
    ⓒ prunounciation
    ⓓ pronunciation

15. ⓐ facimile
    ⓑ facsimile
    ⓒ fascimile
    ⓓ facsimmile

16. ⓐ monachrome
    ⓑ monocrome
    ⓒ monnochrome
    ⓓ monochrome

17. ⓐ semi-conductor
    ⓑ semi-conducter
    ⓒ semiconductor
    ⓓ semiconducter

18. ⓐ paraphanalia
    ⓑ paraphernalia
    ⓒ paraphenalia
    ⓓ parephernalia

19. ⓐ denunciation
    ⓑ denounciation
    ⓒ denownciation
    ⓓ denunsiation

20. ⓐ poschumous
    ⓑ posthumus
    ⓒ posthumous
    ⓓ poschumus

Prewriting Ideas: Research Report

Choosing a Topic   Listed below are some topics that one student thought of for writing a research report. What topics of your own are you curious about?

On the lines below *My Five Ideas*, list five topics for a research report. Which ones do you want to know more about? Which ones will interest your readers? Circle the topic that you would like to write about.

Ideas for Writing

The woolly mammoth
The La Brea pits
How a person can be knighted today
How a camera works
Organic gardening
How a compact disk works
Black holes in the universe
Dream interpretation

My Five Ideas

1. _____

2. _____

3. _____

4. _____

5. _____

Exploring Your Topic   Use an inverted triangle to help narrow your topic. Write the topic you chose at the top of the inverted triangle. Ask yourself questions about your topic to narrow it further and further. Write each narrowed idea underneath your first topic. At the bottom of the triangle write the narrowed topic you will write about.

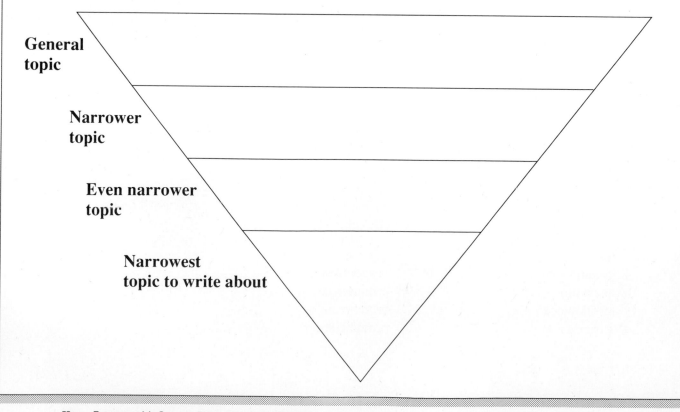

General topic

Narrower topic

Even narrower topic

Narrowest topic to write about

Use: For use with Step 1: Prewriting on page 227.

End-of-Year Test

Find the word that is spelled incorrectly. Fill in the letter beside the misspelled word.

Sample:
  ⓐ collision
  ● sosiology
  ⓒ armada
  ⓓ personality

---

1. ⓐ abstract
  ⓑ saute
  ⓒ proppaganda
  ⓓ succession

2. ⓐ transpertation
  ⓑ counteract
  ⓒ pueblo
  ⓓ prosecute

3. ⓐ strategy
  ⓑ curiousity
  ⓒ punctuality
  ⓓ pliers

4. ⓐ century
  ⓑ spaghetti
  ⓒ pharmacist
  ⓓ symbal

5. ⓐ persperation
  ⓑ reference
  ⓒ production
  ⓓ cashmere

6. ⓐ committee
  ⓑ proclamation
  ⓒ inventive
  ⓓ pastuerize

7. ⓐ zoology
  ⓑ tremendus
  ⓒ antibiotic
  ⓓ algebra

8. ⓐ mischeivous
  ⓑ transpire
  ⓒ synthetic
  ⓓ psyche

9. ⓐ intercept
  ⓑ choral
  ⓒ detention
  ⓓ dillemma

10. ⓐ agressive
  ⓑ chronology
  ⓒ alternate
  ⓓ frequency

11. ⓐ robotics
  ⓑ management
  ⓒ pertinent
  ⓓ referrel

12. ⓐ italics
  ⓑ mountinous
  ⓒ complexity
  ⓓ gondola

13. ⓐ politician
  ⓑ submission
  ⓒ aquaintance
  ⓓ substance

14. ⓐ intersection
  ⓑ abundent
  ⓒ exclamation
  ⓓ concession

15. ⓐ protoplasm
  ⓑ transfusion
  ⓒ indicative
  ⓓ imaculate

(continued)

End-of-Year Test (continued)

16. (a) opake
    (b) succumb
    (c) introduce
    (d) microwave

17. (a) preferable
    (b) mosiac
    (c) dissent
    (d) theology

18. (a) prominent
    (b) acomplice
    (c) pimento
    (d) symbolism

19. (a) conformist
    (b) ridiculous
    (c) rinestone
    (d) harass

20. (a) decathlon
    (b) maneuver
    (c) anniversary
    (d) sourkraut

21. (a) humidity
    (b) preposition
    (c) prespective
    (d) syndicate

22. (a) aggravate
    (b) indigo
    (c) remediel
    (d) popularity

23. (a) pneumonia
    (b) rendayvous
    (c) syllabication
    (d) versatile

24. (a) trespass
    (b) amplifier
    (c) transmision
    (d) guardian

25. (a) sensor
    (b) regimen
    (c) pathalogical
    (d) mentor

Additional Resources

Individual Progress Chart
Class Progress Chart
Scoring Chart
Proofreading Marks
Proofreading Checklist
Handwriting Models

Additional Resources

★ Individual Progress Chart ★

Prebook Test (TRB)	Midyear Test (TRB)	End-of-Year Test (TRB)

	Pretest (TE)	Unit Evaluation (TE)	Unit Test (TRB)			Pretest (TE)	Unit Evaluation (TE)	Unit Test (TRB)
Unit 1					Unit 19			
Unit 2					Unit 20			
Unit 3					Unit 21			
Unit 4					Unit 22			
Unit 5					Unit 23			
Unit 6 Review			A B C		Unit 24 Review			A B C
Unit 7					Unit 25			
Unit 8					Unit 26			
Unit 9					Unit 27			
Unit 10					Unit 28			
Unit 11					Unit 29			
Unit 12 Review			A B C		Unit 30 Review			A B C
Unit 13					Unit 31			
Unit 14					Unit 32			
Unit 15					Unit 33			
Unit 16					Unit 34			
Unit 17					Unit 35			
Unit 18 Review			A B C		Unit 36 Review			A B C

Class Progress Chart

Name	Extra Test	Unit __			Unit __			Unit __			Unit __			Unit __			Review Unit __					Extra Tests	
	Prebook Test (TRB)	Pretest (TE)	Unit Evaluation (TE)	Unit Test (TRB)	Pretest (TE)	Unit Evaluation (TE)	Unit Test (TRB)	Pretest (TE)	Unit Evaluation (TE)	Unit Test (TRB)	Pretest (TE)	Unit Evaluation (TE)	Unit Test (TRB)	Pretest (TE)	Unit Evaluation (TE)	Unit Test (TRB)	Pretest (TE)	Unit Evaluation (TE)	Review Test A (TRB)	Review Test B (TRB)	Review Test C (TRB)	Midyear Test (TRB)	End-of-Year Test (TRB)
1.																							
2.																							
3.																							
4.																							
5.																							
6.																							
7.																							
8.																							
9.																							
10.																							
11.																							
12.																							
13.																							
14.																							
15.																							
16.																							
17.																							
18.																							
19.																							
20.																							
21.																							
22.																							
23.																							
24.																							
25.																							
26.																							
27.																							
28.																							
29.																							
30.																							
31.																							
32.																							
33.																							
34.																							
35.																							

Scoring Chart

181

Use the scoring bars below to convert the raw score for each test to a percentage.

For 5-item tests, number and percent correct:

Number	3	4	5
Percent	60	80	100

For 9-item tests, number and percent correct:

Number	5	6	7	8	9
Percent	56	67	78	89	100

For 10-item tests, number and percent correct:

Number	5	6	7	8	9	10
Percent	50	60	70	80	90	100

For 11-item tests, number and percent correct:

Number	6	7	8	9	10	11
Percent	55	64	73	82	91	100

For 12-item tests, number and percent correct:

Number	6	7	8	9	10	11	12
Percent	50	58	67	75	83	92	100

For 13-item tests, number and percent correct:

Number	7	8	9	10	11	12	13
Percent	54	62	69	77	85	92	100

For 14-item tests, number and percent correct:

Number	7	8	9	10	11	12	13	14
Percent	50	57	64	71	79	86	93	100

For 15-item tests, number and percent correct:

Number	8	9	10	11	12	13	14	15
Percent	53	60	67	73	80	87	93	100

For 16-item tests, number and percent correct:

Number	8	9	10	11	12	13	14	15	16
Percent	50	56	63	69	75	81	88	94	100

For 20-item tests, number and percent correct:

Number	10	11	12	13	14	15	16	17	18	19	20
Percent	50	55	60	65	70	75	80	85	90	95	100

For use with Levels 2–8

Scoring Chart (continued)

For 24-item tests, number and percent correct:

Number	12	13	14	15	16	17	18	19	20	21	22	23	24
Percent	50	54	58	63	67	71	75	79	83	88	92	96	100

For 25-item tests, number and percent correct:

Number	13	14	15	16	17	18	19	20	21	22	23	24	25
Percent	52	56	60	64	68	72	76	80	84	88	92	96	100

For 26-item tests, number and percent correct:

Number	13	14	15	16	17	18	19	20	21	22	23	24	25	26
Percent	50	54	58	62	65	69	73	77	81	85	88	92	96	100

For 28-item tests, number and percent correct:

Number	14	15	16	17	18	19	20	21	22	23	24	25	26	27	28
Percent	50	54	57	61	64	68	71	75	79	82	86	89	93	96	100

For 29-item tests, number and percent correct:

Number	15	16	17	18	19	20	21	22	23	24	25	26	27	28	29
Percent	52	55	59	62	66	69	72	76	79	83	86	90	93	97	100

For 30-item tests, number and percent correct:

Number	15	16	17	18	19	20	21	22	23	24	25	26	27	28	29	30
Percent	50	53	57	60	63	67	70	73	77	80	83	87	90	93	97	100

For 34-item tests, number and percent correct:

Number	17	18	19	20	21	22	23	24	25	26	27	28	29	30	31	32	33	34
Percent	50	53	56	59	62	65	68	71	74	76	79	82	85	88	91	94	97	100

For 35-item tests, number and percent correct:

Number	18	19	20	21	22	23	24	25	26	27	28	29	30	31	32	33	34	35
Percent	51	54	57	60	63	66	69	71	74	77	80	83	86	89	91	94	97	100

For 36-item tests, number and percent correct:

Number	18	19	20	21	22	23	24	25	26	27	28	29	30	31	32	33	34	35	36
Percent	50	53	56	58	61	64	67	69	72	75	78	81	83	86	89	92	94	97	100

For 50-item tests, number and percent correct:

Number	25	26	27	28	29	30	31	32	33	34	35	36	37	38	39	40	41	42	43	44
Percent	50	52	54	56	58	60	62	64	66	68	70	72	74	76	78	80	82	84	86	88

Number	45	46	47	48	49	50
Percent	90	92	94	96	98	100

For use with Levels 2–8.

★ *Proofreading Marks* ★

Mark	Explanation	Example
¶	Begin a new paragraph. Indent the paragraph.	¶ The space shuttle landed safely after its five-day voyage. It glided to a smooth, perfect halt.
∧	Add letters, words, or sentences.	People _{who} are lively are said to have charisma.
∧,	Add a comma.	Carlton, my Siamese cat, has a mind of his own.
⌄⌄ ⌄⌄	Add quotation marks.	"Where do you want us to put the piano?" asked the gasping movers.
⊙	Add a period.	Don't forget to put a period at the end of every statement⊙
ℐ	Take out words, sentences, and punctuation marks. Correct spelling.	She likes movies more better than plays.
/	Change a capital letter to a small letter.	We are studying about the Louisiana Purchase in History class.
≡	Change a small letter to a capital letter.	The Nile river in africa is the longest river in the world.
∼	Reverse letters or words.	To complete the task successfully, you must follow carefully the steps.

183

Proofreading Checklist

Does your paper have mistakes that might make it difficult to read and understand? Use the questions below to check your paper. Read each question; then correct any mistakes that you find in your paper. After you have corrected the mistakes, put a check mark in the box next to the question.

☐   **1.** Did I spell all words correctly?

☐   **2.** Did I indent correctly?

☐   **3.** Did I correct all fragments and run-ons?

☐   **4.** Did I use capital letters correctly?

☐   **5.** Did I end each sentence with the correct punctuation mark?

☐   **6.** Did I use commas, apostrophes, quotation marks, underlining, hyphens, dashes, parentheses, colons, and semicolons correctly?

☐   **7.** Did I use abbreviations and numbers correctly?

☐   **8.** Did I use the correct forms of nouns and pronouns?

☐   **9.** Did I use verbs and verb forms correctly?

☐ **10.** Did I use modifiers correctly?

Are there any special problems you should be careful of? Make your own proofreading checklist.

☐ _____

☐ _____

☐ _____

☐ _____

☐ _____

☐ _____

☐ _____

☐ _____

☐ _____

Handwriting Models

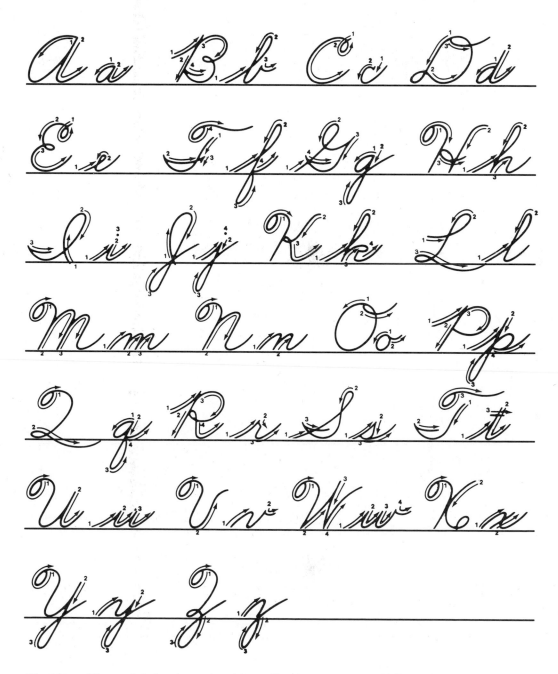

The Zaner-Bloser alphabet is reprinted from *Handwriting: Basic Skills and Application*. Copyright © 1989. Reprinted with permission of Zaner-Bloser, Inc., Columbus, OH.

★ *Handwriting Models* ★

Aa Bb Cc Dd

Ee Ff Gg Hh

Ii Jj Kk Ll

Mm Nn Oo Pp

Qq Rr Ss Tt

Uu Vv Ww Xx

Yy Zz

Handwriting style reprinted from HBJ HANDWRITING, copyright © 1987 by
Harcourt Brace Jovanovich, Inc. Reproduced by permission of the publisher.

★ *Handwriting Models* ★

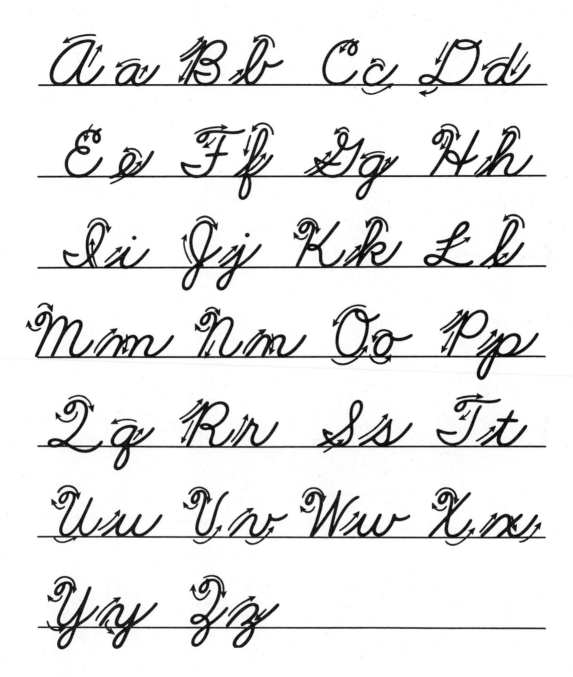

The McDougal, Littell alphabet is used with permission from *McDougal, Littell Handwriting*. Copyright © 1990 by McDougal, Littell and Company, Evanston, Illinois.

★ *Handwriting Models* ★

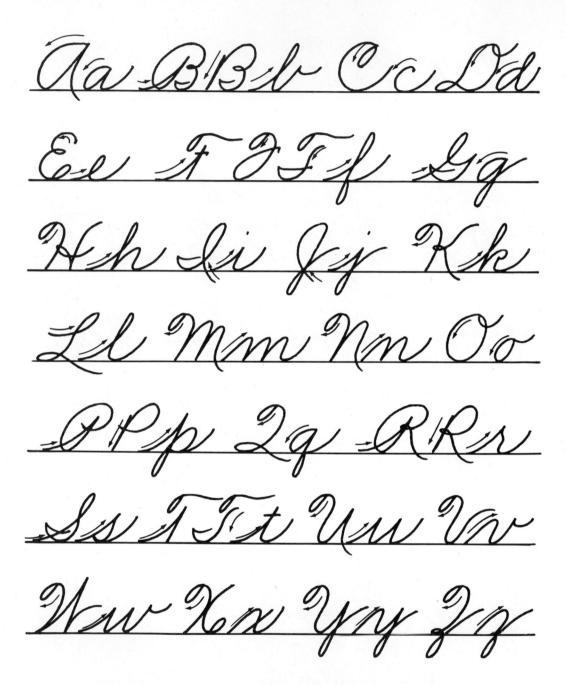

The Palmer alphabet is reprinted with permission of Macmillan/McGraw-Hill
School Publishing Company from *Palmer Method Handwriting*, Centennial
Edition. Copyright © 1987 by Macmillan Publishing Company.

Practice Master and Test Answers

Placement and Cumulative Evaluation
Prebook Test (Unit 1)
Midyear Test (Unit 18)
End-of-Year Test (Unit 36)
Basic Units
Practice Masters
Practice A (Easy)
Practice B (Average)
Practice C (Challenging)
Unit Test
Review Units
Tests
Review Test A
Review Test B
Review Test C

Name _____

Prebook Test

Find the word that is spelled incorrectly. Fill in the letter beside the misspelled word.

Sample:
- a succeed
- **b inevitible**
- c cymbal
- d counterfeit

1.
- a synagogue
- b sensor
- c comedien
- d adjourn

2.
- a omelet
- b inference
- c embarass
- d calculator

3.
- a limuosine
- b exquisite
- c advertisement
- d hypnosis

4.
- a subscription
- b collaberate
- c anthology
- d mosquito

5.
- a familiarity
- b neutrality
- c kindergarden
- d avocation

6.
- a deprevation
- b abstention
- c acclamation
- d sacrifice

7.
- a monotonous
- b consede
- c descent
- d interchangeable

8.
- a consumption
- b conscientous
- c laboratory
- d synonym

9.
- a suburban
- b intrigue
- c accordian
- d persecute

10.
- a mannerism
- b recommend
- c transistor
- d extrordinary

11.
- a colleague
- b technology
- c savanna
- d hygeine

12.
- a sequential
- b contraversy
- c sensible
- d disastrous

13.
- a artificial
- b turquoise
- c sustenence
- d efficient

14.
- a monopoly
- b vegatation
- c disposal
- d anxiety

15.
- a sophomore
- b intravenous
- c pathological
- d sylabication

(continued)

Name _____

Prebook Test (continued)

16.
- a remission
- b psychiatrist
- c summary
- d maintenence

17.
- a manipulate
- b diskett
- c allegiance
- d transition

18.
- a avacado
- b accede
- c camouflage
- d endeavor

19.
- a criticism
- b accomplice
- c strenuous
- d inturmural

20.
- a trilogy
- b canvass
- c alternative
- d preference

21.
- a democracy
- b conspiracy
- c grafitti
- d resumption

22.
- a miscelaneous
- b magenta
- c centennial
- d commission

23.
- a ascent
- b accesory
- c retention
- d dilemma

24.
- a illustrative
- b barbecue
- c accommodate
- d chauffer

25.
- a contageous
- b convenient
- c mathematics
- d pedestrian

Practice Master and Test Answers

PRACTICE B
Consonant Changes

Crossword Puzzle Complete the puzzle by writing the Basic Word that fits each clue.

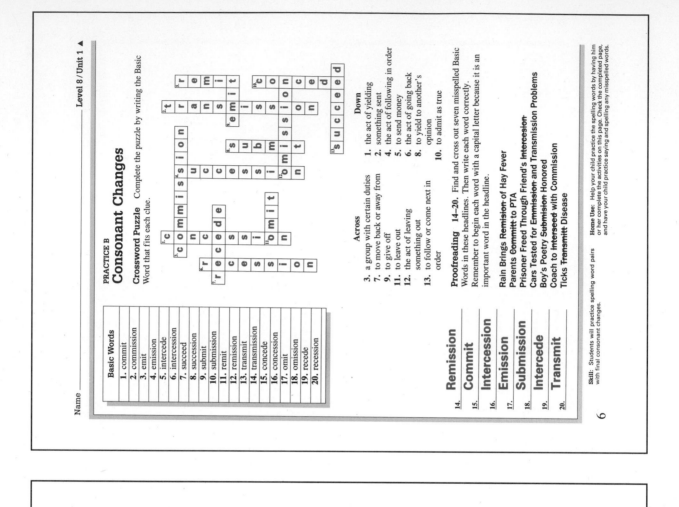

Basic Words
1. commit
2. commission
3. emit
4. emission
5. intercede
6. intercession
7. succeed
8. succession
9. submit
10. submission
11. remit
12. remission
13. transmit
14. transmission
15. concede
16. concession
17. omit
18. omission
19. recede
20. recession

Across

3. a group with certain duties
7. to move back or away from
9. to give off
11. to leave out
12. the act of leaving something out
13. to follow or come next in order

Down

1. the act of yielding
2. something sent
4. the act of following in order
5. to send money
6. the act of going back
8. to yield to another's opinion
10. to admit as true

Proofreading 14–20. Find and cross out seven misspelled Basic Words in these headlines. Then write each word correctly. Remember to begin each word with a capital letter because it is an important word in the headline.

Rain Brings Remision of Hay Fever
Parents Committ to PTA
Prisoner Freed Through Friend's Intercesion
Cars Tested for Emmision and Transmission Problems
Boy's Poetry Submision Honored
Coach to Intersed with Commission
Ticks Transmitt Disease

14. _____ Remission
15. _____ Commit
16. _____ Intercession
17. _____ Emission
18. _____ Submission
19. _____ Intercede
20. _____ Transmit

PRACTICE A
Consonant Changes

> **Summing Up**
>
> Knowing how consonants change in one pair of words may help you predict changes in words with similar spelling patterns.

Digging for Success 1–10. Professor Wyse dug up these pieces of pottery. On each one is a clue to the spelling of the letters missing from the Basic Words below. Fill in the missing letter or letters in each word on the shovels. Then write the Basic Word pairs under the correct category. **Order of answers may vary.**

final **t** changes to **ss**

emi **t**
emi **ss** ion

commi **t**
commi **ss** ion

submi **t**
submi **ss** ion

interce **d** e
interce **ss** ion

succee **d**
succe **ss** ion

final **t** changes to **ss**

1. _____ commit
2. _____ commission
3. _____ emit
4. _____ emission
5. _____ submit
6. _____ submission

final **d** changes to **ss**

7. _____ intercede
8. _____ intercession
9. _____ succeed
10. _____ succession

Basic Words
1. commit
2. commission
3. emit
4. emission
5. intercede
6. intercession
7. succeed
8. succession
9. submit
10. submission

At the Dig Write the Basic Words to complete this reporter's story about Professor Wyse's expedition.

The crew broke the seal on the old door and stood back as the cave began to __(11)__ a strange odor. "Don't breathe that gas!" shouted someone from the archaeology __(12)__. "The __(13)__ might be harmful."

Soon they could enter the cave. "Be careful, please," said the professor. "To damage anything would be to __(14)__ a terrible act. If we are to __(15)__ in our work, we must be very cautious."

The archaeologists entered several caves in __(16)__. Some wall drawings told a story of a man who tried to __(17)__ for a friend who was in trouble because he would not __(18)__ to the law. His __(19)__ did not work, however. The last picture showed the friend kneeling in __(20)__ to the king.

11. _____ emit
12. _____ commission
13. _____ emission
14. _____ commit
15. _____ succeed
16. _____ succession
17. _____ intercede
18. _____ submit
19. _____ intercession
20. _____ submission

192

Unit 1 Test: Consonant Changes

Each item below gives four possible spellings of a word. Fill in the letter beside the correct spelling.

Sample:
- ⓐ voilation
- ● violation
- ⓒ violashun
- ⓓ vialation

Items 1–10 test Basic Words 1–10. Items 11–20 test Basic Words 11–20.

1. ⓐ comision ⓑ comission ⓒ commision ⓓ● commission
2. ⓐ suceed ⓑ succede ⓒ● succeed ⓓ sucseed
3. ⓐ emishun ⓑ● emission ⓒ emmision ⓓ emmission
4. ⓐ submitt ⓑ● submit ⓒ submit ⓓ submitt
5. ⓐ● commit ⓑ committ ⓒ comitt ⓓ comit
6. ⓐ succesion ⓑ sucession ⓒ sucesion ⓓ● succession
7. ⓐ● submission ⓑ submmission ⓒ submision ⓓ submmision

8. ⓐ emmit ⓑ● emit ⓒ emitt ⓓ emmitt
9. ⓐ intercesion ⓑ interccesion ⓒ● intercession ⓓ intricession
10. ⓐ● intercede ⓑ intersede ⓒ interceed ⓓ interseed
11. ⓐ remision ⓑ● remission ⓒ remmision ⓓ remmission
12. ⓐ● remit ⓑ remitt ⓒ remmite ⓓ remmitt
13. ⓐ● concession ⓑ concesion ⓒ consesion ⓓ consession
14. ⓐ resesion ⓑ● recession ⓒ resession ⓓ recesion

15. ⓐ omitt ⓑ omite ⓒ ommit ⓓ● omit
16. ⓐ● transmit ⓑ transmitt ⓒ transsmit ⓓ transmitt
17. ⓐ consede ⓑ conced ⓒ● concede ⓓ conceede
18. ⓐ● transmission ⓑ transmision ⓒ remmission ⓓ transsmission
19. ⓐ receed ⓑ● recede ⓒ recede ⓓ reecede
20. ⓐ ommission ⓑ ommision ⓒ omision ⓓ● omission

PRACTICE C

Consonant Changes

Super Analogies Write the Challenge and Vocabulary Words that best complete each analogy.

1–2. irritate : _____ :: irritation : _____
3–4. protection : _____ :: dangerous : _____
5–6. remainder : _____ :: poisons : _____
7–8. cancel : _____ :: cancellation : _____

1. provoke
2. provocation
3. conservation
4. hazardous
5. by-product
6. toxins
7. revoke
8. revocation

Challenge Words
1. revoke
2. revocation
3. provoke
4. provocation
Theme Vocabulary
5. conservation
6. endangered
7. contaminate
8. toxins
9. by-product
10. hazardous
11. biodegradable
12. aquifer

Earth Awareness In the space below, design a two-page flier about an Earth Day seminar at your school. What will be the topics of the seminar sessions? Write a time, a title, and a brief description for each session. Use the Vocabulary Words *endangered, biodegradable, contaminate, aquifer,* and *conservation* and any other Challenge or Vocabulary Words you wish in your flier. **Answers will vary.**

Skill: Students will practice spelling word pairs with final consonant changes and words related to the theme of ecology.

Home Use: Help your child practice the spelling words by having him or her complete the activities on this page. Check the completed page, and have your child practice saying and spelling any misspelled words.

Practice Master and Test Answers

PRACTICE A
Greek Word Parts I

Summing Up

Many English words contain the Greek word parts *path*, *syn* (or *sym*), *gen*, and *prot*.

Word Part Match 1–11. Write each Basic Word under the Greek word part contained in that Basic Word. Write one Basic Word under two word parts. **Order of answers may vary.**

Basic Words
1. pathology
2. symptom
3. syndrome
4. synthetic
5. protein
6. oxygen
7. hydrogen
8. homogenized
9. synonym
10. sympathy

path = disease; feeling

1. pathology (C)
2. sympathy (G)

prot = first

3. protein (F)

syn/sym = together; same

4. symptom (A)
5. synthetic (B)
6. syndrome (D)
7. sympathy (G)
8. synonym (H)

gen = born; produced

9. hydrogen (E)
10. homogenized (I)
11. oxygen (J)

Next to each Basic Word that you wrote, write the letter of its definition.

Definitions
A. a sign of illness
B. artificial
C. the study of disease
D. a set of symptoms
E. the lightest gas
F. a class of food
G. an understanding between persons
H. a word with a meaning similar to that of another word
I. spread evenly through a fluid
J. a gas needed for human life

Word Search 12–20. Circle the nine Basic Words hidden in this puzzle. The words may cross each other and may appear horizontally, vertically, or diagonally. Then write each word. **Order of answers may vary.**

```
t s y m p a t h y d a y l g u s e t s
e y y p a r e p a t h o l o g y h h y
o n t m t o o s r y n o g o r y o v n
t d h e p y r e d o u l x o r n e o
r v o u t s o r i u s y t p l a n
x o h y d r o g e n o e n b g o n i y
n l o u s t h m e y l a i c k e g e m
n e e l w a y s t e m u c i n j s
s y n t h e t i c r o r r a n s i m l
```

12. synthetic
13. protein
14. hydrogen
15. sympathy
16. symptom
17. oxygen
18. synonym
19. pathology
20. syndrome

Skill: Students will practice spelling words that have the Greek word parts *path*, *syn*, *gen*, and *prot*.

Home Use: Help your child practice the spelling words on this page. Check the completed page, and have your child practice saying and spelling any misspelled words.

PRACTICE B
Greek Word Parts I

Basic Words
1. pathology
2. symptom
3. syndrome
4. synthetic
5. protein
6. oxygen
7. hydrogen
8. homogenized
9. synonym
10. sympathy
11. pathetic
12. apathy
13. photogenic
14. synagogue
15. genealogy
16. empathy
17. pathological
18. symmetrical
19. protoplasm
20. syndicate

Code Load While in Greece, Alex made up a code. Use his code to figure out and write the Basic Words. A △ stands for a vowel or *y*.

CODE:	5	7	10	3	12	1	9	2	11	8	4	6	△	△	△	△	△	△
LETTER:	c	d	g	h	l	m	n	p	r	s	t	z	a	e	i	o	u	y

1. 8-△-9-7-△-5-△-4-△
2. 8-△-9-7-11-△-1-△
3. 8-△-9-△-10-△-10-△-△
4. 2-△-4-3-△-12-△-10-△
5. △-1-2-△-4-3-△

6. 2-△-4-3-△-12-△-10-△-5-△-12
7. 3-△-7-11-△-10-△-9
8. 3-△-1-△-10-△-9-△-6-△-7
9. 2-11-△-4-△-2-12-△-8-1
10. 8-△-9-△-9-△-1

1. syndicate
2. syndrome
3. synagogue
4. empathy
5. pathology

6. pathological
7. hydrogen
8. homogenized
9. protoplasm
10. synonym

Greetings from Greece Write ten Basic Words to complete the letter Alex sent from Greece to his friend Charlie.

Dear Charlie,

My study of family __(11)__ excited me so much that I had to explore my Greek background firsthand. Greece is wonderful! At first, I found the old buildings sad and __(12)__ because they were decayed, but now I find them magical. Many have beautiful columns that make the most uneven building look balanced and __(13)__ . I'm taking a lot of pictures of people because they are so __(14)__ . I bought clothes made of wool, not anything __(15)__ . The food is delicious. The lamb is a good source of __(16)__ .

Yesterday we climbed a mountain. The guide told us to report dizziness or any other __(17)__ that we might feel because there is less __(18)__ at higher altitudes.

I once felt __(19)__ for other cultures, but now I care very much about what goes on in the rest of the world. I feel __(20)__ for anyone who is unable to visit Greece.

See you soon,
Alex

11. genealogy
12. pathetic
13. symmetrical
14. photogenic
15. synthetic
16. protein
17. symptom
18. oxygen
19. apathy
20. sympathy

Skill: Students will practice spelling words that have the Greek word parts *path*, *syn*, *gen*, and *prot*.

Home Use: Help your child practice the spelling words that have the Greek word parts *path*, *syn*, *gen*, and *prot*. Help your child practice the spelling words by having him or her complete the activities on this page. Check the completed page, and have your child practice saying and spelling any misspelled words.

194

PRACTICE C
Greek Word Parts I

Rights and Wrongs Decide whether the underlined Challenge or Vocabulary Word in each sentence is used correctly. If the word is correct, write it on the answer line. If the word is incorrect, write the correct Challenge or Vocabulary Word instead.

1. The doctor wore a <u>microbe</u> around her neck.
2. In the laboratory, scientists are working on the <u>biopsy</u> of separate elements to form a new substance.
3. Doctor Sinclair examined the <u>prognosis</u> through a high-powered microscope.
4. Kyle stayed home from school because he had caught the <u>diagnostic</u> disease that had spread through the town.
5. The <u>pathos</u> of the movie made Ernie cry.
6. The <u>synthesis</u> for Bob's immediate recovery looks very good.
7. The <u>inflammation</u> on Enid's knee caused the skin to redden.
8. The <u>protagonist</u> in that drama is a boy who saves a baby.
9. I saw an unusual x-ray in the <u>protocol</u> department today.
10. The doctor did a <u>biopsy</u> of the patient's muscle tissue.
11. The head nurse will <u>synthesis</u> her watch with the hospital clock to make sure that she is on time.
12. The interns followed proper <u>protocol</u> when greeting the visiting Count Von Diefendorf.
13. Dr. Klikka ran a series of <u>infectious</u> tests on the patient to identify the disease.

1.	**stethoscope**	5.	**pathos**
2.	**synthesis**	6.	**prognosis**
3.	**microbe**	7.	**inflammation**
4.	**infectious**	8.	**protagonist**
		9.	**radiology**
		10.	**biopsy**
		11.	**synchronize**
		12.	**protocol**
		13.	**diagnostic**

Challenge Words

1. synthesis
2. protocol
3. synchronize
4. pathos
5. protagonist

Theme Vocabulary

6. diagnostic
7. prognosis
8. stethoscope
9. biopsy
10. radiology
11. infectious
12. microbe
13. inflammation

Limericks Write a Vocabulary Word to complete each limerick. Then write three limericks of your own, using any three Challenge or Vocabulary Words. **Limericks will vary.**

14. A lady who lived near the Rhine
  Collected x-rays of the spine.
    She made no apology.
    She loved _____
  She simply found x-rays divine!

15. A cartographer two inches tall
  Drew maps one could not see at all.
    He worked years on a globe
    The size of a _____
  Because he preferred the world small.

14.	**radiology**	15.	**microbe**

Skill: Students will practice spelling words that have the Greek word parts *path*, *syn*, *gen*, and *prot* and words related to the theme of medicine.

Home Use: Help your child practice the spelling words by having him or her complete the activities on this page. Check the completed page, and have your child practice saying and spelling any misspelled words.

11

Unit 2 Test: Greek Word Parts I

Find the correctly spelled word to complete each phrase. Fill in the letter beside the correct spelling.

Sample:

to conduct a _____
  ⓐ simphony   ⓒ symfony
  ● symphony   ⓓ symphuny

Items 1–10 test Basic Words 1–10. Items 11–20 test Basic Words 11–20.

1. a food containing _____
  ● protein   ⓒ protien
  ⓑ protien   ⓓ protene

2. hydrogen and _____ gases
  ⓐ oxigen   ⓒ oxygene
  ⓑ oxegen   ● oxygen

3. the treatment for the _____
  ● syndrome   ⓒ sindrome
  ⓑ syndrom   ⓓ sindrom

4. to show _____ for
  ⓐ simpathy   ⓒ symmpathy
  ⓑ simpathy   ● sympathy

5. a bottle of _____ milk
  ⓐ homaginized   ⓒ homoginised
  ● homogenized   ⓓ hamogenized

6. the study of _____
  ⓐ patholigy   ● pathology
  ⓑ pathologie   ⓓ pathalogy

7. a _____ for a word
  ⓐ synanym   ⓒ synonym
  ⓑ synonim   ● synonym

8. a _____ fiber
  ⓐ synthetick   ⓒ sinthetic
  ● synthetic   ⓓ synthetic

9. a _____ atom
  ⓐ hydrogen   ⓒ hidrogen
  ⓑ hydrogin   ⓓ hydragen

10. a _____ of the disease
  ⓐ simptom   ⓒ symptom
  ⓑ symmptom   ⓓ symptum

11. two _____ sides
  ⓐ symetrical   ⓒ symmetricle
  ⓑ symmetricel   ● symmetrical

12. the _____ of a cell
  ⓐ protplasm   ⓒ protoplasim
  ● protoplasm   ⓓ protaplasm

13. a _____ sigh
  ⓐ pethetic   ● pathetic
  ⓑ puthetic   ⓓ pathetick

14. to feel _____ for
  ⓐ ampathy   ⓒ empethy
  ● empathy   ⓓ ampethy

15. people in a _____
  ● syndicate   ⓒ sindicate
  ⓑ syndikit   ⓓ syndikat

16. a _____ smile
  ⓐ fotogenic   ⓒ photogenik
  ● photogenic   ⓓ fotogenic

17. _____ voter
  ⓐ apethy   ⓒ apathie
  ⓑ appathy   ● apathy

18. a _____ condition
  ⓐ pathological   ⓒ pathalogical
  ● pathological   ⓓ pathologicel

19. the congregation at the _____
  ⓐ sinagogue   ⓒ synogog
  ⓑ synogogue   ● synagogue

20. to trace the _____
  ● geneology   ⓒ genealogy
  ⓑ geniology   ⓓ genelogy

12

PRACTICE B
Latin Prefixes I

Prefix Time Match each definition below with a Basic Word formed from the prefix *trans-* or *sub-* and a base word or a word root shown on the clock. Write the Basic Word. Then write the hour shown if the clock's hands were pointing to that Basic Word.
Example: to rent from a lease holder *sublet* 6:00

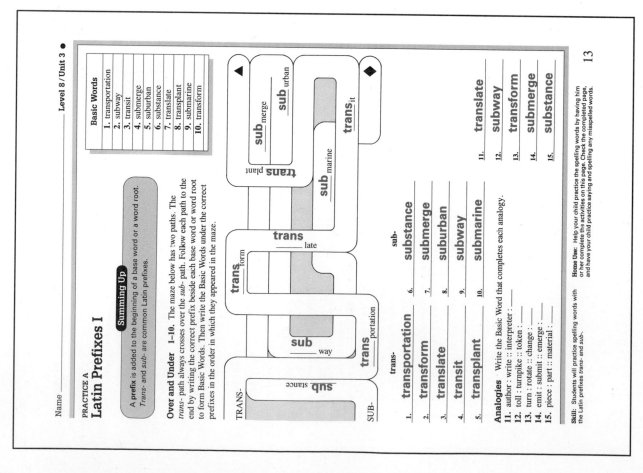

Clock labels: 12 trans-, 11 parent, 10 sub-, stance, 9 marine, action 8, plant 7, let 6, late 5, urban 4, merge 3, portation 2, way 1

1. the gist of something
2. to express in another language
3. to move something from one place to another
4. the act of carrying from one place to another
5. an underground railroad
6. to place under water
7. able to be seen through
8. of an area outside a city
9. an underwater ship
10. a business deal

Basic Words
1. transportation
2. subway
3. transit
4. submerge
5. suburban
6. substance
7. translate
8. transplant
9. submarine
10. transfusion
11. transfusion
12. subdivide
13. sublet
14. subscription
15. transparent
16. subtotal
17. transaction
18. subtitle
19. subside
20. transition

1. substance 10:00
2. translate 5:00
3. transplant 7:00
4. transportation 2:00
5. subway 1:00
6. submerge 3:00
7. transparent 11:00
8. suburban 4:00
9. submarine 9:00
10. transaction 8:00

Movie Message **11–20.** Read from left to right to find the Basic Words that appear on these strips of film. Circle and write the Basic Words. Then write the remaining letters to find a movie title. Remember to start each important word with a capital letter.
Example: asjhaamreosn(tran scribe)mraarnoes *transcribe*

Film strips: i(transition)wasasp(subdivide)(transform)e(sub let) h(transfusion) p(subscription) t(transit) ow(subtotal)(subtitle)subsideway

11. transition
12. subdivide
13. transform
14. sublet
15. transfusion
16. subscription
17. transit
18. subtotal
19. subtitle
20. subside

The name of the movie is __I Was a Spaceship Stowaway__.

Skill: Students will practice spelling words with the Latin prefixes *trans-* and *sub-*.

Home Use: Help your child practice the spelling words by having him or her complete the activities on this page. Check the completed page, and have your child practice saying and spelling any misspelled words.

14

PRACTICE A
Latin Prefixes I

> **Summing Up**
>
> A **prefix** is added to the beginning of a base word or a word root. *Trans-* and *sub-* are common Latin prefixes.

Over and Under 1–10. The maze below has two paths. The *trans-* path always crosses over the *sub-* path. Follow each path to the end by writing the correct prefix beside each base word or word root to form Basic Words. Then write the Basic Words under the correct prefixes in the order in which they appeared in the maze.

Basic Words
1. transportation
2. subway
3. transit
4. submerge
5. suburban
6. substance
7. translate
8. transplant
9. submarine
10. transform

Maze words: sub merge, sub urban, trans plant, sub marine, trans it, trans late, trans form, sub way, trans portation, sub stance

TRANS-

SUB-

trans-
1. transportation
2. transform
3. translate
4. transit
5. transplant

sub-
6. substance
7. submerge
8. suburban
9. subway
10. submarine

Analogies Write the Basic Word that completes each analogy.
11. author : write :: interpreter : __translate__
12. toll : turnpike :: token : __subway__
13. turn : rotate :: change : __transform__
14. emit : submit :: emerge : __submerge__
15. piece : part :: material : __substance__

Skill: Students will practice spelling words with the Latin prefixes *trans-* and *sub-*.

Home Use: Help your child practice the spelling words by having him or her complete the activities on this page. Check the completed page, and have your child practice saying and spelling any misspelled words.

13

Unit 3 Test: Latin Prefixes I

Each item below gives four possible spellings of a word. Fill in the letter beside the correct spelling.

Sample:
- (a) arival
- **(b) arrival**
- (c) arrivel
- (d) arivil

Items 1–10 test Basic Words 1–10. Items 11–20 test Basic Words 11–20.

1. **(a) transform**
   (b) transsform
   (c) transforem
   (d) transforme

2. (a) tranzplant
   (b) transplante
   (c) transplant
   (d) transplent

3. (a) substince
   (b) substense
   (c) substanse
   (d) substance

4. **(a) submerge**
   (b) submurge
   (c) submirge
   (d) submmerge

5. (a) sub-way
   (b) subway
   (c) subwaye
   (d) subbway

6. (a) transportashun
   (b) transportashun
   (c) transportacion
   (d) transportation

7. (a) transit
   (b) transit
   (c) transitt
   (d) transsit

8. (a) suberban
   (b) suberben
   (c) suburban
   (d) suburben

9. **(a) translate**
   (b) translait
   (c) trenslate
   (d) translaite

10. (a) submurine
    (b) submerine
    (c) submarine
    (d) submarrine

11. (a) subdivid
    (b) subbdivide
    (c) subdevide
    (d) subdivide

12. **(a) transfusion**
    (b) trans-fusion
    (c) tranzfusion
    (d) transfusion

13. (a) subscripshun
    (b) subscription
    (c) supscription
    (d) subscribtion

14. (a) sub-let
    (b) sublet
    (c) sublett
    (d) sublette

15. (a) transparrant
    (b) transparrent
    (c) transparent
    (d) transparant

16. **(a) transaction**
    (b) transsaction
    (c) transacsion
    (d) trensacssion

17. (a) subtotel
    (b) subtotal
    (c) subtotle
    (d) sub-total

18. (a) transision
    (b) transsition
    (c) trannsition
    (d) transition

19. (a) sub-title
    (b) subtitle
    (c) subtitel
    (d) subtile

20. **(a) subside**
    (b) sub-side
    (c) subsid
    (d) subcide

16

PRACTICE C
Latin Prefixes I

Word Puzzle Write seven Challenge or Vocabulary Words so that the letters in the box spell a word that means "a group of four." Then write a clue for each numbered word.

1. s u b s e **q** u e n t
2. s **u** b c o n s c i o u s
3. e l e v **a** t e d
4. t **r** a n s i e n t
5. m e **t** r o p o l i t a n
6. s u b t **e** r r a n e a n
7. s u b c u l t u **r** e

Clues will vary.
1. _____
2. _____
3. _____
4. _____
5. _____
6. _____
7. _____

Rhyming Pairs Write a Challenge or Vocabulary Word and another rhyming word to answer each question.
Example: What do you call a foreigner who lives underground?
subterranean alien

8. What is a merry streetcar? **jolly trolley**
9. What is a shattered piece of stamped metal used as a substitute for currency? **broken token**
10. What is a dish for a tax collected for passing over a bridge? **toll bowl**
11. What is a simple song sung between towns? **intercity ditty**
12. What do you call a teacher of those who travel regularly between home and work? **commuter tutor**
13. What is a device for admitting people to an African river? **Nile turnstile**

Challenge Words
1. subterranean
2. transient
3. subsequent
4. subculture
5. subconscious
Theme Vocabulary
6. metropolitan
7. commuter
8. intercity
9. elevated
10. trolley
11. toll
12. token
13. turnstile

Skill: Students will practice spelling words with the Latin prefixes *trans-* and *sub-* and words related to the theme of transportation.

Home Use: Help your child practice the spelling words by having him or her complete the activities on this page. Check the completed page, and have your child practice saying and spelling any misspelled words.

15

Practice Master and Test Answers

197

PRACTICE B
Words from Names

Basic Words
1. atlas
2. mercury
3. narcissus
4. psyche
5. odyssey
6. museum
7. hypnosis
8. Fahrenheit
9. czar
10. pasteurize
11. fate
12. jovial
13. tantalize
14. hygiene
15. mentor
16. psychiatrist
17. mosaic
18. Celsius
19. fury
20. galvanized

Myth Mystery Write the Basic Word that fits each clue. Then write the circled letters in order. Write a colorful mystery word that comes from the name of the Greek goddess of the rainbow.

1. full of fun — jov(i)a(l)
2. to kill germs — pasteu(r)ize
3. a sleeplike condition — hypnos(i)(s)
4. an adventurous journey — (o)dyssey
5. destiny — fat(e)
6. a book of maps — atla(s)
7. a flower name — nar(c)issus
8. a building with exhibits — mus(e)um
9. methods to promote good health — hygi(e)(n)(e)
10. a Russian emperor — (c)zar
11. an advisor or counselor — m(e)(n)tor

Mystery Word: i r i d e s c e n c e

Proofreading 12-20. Find and cross out nine misspelled Basic Words in these advertisements. Then write each word correctly. **Order of answers may vary.**

Whether the mercury plunges in degrees Farenheit or Celsius, we have a down jacket to suit you!

Read *Odyssey of the Mind* by psyehaitrist Jorge Ruiz.

Let us tentelize you with our newest line of cars featuring galvenized body panels.

Join Center East Crafts! Learn to work with mozaic tile.

Full of fewry and rage? Improve your psyeke with a meditation course at Oak College. A lecture on hypnosis is included.

12. mercury
13. Fahrenheit
14. Celsius
15. psychiatrist
16. tantalize
17. galvanized
18. mosaic
19. fury
20. psyche

18

PRACTICE A
Words from Names

Summing Up

Some English words come from the names of mythological figures. Others come from the names of real people.

Basic Words
1. atlas
2. mercury
3. narcissus
4. psyche
5. odyssey
6. museum
7. hypnosis
8. Fahrenheit
9. czar
10. pasteurize

Crossword Puzzle Complete the crossword puzzle by writing the Basic Word that fits each clue.

Across

4. a word from the name of a Greek maiden, meaning "soul"
7. a word from the name of the scientist Louis Pasteur
8. a word from the Latin word *Caesar*, meaning "emperor"
9. a word from the name of the giant who carried the world
10. a word from the name of the Greek warrior Odysseus

Down

1. a word from the name of the Muses of Greek myth
2. a word from the name of a German physicist
3. a word from the name of the Greek youth who loved himself
5. a word from the Greek god of sleep
6. a word from the name of the Roman messenger god

Silly Book Titles Write the Basic Word that completes each silly book title. Remember to use capital letters.

11. *Sleep Therapy Through _____* by Z.Z.Z.
12. *My Days Among the Statues in the _____* by Q. Ray Torr
13. *A Subject in the Court of the _____* by Roy L. Tee
14. *Ninety Degrees _____* by Hy Temps
15. *The Squirrel in the _____ Garden* by Flora N. Fauna

11. Hypnosis
12. Museum
13. Czar
14. Fahrenheit
15. Narcissus

17

198

PRACTICE C
Words from Names

Word Merge Use the clues below to write two words on each line. One word will be a Vocabulary Word. Letters at the end of the first word will also begin the second word. Circle the common letters. You may want to use a class dictionary.

Example: n e m e (s i s t) e r

1-2. e p i c t u r e
3-4. M u s (e t t) l e
5-6. c o n n e c t a r
7-8. l a b y r i n t h i n k
9-10. s l (a m b r o s i a)
11-12. i m m o r t a l l y
13-14. h y p h e n o m e n a
15-16. l u n (c h a r i o t)

Clues
1. a long poem about heroes
2. an illustration
3. a Greek goddess of the arts and sciences
4. to establish residence
5. to join
6. the drink of the gods
7. a maze
8. to contemplate
9. to close loudly
10. the food of the gods
11. living forever
12. to count
13. a punctuation mark
14. facts perceived by the senses
15. the midday meal
16. a horse-drawn vehicle

Words and Names Write the names of the characters described. Then write the Challenge Word that comes from each name. Use the etymologies in your Spelling Dictionary.
17-18. Greek goddess of the rainbow
19-20. Greek poet of the sixth century B.C., said to be the originator of Greek tragedy
21-22. fictional giant king noted for his huge appetite
23-24. Greek goddess of vengeance
25-26. Greek thinker who believed that the goal of life should be pleasure and luxurious living

17. __Iris__   19. __Thespis__   21. __Gargantua__
18. __iridescent__ 20. __thespian__   22. __gargantuan__

23. __Nemesis__
24. __nemesis__

25. __Epicurus__
26. __epicure__

Challenge Words
1. iridescent
2. nemesis
3. thespian
4. epicure
5. gargantuan

Theme Vocabulary
6. epic
7. immortal
8. phenomena
9. Muse
10. nectar
11. ambrosia
12. chariot
13. labyrinth

Skill: Students will practice spelling words that come from names and words related to the theme of mythology.

Home Use: Help your child practice the spelling words by having him or her complete the activities on this page. Check the completed page, and have your child practice saying and spelling any misspelled words.

Unit 4 Test: Words from Names

Find the correctly spelled word to complete each phrase. Fill in the letter beside the correct spelling.

Sample:
to draw a _____
ⓐ silouette   ⓒ sillouette
● silhouette   ⓓ silloette

Items 1–10 test Basic Words 1–10. Items 11–20 test Basic Words 11–20.

1. to put under _____
ⓐ hipnosis   ⓒ hypnosis
ⓑ hypnosis   ⓓ hypnosiss

2. the liquid metal _____
ⓐ murcury   ⓒ mercury
ⓑ mercurie   ⓓ mercuery

3. a person's _____
ⓐ psyche   ⓒ syche
ⓑ psiche   ⓓ psycke

4. ninety degrees _____
ⓐ Farenheit   ⓒ Fahrenheit
ⓑ farenhiet   ⓓ fahrenhiet

5. a map in the _____
ⓐ atlis   ⓒ atlass
ⓑ atlas   ⓓ attlas

6. to smell the _____
ⓐ narsissus   ⓒ narcissus
ⓑ narcissuss ⓓ narcissus

7. to _____ the milk
ⓐ pasteurize ⓒ pasteurize
ⓑ pasturize   ⓓ pastuerize

8. a visit to the _____
ⓐ museum   ⓒ museum
ⓑ museumm   ⓓ museumm

9. the palace of the _____
ⓐ zar   ⓒ czarr
ⓑ zarr   ⓓ czar

10. the family's _____
ⓐ odysey   ⓒ oddisey
ⓑ oddyssey   ⓓ odyssey

11. a _____ manner
ⓐ joviul   ⓒ joviel
ⓑ jovial   ⓓ joviale

12. studied to be a _____
ⓐ sychiatrist ⓒ psykiatrist
ⓑ psichiatrist ⓓ psychiatrist

13. a type of _____ metal
ⓐ galvanized ⓒ galvanized
ⓑ galvannized ⓓ galvannized

14. to tempt _____
ⓐ fate   ⓒ fait
ⓑ fatte   ⓓ faet

15. a lesson on good _____
ⓐ hygeine   ⓒ hygeen
ⓑ hygiene   ⓓ hygeene

16. the _____ of the storm
ⓐ furie   ⓒ fury
ⓑ feury   ⓓ furee

17. a _____ of tiles
ⓐ mosiac   ⓒ mosaic
ⓑ mosaick   ⓓ mozaic

18. a teacher and a _____
ⓐ mentor   ⓒ menter
ⓑ mentorr   ⓓ menntor

19. on the _____ scale
ⓐ Selsius   ⓒ Celcius
ⓑ Selcius   ⓓ Celsius

20. to _____ the senses
ⓐ tantulize   ⓒ tantulize
ⓑ tantalize   ⓓ tantalise

Practice Master and Test Answers

PRACTICE B
Homophones

Homophone Cartoons Write the Basic Words that correctly complete each speech balloon in the cartoons.

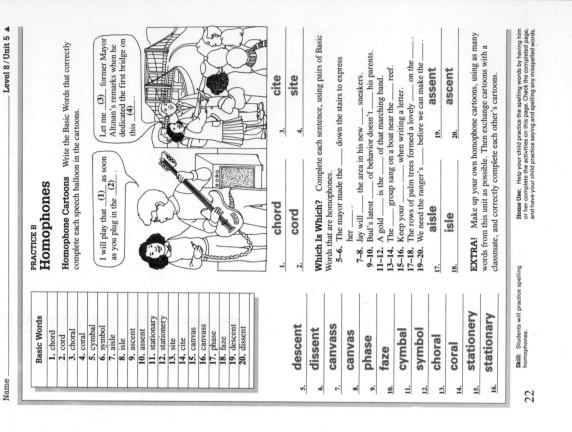

I will play that __(1)__ as soon as you plug in the __(2)__.

Let me __(3)__ former Mayor Altman's remarks when he dedicated the first bridge on this __(4)__.

Basic Words
1. chord
2. cord
3. choral
4. coral
5. cymbal
6. symbol
7. aisle
8. isle
9. ascent
10. assent
11. stationary
12. stationery
13. site
14. cite
15. canvas
16. canvass
17. phase
18. faze
19. descent
20. dissent

1. **chord**
2. **cord**
3. **cite**
4. **site**

Which Is Which? Complete each sentence, using pairs of Basic Words that are homophones.

5–6. The mayor made the ____ her ____ down the stairs to express

7–8. Jay will ____ the area in his new ____ sneakers.

9–10. Bud's latest ____ of behavior doesn't ____ his parents.

11–12. A gold ____ is the ____ of that marching band.

13–14. The ____ group sang on a boat near the ____ reef.

15–16. Keep your ____ when writing a letter.

17–18. The rows of palm trees formed a lovely ____ on the ____.

19–20. We need the ranger's ____ before we can make the ____.

5. **descent**
6. **dissent**
7. **canvass**
8. **canvas**
9. **phase**
10. **faze**
11. **cymbal**
12. **symbol**
13. **choral**
14. **coral**
15. **stationery**
16. **stationary**
17. **aisle**
18. **isle**
19. **assent**
20. **ascent**

EXTRA! Make up your own homophone cartoons, using as many words from this unit as possible. Then exchange cartoons with a classmate, and correctly complete each other's cartoons.

22

Skill: Students will practice spelling homophones.

Home Use: Help your child practice the spelling words by having him or her complete the activities on this page. Check the completed page, and have your child practice saying and spelling any misspelled words.

PRACTICE A
Homophones

Summing Up

Homophones are words that sound alike but differ in spelling and meaning.

Puzzling Pairs Use the clues to complete each puzzle with a pair of homophones. Fill in any boxes that you do not need for letters.

Basic Words
1. chord
2. cord
3. choral
4. coral
5. cymbal
6. symbol
7. aisle
8. isle
9. ascent
10. assent

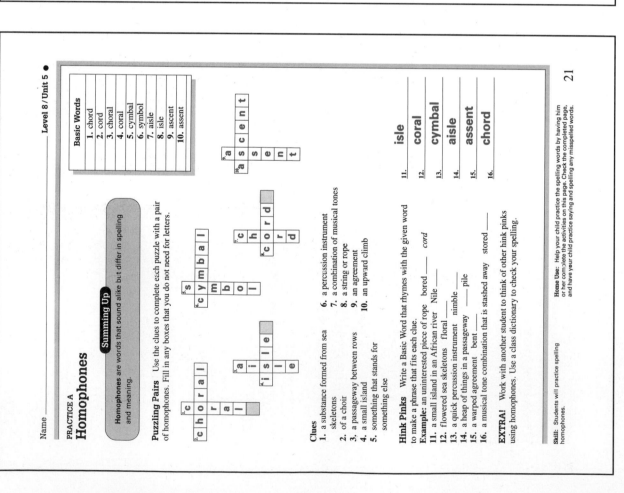

Clues
1. a substance formed from sea skeletons
2. of a choir
3. a passageway between rows
4. a small island
5. something that stands for something else
6. a percussion instrument
7. a combination of musical tones
8. a string or rope
9. an agreement
10. an upward climb

Hink Pinks Write a Basic Word that rhymes with the given word to make a phrase that fits each clue.

Example: an uninterested piece of rope bored ____ *cord*

11. a small island in an African river Nile ____ **isle**
12. flowered sea skeletons floral ____ **coral**
13. a quick percussion instrument nimble ____ **cymbal**
14. a heap of things in a passageway pile ____ **aisle**
15. a warped agreement bent ____ **assent**
16. a musical tone combination that is stashed away stored ____ **chord**

EXTRA! Work with another student to think of other hink pinks using homophones. Use a class dictionary to check your spelling.

21

Skill: Students will practice spelling homophones.

Home Use: Help your child practice the spelling words by having him or her complete the activities on this page. Check the completed page, and have your child practice saying and spelling any misspelled words.

200

Practice Master and Test Answers

Name _____ Level 8 / Unit 5 ●▲

Unit 5 Test: Homophones

Read each sentence. Decide if the underlined word is the right word or the wrong word for that sentence. Fill in the circle for the correct answer in the answer column.

ANSWERS
Right Wrong

Sample:

Jen paid Rob a compliment. ● ○

Items 1–10 test Basic Words 1–10. Items 11–20 test Basic Words 11–20.

1. Elsa wore the coral bracelet to the party.   1. ● ○
2. You can find the carrots in the vegetable isle.   2. ○ ●
3. Jim wrote to Sharon on plain stationery.   3. ● ○
4. Sara tied the boxes together with a thin chord.   4. ○ ●
5. Craig hit the symbol with his drumstick.   5. ○ ●
6. We voiced our assent.   6. ● ○
7. Please exit down the center aisle.   7. ● ○
8. My father gave me his ascent.   8. ○ ●
9. Fred joined the choral singing group.   9. ● ○
10. Martina dropped her cymbal during the last song.   10. ● ○
11. We voiced our descent.   11. ○ ●
12. Twelve carpenters were working at the building cite.   12. ○ ●
13. The sea is so calm that the water seems stationary.   13. ● ○
14. Chet's sneakers were made of canvas.   14. ● ○
15. The new procedure did not seem to phase Liza.   15. ○ ●
16. The cord was made of nylon.   16. ● ○
17. The sails are made of a sturdy canvass fabric.   17. ○ ●
18. Next fall, we will begin a new faze of construction.   18. ○ ●
19. That grassy hill marks the site of the battle.   19. ● ○
20. The elevator began its dissent.   20. ○ ●

24

Name _____ Level 8 / Unit 5 ■

PRACTICE C
Homophones

Making Choices Complete the answer to each question. First, write the correct Challenge Word. Then write an explanation telling why the word you chose is correct. **Explanations will vary.**

1. Might you find a callous or a callus on your hand?

   I might find a __callus__ because _____

2. Would a person more likely be callus or callous?

   A person would more likely be __callous__ because _____

3. Can a precious stone be bought by the carat or the caret?

   A precious stone can be bought by the __carat__ because _____

4. Would you more likely write a caret or a carat?

   I would more likely write a __caret__ because _____

Opera Lovers Write the Vocabulary Words to complete these clues about four opera singers. Then complete the chart to match the singers with their parts and their favorite composers. Put a check mark in each correct box and an X in each incorrect box.

- Richard and the man who likes Wagner teach at the __(5)__ .
- The woman who likes Verdi is in the alto section of the __(6)__ .
- Lorenzo can sing almost an __(7)__ higher than Richard. He will play Lieutenant Pinkerton, the __(8)__ in *Madame Butterfly*.
- At a recent concert, Paula, a famous __(9)__ , sang an __(10)__ from *Madame Butterfly*. This opera is by her favorite composer, whose name begins with the same letter as Paula's. The bus carrying the orchestra broke down, and Paula was forced to sing __(11)__ .
- The __(12)__ saw *Amadeus*, a movie about his favorite composer.

5. __conservatory__   8. __tenor__
6. __chorus__   9. __diva__
7. __octave__   10. __aria__
11. __a cappella__
12. __baritone__

	Paula	Beverly	Richard	Lorenzo
soprano	✓	X	X	X
tenor	X	X	X	✓
baritone	X	X	✓	X
alto	X	✓	X	X
Wagner	X	X	✓	X
Verdi	X	✓	X	X
Mozart	X	X	✓	X
Puccini	✓	X	X	X

Challenge Words
1. callous
2. callus
3. caret
4. carat

Theme Vocabulary
5. chorus
6. tenor
7. baritone
8. a cappella
9. octave
10. diva
11. aria
12. conservatory

Skill: Students will practice spelling homophones and words related to the theme of music.

Home Use: Help your child practice the spelling words by having him or her complete the activities on this page. Check the completed page, and have your child practice saying and spelling any misspelled words.

23

Unit 6 Review: Test B

Read each sentence. If one of the underlined words is misspelled, fill in the letter for that word in the answer column. If neither word is misspelled, fill in the letter for none in the answer column.

ANSWERS

Sample:
Be jovial when you canvas the neighborhood.   none
  a   b   c

This test reviews Basic Words 11–20 in Units 1–5.

1. Please remit a check to renew your subscription.   none
2. The psychietrist felt empathy for her patient.   none
3. It was pathetic to watch the captain consede defeat.   none
4. Jo had to transmit the message on plain stationary.   none
5. The transaction was made at the building site.   none
6. The subtitle of May's book refered to her mentor.   none
7. In the first faze, they will subdivide the lot.   none
8. Make a concession to buy him a stationery bicycle.   none
9. A symmetrical pattern of mosiac tiles lined the pool.   none
10. The subtotal showed the omission of printing costs.   none
11. A transfusion involves the transmision of fluids.   none
12. With proper oral hygeine, gums should not recede.   none
13. Tom felt apathy for the fait of the prisoner.   none
14. A galvanized railing helped us in our descent.   none
15. His pathological symptoms did not phaze his doctor.   none
16. A canvas sheet covered some chairs in the synagogue.   none
17. Nora will site the scientist Celsius in her report.   none
18. The fury of the storm began to subbside.   none
19. The family geneology was found on transparent paper.   none
20. The syndicat will omit a name from its membership.   none

---

Unit 6 Review: Test A

Read each sentence. If one of the underlined words is misspelled, fill in the letter for that word in the answer column. If neither word is misspelled, fill in the letter for none in the answer column.

ANSWERS

Sample:
Misha will translate his lines in the choral concert.   none
  a   c

This test reviews Basic Words 1–10 in Units 1–5.

1. Alfred found a map of the isle in the atlas.   none
2. It was easy to commit the odyssey to memory.   none
3. Peasants had to submit to the law of the czar.   none
4. The substance was found to contain protien.   none
5. A comission was formed to update the transit system.   none
6. Those plants emit healthy quantities of oxygen.   none
7. Pieces of coral were found on top of the submerine.   none
8. Quiet streets are a symbol of a suberban area.   none
9. The pathology department does not use hypnosis.   none
10. Do transform metric degrees to the Farenheit scale.   none
11. We made our acsent to the third floor of the museum.   none
12. She will intercede for someone she has simpathy for.   none
13. He will submerge through a succession of air locks.   none
14. A corde of synthetic fiber is used in rock climbing.   none
15. The bride carried a narcistus down the aisle.   none
16. Someone has spilled mercury in the subway station.   none
17. The transportation of the hydragen gas was risky.   none
18. Amy hoped to succede in striking the right chord.   none
19. Inhaling a toxic emision may cause that syndrome.   none
20. Dr. Prichard gave his assent to treat the symptom.   none

PRACTICE A
Absorbed Prefixes

Basic Words
1. communication
2. announcer
3. commentary
4. accent
5. colleague
6. apparent
7. allude
8. aggressive
9. immerse
10. illusion

Summing Up
The prefixes *ad-*, *in-*, and *con-* can be **absorbed prefixes**.

Absorb the Prefixes 1–9. When the prefix in each puddle is added to the scrambled letters in each sponge, the prefix is absorbed to form a Basic Word. Unscramble the letters, and add the prefix to write a Basic Word. Then underline the letter that changes in the prefix.

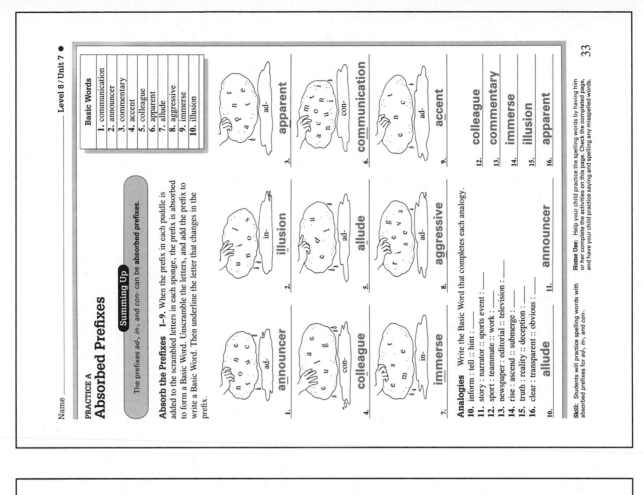

1. ad- / announcer
2. in- / illusion
3. ad- / apparent
4. con- / colleague
5. ad- / allude
6. con- / communication
7. in- / immerse
8. ad- / aggressive
9. ad- / accent

Analogies Write the Basic Word that completes each analogy.
10. inform : tell :: hint : _____
11. story : narrator :: sports event : _____
12. sport : teammate :: work : _____
13. newspaper : editorial :: television : _____
14. rise : ascend :: submerge : _____
15. truth : reality :: deception : _____
16. clear : transparent :: obvious : _____

10. allude
11. announcer
12. colleague
13. commentary
14. immerse
15. illusion
16. apparent

Skill: Students will practice spelling words with absorbed prefixes for *ad-*, *in-*, and *con-*.

Home Use: Help your child practice the spelling words by having him or her complete the activities on this page. Check the completed page, and have your child practice saying and spelling any misspelled words.

33

Unit 6 Review: Test C

Read each sentence. If one of the underlined words is misspelled, fill in the letter for that word in the answer column. If neither word is misspelled, fill in the letter for none in the answer column.

Sample:
The epicure felt pathos in the soup line. none
a   b   c

This test reviews the Challenge Words in Units 1–5.

1. The iridescent gem weighed one carat.   none
   a   b   c
2. The famous thespien played the film's protagonist.   none
   a   b   c
3. Sal's nemesis wanted a revacation of the challenge.   none
   a   b   c
4. Because of provacation, Mel will revoke his offer.   none
   a   b   c
5. Try to syncronize all subsequent trips with us.   none
   a   b   c
6. A tight shoe may give you a gargantuan callous.   none
   a   b   c
7. Ralph's synthesis into the subculture was not easy.   none
   a   b   c
8. He tried to provoke a memory from her subconcious.   none
   a   b   c
9. The transient was treated with callus indifference.   none
   a   b   c
10. Protacol dictates that you use the caret as shown.   none
    a   b   c

ANSWERS
● ⓑ ⓒ

1. ⓐ ⓑ ●
2. ● ⓑ ⓒ
3. ⓐ ● ⓒ
4. ● ⓑ ⓒ
5. ⓐ ⓑ ●
6. ⓐ ● ⓒ
7. ⓐ ⓑ ●
8. ⓐ ● ⓒ
9. ⓐ ● ⓒ
10. ● ⓑ ⓒ

31

PRACTICE C
Absorbed Prefixes

Two-Step Crosswords Fill in all the Challenge and Vocabulary Words in the puzzle. (There is only one way to arrange them.) Then write a short clue for each word.

Challenge Words
1. irrelevant
2. corroborate
3. commemorate
4. alliteration
5. commiserate
Theme Vocabulary
6. disc jockey
7. ad-lib
8. identification
9. prerecorded
10. cartridge
11. antenna
12. static
13. technician

(crossword puzzle with: prerecorded, commiserate, identification, alliteration, corroborate, ad-lib, static)

Across
Clues will vary.

4. _____
6. _____
7. _____
9. _____
10. _____
12. _____
13. _____

Down

1. _____
2. _____
3. _____
5. _____
8. _____
11. _____

Now write the Vocabulary Word that is written as two separate words. 14. __disc jockey__

Skill: Students will practice spelling words with absorbed prefixes for *ad-*, *in-*, and *con-* and words related to the theme of radio broadcasting.

Home Use: Help your child practice the spelling words by having him or her complete the activities on this page. Check the completed page, and have your child practice saying and spelling any misspelled words.

35

PRACTICE B
Absorbed Prefixes

Basic Words
1. communication
2. announcer
3. commentary
4. accent
5. colleague
6. apparent
7. allude
8. aggressive
9. immerse
10. illusion
11. collaborate
12. appliance
13. collision
14. accessory
15. immaculate
16. accumulate
17. allegiance
18. aggravate
19. collapse
20. illuminate

Prefix Switch Each word below begins with one of these prefixes: *re-*, *con-*, *inter-*, *trans-*, or *pro-*. Circle the prefix in each word. Then replace each prefix with a different prefix to form a Basic Word. Write each Basic Word.

1. (re)cent   5. (inte)rlude
2. (trans)parent   6. (col)lusion
3. (re)lapse   7. (com)pliance
4. (an)nouncer   8. (pro)gressive

1. __accent__   5. __allude__
2. __apparent__   6. __illusion__
3. __collapse__   7. __appliance__
4. __announcer__   8. __aggressive__

Headline Completion Write the Basic Word that completes each headline. Capitalize each word.

Cape Canaveral Reestablishes __(9)__ with Spacecraft

New Street Sweepers Make Roads __(10)__

Auction House Sells Antique Dress and __(11)__ for $1,000,000

Icy Roads Cause __(12)__ Near Bridge

Television Newscaster Broadcasts Controversial __(13)__

Train Staff Strike over Dismissal of __(14)__

Escape Artist Plans to __(15)__ Himself in Water for Two Days

Billionaire Shows Others How to __(16)__ Wealth

New Streetlights __(17)__ the City

General Crossfire Pledges __(18)__ to Republic of Oathia

Border Disputes __(19)__ Tension Between Neighboring States

Boris Vetlan and Buck Brady __(20)__ on New Musical

9. __Communication__   13. __Commentary__   17. __Illuminate__
10. __Immaculate__   14. __Colleague__   18. __Allegiance__
11. __Accessory__   15. __Immerse__   19. __Aggravate__
12. __Collision__   16. __Accumulate__   20. __Collaborate__

Skill: Students will practice spelling words with absorbed prefixes for *ad-*, *in-*, and *con-*.

Home Use: Help your child practice the spelling words by having him or her complete the activities on this page. Check the completed page, and have your child practice saying and spelling any misspelled words.

34

204

PRACTICE A
Greek Word Parts II

Summing Up

Some English words contain the Greek word parts *log* and *logy*.

Basic Words
1. chronology
2. terminology
3. catalog
4. technology
5. geology
6. zoology
7. logic
8. biology
9. apology
10. psychology

Word Riddles Write the Basic Word that fits each clue.

1. This log helps you understand all living things.
2. This log teaches you about animals.
3. This log helps you understand rocks.
4. This log is full of regret.
5. This log will help you understand the mind.
6. This log gives you the words you need for a particular trade, science, or art.
7. This log is found in industry.
8. This log is a list.
9. This log is very rational.
10. This log always tells everything in order.

1. <u>biology</u>
2. <u>zoology</u>
3. <u>geology</u>
4. apology
5. <u>psychology</u>
6. (terminology)
7. <u>technology</u>
8. (catalog)
9. (logic)
10. (chronology)

Now circle the Basic Words in which *log* or *logy* relate to the meaning "speech" or "reason." Underline the Basic Words in which *log* or *logy* relate to the meaning "science or study of."

Basic Word Mix-Up Unscramble and write the Basic Word in each phrase.

11. a seed tolacag
12. the latest cogytholen
13. a sincere pogaloy
14. unquestionable golic
15. the study of loogyeg
16. proper trogonimely
17. the gryocholno of events
18. a yiblog class
19. child yogolchyps
20. a course in golzoyo

11. catalog
12. technology
13. apology
14. logic
15. geology
16. terminology
17. chronology
18. biology
19. psychology
20. zoology

Skill: Students will practice spelling words with the Greek word parts *log* and *logy*.

Home Use: Help your child practice the spelling words by having him or her complete the activities on this page. Check the completed page, and have your child practice saying and spelling any misspelled words.

Unit 7 Test: Absorbed Prefixes

Each item below gives four possible spellings of a word. Fill in the letter beside the correct spelling.

Sample:
- (a) apropriate
- ● appropriate
- (c) appropreate
- (d) appropriat

Items 1–10 test Basic Words 1–10. Items 11–20 test Basic Words 11–20.

1. ● communication (b) comunication (c) communiction (d) communacation
2. (a) aksent (b) akcent ● accent (d) ascent
3. ● aggressive (b) agressive (c) aggresive (d) agresive
4. ● allude (b) alude (c) allood (d) alloode
5. (a) anouncer ● announcer (c) announcer (d) announser
6. (a) ilusion (b) elusion (c) ellusion ● illusion
7. (a) aparent (b) apparant (c) aparrent ● apparent
8. (a) commentery (b) comentary ● commentary (d) comentairy
9. (a) colleag (b) coleague ● colleague (d) coleag
10. (a) imerse ● immerse (c) imerce (d) immerce
11. (a) apliance ● appliance (c) aplience (d) applyance
12. (a) accesory (b) accesory ● accessory (d) accesory
13. (a) acumulate (b) accummulate (c) accumulate ● accumulate
14. (a) iluminate ● illuminate (c) illumenate (d) ilumenate
15. ● immaculate (b) imaculate (c) immaculit (d) imaculat
16. (a) collappse (b) collapse ● collapse (d) cullapse
17. ● aggravate (b) agravate (c) aggrevate (d) aggrivate
18. (a) collaborrate (b) colaborate ● collaborate (d) collaberate
19. ● collision (b) colision (c) collission (d) colesion
20. (a) alegiance ● allegiance (c) allegience (d) allegiance

Practice Master and Test Answers

PRACTICE B
Greek Word Parts II

Basic Words
1. chronology
2. terminology
3. catalog
4. technology
5. geology
6. zoology
7. logic
8. biology
9. apology
10. psychology
11. dialogue
12. sociology
13. ecology
14. meteorology
15. theology
16. anthology
17. astrology
18. analogy
19. mythology
20. trilogy

Word Search 1–10. Find and circle ten Basic Words hidden in the puzzle. The words may appear horizontally, vertically, or diagonally. Then write the Basic Words. **Order of answers may vary.**

```
d l a n a l o g y n b d o i f r l t
i d a b s u t h e s o c i o l o g y e
a w y e o t n f t a g t h o e w a r
l l m f t r e f s e h e a l n l d m
o e i o e n t o e p o l r o e v o r b i
g i a d c l u s i l g o o g s g h h n
u l y l g o e t o o a s y i t t u o v
e b l t y a l b h e g i h l d e u l
e j a d u e t o i f y v u l r a l f o
a r m e e s h c g r t a s n a e w r g
t e c h n o l o g y a n t r i l o g y
```

1. terminology
2. technology
3. geology
4. biology
5. dialogue
6. sociology
7. ecology
8. astrology
9. analogy
10. trilogy

Proofreading 11–20. Find and cross out ten misspelled Basic Words in this book review. Then write each word correctly.

BOOK NEWS

This season's ~~catelog~~ from Cornell Publishing features Warner Workman's latest book, *Any Job Will Do,* an ~~anthology~~ of his earlier essays. Workman's previous accounts of trying to succeed in the fields of ~~zoologe~~, ~~psychology~~, and ~~meteorology~~ have been combined in this biography that describes his experiences in several other occupations as well.

Though Workman's job experiences are amusing, it is difficult to follow his job history because the book's ~~chronalogy~~ is so confusing. Also confusing are new essays that are included in the book for no apparent reason. In an essay on ~~theolegy~~, Workman's theory lacks ~~logick~~ and wavers between ~~mythalogy~~ and astrology. Finally, Workman ends the book with scientific terminology when an ~~apolegy~~ to the reader would be more in order!

11. catalog
12. anthology
13. zoology
14. psychology
15. meteorology
16. chronology
17. theology
18. logic
19. mythology
20. apology

PRACTICE C
Greek Word Parts II

Challenge Words
1. archaeology
2. logistics
3. etymology
4. prologue
5. epilogue
Theme Vocabulary
6. expedition
7. excavate
8. civilization
9. strata
10. relic
11. implement
12. shard
13. classification

Word Change Follow the directions below to change Challenge or Vocabulary Words to other words. You may want to use a class dictionary.

1–2. Write the Challenge Word whose prefix means "before." Then change the prefix to write a word that names a long speech delivered by one actor on stage.

3–4. Write the Vocabulary Word that is a plural noun. Then replace the first three letters with one consonant to write a plural noun that means "information."

5–6. Write the Challenge Word that has a prefix meaning "ancient." Then change the prefix to write a word that means the study of animals.

7–8. Write the Vocabulary Word that means "a trip made by an organization." Then drop the suffix and add a vowel to write a word that means "to speed the progress of."

9–10. Write the Challenge Word that has a prefix meaning "on, upon, near, toward, or over." Then change the prefix to write a word that means "a discussion or conversation."

11–12. Write the Challenge Word that is a plural noun. Then change the Greek word part to write a word that means "a collection or set of numerical information."

13–14. Write the Challenge Word that means "the origin and development of a word." Then add a consonant and change the y to a vowel to write a word that means "the scientific study of insects."

15–16. Write a Vocabulary Word that means "a tool used in doing a task." Then change the prefix to write a word that means "something that completes."

1. prologue
2. monologue
3. strata
4. data
5. archaeology
6. zoology
7. expedition
8. expedite
9. epilogue
10. dialogue
11. logistics
12. statistics
13. etymology
14. entomology
15. implement
16. complement

Stop the Presses! Imagine that you are a journalist on an archaeological expedition. On the back of this paper, write at least three headlines that could accompany stories about your expedition. Use the Vocabulary Words *civilization, relic, shard, excavate,* and *classification.* Then write the first sentence of the news story that would follow each headline. Capitalize the first, last, and each important word in each headline. **Headlines and sentences will vary.**

PRACTICE A
Latin Prefixes II

Inter-, intra-, super-, and *counter-* are common Latin prefixes.

Summing Up

Latin Prefix Prix There are three bicycle races in the Latin Prefix Prix. They are the Super Speed, the Counter Contest, and the Inter/Intra Sprint. Determine which Basic Word placed first, second, etc., in each race by writing each word in alphabetical order under the race named for its prefix.

Basic Words
1. intramural
2. interstate
3. supervise
4. interference
5. intercept
6. counteract
7. intermediate
8. superlative
9. counterfeit
10. superficial

Super Speed

1. superficial
2. superlative
3. supervise

Counter Contest

4. counteract
5. counterfeit

Inter/Intra Sprint

6. intercept
7. interference
8. intermediate
9. interstate
10. intramural

Silly Book Titles Write a Basic Word to complete each silly title. Remember to capitalize each word.

11. *How to Identify _____ Cash* by Bill Iz Fake
12. *Conversational German: _____ Level* by U. Ken Learn
13. *How to _____ the Effects of Sunburn* by Sonny Tan Lotion
14. *The History of the _____ Highway System* by Ty Urd Driver
15. *The Catskill College _____ Athletic Program* by Kip Fitt
16. *How to Treat _____ Wounds* by I. Ama Doctor
17. *Penalties for _____: A Referee's Handbook* by Les Playfair
18. *How to _____ the Ball* by Stan Dintheway
19. *Fabulous Main Courses and _____ Desserts* by Sue Perior Cook
20. *How to _____ Children* by I. Canteach

11. Counterfeit
12. Intermediate
13. Counteract
14. Interstate
15. Intramural
16. Superficial
17. Interference
18. Intercept
19. Superlative
20. Supervise

Home Use: Help your child practice the spelling words by having him or her complete the activities on this page. Check the completed page, and have your child practice saying and spelling any misspelled words.

Unit 8 Test: Greek Word Parts II

Find the correctly spelled word to complete each phrase. Fill in the letter beside the correct spelling.

Sample:

___ of glass
ⓐ fragment ● fragment
ⓑ fragmint ⓓ fragmint

Items 1–10 test Basic Words 1–10. Items 11–20 test Basic Words 11–20.

1. scientific ___
ⓐ terminalogy ⓒ terminalogy
● terminology ⓓ terminology

2. to accept an ___
ⓐ apollogy ⓒ apology
ⓑ appology ● appoligy

3. using ___
● logic ⓒ logick
ⓑ loggic ⓓ logik

4. an item in the ___
ⓐ catilog ⓒ catilogue
ⓑ catalogg ● catalog

5. electronics ___
ⓐ tecknology ⓒ tecknology
● technology ⓓ tecnology

6. a ___ of events
ⓐ cronology ⓒ chronology
ⓑ chronnology ● cronnology

7. the study of ___
ⓐ sychology ⓒ psychology
ⓑ psicology ● psycology

8. a ___ class
● biology ⓒ bioligy
ⓑ biulogy ⓓ biologie

9. a professor of ___
ⓐ geologie ⓒ geeology
● geology ⓓ geoligy

10. to learn about ___
ⓐ zology ⓒ zooligy
ⓑ zooology ● zoology

11. books in a ___
ⓐ trilogy ⓒ trilogy
ⓑ trilogie ⓓ triligy

12. to draw an ___
ⓐ analogy ⓒ anelogy
ⓑ anallcgy ⓓ annalcgy

13. the study of ___
ⓐ meteorlogy ⓒ meteoralogy
● meteorology ⓓ meteorrology

14. a telephone ___
ⓐ dialogg ⓒ dialog
ⓑ dialoge ● dialogue

15. to read books on ___
ⓐ theollogy ⓒ theology
ⓑ theologie ● theology

16. to read from an ___
ⓐ anthollogy ⓒ anthology
ⓑ annthology ⓓ enthology

17. ancient Greek ___
ⓐ mythology ⓒ mythology
ⓑ mythology ⓓ mythologie

18. the ___ of the ocean
ⓐ ecology ⓒ ecoology
ⓑ ekology ⓓ ecology

19. an article on ___
ⓐ astrology ⓒ astrology
ⓑ astrollogy ⓓ astrallogy

20. a ___ course
ⓐ sosiology ⓒ sociollogy
ⓑ sociology ⓓ sociology

Practice Master and Test Answers

207

PRACTICE B
Latin Prefixes II

Basic Words
1. intramural
2. interstate
3. supervise
4. interference
5. intercept
6. counteract
7. intermediate
8. superlative
9. counterfeit
10. superficial
11. counterpart
12. intervention
13. intersection
14. intrastate
15. supermarket
16. interchangeable
17. superintendent
18. counterclockwise
19. interpret
20. intravenous

Synonym/Antonym 1–9. Write the Basic Word that is a synonym for or an antonym of the clue word. Then circle *synonym* or *antonym* to show how the Basic Word and the clue word are related.

Clue Word	Basic Word	Synonym or Antonym
1. middle	intermediate	(synonym) antonym
2. unique	interchangeable	synonym (antonym)
3. authentic	counterfeit	synonym (antonym)
4. crossroads	intersection	(synonym) antonym
5. deep	superficial	synonym (antonym)
6. oversee	supervise	(synonym) antonym
7. obstruction	interference	(synonym) antonym
8. support	counteract	synonym (antonym)
9. explain	interpret	(synonym) antonym

Proofreading 10–20. Find and cross out eleven misspelled Basic Words in this sportscast. Then write each word correctly.

Greetings, sports fans! The Babbleton Baboons finally left their ~~intrastate~~ league to cross the state border for the football championships. As the head coach was ill, the school ~~superintendent~~ asked Coach Ted Field to cancel his ~~intramural~~ college coaching activities to supervise the team. As it turned out, he more than matched the brilliant coaching of his ~~counterpart~~, the Germville Gerbils' coach Bob Trophy.

The Baboons began badly. After losing their way in a ~~supermarket~~ parking lot, they took the wrong turn at an ~~intersection~~ on the ~~interstate~~ near the state border and arrived late. In the first two quarters the Gerbils belted the Baboons, who were not able to ~~intercept~~ once.

In the second half the Baboons became brutal after a disagreement prompted the referee's ~~intervention~~. Coach Field's ~~counterclockwise~~ play exhausted the Gerbils, leaving them in need of ~~intravenous~~ injections of spirit. The Baboons bashed the Gerbils in the final minutes, closing with a score of Baboons 410, Gerbils 35. What a ~~superlative~~ bunch of Baboons!

10. intrastate
11. superintendent
12. intramural
13. counterpart
14. supermarket
15. interstate
16. intercept
17. intervention
18. counterclockwise
19. intravenous
20. superlative

Skill: Students will practice spelling words with the Latin prefixes *inter-*, *intra-*, *super-*, and *counter-*.

Home Use: Help your child practice the spelling words by having him or her complete the activities on this page. Check the completed page, and have your child practice saying and spelling any misspelled words.

PRACTICE C
Latin Prefixes II

Challenge Words
1. interscholastic
2. superfluous
3. counterproductive
4. interrogate
5. intersperse
Theme Vocabulary
6. recreational
7. participant
8. competition
9. championship
10. varsity
11. scrimmage
12. defensive
13. offense

Word Substitution Each pair of sentences includes an underlined word or phrase that is a synonym or a definition for a Challenge or Vocabulary Word. Write the Challenge or Vocabulary Word. Then write the letter of the sentence in which the Challenge or Vocabulary Word could be used.

1. a. The Westlake High School football team had a practice game before they played their first game of the season.
   b. Would you like to play a <u>practice game</u> of chess?
2. a. Sheila will scatter the birdseed on the ground.
   b. Let's <u>scatter</u> violets among the daffodils in the garden.
3. a. The police sergeant will question the suspect.
   b. The lost tourist will <u>question</u> the bus driver to get directions to the museum.
4. a. Manuel wished that he had brought extra food on the hike.
   b. Bring only necessities on the hike and nothing <u>extra</u>.
5. a. The struggle for the championship title was fierce.
   b. It was a <u>struggle</u> for Elena to solve the problem.
6. a. The farming technique had a harmful effect on the crops.
   b. Eating an imbalanced diet can be <u>harmful</u> to your health.
7. a. The Springfield Centaurs are the best team in the state.
   b. Our school's best team won top honors in the swim meet.
8. a. The semifinalists will compete in the contest next week.
   b. Jody wrote an essay on the application for the <u>contest</u>.

1. scrimmage (a)
2. intersperse (b)
3. interrogate (a)
4. superfluous (b)
5. competition (a)
6. counterproductive (a)
7. varsity (b)
8. championship(a)

Word Relatives Write a Challenge or Vocabulary Word and a word related in spelling and meaning to the Challenge or Vocabulary Word to complete each sentence. You may want to use a class dictionary.

9–10. The rival team took ___ when the captain of our soccer team was named the best ___ player in the state.
11–12. The lawyer's question made the ___ extremely ___.
13–14. Every ___ in the tournament will ___ in the parade.
15–16. The park has many ___ facilities for all kinds of ___.
17–18. Several ___ from different universities competed in an ___ math contest.
19–20. Clayton, a tough ___, won the swimming ___.

9. offense   11. defendant
10. offensive   12. defensive
13. participant   14. participate
15. recreation   16. recreation
17. scholars   18. interscholastic
19. competitor   20. competition

Skill: Students will practice spelling words with the Latin prefixes *inter-*, *intra-*, *super-*, and *counter-* and words related to the theme of intramural sports.

Home Use: Help your child practice the spelling words by having him or her complete the activities on this page. Check the completed page, and have your child practice saying and spelling any misspelled words.

208

PRACTICE A
Words from Spanish

Summing Up

Many English words are borrowed from Spanish.

Basic Words
1. coyote
2. mesa
3. savanna
4. adobe
5. pueblo
6. stampede
7. lariat
8. bronco
9. barbecue
10. tornado

Word Chain Complete the word chain by writing the Basic Word that matches each definition.

1. a small, wild horse
2. to rush suddenly
3. a lasso
4. a sun-dried brick
5. a small plateau
6. a flat-roofed dwelling
7. a flat, treeless grassland
8. a wolflike animal
9. a cyclone
10. a grill for roasting meat

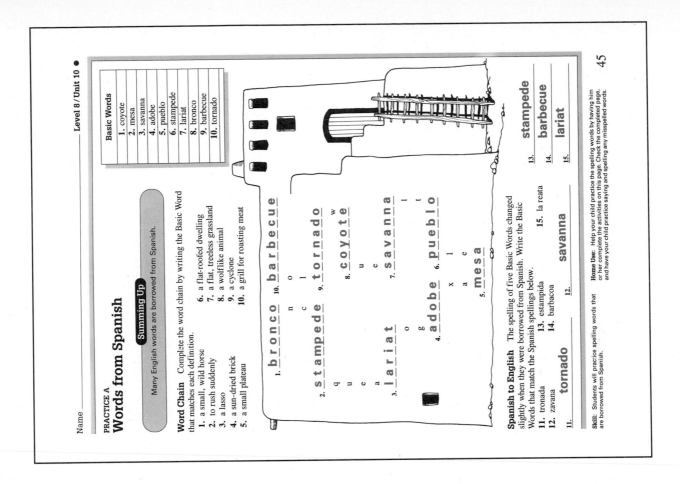

1. b r o n c o   10. b a r b e c u e
    n   o
    c   l
2. s t a m p e d e   9. t o r n a d o
  q   w
  u   8. c o y o t e
  e   u
  a   e
3. l a r i a t   7. s a v a n n a
  o   l
  g   t
  4. a d o b e   6. p u e b l o
    x   e
    a   e
    5. m e s a

Spanish to English The spelling of five Basic Words changed slightly when they were borrowed from Spanish. Write the Basic Words that match the Spanish spellings below.

11. tronada
12. zavana
13. estampida
14. barbacoa
15. la reata

11. **tornado**   12. **savanna**   13. **stampede**

14. **barbecue**   15. **lariat**

Home Use: Help your child practice the spelling words by having him or her complete the activities on this page. Check the completed page, and have your child practice saying and spelling any misspelled words.

Skill: Students will practice spelling words that are borrowed from Spanish.

Unit 9 Test: Latin Prefixes II

Each item below gives four possible spellings of a word. Fill in the letter beside the correct spelling.

Sample:
- ● athletic
- ⓑ athaletic
- ⓒ atheletic
- ⓓ atheltic

Items 1–10 test Basic Words 1–10. Items 11–20 test Basic Words 11–20.

1.
- ⓐ interrstate
- ● interstate
- ⓒ enterstate
- ⓓ intarstate

2.
- ⓐ interfeerence
- ⓑ interfrence
- ● interferense
- ⓓ interrference

3.
- ⓐ counteracte
- ⓑ cownteract
- ● counteract
- ⓓ counterract

4.
- ⓐ superlative
- ⓑ superllative
- ● superlativie
- ⓓ superletive

5.
- ⓐ superfishal
- ● superficial
- ⓒ sooperficial
- ⓓ suparficial

6.
- ● interpret
- ⓑ interprette
- ⓒ interpprett
- ⓓ interrpret

7.
- ⓐ soopervise
- ⓑ supervize
- ● supervise
- ⓓ superrvise

8.
- ● intercept
- ⓑ intersept
- ⓒ intercept
- ⓓ intircept

9.
- ⓐ intirmediate
- ⓑ intermmediate
- ⓒ intermediate
- ● intermediate

10.
- ● counterfeit
- ⓑ counterfiet
- ⓒ counterfit
- ⓓ counterfet

11.
- ⓐ intervenntion
- ⓑ interventon
- ⓒ intervenntion
- ● intervention

12.
- ⓐ entrastate
- ⓑ intrestate
- ● intrastate
- ⓓ intarstate

13.
- ⓐ interchangable
- ⓑ interchangable
- ⓒ interchangeable
- ● interchangeable

14.
- ⓐ conterclockwise
- ● counterclockwise
- ⓒ counter-clockwise
- ⓓ counter-clock-wise

15.
- ⓐ intervenous
- ⓑ intravenus
- ● intravenous
- ⓓ intervenus

16.
- ⓐ counnterparrt
- ⓑ counterparrt
- ● counterpart
- ⓓ counterrpart

17.
- ⓐ intersection
- ⓑ interrsection
- ⓒ inter-section
- ● interssection

18.
- ⓐ super-market
- ● supermarket
- ⓒ supermarkett
- ⓓ supermarkette

19.
- ⓐ superintendent
- ⓑ superintendant
- ⓒ superentendent
- ● superintendent

20.
- ⓐ interpret
- ⓑ interprette
- ⓒ interpprett
- ● interrprett

Practice Master and Test Answers

PRACTICE B
Words from Spanish

Basic Words
1. coyote
2. mesa
3. savanna
4. adobe
5. pueblo
6. stampede
7. lariat
8. bronco
9. barbecue
10. tornado
11. indigo
12. jaguar
13. mosquito
14. sierra
15. avocado
16. alfalfa
17. cafeteria
18. mascara
19. pimento
20. armada

Crossword Puzzle   Complete the puzzle by writing the Basic Word that fits each clue.

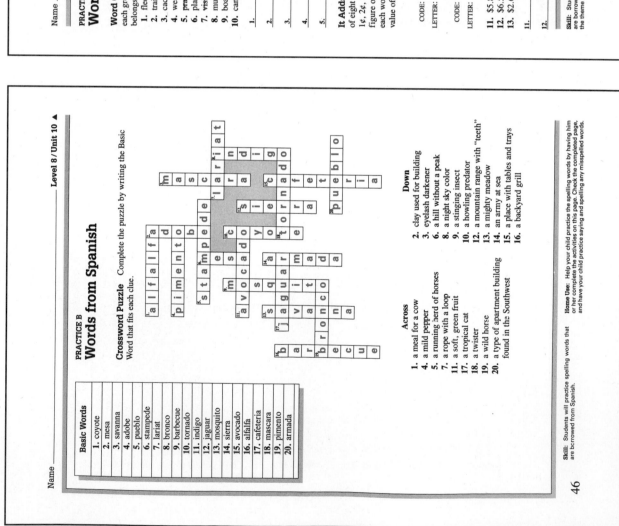

Across
1. a meal for a cow
4. a mild pepper
5. a running herd of horses
7. a rope with a loop
11. a soft, green fruit
17. a tropical cat
18. a twister
19. a wild horse
20. a type of apartment building found in the Southwest

Down
2. clay used for building
3. eyelash darkener
6. a hill without a peak
8. a night sky color
9. a stinging insect
10. a howling predator
12. a mountain range with "teeth"
13. a mighty meadow
14. an army at sea
15. a place with tables and trays
16. a backyard grill

Skill: Students will practice spelling words that are borrowed from Spanish.

Home Use: Help your child practice the spelling words by having him or her complete the activities on this page. Check the completed page, and have your child practice saying and spelling any misspelled words.

46

PRACTICE C
Words from Spanish

Challenge Words
1. bravado
2. renegade
3. incommunicado
4. flotilla
5. aficionado
Theme Vocabulary
6. mesquite
7. butte
8. scorpion
9. saguaro
10. gulch
11. armadillo
12. yucca
13. piñon

Word Categories   Cross out the word that does not belong in each group. Then write the Challenge or Vocabulary Word that belongs with each group. You may want to use a class dictionary.

1. fleet, yacht, armada
2. traitor, outlaw, nonconformist
3. cactus, tumbleweed, prickly pear
4. weasel, eel, elephant
5. praying mantis, black widow, tarantula
6. plateau, mountain, mesa
7. visitor, fan, admirer
8. mute, silent, rude
9. boastfulness, defiance, enthusiastic
10. canyon, cave, ravine

1. _____ flotilla   6. _____ butte

2. _____ renegade   7. _____ aficionado

3. _____ saguaro   8. _____ incommunicado

4. _____ armadillo   9. _____ bravado

5. _____ scorpion   10. _____ gulch

It Adds Up   The code below has been used to determine the values of eight Challenge or Vocabulary Words. The vowels are each worth 1¢, 2¢, 3¢, 4¢, or 5¢, but not in that order. Use the code to help you figure out and write the eight words. (Hint: The number of letters in each word is given in parentheses.) Then figure out and write the value of each vowel in the code box.

CODE:	2¢	4¢	1¢	5¢	3¢	10¢	15¢	20¢	25¢	30¢	35¢	40¢
LETTER:	a	e	i	o	u	b	c	d	f	g	h	l

CODE:	45¢	50¢	75¢	$1.00	$1.50	$2.00	$3.00	$4.00	$5.00
LETTER:	m	n	p	q	r	s	t	v	y

11. $5.89 (7) _____   14. $6.17 (5) _____   17. $3.92 (7) _____
12. $6.57 (8) _____   15. $5.35 (5) _____   18. $1.81 (5) _____
13. $2.64 (8) _____   16. $1.23 (5) _____

11. _____ bravado   13. _____ renegade   15. _____ yucca

12. _____ mesquite   14. _____ butte   16. _____ gulch

                                                                       17. _____ saguaro

                                                                       18. _____ piñon

Skill: Students will practice spelling words that are borrowed from Spanish and words related to the theme of the American Southwest.

Home Use: Help your child practice the spelling words by having him or her complete the activities on this page. Check the completed page, and have your child practice saying and spelling any misspelled words.

47

210

PRACTICE A
Words Often Confused

Basic Words
1. immigrate
2. emigrate
3. adverse
4. averse
5. persecute
6. prosecute
7. accede
8. exceed
9. liable
10. libel

Summing Up

Be careful not to confuse words that have similar spellings or pronunciations.

Write Right 1–10. Underline the correct Basic Word in each pair to complete the story. Then write the Basic Words on lines 1–10.

Tamal Finds a New Life

The Green Knights continued to (persecute/prosecute) the Blue Knights, bullying and mocking them. Still, many Blue Knights remained in Arburn. They were too loyal to (emigrate/immigrate) from their homeland, fearing (adverse/averse) times would befall the Arburnians without their protection.

Green Knights intended to (persecute/prosecute) him unjustly for (liable/libel). Because he would not (accede/exceed) to their demands to pay a large sum for his freedom, relatives in neighboring Carden persuaded him to (emigrate/immigrate) to their country.

Hurriedly Tamal went from merchant to merchant, trying not to (accede/exceed) the time left to him. He had to pay the bills for which he was (liable/libel), as he was (adverse/averse) to leaving debts behind.

At last Tamal mounted his steed and crossed Arburn's border. Once in Carden's forest, he knew he had found a place for a better life!

1. persecute
2. emigrate
3. adverse
4. prosecute
5. libel
6. accede
7. immigrate
8. exceed
9. liable
10. averse

Heads and Tails Add the first syllable of the second word to write a Basic Word. Add the first syllable of the first word to the last syllable of the second word to write a Basic Word.

11. adventure + reverse
12. excite + succeed
13. avert + diverse
14. library + rebel
15. accept + precede

11. adverse
12. exceed
13. averse
14. libel
15. accede

Skill: Students will practice spelling words that are often confused.

Home Use: Help your child practice the spelling words by having him or her complete the activities on this page. Check the completed page, and have your child practice saying and spelling any misspelled words.

49

Unit 10 Test: Words from Spanish

Find the correctly spelled word to complete each phrase. Fill in the letter beside the correct spelling.

Sample:

a string
- ⓐ hammock
- ⓑ hammock
- ⓒ hammuck
- ⓓ hamuck

Items 1–10 test Basic Words 1–10. Items 11–20 test Basic Words 11–20.

1. invitation to a ___
- ⓐ barbacue
- ⓑ barbecue
- ⓒ barbacue
- ⓓ barbicue

2. to swing a ___
- ⓐ lariet
- ⓑ lariat
- ⓒ larriet
- ⓓ lariat

3. trees of the ___
- ⓐ savana
- ⓑ savanna
- ⓒ savana
- ⓓ savannuh

4. atop the ___
- ⓐ maisa
- ⓑ masa
- ⓒ mesa
- ⓓ maysa

5. living in the ___
- ⓐ pweblo
- ⓑ pueblo
- ⓒ pwebloh
- ⓓ pueblo

6. a bucking ___
- ⓐ bronco
- ⓑ bronkoh
- ⓒ bronko
- ⓓ brawnco

7. a howling ___
- ⓐ kiyote
- ⓑ coyote
- ⓒ coyotee
- ⓓ kiotee

8. destruction caused by a ___
- ⓐ tornado
- ⓑ tornadoh
- ⓒ tornado
- ⓓ tornaydo

9. a ___ of cattle
- ⓐ stampeed
- ⓑ stampede
- ⓒ stampede
- ⓓ stampede

10. bricks of ___
- ⓐ adobe
- ⓑ adobee
- ⓒ adobie
- ⓓ adobe

11. an ___ sprout
- ⓐ allfalfa
- ⓑ alphalfa
- ⓒ alfalfa
- ⓓ alfalpha

12. the color ___
- ⓐ inndigo
- ⓑ indigo
- ⓒ indigo
- ⓓ inndigo

13. to eat in a ___
- ⓐ cafeteria
- ⓑ cafeteria
- ⓒ cafeteria
- ⓓ cafeteeria

14. a bite from a ___
- ⓐ musquito
- ⓑ moskeeto
- ⓒ moskito
- ⓓ mosquito

15. a ___ stalking its prey
- ⓐ jagwar
- ⓑ jaguar
- ⓒ jaggwar
- ⓓ jaguar

16. to apply ___
- ⓐ mascara
- ⓑ maskara
- ⓒ masscara
- ⓓ mascarra

17. a ripe ___
- ⓐ avacado
- ⓑ avocado
- ⓒ avacado
- ⓓ avocodo

18. a ___ in a salad
- ⓐ pemento
- ⓑ pimento
- ⓒ pimmento
- ⓓ pimentto

19. a mountain in the ___
- ⓐ siarra
- ⓑ sierra
- ⓒ sierra
- ⓓ searra

20. an ___ of ships
- ⓐ armadda
- ⓑ armada
- ⓒ arrmada
- ⓓ arrmadda

48

PRACTICE B
Words Often Confused

Basic Words
1. immigrate
2. emigrate
3. adverse
4. averse
5. persecute
6. prosecute
7. accede
8. exceed
9. liable
10. libel
11. rational
12. rationale
13. prospective
14. perspective
15. vocation
16. avocation
17. vial
18. vile
19. regimen
20. regiment

Rhyming Lines Write a Basic Word that has the same meaning as the underlined word or phrase to make the two lines in each item rhyme.

1. I'm tired of living in New York state.
   I'll pack my bags and <u>leave a native region</u>.

2. I have always been against
   To skiing downhill in reverse!

3. Just because the suspect is of ill repute
   Does not mean the court will <u>conduct legal action</u>.

4. I made the mess; it's undeniable.
   You're right to say that I am <u>responsible</u>.

5. We thought our friendship was defective,
   Until we got a new way of <u>looking at something</u>.

6. Digging the foundation and pouring the cement
   Would <u>take an enormous group of soldiers</u>.

7. A pilot must practice navigation
   If she's to succeed at her <u>chosen profession</u>.

8. Do not befriend the crocodile!
   His smile is nice, but his breath is <u>disgusting</u>!

1. _____emigrate_____
2. _____averse_____
3. _____prosecute_____
4. _____liable_____
5. _____perspective_____
6. _____regiment_____
7. _____vocation_____
8. _____vile_____

One Word Out Cross out the word in each group that does not belong. Then write the Basic Word that belongs with the group.

9. ~~shorten~~, slander, smear
10. ~~obligation~~, plan, system
11. bottle, ~~plate~~, container
12. bother, ~~impress~~, oppress
13. ~~detect~~, enter, settle
14. ~~collect~~, cutshine, surpass
15. hostile, negative, ~~regal~~
16. expected, ~~finished~~, possible
17. diversion, hobby, ~~job~~
18. explanation, ~~expense~~, reason
19. consent, yield, ~~argue~~
20. logical, ~~interesting~~, reasonable

9. _____libel_____
10. _____regimen_____
11. _____vial_____
12. _____persecute_____
13. _____immigrate_____
14. _____exceed_____
15. _____adverse_____
16. _____prospective_____
17. _____avocation_____
18. _____rationale_____
19. _____accede_____
20. _____rational_____

PRACTICE C
Words Often Confused

Challenge Words
1. antidote
2. anecdote
3. eminent
4. imminent
Theme Vocabulary
5. asylum
6. aliens
7. quota
8. exile
9. refugee
10. assimilation
11. naturalized
12. citizenship

Making Choices Complete the answer to each question. First, write the correct Challenge Word. Then write an explanation telling why the word you chose is correct. **Explanations will vary.**

1. Would an eminent or imminent physician be given an award?
   An ___eminent___ physician would be given an award
   because _____ .

2. Would you warn someone of danger that is eminent or imminent?
   I would warn someone of danger that is ___imminent___
   because _____ .

3. Would one be likely to laugh at an antidote or an anecdote?
   One would be more likely to laugh at an ___anecdote___
   because _____ .

4. Would you use an anecdote or an antidote for a snakebite?
   I would use an ___antidote___ for a snakebite because
   _____ .

Newspaper Capers Help newspaper reporter Skip Scoop finish the first sentence of eight articles. Replace each wordy, underlined phrase with a Vocabulary Word. Then use the new, edited beginning to write the first sentence of a news article on another sheet of paper. **Sentences will vary.**

5. The maximum number that may be admitted to a country for imported watches is . . .

6. Several illegal persons living in one country though they are citizens of another . . .

7. Political activist Geoff Young may choose voluntary separation from his native country rather than . . .

8. One-hundred-year-old Juan Soledad received the status of a citizen with its duties, rights, and privileges today . . .

9. Studies have shown that foreigners who have been given full citizen status . . .

10. Soviet sailor Ivan Tartikov sought a place of refuge . . .

11. Living the life of a person who flees from his country to avoid oppression . . .

12. Many immigrants find the process of being taken into the cultural tradition of a group . . .

5. _____quota_____
6. _____aliens_____
7. _____exile_____
8. _____citizenship_____
9. _____naturalized_____
10. _____asylum_____
11. _____refugee_____
12. _____assimilation_____

Unit 11 Test: Words Often Confused

Read each sentence. Decide if the underlined word is the right word or the wrong word for that sentence. Fill in the circle for the correct answer in the answer column.

ANSWERS
Right   Wrong

Sample:
Jim bought the old radio at the bazaar.

Items 1–10 test Basic Words 1–10. Items 11–20 test Basic Words 11–20.

1. The harsh treatment was meant to persecute the prisoner.
2. Juan and his family want to immigrate from Chile.
3. We drove to the game under adverse conditions.
4. Marcia is liable for service in the army.
5. Esther wants to emigrate to the United States.
6. That medicine had an adverse effect on the patient.
7. Please do not exceed the speed limit.
8. It is libel to rain today.
9. Mr. Craner is the lawyer who will prosecute the case.
10. The candidate plans to accede defeat tonight.
11. Josie has chosen a vocation in medicine.
12. What is the rational for your decision?
13. The vial contains grains of fine, black sand.
14. Dr. Teckman put his patient on a strict diet regiment.
15. Fran made a rationale decision about the repairs.
16. Owen's avocation is collecting post cards.
17. An army regimen marched through the town square.
18. Prospective employees should apply at the front desk.
19. Aunt Margaret always carried a vile of smelling salts.
20. From this perspective, the building looks slanted.

Unit 12 Review: Test A

Read each sentence. If one of the underlined words is misspelled, fill in the letter for that word in the answer column. If neither word is misspelled, fill in the letter for none in the answer column.

ANSWERS
ⓐ ⓑ ●

Sample:
High technology creates the illusion of order.   none
  a   b   c

This test reviews Basic Words 1–10 in Units 7–11.

1. Mike's colleague had to take a psychology course.   none
       a   b   c

2. Sara was the announcer at the intermural game.   none
         a   b   c

3. The agressive boy used to persecute the children.   none
       a   b   c

4. A geology expert spoke on adverse soil conditions.   none
       a   b   c

5. The surface of the interstate road was imaculate.   none
              a   b   c

6. Ann's comentary was on those who want to immigrate.   none
           a   b   c

7. Andrew plans to take an intermediate biology class.   none
                         a   b   c

8. Every teacher must supervise a mock tornado drill.   none
                         a   b   c

9. A zooology student studied animals of the savanna.   none
       a   b   c

10. We found counterfeit money in the pueblo.   none
                a   b   c

11. Try to intercept the catalogg before he sees it.   none
             a   b   c

12. It was apparent that her apology was sincere.   none
             a   b   c

13. The villagers were averrse to using adobe bricks.   none
                         a   b   c

14. Jim will not prosicute the man with the accent.   none
                  a   b   c

15. You must immerse yourself in the math terminalogy.   none
                  a   b   c

16. Is there any logic in suing the magazine for lible?   none
                  a   b   c

17. The length of her lariat seems to exceed the limit.   none
                       a   b   c

18. Pam and Gary threw a superlative barbecue party.   none
                            a   b   c

19. Was anyone held liable for the stampeed?   none
                       a   b   c

20. We heard radio interfernce on the mesa.   none
                      a   b   c

Unit 12 Review: Test B

Read each sentence. If one of the underlined words is misspelled, fill in the letter for that word in the answer column. If neither word is misspelled, fill in the letter for none in the answer column.

Sample:
The leader of the armada met the praspective sailor. none
a   b   c

This test reviews Basic Words 11–20 in Units 7–11.

1. The uniforms of the regiment were immaculate. none
2. I often colaborate with Tom's counterpart in sales. none
3. A vial of indigo fluid was drawn from the plant. none
4. A collision occurred at the main interrsectior. none
5. The superintendant visited our cafeteria last week. none
6. The sociology expert offered rational explanations. none
7. The third book in the trilogy is hard to interpret. none
8. You can buy astrology charts at the supermarkit. none
9. The jagaur is sometimes found in folk mythology. none
10. Al's vocation combines metorology with acting. none
11. The blades on the applience are interchangeable. none
12. A tale of a mosquito swarm was in the anthology. none
13. From this perspective, the sierra looks purple. none
14. A vile odor rose from the rotting avacado. none
15. How did you accumulate so many kinds of mascarra? none
16. Toxic fumes will agravate damage to the ecology. none
17. Please illuminate the meaning of that analogy. none
18. The recovery regimen includes intravenous feecings. none
19. The crew's intervention halted the wall's collapse. none
20. Growing alfalfa has become Maeve's avocation. none

ANSWERS
Sample: ⓐ ● ⓒ
1. ● ⓑ ⓒ
2. ⓐ ● ⓒ
3. ● ⓑ ⓒ
4. ⓐ ● ⓒ
5. ● ⓑ ⓒ
6. ● ⓑ ⓒ
7. ● ⓑ ⓒ
8. ● ⓑ ⓒ
9. ● ⓑ ⓒ
10. ⓐ ● ⓒ
11. ● ⓑ ⓒ
12. ⓐ ● ⓒ
13. ● ⓑ ⓒ
14. ⓐ ● ⓒ
15. ⓐ ● ⓒ
16. ● ⓑ ⓒ
17. ⓐ ● ⓒ
18. ● ⓑ ⓒ
19. ⓐ ● ⓒ
20. ⓐ ● ⓒ

Unit 12 Review: Test C

Read each sentence. If one of the underlined words is misspelled, fill in the letter for that word in the answer column. If neither word is misspelled, fill in the letter for none in the answer column.

Sample:
Phil will commemorate the event in his epilog. none
a   b   c

This test reviews the Challenge Words in Units 7–11.

1. Charmaine used alliteration in her anecdote. none
2. A flotilla escorted the man carrying the antedote. none
3. Myles is an aficianado of interscholastic hockey. none
4. We spoke with an eminent professor of archaeology. none
5. Stu can corroborrate my sighting of the renegade. none
6. Please intersperse relevant quotes in the prolog. none
7. That etymology contains superfluos information. none
8. I could not interogate the incommunicado prisoner. none
9. The logistics of the move seem irrelavant to me. none
10. We commiserate with you on his imminent departure. none

ANSWERS
Sample: ⓐ ● ⓒ
1. ⓐ ⓑ ⓒ
2. ⓐ ⓑ ⓒ
3. ● ⓑ ⓒ
4. ⓐ ⓑ ⓒ
5. ● ⓑ ⓒ
6. ⓐ ● ⓒ
7. ⓐ ● ⓒ
8. ⓐ ● ⓒ
9. ⓐ ● ⓒ
10. ⓐ ● ⓒ

PRACTICE B
Vowel Changes I

Basic Words
1. vegetable
2. vegetation
3. strategy
4. strategic
5. stability
6. stable
7. alternative
8. alternate
9. definition
10. define
11. remedy
12. remedial
13. immunize
14. immune
15. deprivation
16. deprive
17. indicative
18. indicate
19. infinite
20. finite

Anagrams The words in each equation are formed from the letters of one Basic Word. Rearrange the letters to write the Basic Word.
Example: gave + let + be = *vegetable*

1. feed + in **define**
2. rove + tin + paid **deprivation**
3. deem + rail **remedial**
4. dive + per **deprive**
5. tie + fin **finite**
6. tics + grate **strategic**
7. rent + teal + via **alternative**
8. dice + vain + it **indicative**
9. get + stray **strategy**
10. diet + ion + fin **definition**
11. my + reed **remedy**
12. nine + if + it **infinite**

Puzzle Play Write the Basic Word that fits each clue. Then write the circled letters in order. They will spell the name of a flower.

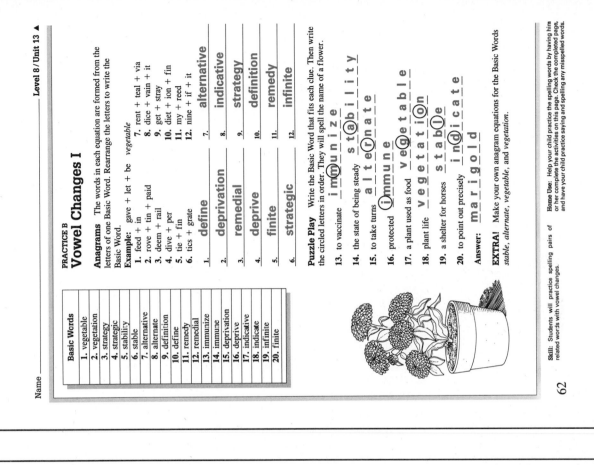

13. to vaccinate **i m m u n i z e**
14. the state of being steady **s t a b i l i t y**
15. to take turns **a l t e r n a t e**
16. protected **i m m u n e**
17. a plant used as food **v e g e t a b l e**
18. plant life **v e g e t a t i o n**
19. a shelter for horses **s t a b l e**
20. to point out precisely **i n d i c a t e**

Answer: **m a r i g o l d**

EXTRA! Make your own anagram equations for the Basic Words *stable, alternate, vegetable,* and *vegetation.*

Skill: Students will practice spelling pairs of related words with vowel changes.

Home Use: Help your child practice the spelling words by having him or her complete the activities on this page. Check the completed page, and have your child practice saying and spelling any misspelled words.

62

PRACTICE A
Vowel Changes I

Basic Words
1. vegetable
2. vegetation
3. strategy
4. strategic
5. stability
6. stable
7. alternative
8. alternate
9. definition
10. define

Summing Up
To remember the spelling of a word with the schwa sound, think of a related word in which the vowel sound is more obvious.

Crossed Words Complete the word crosses with a pair of related Basic Words. The words will cross at the vowel that changes from the schwa sound to a long vowel sound.

1–2. **stability**
3–4. **strategic**
5–6. **vegetation**
7–8. **definition**
9–10. **alternative**

Synonym Switch Write the Basic Word that has the same meaning as the underlined word or words in these ads seen on the sides of city buses.

11. Avoid highway hazards! Public transportation gives you **the choice of** not driving. — **alternative**

12. Are you looking for **security** in your job? Midwest Tech offers training that will guarantee lifetime employment. — **stability**

13. Local programming will **take turns** with network reruns during the summer months. Watch Channel 90 for variety. — **alternate**

14. Help our state achieve a **steady** economy. Support local manufacturers and retailers. — **stable**

Skill: Students will practice spelling pairs of related words with vowel changes.

Home Use: Help your child practice the spelling words by having him or her complete the activities on this page. Check the completed page, and have your child practice saying and spelling any misspelled words.

61

Practice Master and Test Answers

215

Unit 13 Test: Vowel Changes I

Each item below gives four possible spellings of a word. Fill in the letter beside the correct spelling.

Sample:

ⓐ harmonious
● harmonious
ⓒ harmonoius
ⓓ harmonius

Items 1–10 test Basic Words 1–10. Items 11–20 test Basic Words 11–20.

1. ⓐ allternative
● alternative
ⓒ alternitive
ⓓ alternetive

2. ⓐ stratigy
● strategy
ⓒ strategy
ⓓ stragy

3. ⓐ stability
ⓑ stubility
ⓒ stability
● stabbility

4. ● vegetable
ⓑ vegetabal
ⓒ vegatable
ⓓ vegeteble

5. ⓐ stabel
● stable
ⓒ stabbel
ⓓ stayble

6. ⓐ strutegic
ⓑ strategick
ⓒ stretegic
● strategic

7. ⓐ define
ⓑ deafine
● define
ⓓ defyne

8. ⓐ alternate
● alternate
ⓒ altarnate
ⓓ alternitt

9. ⓐ defintion
ⓑ definition
ⓒ definnition
● definition

10. ⓐ vegation
ⓑ veggetation
ⓒ vegitation
● vegetation

11. ● deprive
ⓑ depprive
ⓒ diprive
ⓓ depprive

12. ⓐ remmedy
ⓑ remedie
● remedy
ⓓ remidy

13. ● indicative
ⓑ indicitive
ⓒ indikative
ⓓ indickative

14. ⓐ fynite
● finite
ⓒ finyte
ⓓ finit

15. ⓐ imunize
● immunize
ⓒ immunize
ⓓ imunize

16. ● infinite
ⓑ infinit
ⓒ innfinite
ⓓ infinate

17. ● ramedial
ⓑ remedial
ⓒ remedial
ⓓ remediel

18. ⓐ imune
ⓑ emmune
● immune
ⓓ emune

19. ⓐ deprevation
ⓑ depprivation
● depravation
ⓓ deprivation

20. ● indicate
ⓑ inndicate
ⓒ indecate
ⓓ indacate

PRACTICE C
Vowel Changes I

Sentence Scrambler 1–6. Use the words below to write sentences about agriculture. First, list the words in separate groups according to their box numbers. Then write six statements by unscrambling each group and adding two Challenge or Vocabulary Words to complete each sentence.

4 against	5 in	3 tomato	1 the	2 repaired	6 harvest	
3 university's	2 and	5 making	6 you	2 the	1 Angus	
5 cooperative	5 year	3 new	4 a	1 field	6 swinging	
4 scientists	5 the	5 farmers'	3 by	4 Aaron	4 issued	
4 controversial	5 the	5 the	6 that	5 in	2 motors	
5 procedure	2 in	1 the	4 will	6 the	6 can	
4 government	3 the	4 spraying	6 the	5 the	5 the	
3 created	5 new	4 the	3 a	3 department	1 next	

1. <u>Angus will cultivate the fallow field next year.</u>

2. <u>Aaron repaired the motors in the thresher and the reaper.</u>

3. <u>Scientists in the university's agriculture department</u>
    <u>created a new hybrid tomato.</u>

4. <u>The government issued a mandate against spraying the</u>
    <u>controversial pesticide.</u>

5. <u>The farmers' cooperative took the initiative in making the</u>
    <u>new procedure mandatory.</u>

6. <u>You can initiate the harvest by swinging that scythe.</u>

Challenge Words

1. mandatory
2. mandate
3. initiative
4. initiate

Theme Vocabulary

5. agriculture
6. cultivate
7. pesticide
8. hybrid
9. reaper
10. scythe
11. thresher
12. fallow

Skill: Students will practice spelling pairs of related words with vowel changes and words related to the theme of agriculture.

Home Use: Help your child practice the spelling words by having him or her complete the activities on this page. Check the completed page, and have your child practice saying and spelling any misspelled words.

PRACTICE A
Latin Roots I

Summing Up

Three common Latin roots are *fer*, *pos*, and *tract*.

Word Root Robots Each robot is programmed only with words having a certain word root. On each robot, write the Basic Word that have its word root. Then match each Basic Word with its definition by writing the number of its definition next to the Basic Word.

Basic Words
1. reference
2. transfer
3. abstract
4. traceable
5. disposal
6. purpose
7. differ
8. proposal
9. contract
10. opposite

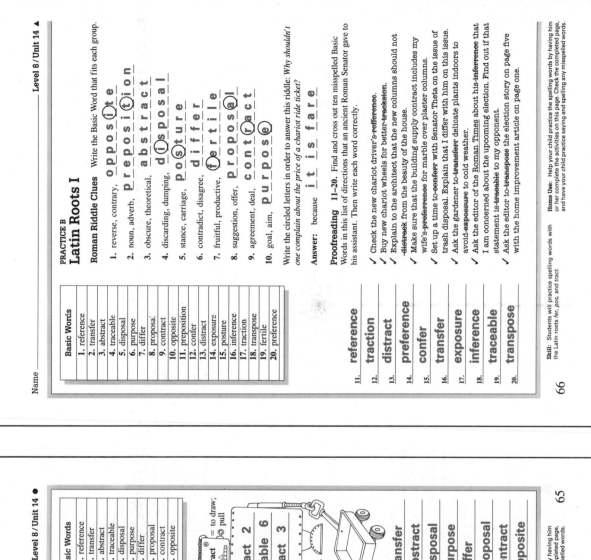

fer = to carry
reference 8
transfer 10
differ 7

pos = to put; place
disposal 9
purpose 4
proposal 5
opposite 1

tract = to draw; pull
abstract 2
traceable 6
contract 3

Definitions
1. contrary in nature
2. not concrete
3. a formal agreement
4. a goal
5. a suggestion
6. able to be followed
7. to be unlike
8. the source of information
9. the act of throwing away
10. to move from one place to another

Word Search 11–18. Find eight Basic Words hidden in the puzzle. The words may cross each other and appear horizontally, vertically, or diagonally. Circle each word, and then write it.
Order of answers may vary.

```
w p h e h o g y t h c t w o n t o s w
o r t e e p s t j d o p u r p o s e
a o s d i s p o s a l r k h p w a
p p r f m i h e o o d c e t i a g n x
a o t e e f f s t a b s t r a c t
j s t r a n s f e r i s a a n g r
s a b s o h e m o l s f m x c h o
e l c t o l i n h a e a e l l t a
```

11. transfer
12. abstract
13. disposal
14. purpose
15. differ
16. proposal
17. contract
18. opposite

PRACTICE B
Latin Roots I

Roman Riddle Clues Write the Basic Word that fits each group.

Basic Words
1. reference
2. transfer
3. abstract
4. traceable
5. disposal
6. differ
7. proposal
8. contract
9. opposite
10. preposition
11. confer
12. distract
13. exposure
14. posture
15. inference
16. traction
17. transpose
18. fertile
19. preference
20. purpose

1. reverse, contrary, ___ **o p p o s i t e**
2. noun, adverb, ___ **p r e p o s i t i o n**
3. obscure, theoretical, ___ **a b s t r a c t**
4. discarding, dumping, ___ **d i s p o s a l**
5. stance, carriage, ___ **p o s t u r e**
6. contradict, disagree, ___ **d i f f e r**
7. fruitful, productive, ___ **f e r t i l e**
8. suggestion, offer, ___ **p r o p o s a l**
9. agreement, deal, ___ **c o n t r a c t**
10. goal, aim, ___ **p u r p o s e**

Write the circled letters in order to answer this riddle: *Why shouldn't one complain about the price of a chariot ride ticket?*

Answer: because **i t i s f a r e**

Proofreading 11–20. Find and cross out ten misspelled Basic Words in this list of directions that an ancient Roman Senator gave to his assistant. Then write each word correctly.

✓ Check the new chariot driver's ~~refrence~~.
✓ Buy new chariot wheels for better ~~trackion~~.
✓ Explain to the architect that the new columns should not ~~distrack~~ from the beauty of the house.
✓ Make sure that the building supply contract includes my wife's ~~prefrence~~ for marble over plaster columns.
Set up a time to ~~confer~~ with Senator Theta on the issue of trash disposal. Explain that I differ with him on this issue.
Ask the gardener to ~~transfer~~ delicate plants indoors to avoid ~~exposuer~~ to cold weather.
Ask the editor of the Roman Times about his ~~inferrence~~ that I am concerned about the upcoming election. Find out if that statement is ~~traceble~~ to my opponent.
✓ Ask the editor to ~~transpoze~~ the election story on page five with the home improvement article on page one.

11. **reference**
12. **traction**
13. **distract**
14. **preference**
15. **confer**
16. **transfer**
17. **exposure**
18. **inference**
19. **traceable**
20. **transpose**

Practice Master and Test Answers

217

Page 67

PRACTICE C
Latin Roots I

Hidden Words Use the clues below to find little words hidden in seven Challenge or Vocabulary Words. Write each hidden word and the Challenge or Vocabulary Word in which it is found.

Example: auto *car* carrel

1. to hit lightly   4. a brim or edge   6. an antonym for *out*
2. to create music   5. a wager   7. a location or place
3. a farm vehicle

	Hidden Word	Challenge/Vocabulary Word
1.	tap	juxtapose
2.	compose	decompose
3.	tractor	protractor
4.	rim	superimpose
5.	bet	alphabetical
6.	in	index
7.	site	composite

On the back of this paper, write the definitions for the Challenge and Vocabulary Words that you wrote above.

Library Locations Write a Vocabulary Word to complete each clue. Then identify the parts of the library on the floor plan by writing the number of each clue in the correct location.

8. Check out books at the _____ desk just east of the entrance.
9. Magazines are on the _____ shelves in the southwest corner.
10. Use microfilm readers with the _____ in the northwest corner.
11. You can study in a _____ located just north of the magazines.
12. History books are in the _____ section, east of the study area.
13. Novels are in the _____ section, located in the northeast corner.

Challenge Words
1. composite
2. juxtapose
3. protractor
4. decompose
5. superimpose
Theme Vocabulary
6. index
7. periodical
8. alphabetical
9. microfiche
10. carrel
11. circulation
12. fiction
13. nonfiction

8. circulation
9. periodical
10. microfiche
11. carrel
12. nonfiction
13. fiction

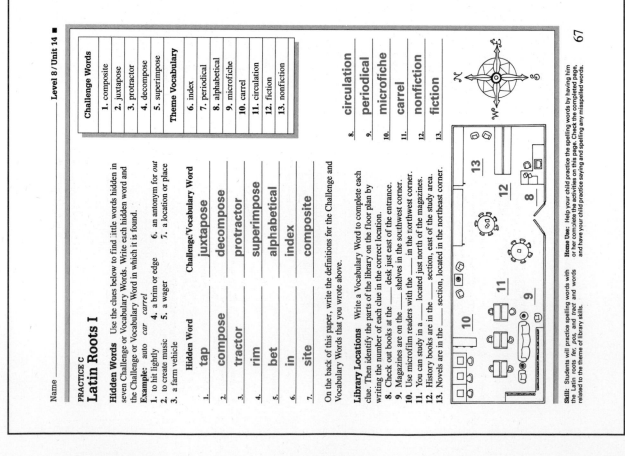

Skill: Students will practice spelling words with the Latin roots *fer*, *pos*, and *tract* and words related to the theme of library skills.

Home Use: Help your child practice the spelling words by having him or her complete the activities on this page. Check the completed page, and have your child practice saying and spelling any misspelled words.

Page 68

Unit 14 Test: Latin Roots I

Find the correctly spelled word to complete each phrase. Fill in the letter beside the correct spelling.

Sample:

to look up in a _____
ⓐ dictionery   ⓒ dicshunary
● dictionary   ⓓ dicshunery

Items 1–10 test Basic Words 1–10. Items 11–20 test Basic Words 11–20.

1. the garbage _____
ⓐ disposal   ⓒ disposel
ⓑ disposol   ⓓ disposal

2. to serve a _____
ⓐ purpose   ⓒ purpess
ⓑ perpose   ⓓ purpuse

3. to request a _____
ⓐ transfer   ⓒ transfer
ⓑ transferr   ⓓ transfer

4. to make a _____ to
ⓐ reference   ⓒ reference
ⓑ reference   ⓓ reference

5. to _____ from one another
ⓐ difer   ⓒ diffir
ⓑ differr   ⓓ differ

6. signed the _____
ⓐ contracte   ⓒ contract
ⓑ kontract   ⓓ conntract

7. to accept the _____
ⓐ propsal   ⓒ propole
ⓑ proposal   ⓓ proposal

8. a piece of _____ art
ⓐ abstract   ⓒ abstracte
ⓑ abstrack   ⓓ abstracte

9. on the _____ side
ⓐ oposite   ⓒ oposite
ⓑ opposite   ⓓ opposite

10. something _____ to its source
ⓐ traceable   ⓒ trasable
ⓑ tracable   ⓓ traceable

11. to have good _____
ⓐ poschure   ⓒ postcher
ⓑ posture   ⓓ poscher

12. the object of a _____
ⓐ preposition   ⓒ prepasition
ⓑ preposition   ⓓ preposetion

13. a double _____
ⓐ eksposure   ⓒ exposure
ⓑ ecksposure   ⓓ exposure

14. to have a _____ for
ⓐ preference   ⓒ preference
ⓑ preferance   ⓓ preference

15. to _____ with the others
ⓐ confer   ⓒ comfer
ⓑ conferr   ⓓ cumfer

16. to _____ two words
ⓐ transpose   ⓒ transpose
ⓑ transpose   ⓓ trenspose

17. to _____ one's opponent
ⓐ distract   ⓒ disteract
ⓑ disstract   ⓓ distrect

18. gaining _____ on the icy slope
ⓐ traction   ⓒ trection
ⓑ tracton   ⓓ tracton

19. the _____ soil
ⓐ fertill   ⓒ fertile
ⓑ ferrile   ⓓ fertall

20. to make an _____
ⓐ inference   ⓒ inferance
ⓑ inference   ⓓ inferance

Name

PRACTICE B
Noun Suffixes I

Basic Words
1. nationality
2. hospitality
3. agency
4. society
5. curiosity
6. generosity
7. familiarity
8. majority
9. privacy
10. frequency
11. popularity
12. accuracy
13. minority
14. urgency
15. democracy
16. emergency
17. personality
18. maturity
19. anxiety
20. humidity

Mystery Titles Read these book titles and descriptions. Unscramble the Basic Words in each title to write a book title that matches each description. Capitalize each important word.

1–2. *The Saltyhipoti of a Torymini*
Only a few townspeople welcome the mysterious newcomer.

3–4. *The Yergosenti of Yetsoci*
Earthquake victims are overwhelmed by financial support.

5–6. *A Roitycusi About Alatniotiny*
While vacationing in Switzerland, Barney Bosco loses his passport and his memory. What country does he come from? Barney must know the truth.

7–8. *The Dumlihity Germeceny*
A mad scientist finds a way to control the moisture content of the world's air—with devastating results.

9–10. *An Ecgany of Rodymecac*
An office in the capital of Westania is opened to teach citizens about the new system of government elections.

1–2. __The Hospitality of a Minority__
3–4. __The Generosity of Society__
5–6. __A Curiosity About Nationality__
7–8. __The Humidity Emergency__
9–10. __An Agency of Democracy__

Sports Article Write ten Basic Words to complete this excerpt from an article in a sports magazine.

In the __(11)__ of his room, Matt Miller talks about the crowd that will be at the tie-breaking meet. He will be mobbed, for he enjoys immense __(12)__. With his cheerful, friendly __(13)__ and the __(14)__ of his victories, Miller has made quite a name for himself. His fans, at least the __(15)__ of them, think of him as an old friend and greet him with __(16)__ wherever he goes.

A sportswriter once called him an amateur in search of glory. There is a degree of __(17)__ in that observation—Miller has always taken his fame more seriously than his running, but he does not any-more. He has grown up and achieved __(18)__. He still suffers __(19)__ about losing, but he no longer feels the pressure or the __(20)__ to succeed. Although he still loves to win, he now knows that there is more to sport than victory.

11. __privacy__
12. __popularity__
13. __personality__
14. __frequency__
15. __majority__
16. __familiarity__
17. __accuracy__
18. __maturity__
19. __anxiety__
20. __urgency__

70

Skill: Students will practice spelling words with the suffixes -cy, -ty, and -ity.
Home Use: Help your child practice the spelling words by having him or her complete the activities on this page. Check the completed page, and have your child practice saying and spelling any misspelled words.

Name

PRACTICE A
Noun Suffixes I

Summing Up
The suffixes -cy, -ty, and -ity form nouns.

Basic Words
1. nationality
2. hospitality
3. agency
4. society
5. curiosity
6. generosity
7. familiarity
8. majority
9. privacy
10. frequency

Bumper Stickers Help finish printing the bumper stickers by writing the Basic Word that fits in each blank. On the lines below each sticker, write the other Basic Words that have the same suffix as each word you wrote in the sticker.
Order of answers may vary.

-cy
Warning! I brake for ice cream shops with unusual __frequency__.
1. __frequency__
2. __agency__
3. __privacy__

-ity
Most drivers are safe drivers. Be part of that __majority__.
4. __majority__
5. __nationality__
6. __hospitality__
7. __curiosity__

-ty
Do your part! Become an active member of __society__.
10. __society__
8. __generosity__
9. __familiarity__

Word Riddles Write the Basic Word that answers each riddle.
11. You can find me only when you are alone.
12. Everyone is a part of me.
13. I am the number of occurrences within a given period.
14. I am characteristic of someone who likes to give.
15. I am indicated on your passport.
16. I am a business that acts for others.
17. I am what you feel when you want to know something.
18. I exist when you know someone or something well.
19. I am the greater number or part of something.
20. I am what every guest expects.

11. __privacy__
12. __society__
13. __frequency__
14. __generosity__
15. __nationality__
16. __agency__
17. __curiosity__
18. __familiarity__
19. __majority__
20. __hospitality__

69

Skill: Students will practice spelling words with the suffixes -cy, -ty, and -ity.
Home Use: Help your child practice the spelling words by having him or her complete the activities on this page. Check the completed page, and have your child practice saying and spelling any misspelled words.

Practice Master and Test Answers

PRACTICE C
Noun Suffixes I

Word Merge Use the clues to write two words on each line. One word will be a Challenge or Vocabulary Word. The letters at the end of the first word will be the letters that also begin the second word. You may want to use a class dictionary. Circle the common letters.

Example: _c u l t u r a l l i a n c e_

1–2. s e m e s t e r m i n a t e

3–4. t u i t i o n i o n

5–6. r e c i p i e n t e r t a i n

7–8. a b r o a d b l o c k

9–10. b e a c o n s i s t e n c y

11–12. r e c i p r o c a t e r m i t e

13–14. v i s a f e g u a r d

15–16. s c h o l a r s h i p p o p o t a m u s

Clues
1. a school term
2. to put an end to
3. a school fee
4. a strong-smelling vegetable
5. someone who acquires
6. to amuse
7. in foreign places
8. a barrier across a highway
9. a light for guiding ships
10. conformity
11. to give in return
12. an insect that eats wood
13. a travel permit
14. to protect
15. money awarded to a student
16. a large African river animal

Read All About It 17–21. A wealthy citizen has secretly donated a fortune to a museum. Write five headlines about the donation, using these Challenge and Vocabulary Words: *cultural, prosperity, anonymity, spontaneity, eccentricity.*

Headlines will vary.

17. _____

18. _____

19. _____

20. _____

21. _____

Challenge Words
1. prosperity
2. anonymity
3. consistency
4. spontaneity
5. eccentricity

Theme Vocabulary
6. scholarship
7. recipient
8. abroad
9. visa
10. reciprocate
11. semester
12. cultural
13. tuition

Skill: Students will practice spelling words with the noun suffixes -cy, -ty, and -ity and words related to the theme of student exchange programs.

Home Use: Help your child practice the spelling words by having him or her complete the activities on this page. Check the completed page, and have your child practice saying and spelling any misspelled words.

71

Unit 15 Test: Noun Suffixes I

Each item below gives four possible spellings of a word. Fill in the letter beside the correct spelling.

Sample:
- (a) varriety
- (b) variety
- (c) **variety**
- (d) varriaty

Items 1–10 test Basic Words 1–10. Items 11–20 test Basic Words 11–20.

1.
- (a) frequency
- (b) frequencie
- (c) **frequancy**
- (d) freequency

2.
- (a) hospitalety
- (b) hospetality
- (c) **hospitality**
- (d) hospitelity

3.
- (a) sosiety
- (b) sociaty
- (c) **society**
- (d) societie

4.
- (a) familarity
- (b) familarety
- (c) familyarity
- (d) **familiarity**

5.
- (a) angsiety
- (b) angziety
- (c) **anxiety**
- (d) anxiaty

6.
- (a) machurity
- (b) **maturity**
- (c) muchurity
- (d) matureity

7.
- (a) **nationality**
- (b) nationallity
- (c) nationnality
- (d) nationalety

8.
- (a) curriosity
- (b) curiositie
- (c) cureiosity
- (d) **curiosity**

9.
- (a) **agency**
- (b) agemcy
- (c) ajency
- (d) agencie

10.
- (a) privicy
- (b) privecy
- (c) **privacy**
- (d) privacie

11.
- (a) minority
- (b) minoraty
- (c) mynority
- (d) **minority**

12.
- (a) **angsiety**
- (b) angziety
- (c) anxiety
- (d) anxiaty

13.
- (a) machurity
- (b) **maturity**
- (c) muchurity
- (d) matureity

14.
- (a) **democracy**
- (b) democrecy
- (c) demacracy
- (d) dimocracy

15.
- (a) poppularity
- (b) **popularity**
- (c) popularetiy
- (d) popularity

16.
- (a) **humididy**
- (b) humidity
- (c) humiddity
- (d) humiditey

17.
- (a) **urgency**
- (b) ergensy
- (c) urgensy
- (d) urgency

18.
- (a) emergency
- (b) **emmergency**
- (c) emergency
- (d) emerrgency

19.
- (a) pursonality
- (b) personelity
- (c) **personality**
- (d) personality

20.
- (a) **accuracy**
- (b) accuarcy
- (c) accuracy
- (d) accurecy

72

PRACTICE B
Words from French

Word Associations Write the Basic Word associated with each situation below.

Basic Words
1. chef
2. gourmet
3. buffet
4. saute
5. fillet
6. parfait
7. omelet
8. foyer
9. brochure
10. suite
11. etiquette
12. mustache
13. memoir
14. souvenir
15. camouflage
16. chauffeur
17. opaque
18. intrigue
19. rendezvous
20. elite

1. driving a limousine
2. introducing strangers
3. meeting a friend
4. waiting at a hotel entrance
5. remembering a vacation
6. scheming in secrecy
7. finding travel information
8. blocking out light
9. decorating a series of rooms
10. writing an autobiography
11. hiding in the jungle
12. shaving above the lip

1. ___chauffeur___
2. ___etiquette___
3. ___rendezvous___
4. ___foyer___
5. ___souvenir___
6. ___intrigue___
7. ___brochure___
8. ___opaque___
9. ___suite___
10. ___memoir___
11. ___camouflage___
12. ___mustache___

Proofreading 13–20. Find and cross out eight misspelled Basic Words in this newspaper advertisement. Then write each word correctly.

GRETA'S GRACIOUS GROCERY

Eggs à la Snob—Eggs for the ~~gourmay eleet~~! The most exquisite eggs you'll find this side of Paris. Poach them, scramble them, or use them to make the ultimate ~~omelett~~. At $50 per dozen, these are a special bargain.

White Fish Superior—Buy it whole or let us ~~fillett~~ it for you. Bake it, ~~sautee~~ it, cover it with ketchup—nothing can camouflage the overpowering taste of this unforgettable fish. $67.99 per pound.

Too weary to shop? Send your chauffeur round to inspect our new ~~buffay~~. Our dessert section is superb, with everything from sophisticated Creme Cremoo to an ordinary ~~parfate~~ prepared for you by a French ~~cheff~~.

13. ___gourmet___
14. ___elite___
15. ___omelet___
16. ___fillet___
17. ___saute___
18. ___buffet___
19. ___parfait___
20. ___chef___

Skill: Students will practice spelling words borrowed from French.

Home Use: Help your child practice the spelling words by having him or her complete the activities on this page. Check the completed page, and have your child practice saying and spelling any misspelled words.

74

PRACTICE A
Words from French

> **Summing Up**
> Many French words have become part of the English language.

Parlez-vous Franglais? Your French cousin wants to practice speaking English and refuses to use any French words. Underline the word or words in each of your cousin's sentences that can be replaced by a Basic Word. Then write the Basic Word.

Basic Words
1. chef
2. gourmet
3. buffet
4. saute
5. fillet
6. parfait
7. omelet
8. foyer
9. brochure
10. suite

1. The small pamphlet mentioned a special restaurant.
2. I left my series of connected rooms in the hotel to find it.
3. I called a taxi from the hotel lobby.
4. When I arrived, the manager told me that a world-famous chief cook of a large kitchen staff was in the kitchen.
5. She knew that I was a person who liked fine food.
6. The restaurant had a counter from which food was served.
7. First, I had a cheese dish of beaten eggs.
8. From where I was sitting I could watch the cooks fry lightly my main dish.
9. I had a delicious boneless piece of salmon.
10. Last, I had a superb dessert of layers of ice cream with various toppings, served in a tall glass.

1. ___brochure___   6. ___buffet___
2. ___suite___   7. ___omelet___
3. ___foyer___   8. ___saute___
4. ___chef___   9. ___fillet___
5. ___gourmet___   10. ___parfait___

Tongue Twisters Write the Basic Word that completes each tongue twister. The Basic Word should begin with the same sound(s) as most of the other words in the sentence. See how quickly you can say each sentence.

11. Cheryl Chevron showed the shellfish to the shocked _____.
12. Gorgeous Gordon Gormless is a great _____ at a party.
13. Parsival Parsnip ate part of a _____ the snails.
14. Snarling Sonya Snapper sought to _____ the snails.
15. Freddy Farley found the fish _____ fantastic.
16. Brooding Billy brought a British _____ in his briefcase.
17. Bob Baley's band blew brass bugles at the brunch _____.
18. Superstar Susie Swazy sweltered in her swanky Swedish _____.

11. ___chef___
12. ___gourmet___
13. ___parfait___
14. ___saute___
15. ___fillet___
16. ___brochure___
17. ___buffet___
18. ___suite___

Skill: Students will practice spelling words borrowed from French.

Home Use: Help your child practice the spelling words by having him or her complete the activities on this page. Check the completed page, and have your child practice saying and spelling any misspelled words.

73

Name _____

Unit 16 Test: Words from French

Find the correctly spelled word to complete each phrase. Fill in the letter beside the correct spelling.

Sample:

the _____ tennis player
ⓐ amachure   ⓒ ammachure
● amatuer   ⓓ ammateur

Items 1–10 test Basic Words 1–10. Items 11–20 test Basic Words 11–20.

1. a _____ cook
ⓐ gormet   ⓒ gormay
ⓑ gourmet   ⓓ gourmay

2. the head _____
ⓐ shef   ⓒ cheff
ⓑ sheff   ⓓ chef

3. a strawberry _____
ⓐ parfay   ⓒ parfiait
ⓑ parfait   ⓓ parfay

4. to _____ the onions
ⓐ saute   ⓒ sautay
ⓑ suate   ⓓ suatay

5. a slate floor in the _____
ⓐ foier   ⓒ foyer
ⓑ foyere   ⓓ foiyer

6. a mushroom _____
ⓐ ommelet   ⓒ omelett
ⓑ omelet   ⓓ omalet

7. a _____ of rooms
ⓐ swete   ⓒ swete
ⓑ suite   ⓓ suite

8. a _____ meal
ⓐ buffay   ⓒ buffet
ⓑ bufet   ⓓ buffiett

9. a _____ of fish
ⓐ filett   ⓒ filay
ⓑ fillay   ⓓ fillet

10. a colorful _____
ⓐ brochure   ⓒ brosure
ⓑ broshure   ⓓ brochur

11. the _____ in the car
ⓐ chauffer   ⓒ chauffeur
ⓑ chauffuer   ⓓ choffeur

12. a _____ with destiny
ⓐ rondayvous   ⓒ rendezvoo
ⓑ rondezvous   ⓓ rendezvous

13. an _____ glass
ⓐ opake   ⓒ oppaque
ⓑ opaque   ⓓ opakke

14. a book on proper _____
ⓐ etiquette   ⓒ ettiquette
ⓑ etikette   ⓓ etiquete

15. the man's _____
ⓐ mustache   ⓒ mustach
ⓑ mustashe   ⓓ musstache

16. mystery and _____
ⓐ intreg   ⓒ intrigue
ⓑ intregue   ⓓ intregue

17. having a _____
ⓐ memmwoir   ⓒ memmwoir
ⓑ memoir   ⓓ memmwoir

18. a vacation _____
ⓐ souvenir   ⓒ souvenir
ⓑ soovenir   ⓓ souvennir

19. the _____ of society
ⓐ elite   ⓒ elite
ⓑ ellite   ⓓ ellitte

20. color used as a _____
ⓐ camouflage   ⓒ cammaflage
ⓑ camaflage   ⓓ cammouflage

Name _____

PRACTICE C
Words from French

Dining Out 1–9. Five chefs are preparing to open a restaurant. Write nine Challenge and Vocabulary Words to complete the following clues. Then use the clues to help you figure out what each chef plans. Put a check mark in each correct box and an X in each incorrect box.

Challenge Words
1. hors d'oeuvre
2. connoisseur
3. liaison
4. genre
5. detente
Theme Vocabulary
6. franchise
7. cuisine
8. menu
9. customer
10. entree
11. reservation
12. smorgasbord
13. culinary

- One chef, who is in charge of the main courses, is planning a delicious fish __(1)__.
- Suzanne is a __(2)__ of foreign food. Her expertise will be put to good use.
- A variety of dishes will be offered for the Sunday __(3)__.
- One chef has designed the __(4)__, which lists the food that the restaurant will serve. She is very satisfied with her design.
- Although he has not had much experience in making appetizers, one chef is preparing an __(5)__ of snails in puff pastry.
- One chef will plan all the Spanish and French __(6)__.
- A male chef, whose __(7)__ skill is world-famous, is planning a buffet.
- Chef Edward is making a special trip to the local market to buy trout for Chef Henri's dish. When he returns from the market, he will begin rolling out the dough for his own dish.
- Chef Henri will give a 10 percent discount to each __(8)__ who makes a __(9)__ for dinner at the new restaurant before Tuesday.

	hors d'oeuvre	Spanish and French cuisine	menu	entree	smorgasbord
Henri	X	X	X	✓	X
Rosa	X	X	✓	X	X
Suzanne	X	✓	X	X	X
Edward	✓	X	X	X	X
Lionel	X	X	X	X	✓

1. **entree**
2. **connoisseur**
3. **smorgasbord**
4. **menu**
5. **hors d'oeuvre**
6. **cuisine**
7. **culinary**
8. **customer**
9. **reservation**

Tongue Twisters 10–14. A tongue twister is a sentence in which all or almost all the words begin with the same letter. On the back of this paper, write five tongue twisters. Use each of these Challenge and Vocabulary Words: *connoisseur, liaison, detente, franchise, genre.* **Tongue twisters will vary.**

Tongue twisters will vary.

Skill: Students will practice spelling words borrowed from French and words related to the theme of restaurant management.

Home Use: Help your child practice the spelling words by having him or her complete the activities on this page. Check the completed page, and have your child practice saying and spelling any misspelled words.

PRACTICE B
Words Often Misspelled I

Basic Words
1. playwright
2. tragedy
3. metaphor
4. melancholy
5. propaganda
6. subtle
7. pageant
8. unanimous
9. extraordinary
10. enthusiastic
11. outrageous
12. pneumonia
13. khaki
14. adjourn
15. minuscule
16. siege
17. endeavor
18. prominent
19. wretched
20. flourish

Crossword Puzzle Complete the puzzle by writing the Basic Word that fits each clue.

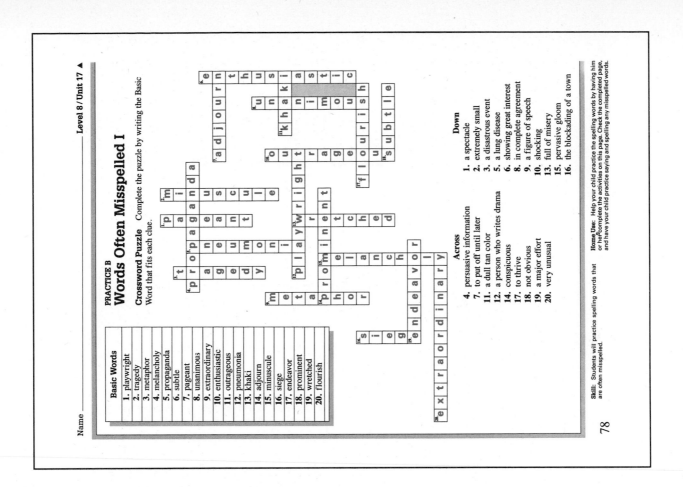

Across
4. persuasive information
7. to put off until later
11. a dull tan color
12. a person who writes drama
14. conspicuous
17. to thrive
18. not obvious
19. a major effort
20. very unusual

Down
1. a spectacle
2. extremely small
3. a disastrous event
5. a lung disease
6. showing great interest
8. in complete agreement
9. a figure of speech
10. shocking
13. full of misery
15. pervasive gloom
16. the blockading of a town

Skill: Students will practice spelling words that are often misspelled.
Home Use: Help your child practice the spelling words by having him or her complete the activities on this page. Check the completed page, and have your child practice saying and spelling any misspelled words.

78

PRACTICE A
Words Often Misspelled I

Basic Words
1. playwright
2. tragedy
3. metaphor
4. melancholy
5. propaganda
6. subtle
7. pageant
8. unanimous
9. extraordinary
10. enthusiastic

Summing Up
Practicing words and learning more about them will help you spell them correctly.

Similar Titles Write the Basic Word that can replace each underlined word or phrase in this bookstore sales promotion letter. Begin each word with a capital letter.

Dear Reader:

Here's an offer you can't refuse! Receive 87% off the price of your next purchase if you buy now. Choose the titles you want to order. Mail the enclosed form in the prepaid envelope.

1. Exceptional *Treasures of the Desert*
2. Watching for *Persuasive Information*
3. Balancing *Joy and Gloom*
4. The Beginning *Dramatist*
5. Comedy and *Misfortune*
6. Dropping *Elusive Hints*
7. How to Organize a Successful *Spectacle*
8. The *Eager* Employee
9. *A Figure of Speech* for Success
10. How to Have *Agreed by All* Appeal

Thank you,
Book Order Sales Department

1. Extraordinary
2. Propaganda
3. Melancholy
4. Playwright
5. Tragedy
6. Subtle
7. Pageant
8. Enthusiastic
9. Metaphor
10. Unanimous

Order of answers may vary.

Which Is It? 11–15. A literary critic is letting you decide which Basic Words deserve thumbs up and which deserve thumbs down. Look at each word given below. If it is a synonym for a Basic Word, write the Basic Word in the thumbs up hand. If it is an antonym, write the Basic Word in the thumbs down hand. Then draw a line to connect each given word with the correct Basic Word in each hand.

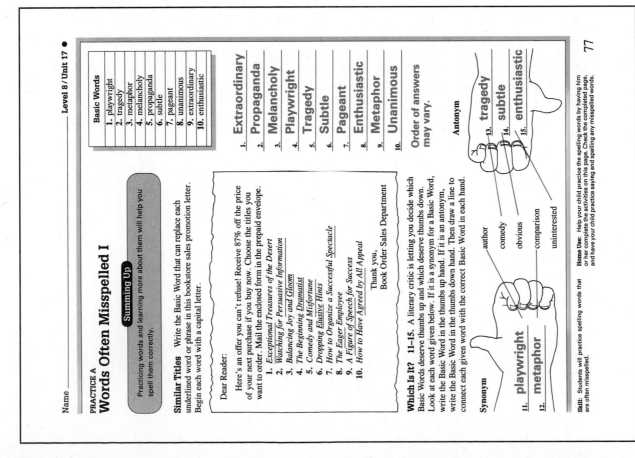

Synonym

author
comedy
obvious
comparison
uninterested

Antonym

11. playwright
12. metaphor
13. tragedy
14. subtle
15. enthusiastic

Skill: Students will practice spelling words that are often misspelled.
Home Use: Help your child practice the spelling words by having him or her complete the activities on this page. Check the completed page, and have your child practice saying and spelling any misspelled words.

77

Practice Master and Test Answers

223

PRACTICE C
Words Often Misspelled I

A Puzzling Predicament   In the dark box in the puzzle, write the Vocabulary Word that is an antonym for *instructor*. Then write ten other Challenge and Vocabulary Words to complete the puzzle. Finally, write a short definition for each word used in the puzzle.

Challenge Words
1. soliloquy
2. rhetoric
3. hypocrite
4. queue
5. susceptible
Theme Vocabulary
6. dramatist
7. Elizabethan
8. sonnet
9. prose
10. blank verse
11. theatrical
12. apprentice
13. repertory

```
        1.
2.  d r a m a t i s t
3.  h y p o c r i t e
    4.  p r o s e
       5.  r e p e r t o r y
    6.  t h e a t r i c a l
  7.  b l a n k   v e r s e
8.  E l i z a b e t h a n
     9.  s o l i l o q u y
    10.  s u s c e p t i b l e
      11.  r h e t o r i c
```

Definitions will vary.

1. _____
2. _____
3. _____
4. _____
5. _____
6. _____
7. _____
8. _____
9. _____
10. _____
11. _____

Hink Pink Challenge   Write a Vocabulary or Challenge Word and another rhyming word to answer each riddle.
Example: What is concise poetry? *terse verse*
12. What is a hat with poetry written on it?
13. What is a line to see a collection of animals?
14. What are lines of ordinary writing?
15. What is a detailed list of a collection of information?

12. **sonnet bonnet**
13. **zoo queue**
14. **prose rows**
15. **repertory inventory**

Skill: Students will practice words that are often misspelled and words related to the theme of Shakespeare.

Home Use: Help your child practice the spelling words by having him or her complete the activities on this page. Check the completed page, and have your child practice saying and spelling any misspelled words.

Unit **17** Test: Words Often Misspelled I

Each item below gives four possible spellings of a word. Fill in the letter beside the correct spelling.

Sample:
- ⓐ campane
- ● campaign
- ⓒ campain
- ⓓ cammpaign

Items 1–10 test Basic Words 1–10. Items 11–20 test Basic Words 11–20.

1. ● propaganda ⓑ propiganda ⓒ proppaganda ⓓ propaggonda
2. ⓐ mellancholy ● melancholy ⓒ melincholy ⓓ melanncholy
3. ⓐ mettaphor ⓑ metafore ⓒ metafor ● metaphor
4. ⓐ tragidy ● tragedy ⓒ tragedy ⓓ traggidy
5. ⓐ playright ⓑ playrite ● playwright ⓓ playwrite
6. ⓐ suptle ● subtle ⓒ sutle ⓓ suddle
7. ⓐ unanimous ● unaninmous ⓒ unanimmous ⓓ unanimos
8. ⓐ enthussiastic ⓑ enthusiastic ⓒ enthoosiastic ● enthusiastic
9. ⓐ pagent ● pagent ⓒ pagient ⓓ pageant
10. ⓐ extrordinary ● extraordinary ⓒ extrordinary ⓓ extrordnary
11. ⓐ flourish ● flurrish ⓒ floresh ⓓ florrish
12. ⓐ wretched ⓑ wreched ⓒ retchid ⓓ reched
13. ⓐ promenant ⓑ promenant ● prominent ⓓ prominant
14. ● endevor ⓑ endeavor ⓒ endeaver ⓓ endaevor
15. ⓐ newmonia ⓑ pneumonia ⓒ nummonia ● pnemonia
16. ⓐ ajourn ⓑ ajume ● adjourn ⓓ adjern
17. ⓐ miniscule ⓑ minniscule ● minuscule ⓓ minnuscule
18. ⓐ outragous ⓑ outrageous ⓒ outrrageous ⓓ outrageus
19. ⓐ siege ⓑ seege ⓒ seige ⓓ seage
20. ⓐ kaki ⓑ kakhi ⓒ khaky ● khaki

Name _____

Unit **18** Review: Test A

Read the four phrases in each item. Find the underlined word that is spelled incorrectly. Fill in the letter for the phrase with the misspelled word in the answer column.

ANSWERS

ⓐ ● ⓒ ⓓ

Sample:
a. the opposite direction   c. a parfait glass
b. a holiday pagent   d. a clear definition

This test reviews Basic Words 1–10 in Units 13–17.

1. a. an enthusiastic reaction   c. a green vegetable
   b. a guormet meal   d. a familiarity with

2. a. strategic planning   c. a job transfer
   b. advertising agency   d. met the playright

3. a. a unanimous vote   c. a delicious omelet
   b. sparse vegetation   d. a reference book

4. a. an alternate form   c. the perpose of
   b. her nationality   d. comedy or tragedy

5. a. a subtle hint   c. a stabel economy
   b. her generosity in giving   d. to saute onions

6. a. a traceable clue   c. a defense strategy
   b. her curiousity about him   d. a melancholy feeling

7. a. a vacation broshure   c. a majority of voters
   b. a marriage proposal   d. a suite of rooms

8. a. to define the word   c. a binding contract
   b. needing privecy   d. the door to the foyer

9. a. an extraordinary meal   c. the head chef
   b. a mixed metaphor   d. an abstract concept

10. a. a sociaty function   c. a garbage disposal
    b. a feeling of stability   d. a fillet of fish

1. ⓐ ● ⓒ ⓓ
2. ⓐ ⓑ ⓒ ●
3. ● ⓑ ⓒ ⓓ
4. ⓐ ⓑ ● ⓓ
5. ⓐ ⓑ ● ⓓ
6. ⓐ ● ⓒ ⓓ
7. ● ⓑ ⓒ ⓓ
8. ⓐ ● ⓒ ⓓ
9. ⓐ ⓑ ● ⓓ
10. ● ⓑ ⓒ ⓓ

85

Name _____

Unit **18** Review: Test B

Read the four phrases in each item. Find the underlined word that is spelled incorrectly. Fill in the letter for the phrase with the misspelled word in the answer column.

ANSWERS

ⓐ ● ⓒ ⓓ

Sample:
a. a home remedy   c. a warm personality
b. suspense and intrigue   d. a prominent figure

This test reviews Basic Words 11–20 in Units 13–17.

1. a. a vacation sovenir   c. to move to adjourn
   b. hired a chauffeur   d. to be immune to

2. a. exposure to radiation   c. an elite class
   b. a finite set   d. attention to acuracy

3. a. an outrageous idea   c. a preference for
   b. those in the minorety   d. indicative of failure

4. a. to transpose the numbers   c. wore khaki trousers
   b. a remedial course of study   d. based on democracy

5. a. under siege   c. heat and humidity
   b. to use a prepasition   d. a wretched feeling

6. a. to indicate a change   c. to confer with them
   b. to reach maturity   d. sensory deprivation

7. a. to flourish there   c. an opake glass
   b. response to an emergency   d. straight posture

8. a. to imunize the group   c. fertile soil
   b. sense of urgency   d. proper etiquette

9. a. a case of pneumonia   c. the man's mustache
   b. to make an inference   d. a miniscule item

10. a. used to camouflage   c. an infinite number
    b. to rendevous with him   d. in anxiety and dread

1. ● ⓑ ⓒ ⓓ
2. ⓐ ⓑ ⓒ ●
3. ● ⓑ ⓒ ⓓ
4. ⓐ ⓑ ⓒ ⓓ
5. ⓐ ● ⓒ ⓓ
6. ⓐ ⓑ ⓒ ⓓ
7. ⓐ ⓑ ● ⓓ
8. ● ⓑ ⓒ ⓓ
9. ⓐ ⓑ ● ⓓ
10. ⓐ ● ⓒ ⓓ

86

Practice Master and Test Answers

225

Midyear Test

Find the word that is spelled incorrectly. Fill in the letter beside the misspelled word.

Sample:
- (a) outrageus ●
- (b) emergency
- (c) transpose
- (d) astrology

Items 1–13 test Basic Words 1–10 in Cycles 1–3. Items 14–25 test Basic Words 11–20 in Cycles 1–3.

1.
- (a) interfarence
- (b) liable
- (c) emission
- (d) oxygen

2.
- (a) mercury
- (b) allude
- (c) definition
- (d) subttle

3.
- (a) chord
- (b) terminalogy
- (c) transform
- (d) bronco

4.
- (a) proposel
- (b) nationality
- (c) brochure
- (d) translate

5.
- (a) psychology
- (b) symptom
- (c) Farhenheit
- (d) aisle

6.
- (a) superletive
- (b) stampede
- (c) tragedy
- (d) emigrate

7.
- (a) communication
- (b) submit
- (c) strategic
- (d) traceble

8.
- (a) generocity
- (b) buffet
- (c) coyote
- (d) interstate

9.
- (a) enthusiastic
- (b) narciscus
- (c) immerse
- (d) reference

10.
- (a) intercession
- (b) choral
- (c) adverse
- (d) parfay

11.
- (a) society
- (b) stability
- (c) biology
- (d) submurge

12.
- (a) protein
- (b) oddysey
- (c) vegetable
- (d) opposite

13.
- (a) commit
- (b) assent
- (c) homoginized
- (d) submarine

14.
- (a) canvas
- (b) superintendant
- (c) immune
- (d) maturity

15.
- (a) khaki
- (b) mythology
- (c) omission
- (d) symetrical

(continued)

Unit 18 Review: Test C

Find the correctly spelled word to complete each phrase. Fill in the letter beside the correct spelling.

Sample:
known by her ___
- (a) eccentricity ●
- (b) eccentrisity
- (c) ecsentricity
- (d) eccentricity

This test reviews the Challenge Words in Units 13–17.

1. to ___ the game
- (a) initiate
- (b) inisheate
- (c) initiate
- (d) inisheate

2. to ___ two photographs
- (a) juckstapose
- (b) juxtapose
- (c) jukstapose
- (d) juxtepose

3. that country's ___
- (a) prosperity
- (b) prosparity
- (c) prosperity
- (d) prossparity

4. a ___ of stews
- (a) connoisseur
- (b) connoiseur
- (c) conoisseur
- (d) connoissuer

5. a ___ out to the street
- (a) queeu
- (b) queue
- (c) queeu
- (d) quewe

6. to be ___ to failure
- (a) susceptible
- (b) susceptible
- (c) susceptible
- (d) suseptible

7. to issue a ___
- (a) manndait
- (b) mandate
- (c) mandait
- (d) mandate

8. a ___ sketch
- (a) commposite
- (b) composit
- (c) composite
- (d) compositt

9. to behave like a ___
- (a) hipocrite
- (b) hypocrit
- (c) hypocrite
- (d) hypocrite

10. the book's ___
- (a) jenre
- (b) genre
- (c) genra
- (d) genre

11. the ___ of the soup
- (a) consistancy
- (b) consistency
- (c) concistency
- (d) connsistency

12. to ___ the picture
- (a) superimmpose
- (b) super-impose
- (c) superempose
- (d) superimpose

13. a beautiful ___
- (a) soliloquy
- (b) saliloquy
- (c) soliloquy
- (d) soliloquy

14. to act as a ___
- (a) liaison
- (b) liason
- (c) liaison
- (d) lieison

15. quest for ___
- (a) anoinmity
- (b) anonymmity
- (c) anoinmity
- (d) anonymity

16. a ___ restriction
- (a) mandatory
- (b) mandutory
- (c) manndatory
- (d) mandetory

17. to use a ___
- (a) protracter
- (b) protracktor
- (c) protractor
- (d) protractor

18. ate an ___
- (a) hors d'oeurve
- (b) hors d'oeuvre
- (c) hor d'oeuvre
- (d) hors d'ouevre

19. to take the ___
- (a) inisheative
- (b) initiative
- (c) iniative
- (d) inishiative

20. showed real ___
- (a) spontaneity
- (b) spontanaity
- (c) spontanity
- (d) sponteneity

PRACTICE A
Vowel Changes II

Basic Words
1. restoration
2. restore
3. original
4. origin
5. illustrate
6. illustrative
7. sequence
8. sequential
9. punctual
10. punctuality

Summing Up

To remember the spelling of a word with the schwa sound, think of a related word in which the vowel sound is more obvious.

Word Pairs Complete each sentence by writing a pair of related Basic Words. Then underline the vowels that change from /ə/ to a short vowel sound in each pair. (More than one vowel should be underlined in one pair of words.)

1–2. Betsy is always ____ about turning in her schoolwork because she knows that her teacher values ____.

3–4. The author has used many ____ examples in the book, and the artist will ____ each one.

5–6. Once the ____ of the first painting is finished, the expert will begin to ____ the second painting.

7–8. José wrote a very ____ story about the ____ of the world.

9–10. Because the episodes in the book are not ____, it is very difficult to understand the ____ of events.

1. __punctual__
2. __punctuality__
3. __illustrative__
4. __illustrate__
5. __restoration__

6. __restore__
7. __original__
8. __origin__
9. __sequential__
10. __sequence__

Wrong Words The wrong Basic Word has been used in each of the following sentences. Cross out the word that does not belong, and write the correct Basic Word.

11. That car is being sold by its sequential owner.
12. Edwin will illustrate the old house to its former condition.
13. We expect Jane at exactly five o'clock because she is known for her originality.
14. The airline's short film of emergency procedures was helpful and punctual, clearly showing us exactly what to do.
15. After Marina finishes her story, she will restore it in watercolors.
16. Dr. Riddle was asked to determine the sequence of the rock.
17. Do you remember the punctuality of events in that book?
18. The museum has sent several paintings out for origin.
19. Charlie bought a new watch to make sure he is original.
20. I will do those tasks in illustrative order.

11. __original__
12. __restore__
13. __punctuality__
14. __illustrative__
15. __illustrate__
16. __origin__
17. __sequence__
18. __restoration__
19. __punctual__
20. __sequential__

Skill: Students will practice spelling pairs of related words with vowel changes.

Home Use: Help your child practice the spelling words by having him or her complete the activities on this page. Check the completed page, and have your child practice saying and spelling any misspelled words.

91

Midyear Test (continued)

16. (a) subdivide (b) Celsius (c) collapse (d) cafateria
17. (a) regiment (b) exposure (c) etiquette (d) elite
18. (a) flourish (b) accummulate (c) transmit (d) jaguar
19. (a) prospective (b) imunize (c) distract (d) mustache
20. (a) miniscule (b) urgency (c) fertile (d) infinite

21. (a) recession (b) counterclockwise (c) allfalfa (d) photogenic
22. (a) transaction (b) tantilize (c) stationary (d) meterology
23. (a) accurracy (b) rationale (c) intervention (d) dialogue
24. (a) appliance (b) phase (c) galvinized (d) subtitle
25. (a) illuminate (b) souvenir (c) geneology (d) sierra

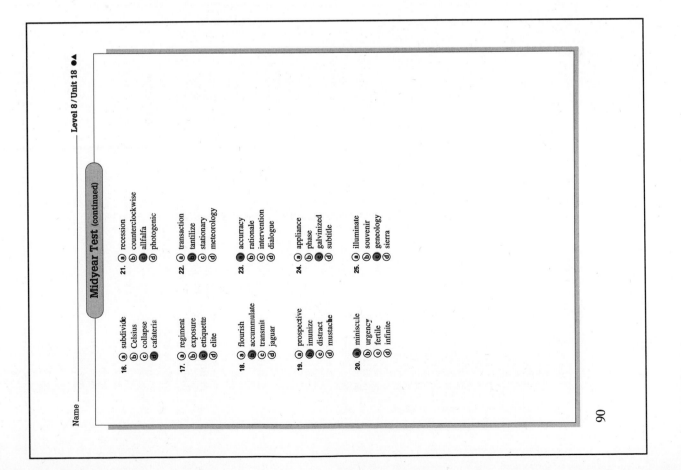

90

Practice Master and Test Answers

227

Basic Words
1. restoration
2. restore
3. original
4. origin
5. illustrate
6. illustrative
7. sequence
8. sequential
9. punctual
10. punctuality
11. symbolism
12. symbolic
13. tranquil
14. tranquility
15. syllable
16. syllabication
17. neutral
18. neutrality
19. trivial
20. triviality

PRACTICE B
Vowel Changes II

Puzzle Play Write the Basic Word that fits each clue.

1. a part of a word   s y l (l) a b l e
2. first   o r i g i n a l
3. 1, 2, 3, 4 . . .   s e q u (e) n c e
4. insignificance   (t) r i v i a l i t y
5. representative   s y m b o l i c
6. peaceful   (t) r a n q u i l
7. impartiality   n (e) u t r a l i t y
8. promptness   p u n c t u a l i t y
9. the source of something   o (r) i g i n
10. the use of symbols   s y m b (o) l i s m

Now write the letters in the circles in order to answer this riddle:
What occurs once in every minute, twice in every moment, but not once in a thousand years?

Answer: the   l e t t e r   m

Word Squeeze Each group of three words contains a hidden Basic Word. To find the word, cross out one letter in each of the three words. Then squeeze the remaining letters together to write the Basic Word.

Example: try and quilt   *tranquil*

11. spun cat dual
12. trafn quail city
13. are story nation
14. sequel not dial
15. syllabie cast iron
16. kill must grate
17. trim vie all
18. new hut raft
19. red stop are
20. ail luster native

11. _punctual_
12. _tranquility_
13. _restoration_
14. _sequential_
15. _syllabication_
16. _illustrate_
17. _trivial_
18. _neutral_
19. _restore_
20. _illustrative_

EXTRA! Write your own Word Squeeze activity for at least five Basic Words.

Home Use: Help your child practice the spelling words by having him or her complete the activities on this page. Check the completed page, and have your child practice saying and spelling any misspelled words.

Skill: Students will practice spelling pairs of related words with vowel changes.

PRACTICE C
Vowel Changes II

In Other Words Find and underline a synonym or an antonym of a Challenge or Vocabulary Word in each sentence. Write the answer as a synonym or an antonym of the underlined word. Then write S or A to identify each Challenge or Vocabulary Word.

1. Leo put a lot of significance on the main argument in his speech.
2. Gloria showed extravagance in spending her allowance.
3. Steve took an interesting finance course this semester.
4. "Stop environmental pollution!" the senator proclaimed in an impassioned voice.
5. Acid rain has caused those statues to decay over the years.
6. The careless worker's habits were widely known.
7. Melanie demonstrated her incompetence in cooking.
8. The painter stood on a platform to reach the ceiling.

1. emphasis   S   5. deteriorate   S
2. economy   A   6. meticulous   A
3. economics   S   7. expertise   A
4. emphatic   S   8. scaffold   S

Art Advice Imagine that you are a student of the great artist Michelangelo. What advice might he give you about painting frescoes? In the speech balloons, write several suggestions that Michelangelo might have made. Use the Vocabulary Words *fresco, varnish, plaster, pigment,* and *scaffold.* **Sentences will vary.**

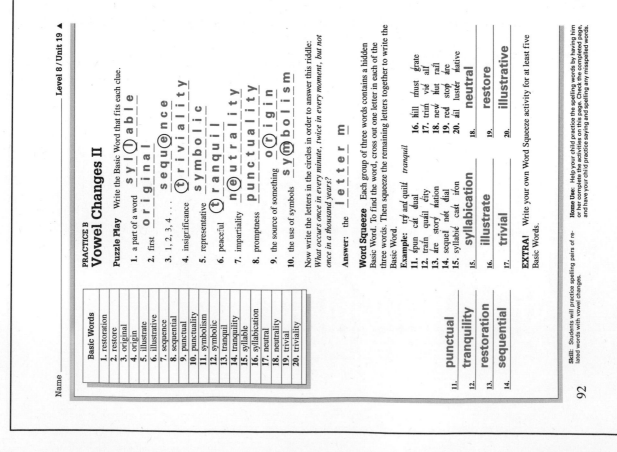

Challenge Words
1. emphasis
2. emphatic
3. economy
4. economics

Theme Vocabulary
5. fresco
6. varnish
7. deteriorate
8. expertise
9. plaster
10. pigment
11. scaffold
12. meticulous

Skill: Students will practice spelling pairs of related words with vowel changes and words related to the theme of painting restoration.

Home Use: Help your child practice the spelling words by having him or her complete the activities on this page. Check the completed page, and have your child practice saying and spelling any misspelled words.

PRACTICE A
Latin Roots II

Basic Words
1. conspiracy
2. diversion
3. transpire
4. convert
5. expire
6. advertisement
7. universal
8. reverse
9. perspiration
10. extrovert

Summing Up

Many English words contain the Latin roots *ver* and *spir*.

Root Tick-Tack-Toe Add the correct Latin root to form a Basic Word in the tick-tack-toe grid. Draw a line through the boxes that make tick-tack-toe, and write those Basic Words on lines 1–3.
Order of answers 1–3 may vary.

re __ver__ se   con __spir__ acy   ad __ver__ tisement

tran __spir__ e   di __ver__ sion   uni __ver__ sal

con __ver__ t   extro __ver__ t   per __spir__ ation

1. __convert__   2. __diversion__   3. __advertisement__

Now write each of the ten Basic Words under the correct word root below. **Order of answers may vary.**

ver = to turn   **spir** = to breathe

4. __reverse__   10. __conspiracy__

5. __advertisement__   11. __transpire__

6. __diversion__   12. __perspiration__

7. __universal__   13. __expire__

8. __convert__

9. __extrovert__

Silly Book Titles Write the Basic Word that completes each silly title. Remember to capitalize each word.

14. An ____ Tells *How to Make Friends* by I. M. Outgoing

15. A ____ *Revealed* by Kip No Secrets

16. A *Distracting* ____ by N. Tertainment

17. The ____ *Need for Sleep: A Worldwide Study* by I. M. Tired

18. How to ____ *Your Roof into a Sun Deck* by Sonny Bathe

14. __Extrovert__
15. __Conspiracy__
16. __Diversion__
17. __Universal__
18. __Convert__

Skill: Students will practice spelling words with the Latin roots *ver* and *spir*.

Home Use: Help your child practice the spelling words by having him or her complete the activities on this page. Check the completed page, and have your child practice saying and spelling any misspelled words.

Unit 19 Test: Vowel Changes II

Find the correctly spelled word to complete each phrase. Fill in the letter beside the correct spelling.

Sample:
to ____ at sports
● excel   © excell
ⓑ exsell   ⓓ exell

Items 1–10 test Basic Words 1–10. Items 11–20 test Basic Words 11–20.

1. to put in ____ order
ⓐ sequential   © sequential
● sequential   ⓓ sequential

2. to ____ with an example
ⓐ ilustrate   ● illustrate
ⓑ illustrate   ⓓ illistrate

3. known for his ____
ⓐ punctuality   © punnctuality
ⓑ puncuality   ● punctuality

4. the ____ of the building
● restoration   © restoration
ⓑ restoration   ⓓ resteration

5. the ____ of the universe
ⓐ origin   © origen
● origin   ⓓ orrigen

6. to be ____
ⓐ punctual   © puncual
ⓑ punctual   ● punctual

7. an ____ example
ⓐ illustrative   © ilastrative
ⓑ illustrative   ● illastrative

8. to ____ to the original condition
ⓐ restore   © restorr
● restore   ⓓ reastore

9. the ____ of events
ⓐ sequence   © sequence
● sequence   ⓓ seaquence

10. an ____ painting
ⓐ originel   © original
● original   ⓓ originil

11. a position of ____
ⓐ nuetrality   © neutrallity
ⓑ nutrality   ● neutrality

12. a feeling of ____
ⓐ tranquility   © tranquility
● tranquility   ⓓ tranquility

13. to take a ____ position
ⓐ newtrel   © nutral
ⓑ nutrel   ● neutral

14. found ____ in the poem
ⓐ symbolism   ● symbolism
ⓑ simbolism   ⓓ symbolism

15. the ____ of the word
ⓐ sylabication   ● syllabication
ⓑ sillabication   ⓓ sylabbication

16. a ____ piece of information
● trivial   © trivvial
ⓑ triveal   ⓓ triviall

17. a ____ gesture
ⓐ symbolic   © symbollic
ⓑ symbolic   ● simbolic

18. the ____ of the event
ⓐ triviality   © triveality
● triviality   ⓓ trivialllity

19. a ____ landscape
ⓐ tranquil   ● tranquill
ⓑ tranquel   ⓓ tranquil

20. stress on the third ____
ⓐ sylable   © syllable
ⓑ syllable   ● sillable

PRACTICE B
Latin Roots II

Crossword Puzzle Complete the puzzle by writing the Basic Word that fits each clue.

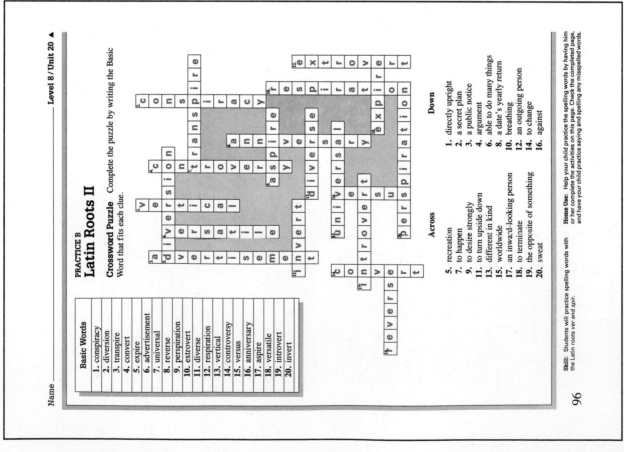

Basic Words
1. conspiracy
2. diversion
3. transpire
4. convert
5. expire
6. advertisement
7. universal
8. reverse
9. perspiration
10. extrovert
11. diverse
12. respiration
13. vertical
14. controversy
15. versus
16. anniversary
17. aspire
18. versatile
19. introvert
20. invert

Across
5. recreation
7. to happen
9. to desire strongly
11. to turn upside down
13. different in kind
15. worldwide
17. an inward-looking person
18. to terminate
19. the opposite of something
20. sweat

Down
1. directly upright
2. a secret plan
3. a public notice
4. argument
6. able to do many things
8. a date's yearly return
10. breathing
12. an outgoing person
14. to change
16. against

Skill: Students will practice spelling words with the Latin roots *ver* and *spir*.

Home Use: Help your child practice the spelling words by having him or her complete the activities on this page. Check the completed page, and have your child practice saying and spelling any misspelled words.

PRACTICE C
Latin Roots II

Synonym Search 1–16. Find eight Challenge and Vocabulary Words hidden in the puzzle. The words may appear horizontally, vertically, or diagonally. Circle each word, and then write it. Then find and circle a synonym for each word you wrote. Write the synonym next to the matching Challenge or Vocabulary Word. **Order of answers may vary.**

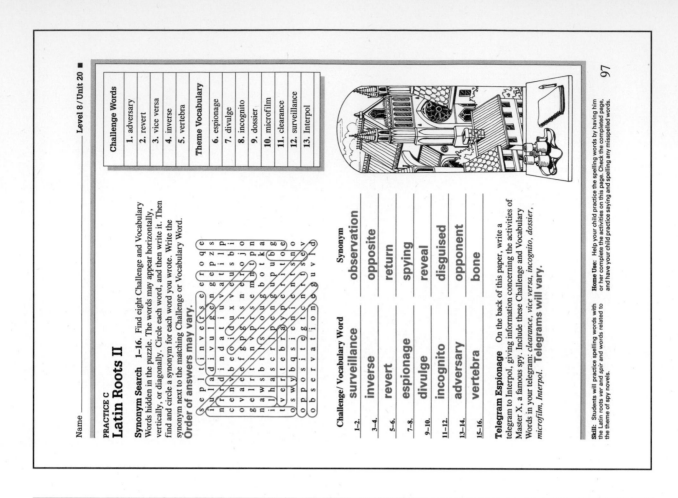

Challenge / Vocabulary Word	Synonym
1–2. surveillance	observation
3–4. inverse	opposite
5–6. revert	return
7–8. espionage	spying
9–10. divulge	reveal
11–12. incognito	disguised
13–14. adversary	opponent
15–16. vertebra	bone

Challenge Words
1. adversary
2. revert
3. vice versa
4. inverse
5. vertebra

Theme Vocabulary
6. espionage
7. divulge
8. incognito
9. dossier
10. microfilm
11. clearance
12. surveillance
13. Interpol

Telegram Espionage On the back of this paper, write a telegram to Interpol, giving information concerning the activities of Master X, a famous spy. Include these Challenge and Vocabulary Words in your telegram: *clearance, vice versa, incognito, dossier, microfilm, Interpol.* **Telegrams will vary.**

Skill: Students will practice spelling words with the Latin roots *ver* and *spir* and words related to the theme of spy novels.

Home Use: Help your child practice the spelling words by having him or her complete the activities on this page. Check the completed page, and have your child practice saying and spelling any misspelled words.

Unit 20 Test: Latin Roots II

Each item below gives four possible spellings of a word. Fill in the letter beside the correct spelling.

Sample:
- ⓐ insperation
- ⓑ insperassion
- ⓒ insperation
- ● inspiration

Items 1–10 test Basic Words 1–10. Items 11–20 test Basic Words 11–20.

1.
- ⓐ transpire
- ⓑ transpier
- ⓒ transspire
- ● transpire

2.
- ⓐ conspiracy
- ● conspiracy
- ⓒ consperecy
- ⓓ consperacy

3.
- ● revirce
- ⓑ reverse
- ⓒ riverse
- ⓓ reverce

4.
- ● exspire
- ⓑ expier
- ⓒ expire
- ⓓ expire

5.
- ⓐ divursion
- ● diversion
- ⓒ deversion
- ⓓ diverrsion

6.
- ⓐ converte
- ⓑ convurt
- ● convert
- ⓓ convirt

7.
- ⓐ addvertisement
- ⓑ advertisment
- ● advertisement
- ⓓ advertisment

8.
- ⓐ pirspiration
- ⓑ pirspration
- ⓒ persperation
- ● perspiration

9.
- ● universal
- ⓑ unerversal
- ⓒ unaversle
- ⓓ unavarsal

10.
- ● extrovert
- ⓑ extrovurt
- ⓒ extrovirt
- ⓓ extravert

11.
- ⓐ inverte
- ⓑ invertt
- ⓒ invert
- ● invert

12.
- ⓐ contraversy
- ⓑ contraversey
- ⓒ controversey
- ● controversy

13.
- ● introvert
- ⓑ introverte
- ⓒ intravert
- ⓓ inntrovert

14.
- ⓐ vurtacal
- ● vertical
- ⓒ verticle
- ⓓ virtical

15.
- ⓐ resperation
- ⓑ resspiration
- ⓒ resparration
- ● respiration

16.
- ⓐ virsatile
- ⓑ versatile
- ● versatile
- ⓓ versitile

17.
- ⓐ anniversery
- ● anniversary
- ⓒ aniversary
- ⓓ aniversery

18.
- ⓐ versus
- ● versus
- ⓒ verses
- ⓓ versus

19.
- ⓐ deverse
- ⓑ diverse
- ⓒ divurse
- ● divirse

20.
- ● aspire
- ⓑ aspier
- ⓒ aspiere
- ⓓ ascpier

PRACTICE A
Noun Suffixes II

Basic Words
1. historian
2. politician
3. comedian
4. pianist
5. librarian
6. novelist
7. pharmacist
8. custodian
9. criticism
10. idealism

Summing Up

The endings *-ian, -ist,* and *-ism* are noun suffixes.

Suffix Puzzle 1–10. Find and circle ten words that can be combined with the suffixes *-ian, -ist,* and *-ism* to form the Basic Words. Then write the Basic Words.
Order of answers may vary.

```
a b n a n o v a r c t u v w
d e p o v r w c c n o b c l
e t h w v i c a i w v n m i
w a p c b e p u m z t c d s
p o i d s a i n s b i o j h
p h a r m a c y a t o m z s
p i n a f i r h s g o e h i
a s o g e w i g h t o d p w
b t t m o n t b e c a v v m
p o t i m y l i r h k a l c
r r t i y t c h k a e n w z
a y d e m l i b m b r v c x
a i d e a l v m o q e p t
q n w b r t m r w o i e q t
p t e i p o l i t i c x b n
```

1. _historian_
2. _politician_
3. _comedian_
4. _pianist_
5. _librarian_
6. _novelist_
7. _pharmacist_
8. _custodian_
9. _criticism_
10. _idealism_

Tongue Twisters Write the Basic Word that best completes each tongue twister. The word should begin with the same sound that begins most of the other words in the sentence. See how quickly you can say each sentence.

11. Carrie coaxed the colorful _____ into coming to the countryside for a crazy comic convention.
12. Patty painted a perfect picture of her pal Peter, the _____ who also plays percussion.
13. Lorna listened to the _____ lecture on literature.
14. Please pay the _____ for the pamphlet on his party's previous campaign pledges.
15. Perhaps Phil's _____ can fly to Philadelphia to find a physician.
16. Henry hired the _____ to help him with his history homework.
17. Cathy's casual _____ of Curt's cat's conduct caused a considerable catastrophe.
18. The cathedral's conscientious _____ carefully cleaned up the choir chambers.

11. _comedian_
12. _pianist_
13. _librarian_
14. _politician_
15. _pharmacist_
16. _historian_
17. _criticism_
18. _custodian_

Skill: Students will practice spelling words with the noun suffixes *-ian, -ist,* and *-ism.*

Home Use: Help your child practice the spelling words by having him or her complete the activities on this page. Check the completed page, and have your child practice saying and spelling any misspelled words.

Practice Master and Test Answers

231

PRACTICE B
Noun Suffixes II

Basic Words
1. historian
2. politician
3. comedian
4. pianist
5. librarian
6. novelist
7. pharmacist
8. custodian
9. criticism
10. idealism
11. guitarist
12. soloist
13. realism
14. civilian
15. conformist
16. perfectionist
17. mannerism
18. pedestrian
19. guardian
20. individualist

Analogies Write the Basic Word that completes each analogy.

1. hospital : doctor :: drugstore : _____
2. present : reporter :: past : _____
3. script : playwright :: manuscript : _____
4. race : runner :: campaign : _____
5. reed : clarinetist :: strings : _____
6. knowledge : teacher :: protection : _____
7. information : professor :: joke : _____
8. money : banker :: books : _____
9. sew : tailor :: clean : _____
10. drive : motorist :: walk : _____

1. **pharmacist**
2. **historian**
3. **novelist**
4. **politician**
5. **guitarist**

6. **guardian**
7. **comedian**
8. **librarian**
9. **custodian**
10. **pedestrian**

Proofreading 11–20. Find and cross out ten misspelled Basic Words in this letter. Then write each word correctly.

Dear Sophie,

I'm really enjoying college! I love my literary ~~critisism~~ class. The professor, Dr. Sterne, is a ~~perfectionist~~. He keeps us on our toes. He has a startling ~~manerism~~, a sharp cough. I jump every time I hear it! Dr. Sterne was once a military man and has carried a sense of discipline into his ~~civilian~~ life.

My roommate Charmaine is a ~~pianist~~ and a ~~soloist~~ in the choir. She is a real ~~individualist~~. It is nice to see someone so unique when it is easier to be a ~~conformist~~. The ~~idealism~~ I'd had about college life is not too far off the mark. It is a charmed existence. Father tells me to enjoy it while it lasts because I'll have to approach life with ~~realism~~ soon enough. I think I'll take his advice. I still have time to decide whether I want to be a pharmacist or a librarian. Write soon!

Your sister,
Alera

11. **criticism**
12. **perfectionist**
13. **mannerism**
14. **civilian**
15. **pianist**
16. **soloist**
17. **individualist**
18. **conformist**
19. **idealism**
20. **realism**

Skill: Students will practice spelling words with the noun suffixes -ian, -ist, and -ism.

Home Use: Help your child practice the spelling words by having him or her complete the activities on this page. Check the completed page, and have your child practice saying and spelling any misspelled words.

PRACTICE C
Noun Suffixes II

Challenge Words
1. linguist
2. equestrian
3. optimism
4. pessimism
5. skepticism

Theme Vocabulary
6. electrician
7. curator
8. photographer
9. stockbroker
10. optometrist
11. caterer
12. chiropractor
13. cartographer

Overachievers Anton, Roberto, Laureen, Mamie, and Willard each have two careers. Read the clues. Then complete the chart. Put a check mark in each correct box and an X in each incorrect box.

- Mamie, whose brother is a linguist, dislikes animals.
- Willard uses lenses in both of his occupations.
- Anton's area of expertise is modern art.
- Roberto, who works on Wall Street, failed French in college.
- The chiropractor asked her stockbroker to invest some of her money. She also asked Mamie to install a chandelier in her dining room.
- The stockbroker has developed a new hors d'oeuvre recipe.
- At lunch yesterday, the equestrian, the cartographer, and the optometrist discussed the stock market.

"My stockbroker predicts that the market will make enormous gains this year," said the equestrian. "I agree with him."
"I'm not sure about that," said the optometrist.
"A worldwide depression is coming," the cartographer said. "My brother works as a translator for foreign businesspeople, who are all predicting the worst. He agrees with them."

	cartographer	caterer	chiropractor	curator	electrician	equestrian	linguist	optometrist	photographer	stockbroker
Anton	X	X	X	✓	X	X	✓	X	X	X
Roberto	X	✓	X	X	X	X	X	X	X	✓
Laureen	X	X	✓	X	X	✓	X	X	X	X
Mamie	✓	X	X	X	✓	X	X	X	X	X
Willard	X	X	X	X	X	X	X	✓	✓	X

Now write the Challenge and Vocabulary Words that name each person's careers. Then write the Challenge Word that best describes his or her attitude toward the stock market.

	Career	Career	Attitude
1–3. Anton	curator	linguist	pessimism
4–6. Roberto	caterer	stockbroker	optimism
7–9. Laureen	chiropractor	equestrian	optimism
10–12. Mamie	cartographer	electrician	pessimism
13–15. Willard	optometrist	photographer	skepticism

Skill: Students will practice spelling words with the noun suffixes -ian, -ist, and -ism and words related to the theme of careers.

Home Use: Help your child practice the spelling words by having him or her complete the activities on this page. Check the completed page, and have your child practice saying and spelling any misspelled words.

PRACTICE A
Words from Other Languages

Summing Up
English has borrowed words from many languages.

Basic Words
1. villa
2. pizza
3. spaghetti
4. gondola
5. accordion
6. balcony
7. opera
8. waltz
9. macaroni
10. tycoon

Crossword Puzzle Complete the puzzle by writing the Basic Word that fits each clue.

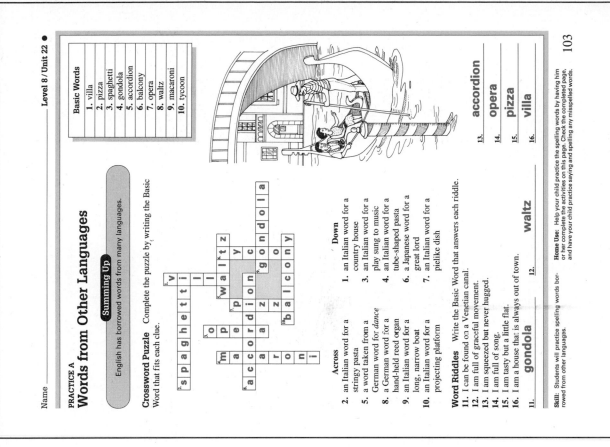

Across
2. an Italian word for a stringy pasta
5. a word taken from a German word for *dance*
8. a German word for a hand-held reed organ
9. an Italian word for a long, narrow boat
10. an Italian word for a projecting platform

Down
1. an Italian word for a country house
3. an Italian word for a play sung to music
4. an Italian word for a tube-shaped pasta
6. a Japanese word for a great lord
7. an Italian word for a pielike dish

Word Riddles Write the Basic Word that answers each riddle.
11. I can be found on a Venetian canal.
12. I am full of graceful movement.
13. I am squeezed but never hugged.
14. I am full of song.
15. I am tasty but a little flat.
16. I am a house that is always out of town.

11. **gondola**   12. **waltz**   13. **accordion**
14. **opera**
15. **pizza**
16. **villa**

Skill: Students will practice spelling words borrowed from other languages.

Home Use: Help your child practice the spelling words by having him or her complete the activities on this page. Check the completed page, and have your child practice saying and spelling any misspelled words.

103

Unit 21 Test: Noun Suffixes II

Find the correctly spelled word to complete each phrase. Fill in the letter beside the correct spelling.

Sample:
a newspaper ___
ⓐ reportor   ⓒ reportor
ⓑ riporter   ● reporter

Items 1–10 test Basic Words 1–10. Items 11–20 test Basic Words 11–20.

1. to ask the ___
   ⓐ farmacist   ⓒ pharmmacist
   ● pharmacist   ⓓ pharmasist

2. the ___ of the building
   ● custodian   ⓒ custodan
   ⓑ custodiane   ⓓ custodain

3. a talented ___
   ⓐ peanist   ⓒ piannist
   ● pianist   ⓓ pianiste

4. constructive ___
   ● criticism   ⓒ criticsm
   ⓑ critisism   ⓓ criticism

5. a sense of ___
   ⓐ idelism   ⓒ iddealism
   ● idealism   ⓓ idealism

6. the school ___
   ● librarian   ⓒ librarion
   ⓑ libbrarian   ⓓ librairian

7. the family ___
   ⓐ historyian   ⓒ histrian
   ⓑ histroyan   ● historian

8. a ___ running for office
   ● politician   ⓒ politisian
   ⓑ politican   ⓓ polatician

9. a famous ___
   ⓐ novellist   ● novelist
   ⓑ novalist   ⓓ novilist

10. a stand-up ___
    ⓐ comedien   ⓒ comedian
    ● comedian   ⓓ comedan

11. an outlook of ___
    ● realism   ⓒ reelism
    ⓑ raelism   ⓓ realisme

12. wearing ___ clothing
    ⓐ civillian   ⓒ civilien
    ● civilian   ⓓ civilian

13. an interesting ___
    ⓐ imdividualist   ● individualist
    ⓑ indivijualist   ⓓ inmdivijualist

14. being a ___
    ● conformist   ⓒ conformist
    ⓑ conformist   ⓓ cunformist

15. to be a ___
    ⓐ perfectionist   ● perfectionist
    ⓑ perfectionist   ⓓ purfectionist

16. a famous ___
    ● guitarist   ⓒ gittarist
    ⓑ gitarist   ⓓ guitarist

17. a strange ___
    ⓐ manerism   ⓒ mannerism
    ⓑ manirism   ● mannerism

18. reserved for ___ traffic only
    ⓐ pedistrian   ⓒ pedestrien
    ⓑ peddestrian   ● pedestrian

19. a song by the ___
    ⓐ solloist   ⓒ soloiste
    ⓑ soleoist   ● soloist

20. parent or ___
    ● guardian   ⓒ ghardian
    ⓑ gardian   ⓓ guardien

102

PRACTICE B
Words from Other Languages

Basic Words
1. villa
2. pizza
3. spaghetti
4. gondola
5. accordion
6. balcony
7. opera
8. waltz
9. macaroni
10. tycoon
11. finale
12. violin
13. confetti
14. pretzel
15. kindergarten
16. kimono
17. influenza
18. umbrella
19. sauerkraut
20. graffiti

Rhyming Pairs Write the Basic Word that rhymes with the given word to answer each riddle.

1. What is a country house for apes? gorilla _____
2. What is tube pasta for small horses? pony _____
3. What is a conclusion in a canyon? valley _____
4. What is the name of a parasol carried by a fairy tale character in glass slippers? Cinderella _____
5. What is a bulky, tangy cabbage? stout _____
6. What is trivial, stringy pasta? petty _____
7. What is a robe from the island of Nakono? Nakono _____
8. What is a large, wealthy monkey? baboon _____

1. villa   5. sauerkraut
2. macaroni   6. spaghetti
3. finale   7. kimono
4. umbrella   8. tycoon

Proofreading 9–20. Find and cross out twelve misspelled Basic Words in this travel itinerary. Then write each word correctly.

Saturday: Arrive in Verona, Italy. Transfer by motor coach to our private villa on the Adige River. After a quick visit to the main points of interest in town, we will dine on spaghetti and walse to violin and accordian music. After dinner, join us in our balconie seats at the opera.

Sunday: Leave for Venice at 4:00 A.M. Check into the hotel before our day of sightseeing. Our leisurely stroll through the city will include a ten-second visit to St. Mark's Cathedral and a five-second gondolla ride. We will also visit an exhibition of kindergarden graffiti art and a medieval pretsel factory.

Monday: After visiting a few Renaissance palaces, we will be ready for the highlight of our tour—a six-hour visit to a paper factory to study how confeti is made. Then join us for our farewell dinner of tiny slices of peetza and delicious bottled water. Leave the city at 11:00 P.M. for the flight home.

Precautions: Due to a recent outbreak of influensa, all travelers are advised to receive vaccinations before departure.

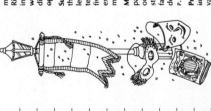

9. waltz
10. violin
11. accordion
12. balcony
13. opera
14. gondola
15. kindergarten
16. graffiti
17. pretzel
18. confetti
19. pizza
20. influenza

Challenge Words
1. pistachio
2. tempera
3. wanderlust
4. hibachi
5. delicatessen

Theme Vocabulary
6. pasta
7. cathedral
8. tomb
9. cafe
10. forum
11. catacombs
12. carnival
13. regatta

PRACTICE C
Words from Other Languages

Happy Endings Each short story description below includes a clue to a Challenge or Vocabulary Word. On another sheet of paper, write a sentence that might conclude each story, using the Challenge or Vocabulary Word suggested by each description.

Example: A young couple marry in a magnificent church.
The last of the confetti gusted across the cathedral steps.

1. Nigel Newport enters his yacht in the boat race.
2. A famous actor inherits a nut plantation.
3. Giselle Ferrez creates a fantastic costume for the festival.
4. A Japanese family buys a new stove.
5. A Bavarian schoolboy is overcome with the urge to travel.
6. Archaeologists discover the remains of a public square.
7. Artist Bernard Brush's new painting brings him sudden fame.
8. Leonora Borgia wins first prize in a macaroni competition.
9. Explorers uncover the burial place of an Egyptian pharaoh.
10. Kyle Kluss opens a store selling salads and cooked meats.

1. regatta   2. pistachio   3. carnival   4. hibachi
5. wanderlust   6. forum   7. tempera   8. pasta

Souvenirs of Italy The Bernini family has returned from a vacation in Italy with eight souvenirs. Figure out the code to write the descriptions of their souvenirs. Each description includes one Vocabulary Word. Write the letters for the code in the code box.

CODE:

?	%	X	*	=	Y	+	@	!	4	Q	&	6	J	2	9	8	Z	#
a	b	c	d	e	f	g	h	i	j	k	l	m	n	o	p	r	s	t	u	v

LETTER:

11. post card of a forum
    2 J 9 8   X ? ? 5 *   J Y   ?   Y J S   &

12. cookbook of pasta recipes
    X J J 4   % J J 4   J Y   ? ? 9 8 ? $ = X Y ! 2 = 9

13. matchbook from a cafe
    & ? 8 X @ % J J 4   Y 5 J &   ?   X ? Y =

14. map of the catacombs
    & ? 2 J   J Y   8 @ =   X ? 8 ? X J & 9

15. pictures of the cathedral
    2 ! X 8 Z ? 5 9   J Y   8 @ =   X ? 8 @ = * $! Q

16. carnival masks
    X ? 5 6 ! ? # ? Q   & ? 9 4 9

17. photo of the regatta
    2 @ J 8 J   J Y   8 @ =   5 = + ? 8 8 ?

Name _____

PRACTICE A
Words Often Misspelled II

Summing Up

The more you learn about words, the easier it is to remember how to spell them.

Mother Goose Times Write the Basic Words to complete these headlines. Capitalize the words except for those used in direct quotations.

Mother Goose Times

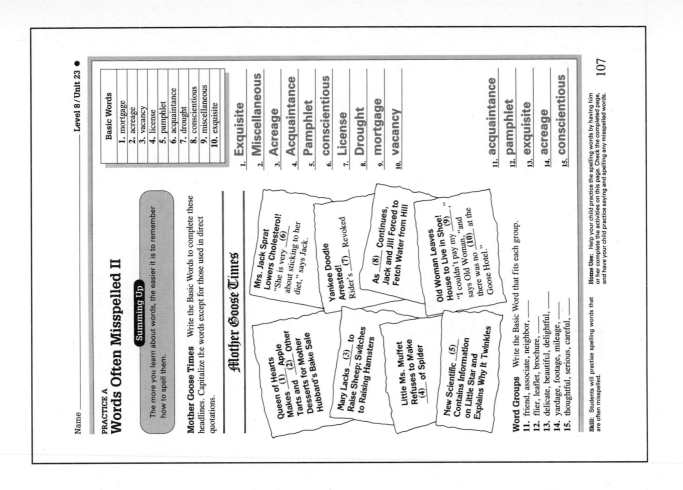

Queen of Hearts Makes (1) Apple Tarts and (2) Other Desserts for Mother Hubbard's Bake Sale

Mary Lacks (3) to Raise Sheep; Switches to Raising Hamsters

Little Ms. Muffet Refuses to Make (4) of Spider

New Scientific (5) Contains Information on Little Star and Explains Why It Twinkles

Mrs. Jack Sprat Lowers Cholesterol! "She is very (6) about sticking to her diet," says Jack.

Yankee Doodle Arrested! Rider's (7) Revoked

As (8) Continues, Jack and Jill Forced to Fetch Water from Hill

Old Woman Leaves House to Live in Shoe! "I couldn't pay my (9)," and says Old Woman, "(10) at the there was no Goose Hotel."

Basic Words
1. mortgage
2. acreage
3. vacancy
4. license
5. pamphlet
6. acquaintance
7. drought
8. conscientious
9. miscellaneous
10. exquisite

1. **Exquisite**
2. **Miscellaneous**
3. **Acreage**
4. **Acquaintance**
5. **Pamphlet**
6. **conscientious**
7. **License**
8. **Drought**
9. **mortgage**
10. **vacancy**

11. **acquaintance**
12. **pamphlet**
13. **exquisite**
14. **acreage**
15. **conscientious**

Word Groups Write the Basic Word that fits each group.
11. friend, associate, neighbor, _____
12. flier, leaflet, brochure, _____
13. delicate, beautiful, delightful, _____
14. yardage, footage, mileage, _____
15. thoughtful, serious, careful, _____

Skill: Students will practice spelling words that are often misspelled.

Home Use: Help your child practice the spelling words by having him or her complete the activities on this page. Check the completed page, and have your child practice saying and spelling any misspelled words.

107

Name _____

Unit 22 Test: Words from Other Languages

Each item below gives four possible spellings of a word. Fill in the letter beside the correct spelling.

Sample:
- ⓐ mammath
- ● mammoth
- ⓒ mamoth
- ⓓ mammathe

Items 1–10 test Basic Words 1–10. Items 11–20 test Basic Words 11–20.

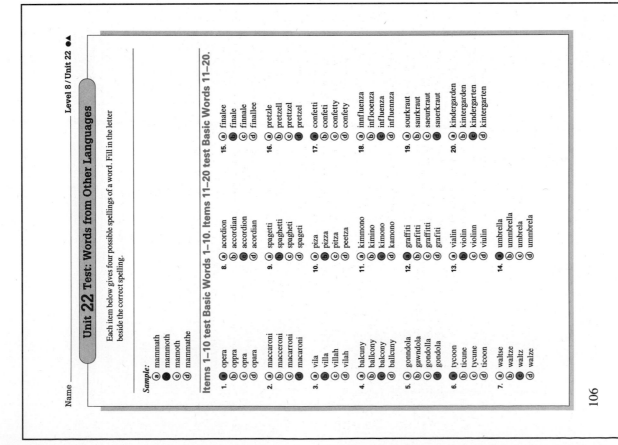

1. ● opera
   ⓑ oppra
   ⓒ opra
   ⓓ opara

2. ⓐ maccaroni
   ⓑ macceroni
   ⓒ macarroni
   ● macaroni

3. ⓐ vila
   ● villa
   ⓒ villah
   ⓓ vilah

4. ⓐ balcuny
   ⓑ ballcony
   ● balcony
   ⓓ ballcuny

5. ● gondola
   ⓑ gawndola
   ⓒ gondolla
   ⓓ gondola

6. ⓐ tycoon
   ⓑ ticune
   ⓒ tycune
   ⓓ ticoon

7. ⓐ waltse
   ⓑ waltze
   ● waltz
   ⓓ walze

8. ⓐ acordion
   ⓑ accordian
   ● accordion
   ⓓ acordian

9. ⓐ spagetti
   ⓑ spaghetti
   ⓒ spagheti
   ⓓ spageti

10. ⓐ piza
    ⓑ pizza
    ⓒ pitza
    ⓓ peetza

11. ⓐ kimmono
    ⓑ kimino
    ● kimono
    ⓓ kamono

12. ● graffiti
    ⓑ grafitti
    ⓒ graffitti
    ⓓ grafiti

13. ⓐ vialin
    ● violin
    ⓒ violinn
    ⓓ viulin

14. ⓐ umbrella
    ⓑ ummbrella
    ⓒ umbrela
    ⓓ ummbrela

15. ⓐ finalee
    ⓑ finale
    ⓒ finmale
    ⓓ finallee

16. ⓐ pretzle
    ⓑ pretzell
    ⓒ prettzel
    ● pretzel

17. ⓐ confetti
    ⓑ confeti
    ⓒ confetty
    ⓓ confety

18. ⓐ imfluenza
    ⓑ inflooenza
    ● influenza
    ⓓ influennza

19. ⓐ sourkraut
    ⓑ saurkraut
    ⓒ saeurkraut
    ● sauerkraut

20. ⓐ kindergarden
    ⓑ kintergarden
    ⓒ kindergaten
    ● kindergarten

106

PRACTICE B
Words Often Misspelled II

Basic Words
1. mortgage
2. acreage
3. vacancy
4. license
5. pamphlet
6. acquaintance
7. drought
8. conscientious
9. miscellaneous
10. exquisite
11. aerial
12. catastrophe
13. inevitable
14. forfeit
15. lieutenant
16. abundant
17. colossal
18. quarantine
19. succumb
20. anxious

Synonym / Antonym Switch Each sentence below contains a synonym or an antonym of a Basic Word. Cross out each synonym or antonym, and write a Basic Word to replace it. Write *A* (for *antonym*) or *S* (for *synonym*) to show the words' relationship.

1. Aunt Vinnie knew that I would ~~resist~~ and turn on the radio.
2. The company made an effort to reward ~~dutiful~~ employees.
3. Thomas Paine wrote a famous ~~brochure~~ titled "Common Sense."
4. The crops were ruined by the previous summer's ~~flood~~.
5. The mountain climbers' ~~meager~~ supply of food lasted weeks.
6. We found some books and ~~various~~ antiques in the attic.
7. The ~~tiny~~ statue stood at the harbor of ancient Rhodes.
8. The captain ~~released~~ after hearing the storm warning.

1. succumb A
2. conscientious S
3. pamphlet S
4. drought A
5. abundant A
6. miscellaneous S
7. colossal A
8. anxious A

Hidden Words 9–20. Read from left to right to find twelve Basic Words in this puzzle. Circle the letters in each Basic Word. Then write the words in the order they appear in the puzzle.

Example: t n s u c u t *succumb*
m b t y o l

9. catastrophe
10. lieutenant
11. mortgage
12. exquisite
13. inevitable
14. acreage
15. quarantine
16. aerial
17. vacancy
18. license
19. acquaintance
20. forfeit

Write the remaining letters in order to spell the body of water that separates the tip of South America from Tierra del Fuego.

Answer: Strait of Magellan

PRACTICE C
Words Often Misspelled II

Challenge Words
1. aesthetic
2. bureaucrat
3. continuum
4. disheveled
5. bouillon
Theme Vocabulary
6. Realtor
7. appraisal
8. zoning
9. surveyor
10. negotiate
11. deed
12. evict
13. tenant

Two-Step Crosswords Fill in all the Challenge and Vocabulary Words in the puzzle. (There is only one way to arrange them.) Then write a short clue for each word.

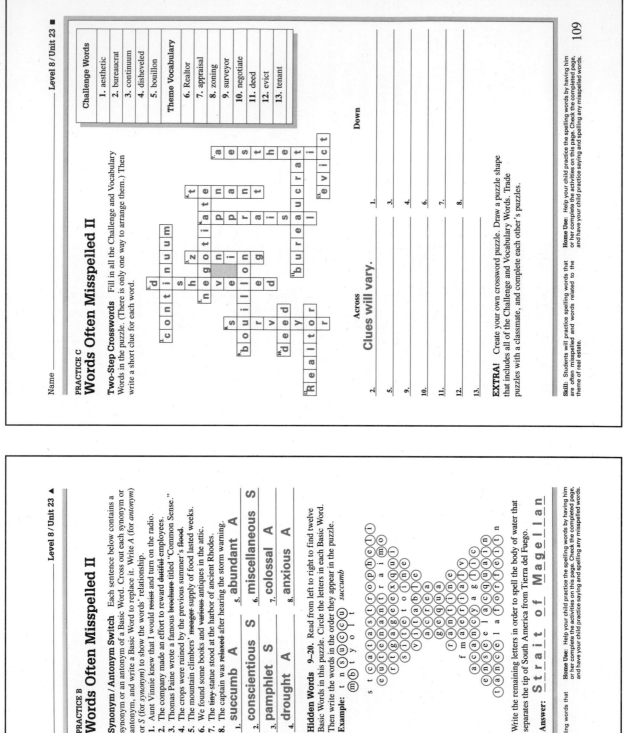

Across
Clues will vary.
2. _____
5. _____
9. _____
10. _____
11. _____
12. _____
13. _____

Down
1. _____
3. _____
4. _____
6. _____
7. _____
8. _____

EXTRA! Create your own crossword puzzle. Draw a puzzle shape that includes all of the Challenge and Vocabulary Words. Trade puzzles with a classmate, and complete each other's puzzles.

Unit 23 Test: Words Often Misspelled II

Find the correctly spelled word to complete each phrase. Fill in the letter beside the correct spelling.

Sample:

a ___ of quality
ⓐ garentee ⓒ garentee
ⓑ guarentee ● guarantee

Items 1–10 test Basic Words 1–10. Items 11–20 test Basic Words 11–20.

1. a box of ___ items
ⓐ misellaneous ⓒ miselaneous
ⓑ miscelaneous ● miscellaneous

2. a ___ worker
ⓐ consientious ⓒ conscientius
ⓑ conshientious ● conscientious

3. either flood or ___
● drought ⓒ drowt
ⓑ drout ⓓ drought

4. a driver's ___
ⓐ lisense ⓒ licence
● license ⓓ lisense

5. to have ___ taste
ⓐ exwisite ● exquisite
ⓑ exquisit ⓓ exquisitt

6. a four-page ___
ⓐ pamflet ⓒ pamphlett
● pamphlet ⓓ pamflett

7. through an ___
ⓐ aquaintance ⓒ acquaintence
ⓑ aquaintence ● acquaintance

8. no ___
● vacancy ⓒ vacansy
ⓑ vacency ⓓ vacensy

9. plenty of ___
● acreage ⓒ acredge
ⓑ acrege ⓓ acrege

10. a ___ on the house
ⓐ morgege ⓒ morgege
● mortgage ⓓ mortgage

11. a ___ error
ⓐ collossal ⓒ colossel
ⓑ collosal ● colossal

12. to have ___ resources
ⓐ abundent ● abundant
ⓑ abundint ⓓ abbundant

13. a ___ in the army
ⓐ leutenant ⓒ lieutenent
● lieutenant ⓓ leutenant

14. to feel ___
ⓐ anxius ● anxious
ⓑ anxcus ⓓ anxuis

15. to ___ the prize
● forfeit ⓒ forfit
ⓑ forfet ⓓ forfiet

16. to be ___
ⓐ inevitabel ⓒ inevitble
ⓑ inevatable ● inevitable

17. to avoid ___
ⓐ catastrophy ● catastrophe
ⓑ catastraphy ⓓ catastrophie

18. an ___ view
ⓐ areal ● aerial
ⓑ aireal ⓓ arial

19. to put into ___
ⓐ quarentine ⓒ quaranteen
● quarantine ⓓ quarentene

20. to ___ to an attack
● succumb ⓒ sucumm
ⓑ sucumb ⓓ succummb

Unit 24 Review: Test A

Find the word that is spelled incorrectly. Fill in the letter beside the misspelled word.

Sample:
ⓐ punctuality
ⓑ convert
● critisism
ⓓ gondola

This test reviews Basic Words 1–10 in Units 19–23.

1. ⓐ exquisite ● idelism ⓒ universal ⓓ punctual
2. ⓐ conspiracy ⓑ historian ● accordian ⓓ mortgage
3. ⓐ restoration ● extravert ⓒ comedian ⓓ acreage
4. ● miscelaneous ⓑ tycoon ⓒ sequence ⓓ reverse
5. ⓐ opera ⓑ pharmacist ⓒ origin ● conscientius
6. ⓐ drought ● advertisment ⓒ restore ⓓ villa
7. ● sequentiel ⓑ perspiration ⓒ librarian ⓓ waltz
8. ⓐ original ⓑ transpire ⓒ politician ● macarroni
9. ⓐ vacancy ⓑ pizza ● custodien ⓓ illustrate
10. ⓐ balcony ⓑ diversion ● novilist ⓓ license

Unit 24 Review: Test B

Find the word that is spelled incorrectly. Fill in the letter beside the misspelled word.

Sample:
- ⓐ anniversary
- ⓑ realism
- ● kindergarden
- ⓓ abundant

This test reviews Basic Words 11–20 in Units 19–23.

1.
- ⓐ symbolic
- ⓑ versus
- ⓒ individualist
- ⓓ grafitti

2.
- ⓐ liuetenant
- ⓑ umbrella
- ⓒ guitarist
- ⓓ triviality

3.
- ⓐ diverse
- ⓑ aerial
- ⓒ triviel
- ⓓ mannerism

4.
- ⓐ tranquil
- ⓑ anxious
- ⓒ kimono
- ⓓ intravert

5.
- ⓐ nuetrality
- ⓑ vertical
- ⓒ civilian
- ⓓ finale

6.
- ⓐ catastrophe
- ⓑ pretzel
- ⓒ guardien
- ⓓ aspire

7.
- ⓐ forfeit
- ⓑ contraversy
- ⓒ perfectionist
- ⓓ influenza

8.
- ⓐ collosal
- ⓑ syllable
- ⓒ pedestrian
- ⓓ invert

9.
- ⓐ tranquility
- ⓑ resperation
- ⓒ soloist
- ⓓ inevitable

10.
- ⓐ quarantine
- ⓑ neutral
- ⓒ sauerkraut
- ⓓ conffetti

Unit 24 Review: Test C

Each item below gives four possible spellings of a word. Fill in the letter beside the correct spelling.

Sample:
- ⓐ continuem
- ● continuum
- ⓒ continuam
- ⓓ continum

This test reviews the Challenge Words in Units 19–23.

1.
- ⓐ pesimism
- ● pessimism
- ⓒ pessamism
- ⓓ pessemism

2.
- ⓐ emfasis
- ⓑ emmphasis
- ● emphasis
- ⓓ emphesis

3.
- ⓐ pestachio
- ⓑ pistacchio
- ⓒ pistachioe
- ● pistachio

4.
- ⓐ diseveled
- ⓑ dishevelled
- ● disheveled
- ⓓ dishevled

5.
- ● vice versa
- ⓑ viceversa
- ⓒ vice-versa
- ⓓ vice vursa

6.
- ⓐ ecanomics
- ● economics
- ⓒ economics
- ⓓ econommics

7.
- ⓐ equestrien
- ⓑ equestriene
- ⓒ equesttrian
- ● equestrian

8.
- ⓐ hibbachi
- ⓑ habachi
- ● hibachi
- ⓓ hibacchi

9.
- ⓐ asthetic
- ⓑ esthetic
- ⓒ easthetic
- ● aesthetic

10.
- ● optimism
- ⓑ optemism
- ⓒ optamism
- ⓓ opptimism

11.
- ⓐ adversary
- ⓑ adversery
- ⓒ adverrsary
- ● adversary

12.
- ⓐ emmphatic
- ● emphatic
- ⓒ emphatic
- ⓓ emfatic

13.
- ● vertebra
- ⓑ vertabra
- ⓒ vertebre
- ⓓ verrtebra

14.
- ⓐ limguist
- ● linguist
- ⓒ lingwist
- ⓓ linguest

15.
- ● wanderlust
- ⓑ wonderluste
- ⓒ wanderluste
- ⓓ wanderlust

16.
- ● bureaucrat
- ⓑ bureucrat
- ⓒ buraucrat
- ⓓ bureacrat

17.
- ⓐ delicatesen
- ⓑ delicatesan
- ⓒ delicatessan
- ● delicatessen

18.
- ⓐ econnomy
- ⓑ econommy
- ● economy
- ⓓ economie

19.
- ⓐ boullon
- ⓑ bouillion
- ● bouillon
- ⓓ boillion

20.
- ● inverse
- ⓑ inverse
- ⓒ invirse
- ⓓ imvurse

PRACTICE A
Vowel Changes III

Summing Up

Learning how the vowels change in one word pair may help you predict changes in other pairs with the same root.

Word Equations Write the Basic Word that completes each equation. Keep in mind that the addition or subtraction of *tion* may involve additional spelling changes in each Basic Word.

1. retain + tion =
2. produce + tion =
3. consumption − tion =
4. detention − tion =
5. consume + tion =
6. production − tion =
7. reduce + tion =
8. retention − tion =
9. detain + tion =
10. reduction − tion =

1. retention
2. production
3. consume
4. detain
5. consumption
6. produce
7. reduction
8. retain
9. detention
10. reduce

News Clues Write the pair of Basic Words that completes each pair of headlines. Capitalize each word.

Dromian Parliament Will **(11)** the Price of Grain
Ministers Say Price **(12)** Will Help the Economy

Police **(13)** "Spudsy" Harrison for Questioning
Spudsy's Lawyers Vow to End His **(14)**

Envian Empire Agrees to Return Batland but Will **(15)** Dravia
World Leaders Say **(16)** of Dravian Territory Is Illegal

Morcar Motors Will **(17)** Smaller, Cleaner Car by Spring
Company Hopes That **(18)** Will Meet Demand

Study Shows Families **(19)** Less Fat Than Ten Years Ago
Report Credits Health Education Campaign for Decline in **(20)**

11. Reduce
12. Reduction
13. Detain
14. Detention
15. Retain
16. Retention
17. Produce
18. Production
19. Consume
20. Consumption

Basic Words
1. produce
2. production
3. consume
4. consumption
5. reduce
6. reduction
7. retain
8. retention
9. detain
10. detention

Skill: Students will practice spelling pairs of related words with vowel changes.

Home Use: Help your child practice the spelling words by having him or her complete the activities on this page. Check the completed page, and have your child practice saying and spelling any misspelled words.

119

PRACTICE B
Vowel Changes III

Tongue Twisters Write the Basic Word that completes each tongue twister. The Basic Word should begin with the same sound as most of the other words in the sentence. See how quickly you can say each sentence.

1. The ranchers will rapidly _____ rebuilding the railroad.
2. Carole could quickly _____ Curt's carrot cake.
3. Representatives wished to _____ the rate of redevelopment.
4. Paul's _____ that Polly had painted the parlor was premature.
5. The divers will _____ the dolphin to diagnose its disease.
6. Richard was relieved at the _____ in rehearsal hours.
7. It was easy indeed to _____ Ingrid to inspect the insects.
8. Patty promised to _____ a priceless painting on porcelain.
9. The innkeeper included an _____ written in India ink.
10. Ruby reassured Ruth that Rick will _____ Robert's respect.

1. resume
2. consume
3. reduce
4. presumption
5. detain
6. reduction
7. induce
8. produce
9. introduction
10. retain

Telephone Code Ten Basic Words are written in code, based on the numbers of a telephone keypad. Use the following number key to figure out each word. The vowels are underlined. Write the decoded words correctly.

Example: 7 3 7 8 6 3 *resume*

11. 7 7 6 3 8 2 8 4 6 6
12. 7 7 3 7 8 6 3
13. 3 3 8 3 6 8 4 6 6
14. 7 3 8 3 6 8 4 6 6
15. 2 2 7 8 3 6 8 4 6 6
16. 4 6 8 7 6 3 8 2 3
17. 7 3 7 8 6 7 8 4 6 6
18. 2 2 7 8 2 4 6
19. 4 6 3 8 2 8 4 6 6
20. 2 6 6 7 8 6 7 8 4 6 6

11. **production**
12. **presume**
13. **detention**
14. **retention**
15. **abstention**
16. **introduce**
17. **resumption**
18. **abstain**
19. **induction**
20. **consumption**

Basic Words
1. produce
2. production
3. consume
4. consumption
5. reduce
6. reduction
7. retain
8. retention
9. detain
10. detention
11. introduce
12. introduction
13. resume
14. resumption
15. induce
16. induction
17. abstain
18. abstention
19. presume
20. presumption

Skill: Students will practice spelling pairs of related words with vowel changes.

Home Use: Help your child practice the spelling words by having him or her complete the activities on this page. Check the completed page, and have your child practice saying and spelling any misspelled words.

120

Practice Master and Test Answers

Unit 25 Test: Vowel Changes III

Each item below gives four possible spellings of a word. Fill in the letter beside the correct spelling.

Sample:
● grateful
ⓑ greatful
ⓒ gratfull
ⓓ gradefull

Items 1–10 test Basic Words 1–10. Items 11–20 test Basic Words 11–20.

1. ⓐ prodution ● production ⓒ producsion ⓓ produssion
2. ⓐ ditain ● detane ⓒ detain ⓓ ditane
3. ● retain ⓑ ritain ⓒ retane ⓓ ritane
4. ⓐ consoom ⓑ consoume ⓒ consum ● consume
5. ● consmption ⓑ consumption ⓒ consumtion ⓓ consoumtion
6. ⓐ produss ⓑ produse ● produce ⓓ produsse
7. ⓐ detantion ⓑ ditention ● detention ⓓ detaintion
8. ● retention ⓑ reatention ⓒ reetention ⓓ ritention
9. ● reduse ⓑ reduce ⓒ reduss ⓓ reduse
10. ⓐ redussion ⓑ reducsion ⓒ reduktion ● reduction
11. ● presumption ⓑ persumption ⓒ presemption ⓓ persummtion
12. ⓐ abstaintion ⓑ abstenntion ⓒ abstantion ● abstention
13. ⓐ resumtionm ● resumption ⓒ resumbtion ⓓ resummtion
14. ⓐ intreduse ● introduce ⓒ intraduce ⓓ intraduse
15. ● induse ⓑ induce ⓒ indoose ● induce
16. ⓐ introdution ⓑ intraduction ● introduction ⓓ interducsion
17. ● presume ⓑ persume ⓒ presum ⓓ presumme
18. ● resume ⓑ resoume ⓒ resum ⓓ resoom
19. ● abstain ⓑ abstane ⓒ abstain ⓓ abstaine
20. ● induktion ⓑ induction ⓒ innduction ⓓ inducsion

PRACTICE C
Vowel Changes III

Business News 1–5. Read these summaries of five news articles. Write a headline for each article. Use each Vocabulary Word at least once in your headlines. **Sample heads:**

Challenge Words
1. atrocious
2. atrocity
3. ferocious
4. ferocity

Theme Vocabulary
5. income
6. gross
7. net
8. per capita
9. scarcity
10. surplus
11. inflation
12. unemployment

VOL. 407   No. 21   **BUSINESS EXTRA**   45 CENTS

1. Unemployment Rises

Across the state, more than 50,000 people are out of work. Economists blame the closing of many high-tech industries.

2. Per Capita Income Increases

The Pandora Department of Commerce reports that the average income last year for each resident of Pandora was $16,444, up from $15,482 the previous year.

3. Inflation Higher

Retail prices made a steep jump last month. The Consumer Price Index rose 1.3 percent.

4. Coal Surplus; Oil Scarcity

Officials say that oil reserves fell during the recent cold snap but that coal stockpiles increased.

5. RayMel Gross Sales Increase $2.1 Million; Employees to Benefit from Net Gain

RayMel Corporation reported sales of $14 million for the year just ended. This is an increase of $2.1 million from the previous year. RayMel executive Abel Shirm also reported that after al-lowing for expenses the company will realize a profit of $1.3 million. Shirm announced that a large part of these profits will be shared with company employees.

The Front Page   Complete each headline by writing the correct Challenge Word. Capitalize each word.

Islands Buffeted by (6) _____ Winds
Storm's (7) _____ Catches Residents *Unprepared*

Governor Calls False Accusation an (8) _____
"This (9) _____ Behavior Must Stop!"

On the back of this paper, write the lead for a news story to go with each headline you completed. Answer the questions *Who? What? When? Where?* and *Why?* in your leads. **Leads will vary.**

6. Ferocious
7. Ferocity
8. Atrocity
9. Atrocious

Skill: Students will practice spelling word pairs with vowel changes and words related to the theme of economics.

Home Use: Help your child practice the spelling words by having him or her complete the activities on this page. Check the completed page, and have your child practice saying and spelling any misspelled words.

PRACTICE A
Latin Roots III

Summing Up

Many words contain the Latin roots *plic*, *sens*, and *struct*.

Root Clues Complete each sentence by writing a Basic Word that makes sense in the sentence and that has the same Latin root as the underlined word. Then underline another word in each sentence that is a clue to the meaning of the Latin root.

Example: A builder will _____ the fort at a low construction cost.
A <u>builder</u> will *reconstruct* the fort at a low construction cost.

1. Sam and Kay are looking for a sensitive, yet _____, person who feels able to care for their three young children.
2. I felt a warm _____ as I touched the overheated sensor.
3. These instructions show how to build the entire _____.
4. The _____ of the map's folds made it complicated to close.
5. Is the plastic pliable enough to fold with a pair of _____?
6. We felt that it was senseless to visit the old _____ post.
7. The fence the construction workers are building will not _____ traffic.

1. **sensible**	3. **structure**
2. **sensation**	4. **complexity**

Book Review Write seven Basic Words to complete this review.

Build That House by Dee Construct is full of sound and __(8)__ advice for the first-time builder. The author is knowledgeable about every kind of __(9)__ , from the simple garden shed to the suburban house. The book will help you through every frustrating __(10)__ in your project.

One chapter addresses the difficulty and __(11)__ of some printed instructions. "Throw them away," says the author. "They don't help with small projects. Instead, they just __(12)__ one's progress." The author concedes, however, that there are certain projects that do require careful attention to instructions. "I do not mean to __(13)__ that they never come in handy," admits Dee. "I used them in my most recent effort to __(14)__ a Victorian porch."

Basic Words	
1. structure	
2. complexity	
3. reconstruct	
4. complication	
5. sensible	
6. obstruct	
7. imply	
8. pliers	
9. sentry	
10. sensation	

5. **pliers**	
6. **sentry**	
7. **obstruct**	

8. **sensible**	
9. **structure**	
10. **complication**	
11. **complexity**	
12. **obstruct**	
13. **imply**	
14. **reconstruct**	

Skill: Students will practice spelling words with the Latin roots *plic*, *sens*, and *struct*.

Home Use: Help your child practice the spelling words by having him or her complete the activities on this page. Check the completed page, and have your child practice saying and spelling any misspelled words.

PRACTICE B
Latin Roots III

Basic Words	
1. structure	
2. complexity	
3. reconstruct	
4. complication	
5. sensible	
6. obstruct	
7. imply	
8. pliers	
9. sentry	
10. sensation	
11. accomplice	
12. destruction	
13. resent	
14. sentimental	
15. applicable	
16. sensor	
17. perplex	
18. multiplication	
19. instructor	
20. sensitivity	

Roman Ruins On the stones of the Roman ruin, write the Basic Word that fits each clue.

1. to block
2. a sensing device
3. to suggest
4. to feel angry about
5. a tool
6. reasonable
7. to restore
8. appropriate
9. a teacher
10. emotional
11. a criminal partner
12. 4 × 4

1. o b s t r u c t
2. s e n s o r
3. i m p l y
4. r e s e n t
5. p l i e r s
6. s e n s i b l e
7. r e c o n s t r u c t
8. a p p l i c a b l e
9. i n s t r u c t o r
10. s e n t i m e n t a l
11. a c c o m p l i c e
12. m u l t i p l i c a t i o n

Proofreading 13–20. Find and cross out eight misspelled Basic Words in this account of an ancient Roman archaeological site. Then write each word correctly.

It was easy to reconstruct the city mentally, despite the ~~complicaty~~ of the site and the extensive ~~destrukcion~~. My study proceeded without much ~~complacation~~. The first ~~strucher~~ I noticed was the city gate, where a ~~sentry~~ had once stood. I recognized the temples, the baths, and the shops with a ~~sensation~~ of familiarity. Indeed, I was so well acquainted with Roman city planning that there was little here to ~~perplexs~~ me. The Romans were a sensible people who built with great ~~sensativity~~. There is still much we can learn from them.

13.	**complexity**
14.	**destruction**
15.	**complication**
16.	**structure**
17.	**sentry**
18.	**sensation**
19.	**perplex**
20.	**sensitivity**

Skill: Students will practice spelling words with the Latin roots *plic*, *sens*, and *struct*.

Home Use: Help your child practice the spelling words by having him or her complete the activities on this page. Check the completed page, and have your child practice saying and spelling any misspelled words.

Practice Master and Test Answers

Unit 26 Test: Latin Roots III

Find the correctly spelled word to complete each phrase. Fill in the letter beside the correct spelling.

Sample:

a marble ___
- (a) calumn
- (b) column ●
- (c) collum
- (d) collumn

Items 1–10 test Basic Words 1–10. Items 11–20 test Basic Words 11–20.

1. to have a ___ thought
- (a) sensible
- (b) senseable
- (c) sensable
- (d) senseible

2. a sturdy ___
- (a) structiur
- (b) structure
- (c) structier
- (d) structer

3. the ___ of the design
- (a) commplexity
- (b) cumplexity
- (c) complecsity
- (d) complexity

4. a ___ standing watch
- (a) sentrey
- (b) sentry
- (c) sentrie
- (d) sentary

5. to run into a ___
- (a) commplication
- (b) complication
- (c) complication
- (d) complecation

6. to ___ the building
- (a) reconstruct
- (b) reconstruct
- (c) reconstruck
- (d) reconstruck

7. to use ___
- (a) pliurs
- (b) plyers
- (c) pliers
- (d) plierse

8. an unusual ___
- (a) sennsation
- (b) sennsation
- (c) senscation
- (d) sensation

9. to ___ the view
- (a) obbstruct
- (b) ubstruct
- (c) obstruct
- (d) obsteruct

10. to ___ something else
- (a) immply
- (b) emply
- (c) imply
- (d) implie

11. a heat ___
- (a) sensorr
- (b) sensor
- (c) sensor
- (d) sencer

12. an ___ to the crime
- (a) accomplice
- (b) accomplise
- (c) acompliss
- (d) acomplice

13. to confuse and ___
- (a) perrplex
- (b) perplecs
- (c) perplex
- (d) purplex

14. warmth and ___
- (a) sensitivity
- (b) sensitivity
- (c) sensativity
- (d) senssativity

15. the ___ of the warehouse
- (a) destruction
- (b) disstruction
- (c) destruction
- (d) desstruction

16. to be ___ to everyday life
- (a) applicable
- (b) aplicable
- (c) applicible
- (d) applacable

17. a good ___
- (a) instructer
- (b) enstructer
- (c) instructor
- (d) instructre

18. to ___ the intrusion
- (a) resent
- (b) rasent
- (c) rissent
- (d) resente

19. to learn the ___ tables
- (a) multiplacation
- (b) multeplication
- (c) multiplication
- (d) multiplication

20. to ___ a feeling
- (a) sentamental
- (b) sentimental
- (c) sentimentle
- (d) sentimentel

PRACTICE C
Latin Roots III

Synonym Search One word in each sentence is a synonym for a Challenge or Vocabulary Word. Underline the synonym. Then write the Challenge or Vocabulary Word that can replace it.

1. Karen and Alice took several months to remodel the kitchen.
2. The building had a marble front.
3. The architect reinforced the wall with a support.
4. We found an old plan of the house in the attic.
5. The writer's opinion of pollution is implied in her work.
6. The carpenter built a reproduction of the old gazebo.
7. That lump of modeling clay is very soft.
8. The group stopped arguing and reached a general agreement.
9. The king had a little tower added to the castle wall.
10. The vacuum cleaner came with precise directions.

1. renovate	6. replica
2. facade	7. pliable
3. buttress	8. consensus
4. blueprint	9. turret
5. implicit	10. explicit

Challenge Words
1. replica
2. consensus
3. explicit
4. implicit
5. pliable
Theme Vocabulary
6. blueprint
7. renovate
8. colonnade
9. facade
10. pilaster
11. atrium
12. turret
13. buttress

Word Building 11–16. Write a Vocabulary Word to identify each architectural feature of this design.

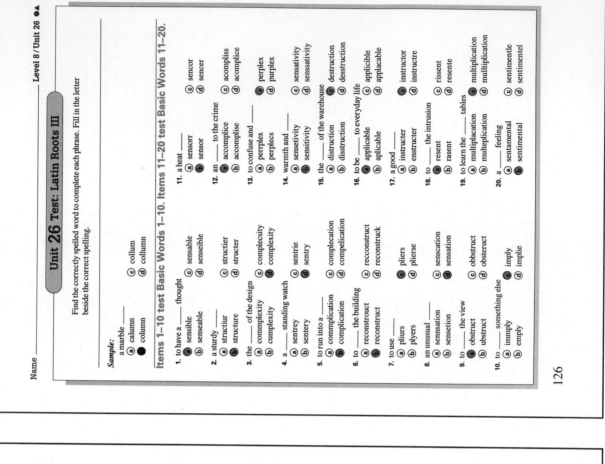

11. facade
12. atrium
13. turret
14. colonnade
15. buttress
16. pilaster

Skill: Students will practice spelling words with the Latin roots *plic*, *sens*, and *struct* and words related to the theme of architecture.

Home Use: Help your child practice the spelling words by having him or her complete the activities on this page. Check the completed page, and have your child practice saying and spelling any misspelled words.

PRACTICE A
Adjective Suffixes

Summing Up

Three common adjective suffixes are *-al*, *-ile*, and *-ous*.

Related Words Complete each sentence by writing the Basic Word that is a form of the underlined noun. Then underline the adjective suffix in the Basic Word.

1. From the top of the mountain, we could see a region even more _____ than the one we were in.
2. I have lived through many natural disasters, but this flood is the most _____ of all.
3. The steep grade of the road soon became a more _____ incline.
4. We used considerable caution as we approached the bear cub, which was clearly as _____ as we were.
5. It was a strain to participate in such _____ exercise.
6. Jo's agility enabled her to outshine the less _____ athletes.
7. The ships on the horizon had _____ stripes on their flags.
8. The Carrolls wanted more mobility on their vacation, so they towed their car behind their _____ home.

1. mountainous		4. cautious	
2. disastrous		5. strenuous	
3. gradual		6. agile	
		7. horizontal	
		8. mobile	

Basic Words
1. mountainous
2. gradual
3. agile
4. cautious
5. strenuous
6. crucial
7. mobile
8. horizontal
9. disastrous
10. tremendous

Word Search 9–18. Find and circle the ten Basic Words hidden in the puzzle. The words may appear horizontally, vertically, or diagonally. Write the words. **Order of answers may vary.**

```
a b g r a d u a l c c f
v m h n m r e g o m a x
a s o o b i w i g d u h
w t t s u r m u i g d t l i
z f m f r w n i b e c c i c o p
v s e o e u k t z w o e o r c j l
t y b n b n y m f r a o g i u u x r i l
e t a i u u t e x w i n c s c d n e
u h l o o p t n j o n t y i c m
u c u i p s s d d e o a a r
t s e n e y b o k m u l
q w a r t c v e u n a s y t
d i s a s t r o u s y t
```

9. gradual			
10. agile			
11. cautious			
12. horizontal			
13. mountainous			
14. tremendous			
15. crucial			
16. strenuous			
17. mobile			
18. disastrous			

Skill: Students will practice spelling words with the adjective suffixes *-al*, *-ile*, and *-ous*.

Home Use: Help your child practice the spelling words by having him or her complete the activities on this page. Check the completed page, and have your child practice saying and spelling any misspelled words.

PRACTICE B
Adjective Suffixes

Antonym Crossword Complete the puzzle by writing the Basic Word that is the antonym of each clue.

Basic Words
1. mountainous
2. gradual
3. agile
4. cautious
5. strenuous
6. crucial
7. mobile
8. horizontal
9. disastrous
10. tremendous
11. occasional
12. artificial
13. fragile
14. precious
15. juvenile
16. ridiculous
17. impartial
18. social
19. hysterical
20. contagious

Across
3. worthless
6. real
8. sturdy
10. calm
12. sudden
13. clumsy
14. motionless

Down
1. mature
2. unfriendly
4. vertical
5. sensible
7. prejudiced
9. easy
11. careless

Proofreading 15–20. Find and cross out six misspelled Basic Words in this notice to campers. Then write each word correctly.

ATTENTION CAMPERS! We have captured a sick bear in the mounteinous area of the park. This is not a tremendus problem! The bear is not contagius. However, please be cautious. An occasonal bear near the campsite does not present a cruseal problem. Park rangers have completed strenuous training classes that enable them to deal with such problems. Our mobile units will patrol the park, though we do not expect to find anything disastrus. Please enjoy your stay here!

15. **mountainous**	18. **occasional**	
16. **tremendous**	19. **crucial**	
17. **contagious**	20. **disastrous**	

Skill: Students will practice spelling words with the adjective suffixes *-al*, *-ile*, and *-ous*.

Home Use: Help your child practice the spelling words by having him or her complete the activities on this page. Check the completed page, and have your child practice saying and spelling any misspelled words.

Practice Master and Test Answers

243

Unit 27 Test: Adjective Suffixes

Each item below gives four possible spellings of a word. Fill in the letter beside the correct spelling.

Sample:

  ⓐ abnormle
  ⓑ abbnormal
  ⓒ abnormall
  ● abnormal

Items 1–10 test Basic Words 1–10. Items 11–20 test Basic Words 11–20.

1. ⓐ mobbile   ● mobile   ⓒ mobill   ⓓ mobille
2. ● aggile   ⓑ agile   ⓒ ajile   ⓓ agyle
3. ⓐ strennuous   ⓑ sterenuous   ⓒ strenuous   ● strenous
4. ● mountainous   ⓑ mountenous   ⓒ montainous   ⓓ mountaimious
5. ● crucial   ⓑ crucial   ⓒ crusial   ⓓ cruciel
6. ⓐ cotious   ⓑ causious   ⓒ causias   ● cautious
7. ⓐ tremindous   ⓑ tremmendous   ● tremendous   ⓓ tremendious
8. ⓐ horizontal   ● horizontal   ⓒ horizontle   ⓓ horizontel
9. ● dissastrous   ⓑ disastriss   ⓒ disasstrous   ⓓ disastrous
10. ⓐ gradeual   ⓑ graduall   ⓒ graddual   ● gradual
11. ⓐ ridiculous   ⓑ ridiculous   ⓒ rediculous   ● rideculous
12. ● ocasional   ⓑ occasional   ⓒ occasional   ⓓ occasionel
13. ● impartial   ⓑ immpartial   ⓒ impartiel   ⓓ immpartiel
14. ⓐ contagious   ⓑ contagious   ⓒ contagous   ● contageous
15. ⓐ fragale   ⓑ fragil   ● fragile   ⓓ fragel
16. ● hysterical   ⓑ hystarical   ⓒ histerical   ⓓ hystericel
17. ⓐ artifisial   ⓑ artificial   ● artifical   ⓓ artifishel
18. ⓐ pretious   ⓑ precious   ● precious   ⓓ pressous
19. ⓐ juvinel   ⓑ juvinal   ● juvenal   ⓓ juvenile
20. ● social   ⓑ soshal   ⓒ socal   ⓓ sosial

PRACTICE C
Adjective Suffixes

Scaling New Heights 1–3. The director of the Mount Majestic School of Mountaineering has hired you to write a flier describing courses at her school. Write titles and brief descriptions of three courses that the school offers, using all of the Vocabulary Words.

Challenge Words
1. notorious
2. simultaneous
3. volatile
4. ambiguous
5. intellectual

Theme Vocabulary
6. scale
7. rappel
8. summit
9. crevice
10. avalanche
11. piton
12. crampons
13. hypothermia

Mount Majestic School of Mountaineering

Titles and descriptions will vary.

1. _____
2. _____
3. _____

Word Relatives In each pair of sentences, write the Challenge Word that completes the first sentence. Then write a word that is related in spelling and meaning to the Challenge Word to complete the second sentence. You may want to use a class dictionary.

A. A stable leader would not exhibit __(4)__ behavior. Many citizens were shocked by the prime minister's __(5)__ .

B. The exam tested the students' creative and __(6)__ abilities. Every student was able to use his or her __(7)__ .

C. The __(8)__ ringing of the telephone and knocking at the door caused Deng to jump. He tried to answer both __(9)__ .

D. Maggie was __(10)__ for borrowing money and not returning it. She never seemed to understand the cause of her __(11)__ .

E. I cannot figure out what Reggie meant by that __(12)__ statement. His arguments are usually quite free of __(13)__ .

4. volatile
5. volatility
6. intellectual
7. intellect
8. simultaneous
9. simultaneously
10. notorious
11. notoriety
12. ambiguous
13. ambiguity

Skill: Students will practice spelling words with the adjective suffixes -al, -ile, and -ous and words related to the theme of mountain climbing.

Home Use: Help your child practice the spelling words by having him or her complete the activities on this page. Check the completed page, and have your child practice saying and spelling any misspelled words.

PRACTICE A
Words from Places

Summing Up

Many English words come from the names of places.

Word Histories Write the Basic Word that fits each word history.

This word comes from

1. Old French words meaning "Turkish stone," because this stone was first found in Turkestan.
2. the French phrase *gants de suède*, meaning "gloves of Sweden," from *Suède* (Sweden).
3. the name for a woolen sweater peculiar to the fishermen of the British isle of Jersey.
4. the French phrase *serge de Nîmes* that refers to a coarse cloth manufactured in the French town of Nîmes.
5. Zaytün (Arabic for Tseutung), a city in southern China where this cloth was probably first exported.
6. Kashmir, a territory north of India where mountain goats with this soft wool are found.
7. Gaza, where this cloth was supposed to be made.
8. Calicut, a city in India, from which this cloth was first exported.
9. Dungri, a section of Bombay where fabric for these trousers originated.
10. Venice, Italy, where this style of type was introduced in 1501.

1. _turquoise_
2. _suede_
3. _jersey_
4. _denim_
5. _satin_
6. _cashmere_
7. _gauze_
8. _calico_
9. _dungarees_
10. _italics_

Rhyming Pairs Write the Basic Word that rhymes with the given word to complete the answer to each riddle.

11. What is a reason to use a loosely woven cloth often made into bandages? _____ cause
12. What are models of ducks that are all painted a bluish-green color? _____ decoys
13. What is a patterned cotton cloth that is a rich, brown color? cocoa _____
14. What is a 365-day time period during which only a soft, fine wool is worn? _____ year
15. What is a pair of trousers made of a coarse, heavy, cotton fabric worn by an insect? flea's _____
16. What is a smooth and glossy ancient Roman fabric? Latin _____

11. _gauze_
12. _turquoise_
13. _calico_
14. _cashmere_
15. _dungarees_
16. _satin_

Basic Words
1. denim
2. jersey
3. satin
4. suede
5. cashmere
6. gauze
7. calico
8. turquoise
9. dungarees
10. italics

Skill: Students will practice spelling words that come from the names of places.

Home Use: Help your child practice the spelling words by having him or her complete the activities on this page. Check the completed page, and have your child practice saying and spelling any misspelled words.

PRACTICE B
Words from Places

Categories 1–10 Find and circle ten Basic Words in the puzzle. They may appear across, down, or diagonally. Then write each Basic Word you circled under the correct category heading.

```
b n c g n m u s l i n d c l a t
a l o i e n e u a t j p x y
i k r m y d e b a c l l
t s p o s d c l u a
s a d t s t c r o
f i m e l i a h s p a s
d c a l i c o n u h b z s v
a d e n i m c g a u z e p p e y
```

Order of answers 5–10 may vary.

Location   **Fabric**

1. _spa_   5. _muslin_

Transportation

2. _limousine_   6. _gauze_

Print   7. _denim_

3. _italics_   8. _suede_

Nature   9. _calico_

4. _geyser_   10. _satin_

Proofreading 11–20. Find and cross out ten misspelled Basic Words in this fashion script. Then write each word correctly.

If you want to say fashion, say it in *mujenta*! This season's garments are all a tribute to that stunning shade.

Here's Carol, wearing a soft, knee-length *jersy* dress. Notice how her simple accessories complete the outfit.

Chloe wears a cotton *dammask* jacket and matching trousers. What a smashing outfit for work or for play!

And here comes Jacqueline in a pair of *dungarees* with suede trim. We've teamed them with an oversized *Rugbey* shirt. Jacqueline's denim *duffle* bag has *rhinestone* accents.

Finally, Neal and Sandra are dressed for a night on the town. Neal's *tuxedoe* is complemented by a bright satin bow tie and sash combination—a lively alternative to basic black. Sandra steals the show in her *cashemere* gown and *turquoise* cape. Please call a limousine! They're ready!

11. _magenta_
12. _jersey_
13. _damask_
14. _dungarees_
15. _Rugby_
16. _duffel_
17. _rhinestone_
18. _tuxedo_
19. _cashmere_
20. _turquoise_

Basic Words
1. denim
2. jersey
3. satin
4. suede
5. cashmere
6. gauze
7. calico
8. turquoise
9. dungarees
10. italics
11. tuxedo
12. muslin
13. rhinestone
14. magenta
15. damask
16. duffel
17. limousine
18. spa
19. Rugby
20. geyser

Skill: Students will practice spelling words that come from the names of places.

Home Use: Help your child practice the spelling words by having him or her complete the activities on this page. Check the completed page, and have your child practice saying and spelling any misspelled words.

Practice Master and Test Answers

246

Unit 28 Test: Words from Places

Find the correctly spelled word to complete each phrase. Fill in the letter beside the correct spelling.

Sample:

a bottle of ___
- (a) collone
- (b) cologn
- (c) colone
- ● cologne

Items 1–10 test Basic Words 1–10. Items 11–20 test Basic Words 11–20.

1. words in ___
   - (a) italics
   - (b) ittalics
   - (c) itallics
   - (d) ittalics

2. a football ___
   - (a) jerrsey
   - (b) jerzey
   - (c) jersey
   - (d) jerrsy

3. a pair of ___ shoes
   - (a) swade
   - (b) suade
   - (c) suede
   - (d) swaid

4. a ___ pin
   - (a) terquoise
   - (b) turquoise
   - (c) turquoise
   - (d) terquoise

5. a ___ sweater
   - (a) casmere
   - (b) cashmere
   - (c) cashmear
   - (d) cashmere

6. a dress made of ___
   - (a) calico
   - (b) calliko
   - (c) calliko
   - (d) caleco

7. a ___ jacket
   - (a) denim
   - (b) dennim
   - (c) denimm
   - (d) dennem

8. sheer ___ fabric
   - (a) gawze
   - (b) guaze
   - (c) gauz
   - (d) gauze

9. a ___ gown
   - (a) satin
   - (b) sattin
   - (c) satin
   - (d) satine

10. an old pair of ___
    - (a) dungares
    - (b) dungarres
    - (c) dungarees
    - (d) dungurees

11. a pair of ___ earrings
    - (a) rinestone
    - (b) rienstone
    - (c) rhineston
    - (d) rhinestone

12. a ___ match
    - (a) Rugbee
    - (b) Ruggby
    - (c) Rugby
    - (d) Ruggbe

13. the health ___
    - (a) spah
    - (b) spa
    - (c) spaa
    - (d) spaw

14. a tablecloth of ___
    - (a) damask
    - (b) dammask
    - (c) damesk
    - (d) damusk

15. a ___ for the bridegroom
    - (a) tucsedo
    - (b) tuxedo
    - (c) tuxedoe
    - (d) tuxsedo

16. steam from the ___
    - (a) giser
    - (b) geyser
    - (c) geyzer
    - (d) gizer

17. a ___ blouse
    - (a) magenta
    - (b) majenta
    - (c) mugenta
    - (d) maggenta

18. in a ___ bag
    - (a) dufal
    - (b) dufel
    - (c) duffel
    - (d) duffle

19. rented a ___
    - (a) limosine
    - (b) limmousine
    - (c) limozine
    - (d) limousine

20. cloth made of ___
    - (a) muzlin
    - (b) muzzlin
    - (c) muslin
    - (d) muslin

134

Practice Master and Test Answers

PRACTICE A
Single or Double Consonants

Summing Up

Knowing why double consonants occur can help your spelling.

Basic Words
1. personnel
2. applicant
3. referral
4. occupation
5. recommend
6. occurrence
7. committee
8. essential
9. broccoli
10. summary

Word Factory 1–10. Help the factory workers dispense consonants to complete each Basic Word on the conveyor belt. Write a single consonant or double consonants in each blank. Then write the Basic Words in the order they appear on the conveyor belt.

single / double

consonants: b c d f l m n p r s t y

1. a **pp** l i c a n t
2. r e c **o** mm e n d
3. s **u** mm a r y
4. p e r s **o** nn e l
5. e **ss** e n t i a l
6. **o** cc u p **a**t i **o** n
7. b r **o** cc **o** l i
8. r e f e **rr** a l
9. c **o** mmi tt ee
10. o cc u **rr** e n c e

Analogies Write the Basic Word that completes each analogy.

11. fish : cod :: vegetable : _____
12. school : faculty :: company : _____
13. simple : complex :: unnecessary : _____
14. hobby : pastime :: profession : _____
15. presidency : candidate :: job : _____

1. applicant
2. recommend
3. summary
4. personnel
5. essential
6. occupation
7. broccoli
8. referral
9. committee
10. occurrence
11. broccoli
12. personnel
13. essential
14. occupation
15. applicant

135

Skill: Students will practice spelling words with single or double consonants.

Home Use: Help your child practice the spelling words by having him or her complete the activities on this page. Check the completed page, and have your child practice saying and spelling any misspelled words.

PRACTICE B
Single or Double Consonants

Basic Words
1. personnel
2. applicant
3. referral
4. occupation
5. recommend
6. occurrence
7. committee
8. essential
9. broccoli
10. summary
11. tariff
12. trespass
13. possession
14. opossum
15. accommodate
16. embarrass
17. paraffin
18. affectionate
19. shrubbery
20. harass

Job Descriptions Write the Basic Words to complete this newspaper feature story.

Jobs Around Town

Keiko is a zoo keeper. The unusual is an everyday __(1)__ for her. Yesterday, for example, she found a stray __(2)__ nibbling food as it hung from her office lamp. Keiko's job demands patience with both animals and the public. Once she found some students who had wandered into the zoo workshop where employees were using hot __(3)__ to make animal models for a new exhibit. Keiko did not want to humiliate or __(4)__ the curious students, yet she had to warn them not to __(5)__ in restricted areas.

Diego works in a day-care center because he likes working with children. His job requires him to be both firm and __(6)__. One of his most difficult tasks involves helping each child share his or her favorite __(7)__. Diego thinks that it is also very important to teach children to show consideration for others. He tells them that sometimes this means slowing down their walking pace to __(8)__ a slower partner. Diego teaches children to be gentle and patient so that they will not annoy or __(9)__ others.

His job also requires some administrative work. He is a member of the __(10)__ that makes decisions about hiring new __(11)__. Recently, he made a __(12)__ for an __(13)__ whom he could not hire but who had done good work as a volunteer. Diego told us, "I knew it was __(14)__ for this person to find a good job, so I wrote a brief __(15)__ of her volunteer work and sent it to another day-care facility."

Elaine has an enjoyable __(16)__—she works in a plant nursery. Her job requires her to care for flowers, trees, and __(17)__. Customers have many questions and often ask her to __(18)__ the best fertilizers for growing vegetables such as carrots and __(19)__. Elaine is also learning about the financial aspects of running such a business. "There are many expenses incurred when plants are imported," Elaine told us. "For example, a tax or __(20)__ can really add to the cost of a tree imported from South America or Asia. I'm always learning something new about cutting costs while maintaining a high-quality supply of plants."

1. occurrence
2. opossum
3. paraffin
4. embarrass
5. trespass
6. affectionate
7. possession
8. accommodate
9. harass
10. committee
11. personnel
12. referral
13. applicant
14. essential
15. summary
16. occupation
17. shrubbery
18. recommend
19. broccoli
20. tariff

136

Skill: Students will practice spelling words, single or double consonants.

Home Use: Help your child practice the spelling words by having him or her complete the activities on this page. Check the completed page, and have your child practice saying and spelling any misspelled words.

Unit 29 Test: Single or Double Consonants

Each item below gives four possible spellings of a word. Fill in the letter beside the correct spelling.

Sample:

ⓐ nesecary
ⓑ necesary
● necessary
ⓓ nessecary

Items 1–10 test Basic Words 1–10. Items 11–20 test Basic Words 11–20.

1. ⓐ recommend
   ⓑ recomend
   ⓒ reccomend
   ⓓ reccommend

2. ⓐ occupation
   ⓑ occupation
   ⓒ occupation
   ⓓ occuppation

3. ⓐ referal
   ⓑ referel
   ⓒ referel
   ⓓ referral

4. ⓐ aplicant
   ⓑ aplicant
   ⓒ applicant
   ⓓ applicant

5. ⓐ personel
   ⓑ personnell
   ⓒ personnel
   ⓓ personell

6. ⓐ ocurence
   ⓑ occurence
   ⓒ ocurrence
   ⓓ occurrence

7. ⓐ essential
   ⓑ issential
   ⓒ isential
   ⓓ esential

8. ⓐ sumary
   ⓑ sumery
   ⓒ summery
   ⓓ summary

9. ⓐ commite
   ⓑ comitte
   ⓒ comitee
   ⓓ committee

10. ⓐ broccolli
    ⓑ brocoli
    ⓒ brocoli
    ⓓ broccoli

11. ⓐ harass
    ⓑ harrass
    ⓒ harras
    ⓓ harres

12. ⓐ shrubbery
    ⓑ shruberry
    ⓒ shrubery
    ⓓ shrubberry

13. ⓐ affectionate
    ⓑ affectionet
    ⓒ affectionate
    ⓓ affectionet

14. ⓐ parafin
    ⓑ paraffin
    ⓒ parrafin
    ⓓ pareffin

15. ⓐ tarriff
    ⓑ tarif
    ⓒ tariff
    ⓓ tarrif

16. ⓐ tresspass
    ⓑ trespass
    ⓒ trespas
    ⓓ tresspas

17. ⓐ posesion
    ⓑ possesion
    ⓒ poesesion
    ⓓ possession

18. ⓐ oppossum
    ⓑ oposum
    ⓒ opossum
    ⓓ opposum

19. ⓐ acomodate
    ⓑ accomodate
    ⓒ accommodate
    ⓓ acommodate

20. ⓐ embarrass
    ⓑ embarass
    ⓒ embaras
    ⓓ embarass

PRACTICE C
Single or Double Consonants

It's Business Use the words below to write eight statements that might be found in an employee handbook. First, list the words in separate groups according to their box numbers. Then write a statement by unscrambling each group and adding the correct Vocabulary Word that completes each sentence.

Challenge Words
1. succinct
2. renaissance
3. irrevocable
4. collateral
5. reconnaissance
Theme Vocabulary
6. orientation
7. dismissal
8. memorandum
9. discrimination
10. insurance
11. incentive
12. grievance
13. confidential

3 based	2 remain	2 attend	8 employee	3 be	1 from
6 employee	8 records	3 reasons	7 our	2 must	3 specific
4 message	6 an	7 health	1 company	1 workers	2 employees
5 displeased	1 laws	6 a	5 file	4 an	4 by
8 all	7 offers	3 on	2 sessions	6 bonus	3 a
3 must	4 a	4 conveyed	5 a	2 new	4 is
6 is	4 office	5 a	5 protect	5 employee	5 should

1. **Laws protect workers from discrimination.**

2. **New employees must attend orientation sessions.**

3. **A dismissal must be based on specific reasons.**

4. **An office message is conveyed by a memorandum.**

5. **A displeased employee should file a grievance.**

6. **A bonus is an employee incentive.**

7. **Our company offers health insurance.**

8. **All employee records remain confidential.**

Word Categories Cross out the word that does not belong in each group. Then write a Challenge Word that belongs with each group. You may want to use a class dictionary.

9. concise, verbose, condensed, brief ___ **9.** _succinct_

10. inevitable, unavoidable, reversible, unalterable ___ **10.** _irrevocable_

11. rebirth, revival, renewal, ruin ___ **11.** _renaissance_

12. exploration, survey, reconciliation, inspection ___ **12.** _reconnaissance_

13. pledge, subordinate, guarantee, deposit ___ **13.** _collateral_

Skill: Students will practice spelling words with single or double consonants and words related to the theme of personnel management.

Home Use: Help your child practice the spelling words by having him or her complete the activities on this page. Check the completed page, and have your child practice saying and spelling any misspelled words.

Unit 30 Review: Test A

Read the four phrases in each item. Find the underlined word that is spelled incorrectly. Fill in the letter for the phrase with the misspelled word in the answer column.

Sample:

a. a crucial moment
b. formed a comittee
c. football jersey
d. to retain the meaning

ANSWERS
ⓐ ● ⓒ ⓓ

This test reviews Basic Words 1–10 in Units 25–29.

1. a. rate of consumption
   b. strenous activity
   c. a sensible solution
   d. a cashmere sweater

2. a. book summary
   b. a mountainous region
   c. a brief detenntion
   d. to obstruct the view

3. a. primary occupation
   b. increased production
   c. a terquoise stone
   d. used pliers

4. a. a tremendous help
   b. an agile cat
   c. unpleasant sensation
   d. a guaze bandage

5. a. faded dungarrees
   b. price reduction
   c. plate of broccoli
   d. a gradual increase

6. a. major complecation
   b. to produce goods
   c. a personnel manager
   d. words in italics

7. a. a denim jacket
   b. to detaine the speaker
   c. to recommend the dish
   d. to imply otherwise

8. a. a horizontal line
   b. received a referrel
   c. suede gloves
   d. to consume goods

9. a. job applicant
   b. disastrious situation
   c. to stand sentry
   d. a calico dress

10. a. strange occurrence
    b. huge structure
    c. cautius behavior
    d. to reduce in number

ANSWERS
1. ⓐ ● ⓒ ⓓ
2. ⓐ ⓑ ● ⓓ
3. ⓐ ⓑ ● ⓓ
4. ⓐ ⓑ ⓒ ●
5. ⓐ ● ⓒ ⓓ
6. ⓐ ● ⓒ ⓓ
7. ⓐ ● ⓒ ⓓ
8. ⓐ ● ⓒ ⓓ
9. ⓐ ● ⓒ ⓓ
10. ⓐ ⓑ ● ⓓ

Unit 30 Review: Test B

Read the four phrases in each item. Find the underlined word that is spelled incorrectly. Fill in the letter for the phrase with the misspelled word in the answer column.

Sample:

a. a social event
b. to harrass the witness
c. a Rugby match
d. to resent the remark

ANSWERS
ⓐ ● ⓒ ⓓ

This test reviews Basic Words 11–20 from Units 25–29.

1. a. green shrubery
   b. hysterical laughter
   c. a magenta cloak
   d. sensitivity to others

2. a. a resumption of activity
   b. artificial flowers
   c. an acomplice in crime
   d. an import tariff

3. a. in possession of
   b. multiplication tables
   c. an induction ceremony
   d. juvinile behavior

4. a. stretch limousine
   b. abstention from voting
   c. paraffin wax
   d. sentimental reasons

5. a. an occasional visit
   b. to accommodate guests
   c. a rhinestone necklace
   d. made the introduction

6. a. swimming instructor
   b. steam from a gyeser
   c. precious stones
   d. affectionate feelings

7. a. to make a presumption
   b. an impartial jury
   c. light sensor
   d. dammask draperies

8. a. to abstain from
   b. contagious laughter
   c. only where aplicable
   d. black tuxedo

9. a. to presoom innocence
   b. a health spa
   c. did embarrass them
   d. fragile crystal

10. a. to resume work
    b. a baby opossum
    c. complete destruction
    d. a duffell bag

ANSWERS
ⓐ ● ⓒ ⓓ
1. ● ⓑ ⓒ ⓓ
2. ⓐ ⓑ ● ⓓ
3. ⓐ ⓑ ⓒ ●
4. ⓐ ⓑ ⓒ ●
5. ● ⓑ ⓒ ⓓ
6. ⓐ ● ⓒ ⓓ
7. ⓐ ⓑ ⓒ ●
8. ⓐ ⓑ ● ⓓ
9. ● ⓑ ⓒ ⓓ
10. ⓐ ⓑ ⓒ ●

PRACTICE A
Vowel Changes IV

Summing Up

Learning how the vowels change in one pair of related words can help you predict changes in other pairs with the same root.

Basic Words
1. proclaim
2. proclamation
3. deceive
4. deception
5. acclaim
6. acclamation
7. pertain
8. pertinent
9. maintain
10. maintenance

Changing Vowels   1–10. Complete each equation by writing the pair of Basic Words that duplicate the vowel changes shown in each example.

perceive + tion = perception

1. **deceive** + tion = 2. **deception**

abstain + ent = abstinent

3. **pertain** + ent = 4. **pertinent**

sustain + ance = sustenance

5. **maintain** + ance = 6. **maintenance**

reclaim + tion = reclamation

7. **proclaim** + tion = 8. **proclamation**

9. **acclaim** + tion = 10. **acclamation**

Adverbial Connections   Write the Basic Word that completes each sentence. The way each character says something is a clue to the missing word in each sentence.

Example: "The judge issued this _____," said Vera **officially**.
proclamation

11. "How did the suspect _____ you?" asked Sue **trickily**.

12. "The witness has made quite a _____ comment," Jenny said **relevantly**.

13. "I continue to _____ my innocence," said Steve **truthfully**.

14. "The man is a master of _____!" said Mary **misleadingly**.

15. "Other criminals will _____ his talents," said Doug **approvingly**.

16. "I _____ your guilt to all!" said Betty **publicly**.

11. **deceive**   14. **deception**

12. **pertinent**   15. **acclaim**

13. **maintain**   16. **proclaim**

Skill: Students will practice spelling pairs of related words with vowel changes.

Home Use: Help your child practice the spelling words by having him or her complete the activities on this page. Check the completed page, and have your child practice saying and spelling any misspelled words.

Unit **30** Review: Test C

Find the correctly spelled word to complete each phrase. Fill in the letter beside the correct spelling.

Sample:

a _____ smile
● sardonic   © sardonic
ⓑ sardunic   ⓓ sardunic

This test reviews the Challenge Words in Units 25–29.

1. the _____ lion
   ⓐ ferrocious   © ferocious
   ⓑ feroshious   ● ferocious

2. the _____ substance
   ● pliable   © plyable
   ⓑ pliabel   ⓓ plyabel

3. an _____ response
   ⓐ ambiguous   © ammbiguous
   ● ambiguous   ⓓ ambiguois

4. a _____ man
   ⓐ renassance   © renaissance
   ⓑ rennaisance   ● renaissence

5. the wind's _____
   ● ferocity   © ferrocity
   ⓑ ferocety   ⓓ ferocety

6. the general _____
   ⓐ concensus   © concensus
   ● consensus   ⓓ consencus

7. a _____ criminal
   ⓐ notoreous   © notoreous
   ● notorious   ⓓ notorreous

8. a _____ message
   ⓐ lackonic   © lakonic
   ● laconic   ⓓ laconic

9. an _____ contract
   ⓐ irrevocable   ● irrevocable
   ⓑ irrevacable   ⓓ irrevicable

10. _____ stylish
    ⓐ joddpurs   © joddpurs
    ⓑ johdpurs   ⓓ johdpurs

11. to exhibit _____ behavior
    ● atrocious   © atroceous
    ⓑ attrocious   ⓓ atrotious

12. an exact _____
    ⓐ replika   © replika
    ⓑ repplika   ● replica

13. a _____ gas
    ● volatile   © vollatile
    ⓑ volatil   ⓓ voletile

14. a _____ mission
    ⓐ reconnaissance © reconaissance
    ● reconnaissance ⓓ reconnaissence

15. an act of _____
    ⓐ atrosity   © attrocity
    ⓑ attrosity   ● atrocity

16. an _____ direction
    ⓐ explisit   © explicit
    ⓑ explisitt   ● explicit

17. an _____ question
    ⓐ intellectual © intelectual
    ● intellectual ⓓ inntellectual

18. the colorful _____
    ⓐ freize   © friez
    ● frieze   ⓓ freise

19. terse and _____
    ⓐ sucinct   ● succinct
    ⓑ sucsinct   ⓓ suscinct

20. found through _____
    ⓐ sarendipity   © serendipidy
    ⓑ serandipity   ● serendipity

PRACTICE B
Vowel Changes IV

Basic Words
1. proclaim
2. proclamation
3. deceive
4. deception
5. acclaim
6. acclamation
7. pertain
8. pertinent
9. maintain
10. maintenance
11. exclaim
12. exclamation
13. perceive
14. perception
15. conceive
16. conception
17. prevail
18. prevalent
19. sustain
20. sustenance

Proofreading 1–8. Find and cross out eight misspelled Basic Words in this letter. Then write each word correctly.

Dear Mom and Dad,

Have the newspapers given you all the pertainent facts about your son's victory? You should see the crowds that acclaim me!

I ate a big breakfast to sustain myself on the morning of the race. A head of lettuce gave me sustainence. All through the race, I knew I would prevail. After a slow start, I tried to maintane my speed; but I fell so far behind that Hare, confident of winning, fell asleep.

Hare was awakened by the crowd's acclaimation as the judges began to preclam my victory. Without using deceiption, I have destroyed the conseption that tortoises never win. Now perhaps tortoises everywhere will come out of their shells!

Love,
Tommy

1. pertinent
2. sustenance
3. prevail
4. maintain
5. acclamation
6. proclaim
7. deception
8. conception

Syllable Maze 9–20. Trace a path through the maze. Find twelve Basic Words by connecting syllables in order. Move up, down, forward, backward, or diagonally, but use each block only once. Some blocks will not be used. The first word is shown.

START →	sus	per	main	tion	cla	ma
ma	claim	as	cep	lent	ex	tion
proc	ance	ten	main	a	as	con
pre	cep	a	tain	cla	ceive	
la	tion	per	ceive	a	per	claim	cep
ma	sus	per	prev	lent	ex	de	ceive	END

Now write the Basic Words in the order that you connected them.

9. acclaim
10. perception
11. sustain
12. exclamation
13. conceive
14. pertain
15. maintenance
16. proclamation
17. perceive
18. prevalent
19. exclaim
20. deceive

PRACTICE C
Vowel Changes IV

Challenge Words
1. pronounce
2. pronunciation
3. denounce
4. denunciation
Theme Vocabulary
5. generalization
6. persuasive
7. distort
8. exaggeration
9. contradiction
10. substantiate
11. testimonial
12. verification

Proper Propaganda 1–6. Write the Challenge or Vocabulary Word that completes each ad. Then write *generalization, testimonial,* or *exaggeration* to identify the propaganda technique used in each ad.

Hi, I'm cover girl Hannah Hairdo. Are you confused about hair sprays? Try Ironhead Hair Spray. With Ironhead Hair Spray I can make my waist-length hair stand up like an iron beam. Scientists have proved that Ironhead Hair Spray sets like concrete. What other __(1)__ of its effectiveness do you need?

People are talking their way to success! Are you ashamed of the way you speak? Sign up for a Speak Up workshop to improve your expression and __(3)__. Join all the Speak Up graduates who are no longer afraid to open their mouths. Register today!

1. verification   3. pronunciation
2. testimonial   4. generalization

Are you tired of glue that does not hold? Try Glory Glue. Glory Glue bonds within seconds and can hold objects together for several thousand years. Glory Glue has been used to glue mountains and skyscrapers back together. Anyone who has ever bought a tube of Glory Glue will be able to __(5)__ these claims. Buy Glory Glue today!

5. substantiate
6. exaggeration

Prefix Play Read each pair of definitions. Write the Challenge or Vocabulary Word that fits the first definition. Then substitute one of the prefixes below to write another word that fits the second definition. You may want to use a class dictionary.

pre	dis	con	re	e	an

7–8. to articulate a sound; to make known publicly
9–10. the act of disagreeing; the act of foretelling
11–12. having the power to convince; having the power to discourage from a course of action
13–14. to express strong disapproval of; to reject
15–16. to give a false account of; to twist out of shape
17–18. the act of condemning; how a person pronounces words

7. pronounce   11. persuasive
8. announce   12. dissuasive
9. contradiction   13. denounce
10. prediction   14. renounce
                    15. distort
                    16. contort
                    17. denunciation
                    18. enunciation

Practice Master and Test Answers

251

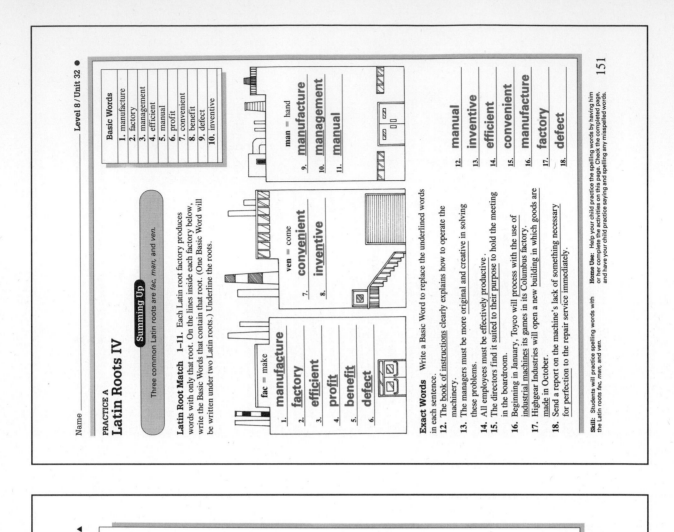

PRACTICE A
Latin Roots IV

Basic Words
1. manufacture
2. factory
3. management
4. efficient
5. manual
6. profit
7. convenient
8. benefit
9. defect
10. inventive

Summing Up

Three common Latin roots are *fac*, *man*, and *ven*.

Latin Root Match 1–11. Each Latin root factory produces words with only that root. On the lines inside each factory below, write the Basic Words that contain that root. (One Basic Word will be written under two Latin roots.) Underline the roots.

fac = make

1. manufacture
2. factory
3. efficient
4. profit
5. benefit
6. defect

ven = come

7. convenient
8. inventive

man = hand

9. manufacture
10. management
11. manual

Exact Words Write a Basic Word to replace the underlined words in each sentence.

12. The book of instructions clearly explains how to operate the machinery. _____

13. The managers must be more original and creative in solving these problems. _____

14. All employees must be effectively productive. _____

15. The directors find it suited to their purpose to hold the meeting in the boardroom. _____

16. Beginning in January, Toyco will process with the use of industrial machines its games in its Columbus factory. _____

17. Highgear Industries will open a new building in which goods are made in October. _____

18. Send a report on the machine's lack of something necessary for perfection to the repair service immediately. _____

12. manual
13. inventive
14. efficient
15. convenient
16. manufacture
17. factory
18. defect

Skill: Students will practice spelling words with the Latin roots *fac, man,* and *ven.*

Home Use: Help your child practice the spelling words by having him or her complete the activities on this page. Check the completed page, and have your child practice saying and spelling any misspelled words.

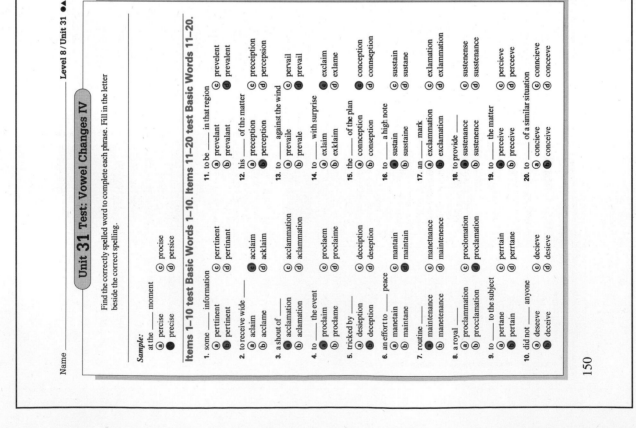

Unit 31 Test: Vowel Changes IV

Find the correctly spelled word to complete each phrase. Fill in the letter beside the correct spelling.

Sample:

at the _____ moment
- ⓐ percise
- ● precise
- ⓒ precise
- ⓓ persice

Items 1–10 test Basic Words 1–10. Items 11–20 test Basic Words 11–20.

1. some _____ information
- ⓐ pertinent
- ⓑ pertinent
- ⓒ pertinant
- ⓓ pertinant

2. to receive wide _____
- ⓐ aclaim
- ● acclaim
- ⓑ acclame
- ⓓ acklaim

3. a shout of _____
- ⓐ acclamation
- ⓑ acclamation
- ⓒ aclammation
- ⓓ acclammation

4. to _____ the event
- ⓐ proclaim
- ⓑ proclaime
- ⓒ proclaem
- ⓓ proclame

5. tricked by _____
- ⓐ desiption
- ● deception
- ⓒ deseption
- ⓓ deseption

6. an effort to _____ peace
- ⓐ mantain
- ⓑ maintane
- ⓒ mantain
- ● maintain

7. routine _____
- ⓐ maintenance
- ⓑ maentenance
- ⓒ manetance
- ⓓ maintenence

8. a royal _____
- ⓐ proclamation
- ⓑ proclamation
- ⓒ proclammation
- ⓓ proclamation

9. to _____ to the subject
- ⓐ pertane
- ⓑ pertain
- ⓒ perrtain
- ⓓ perrtane

10. did not _____ anyone
- ⓐ deseve
- ⓑ desieve
- ⓒ decieve
- ● deceive

11. to be _____ in that region
- ⓐ prevelant
- ⓑ prevalant
- ⓒ prevelent
- ● prevalent

12. his _____ of the matter
- ⓐ preception
- ● perception
- ⓒ preception
- ⓓ percepsion

13. to _____ against the wind
- ⓐ prevaile
- ⓑ prevale
- ⓒ pervail
- ● prevail

14. to _____ with surprise
- ⓐ exlaim
- ⓑ exklaim
- ● exclaim
- ⓓ exlame

15. the _____ of the plan
- ⓐ connception
- ⓑ conseption
- ● conception
- ⓓ connseption

16. to _____ a high note
- ⓐ sustain
- ⓑ sustaine
- ⓒ sustane
- ⓓ sustane

17. an _____ mark
- ⓐ exclammation
- ⓑ exclamation
- ⓒ exlamation
- ⓓ exclammation

18. to provide _____
- ⓐ sustenance
- ⓑ sustenance
- ⓒ sustenense
- ⓓ sustenance

19. to _____ the matter
- ⓐ perceive
- ⓑ preceive
- ⓒ percieve
- ⓓ perceeve

20. to _____ of a similar situation
- ⓐ concieve
- ● conceive
- ⓒ conncieve
- ⓓ conceeve

PRACTICE C
Latin Roots IV

Challenge Words
1. deficit
2. manifest
3. circumvent
4. facsimile
5. artifact

Theme Vocabulary
6. automation
7. assembly
8. inventory
9. specifications
10. prototype
11. uniformity
12. component
13. patent

Word Merge Use the clues to write two words on each line. One word will be a Challenge or Vocabulary Word. Letters at the end of the first word will also begin the second word. Circle the common letters. You may want to use a class dictionary.

Example: p a t (e n) t r a n c e

1–2. d e f i (c i t) a t i o n
3–4. c i r c u m (v e n t) i l a t e
5–6. m a n i (f e s t) i v a l
7–8. f a c s i (m i l e) s t o n e
9–10. s m a r t (i f a c) t
11–12. p l a t e (a u t o m a) t i o n
13–14. s t (u n) i f o r m i t y
15–16. d i s s i (p a t) e n t
17–18. i n v e n t o r (y e)
19–20. a s s e m b (l y r i c s)
21–22. p r o t o t y p e w r i t e r
23–24. c o m p o n e n t r e a t
25–26. s p e c i f i c a t i o n (s l a u g h t)

Clues
1. a shortage
2. a court summons
3. to avoid
4. to air out
5. obvious
6. a celebration
7. a reproduction
8. an important event
9. intelligent
10. a relic
11. elevated, flat land
12. automatic control
13. to daze
14. sameness
15. to scatter
16. an exclusive right to produce something
17. the supply of goods on hand
18. a type of grass used to make flour
19. putting together parts to make a whole
20. the words of a song
21. the first full-scale model of a new item
22. a machine that prints letters
23. a part of the whole
24. to beg
25. statements that describe a product exactly
26. a violent attack

Skill: Students will practice spelling words with the Latin roots *fac*, *man*, and *ven* and words related to the theme of manufacturing.

Home Use: Help your child practice the spelling words by having him or her complete the activities on this page. Check the completed page, and have your child practice saying and spelling any misspelled words.

PRACTICE B
Latin Roots IV

Basic Words
1. manufacture
2. factory
3. management
4. efficient
5. manual
6. profit
7. convenient
8. benefit
9. defect
10. inventive
11. effect
12. manipulate
13. factor
14. convention
15. eventually
16. maneuver
17. feat
18. sacrifice
19. manicure
20. preventive

Scrambled Memo 1–6. Unscramble the underlined Basic Words to complete this company memo. Write the six Basic Words.

MEMO

TO: All gnemmantae personnel
RE: Increasing fotpir margin

To increase our income, we must improve the way we freumautnac our product. Sloppy work will produce a product with a cedtef. Encourage your employees to work in a careful, feintecif manner so that our consumers will continue to recognize our high standards.

When viotnecenn, please list ways to improve production methods.

1. management
2. profit
3. manufacture
4. defect
5. efficient
6. convenient

Word Search 7–20. Find and circle fourteen Basic Words hidden in the puzzle. The words may appear horizontally, vertically, or diagonally.

```
p a w e c a l k f s n f d r o u o h e
m f s b f r u a e a a s d n i a v
a t e e e f f e c d c a m m d t o e
n h a n d c e t s r t r w a k e a n
e a t e e j i o t i i h a n s i t
u l l a f n d u r i w r s h c u r u
v e m n i c t l y o w r e n a i m a a
r m g n a c o n v e n t i o n h e l
m a n i p u l a t e m a n i c u r e y
```

Now write the Basic Words you circled in alphabetical order.

7. benefit
8. convention
9. effect
10. eventually
11. factor
12. factory
13. feat
14. inventive
15. maneuver
16. manicure
17. manipulate
18. manual
19. preventive
20. sacrifice

Skill: Students will practice spelling words with the Latin roots *fac*, *man*, and *ven*.

Home Use: Help your child practice the spelling words by having him or her complete the activities on this page. Check the completed page, and have your child practice saying and spelling any misspelled words.

Practice Master and Test Answers

Unit 32 Test: Latin Roots IV

Each item below gives four possible spellings of a word. Fill in the letter beside the correct spelling.

Sample:

- ⓐ magnificiant
- ⓑ magnificient
- ● magnificent
- ⓓ magnificant

Items 1–10 test Basic Words 1–10. Items 11–20 test Basic Words 11–20.

1.
- ⓐ factery
- ⓑ factory
- ⓒ factorry
- ⓓ factury

2.
- ⓐ deefect
- ⓑ deafect
- ● defect
- ⓓ defecte

3.
- ⓐ convenient
- ⓑ cuvenient
- ● convennient
- ⓓ convenyent

4.
- ⓐ management
- ⓑ managment
- ● management
- ⓓ management

5.
- ⓐ eficient
- ● efficient
- ⓒ efficient
- ⓓ efficient

6.
- ⓐ mannufacture
- ⓑ manafacture
- ● manufacture
- ⓓ manufacure

7.
- ⓐ innventive
- ⓑ facter
- ● inventive
- ⓓ inventiv

8.
- ● benefit
- ⓑ benifit
- ⓒ bennefit
- ⓓ bennefit

9.
- ⓐ manuel
- ⓑ manual
- ⓒ manuell
- ⓓ manuall

10.
- ⓐ profitt
- ⓑ profitt
- ⓒ proffitt
- ● profit

11.
- ⓐ preventive
- ⓑ preeventive
- ⓒ preaventive
- ● prevenntive

12.
- ⓐ manuver
- ⓑ maneuver
- ⓒ maneuever
- ● manneuver

13.
- ⓐ feate
- ⓑ feete
- ● feat
- ⓓ faet

14.
- ⓐ factor
- ⓑ facter
- ⓒ facktor
- ⓓ factorr

15.
- ⓐ manicure
- ⓑ mannicure
- ⓒ mannecure
- ⓓ mannacure

16.
- ⓐ mannipulate
- ⓑ manepulate
- ⓒ manipulate
- ⓓ manipyulate

17.
- ⓐ evenntually
- ⓑ eventaly
- ⓒ eventualy
- ● eventually

18.
- ● sackrifice
- ⓑ sacrifise
- ⓒ sacrifise
- ⓓ sacrafice

19.
- ⓐ convvention
- ● convention
- ⓒ convemtion
- ⓓ cunvention

20.
- ● effect
- ⓑ efect
- ⓒ efecte
- ⓓ effecte

PRACTICE A

Number Prefixes

Basic Words
1. monarch
2. duel
3. dilemma
4. century
5. monk
6. decade
7. monopoly
8. decimal
9. monotone
10. duet

Summing Up

The prefixes *mon-, di-, du-, dec-,* and *cent-* are number prefixes.

Number Network   Complete each sentence by writing a Basic Word that makes sense in the sentence and that contains a number prefix that has the same meaning as the underlined word. Then underline the prefix in the Basic Word.

1. One ____ after another was forced to give up the throne.
2. Under the castle walls, the two knights engaged in a ____ .
3. The previous ten years had been a ____ of prosperity.
4. The lecturer spoke in a ____ that put more than one person in the audience to sleep.
5. Those two singers performed a beautiful ____ .
6. One ____ continued to live in the deserted monastery.
7. After one hundred years of war, there came a ____ of peace.
8. Having to choose between the two colors was a real ____ .
9. One company will no longer have a ____ on the market.
10. After finding ten mistakes, the proofreader checked every ____ in the calculations.

1. __monarch__
2. __duel__
3. __decade__
4. __monotone__
5. __duet__
6. __monk__
7. __century__
8. __dilemma__
9. __monopoly__
10. __decimal__

Hink Pinks   Answer each riddle by writing a Basic Word and a rhyming word from the box below.

rule   saxophone   minimal   bunk   cassette

11. What is a bed in a monastery?
12. What is a regulation governing combat between two people?
13. What is a tape recording of a song sung by two people?
14. What is a wind instrument that emits only one sound?
15. What is the smallest number based on 10?

11. __monk bunk__
12. __duel rule__
13. __duet cassette__
14. __monotone saxophone__
15. __minimal decimal__

Skill: Students will practice spelling words with number prefixes.

Home Use: Help your child practice the spelling words by having him or her complete the activities on this page. Check the completed page, and have your child practice saying and spelling any misspelled words.

PRACTICE B
Number Prefixes

Basic Words
1. monarch
2. duel
3. dilemma
4. century
5. monk
6. decade
7. monopoly
8. decimal
9. monotone
10. duet
11. monotonous
12. diploma
13. decathlon
14. monologue
15. dual
16. centigrade
17. monogram
18. monorail
19. duplex
20. centennial

Word Riddles Write the Basic Word that answers each clue.

1. I am one hundred years old.
2. I am very boring.
3. I can force you to make a difficult choice.
4. I am sought by those who want control.
5. I determine an all-around track and field champion.
6. I am very religious.
7. I have taken place when honor is at stake.
8. I can be found in calculations.
9. I do not participate in conversations.
10. I have a double personality.

1.	century	6.	monk
2.	monotonous	7.	duel
3.	dilemma	8.	decimal
4.	monopoly	9.	monologue
5.	decathlon	10.	dual

Proofreading 11–20. Find and cross out ten misspelled Basic Words in these classified ads. Then write each word correctly. **Order of answers may vary.**

Photographer for hire. During the past ~~deeeade~~ I have photographed everything from a ~~monark~~ to a ~~monarail~~. Call Fred Photo at 555-4777.

Do you speak in a ~~monotone~~? Do you give long, monotonous speeches that put people to sleep? Spectacular Speech School can help. Call us today at 555-5555, and ask about our ~~diploma~~ course.

Researchers needed to study temperatures over the course of the next century. Must be able to live to ripe old age. The ability to convert temperatures from Fahrenheit to ~~centigrade~~ would also be a help. Call Professor Berry at 555-3567.

Friday, March 16: Auction at the ~~duplex~~ of two local antique collectors, 58 Magpie Road. Items include a rare 1900 recording of a famous ~~duet~~ between Lizzy Heartbreak and Matthew Crooner, a ring with the ~~monagram~~ of the Czar of Russia, and a flag made for the 1876 ~~centennial~~ celebration.

11.	decade
12.	monarch
13.	monorail
14.	monotone
15.	diploma
16.	centigrade
17.	duplex
18.	duet
19.	monogram
20.	centennial

156

Skill: Students will practice spelling words with number prefixes.

PRACTICE C
Number Prefixes

Challenge Words
1. decibel
2. centipede
3. digraph
4. diphthong
5. monochrome
Theme Vocabulary
6. medieval
7. chronicle
8. chivalry
9. usurp
10. betrayal
11. sovereign
12. valor
13. conquest

Rhyming Pairs Write a Challenge Word and another rhyming word to answer each riddle.
Example: What was a disturbance in the Middle Ages?
medieval upheaval

1. What is a sudden rush of wormlike, many-legged animals?
2. What is a house painted in different shades of one color?
3. What is a snapshot of a pair of letters with one sound?
4. What is a unit expressing the loudness of sounds that cannot be tolerated?
5. What is a short musical composition meant for singing words with *oy*?

1. centipede stampede
2. monochrome home
3. digraph photograph
4. intolerable decibel
5. diphthong song

Legendary Figures Think of a plot for a story set in the Middle Ages that includes the characters pictured on this page. Write a title for the story. Then write a brief description of each character and his or her role in the story. Use all of the Vocabulary Words in your title and descriptions. Use the back of this paper also, if necessary.

Title: __Titles and descriptions will vary.__

King Aethelgird _____

 King Aethelgird

Prince Segovia _____

 Prince Segovia

Blasé the Fair _____

 Blasé the Fair

157

Skill: Students will practice spelling words with number prefixes and words related to the theme of the legends of King Arthur.

Practice Master and Test Answers

255

PRACTICE A
Words New to English

Summing Up

New words are often created by combining word parts or by forming **compound words**, **blends**, or **acronyms**.

Word Puzzle Write the Basic Word that fits each clue in the numbered rows. The letters in the dark box will spell a word new to English that names a computer language.

1.	s o f t w a r e
2.	d i s k e t t e
3.	p h o t o c o p y
4.	s m o g
5.	r o b o t i c s
6.	a n d r o i d
7.	d i g i t a l
8.	t r a n s i s t o r
9.	a n t i b i o t i c

1. a compound word meaning "data essential for operating computers"
2. a combination of a word part meaning "a round flat object for storing computer data" and a suffix meaning "small"
3. a combination of word parts meaning "light" and "to reproduce"
4. a blend of *smoke* and *fog*
5. a combination of a word meaning "a machine that works automatically" and a suffix meaning "study of"
6. a combination of a word part meaning "manlike" and a suffix meaning "form"
7. a combination of a word part meaning "finger" and a suffix meaning "characterized by"
8. a blend of *transfer* and *resistor*
9. a combination of word parts meaning "effectiveness against" and "made of life"

Analogies Write the Basic Word that completes each analogy.

10. calculator : computer :: typewriter : _____ **word processor**
11. film : photograph :: paper : _____ **photocopy**
12. tapedeck : cassette :: computer : _____ **diskette**
13. real : human :: fake : _____ **android**
14. land : litter :: air : _____ **smog**
15. iron : mineral :: penicillin : _____ **antibiotic**

Basic Words
1. software
2. word processor
3. diskette
4. robotics
5. android
6. digital
7. transistor
8. photocopy
9. smog
10. antibiotic

Home Use: Help your child practice the spelling words by having him or her complete the activities on this page. Check the completed page, and have your child practice saying and spelling any misspelled words.

Skill: Students will practice spelling words that are new to English.

Unit 33 Test: Number Prefixes

Find the correctly spelled word to complete each phrase. Fill in the letter beside the correct spelling.

Sample:
reading great _____
(a) litrature (c) litrature
(b) literature (d) literiture

Items 1–10 test Basic Words 1–10. Items 11–20 test Basic Words 11–20.

1. half a _____ ago
(a) century (c) century
(b) century (d) centurey

2. the last _____
(a) deckade (c) decade
(b) decaid (d) decaide

3. to sing a _____
(a) duet (c) duete
(b) dooet (d) duett

4. a regal _____
(a) monarck (c) monarch
(b) monnarck (d) monnarch

5. the _____ point
(a) decimal (c) decimel
(b) desimal (d) desimel

6. written by a _____
(a) munk (c) munck
(b) monnk (d) monk

7. to fight a _____
(a) duel (c) deul
(b) dool (d) duele

8. bothered by a _____
(a) dillemma (c) dilema
(b) dilemma (d) dillema

9. to gain a _____
(a) minopoly (c) monopoly
(b) monopaly (d) monopoly

10. a _____ voice
(a) moncton (c) monotone
(b) monatone (d) monotone

11. the town's _____
(a) centennial (c) centennial
(b) centennial (d) centenniel

12. to recite the _____
(a) monolog (c) monologue
(b) monnologue (d) monalogue

13. to live in a _____
(a) duplecs (c) duplecks
(b) duplex (d) duplexe

14. to have a _____ purpose
(a) dule (c) dual
(b) dool (d) doole

15. to ride the _____
(a) monorail (c) monarail
(b) monorale (d) monarale

16. received his _____
(a) diploma (c) diploma
(b) diplomma (d) diploma

17. completed the _____
(a) decathalon (c) decathelon
(b) dekathlon (d) decathlon

18. the _____ on her sweater
(a) monogram (c) monagram
(b) monogramm (d) monigram

19. a _____ task
(a) monotonous (c) monotonous
(b) monotonous (d) monotinus

20. forty degrees _____
(a) centigrade (c) centigrade
(b) centigraid (d) centigrad

Name _____

PRACTICE C
Words New to English

Challenge Words
1. semiconductor
2. simulation
3. synthesizer
4. aerospace
5. hologram
Theme Vocabulary
6. electronics
7. hardware
8. database
9. spreadsheet
10. directory
11. tutorial
12. utility
13. keyboard

Hidden Words Write the word that matches each clue below. Then write the Challenge or Vocabulary Word that contains the word that matches the clue.

Example: armed conflict   *war*   *hardware*

1–2. a unit of weight ___ **gram** ___ **hologram**
3–4. to lead ___ **conduct** ___ **semiconductor**
5–6. a step made in walking ___ **pace** ___ **aerospace**
7–8. the past tense of *light* ___ **lit** ___ **utility**

Now write a definition for each Challenge or Vocabulary Word you wrote above. Use the back of this paper.

What's My Job? Write the Challenge and Vocabulary Words that complete the job descriptions. Then identify each person's job on the chart. Put a check mark in each correct box.

9. Dan creates unusual melodies using his _____. — **synthesizer**
10. Judy studies figures on a _____ in order to advise her company on its finances. — **spreadsheet**
11. Cathy helps hire new employees for her company. At the moment she is compiling a _____ of all employees' names and addresses. — **directory**
12–13. Rosa uses many different _____ programs to train airline pilots to handle emergency procedures. One program includes a _____ of a plane with malfunctioning engines. — **tutorial**, **simulation**
14–15. Al's fingers fly over the _____ of his computer when he is entering information for a project's _____. — **keyboard**, **database**
16–17. Before studying computer science, Rod repaired radios in an _____ repair shop. Now he repairs computer _____. — **electronics**, **hardware**

	Cathy	Dan	Rod	Rosa	Judy	Al
financial analyst					✓	
word processing specialist						✓
personnel assistant	✓					
musician		✓				
computer technician			✓			
instructor				✓		

Skill: Students will practice spelling words that are new to English and words related to the theme of computers.

Home Use: Help your child practice the spelling words by having him or her complete the activities on this page. Check the completed page, and have your child practice saying and spelling any misspelled words.

Name _____

PRACTICE B
Words New to English

Basic Words
1. software
2. word processor
3. diskette
4. robotics
5. android
6. digital
7. transistor
8. photocopy
9. smog
10. antibiotic
11. laser
12. calculator
13. space shuttle
14. sonar
15. discotheque
16. microwave
17. amplifier
18. brunch
19. supersonic
20. scuba

Word Origins Write the Basic Word that fits each clue. Use your Spelling Dictionary.

This word comes from
1. the words *sound, navigation,* and *ranging.*
2. the Latin word *calculus,* meaning "small stone."
3. the words *self, contained, underwater, breathing,* and *apparatus.*
4. the words *breakfast* and *lunch.*
5. the Latin words meaning "over" and "sound" and an adjective suffix.
6. the combination of two English words, one of which means "that which processes."
7. the words *light, amplification, stimulated, emission,* and *radiation.*
8. the combination of a Greek word that means "small" and an English word.

1. **sonar**
2. **calculator**
3. **scuba**
4. **brunch**
5. **supersonic**
6. **word processor**
7. **laser**
8. **microwave**

Tongue Twisters Complete each tongue twister with a Basic Word. The Basic Word should begin with the same sound as most of the other words in the sentence. Then see how quickly you can say each one.

9. Sadie sold Sophie some special _____ to solve her schoolwork assignments.
10. An animated _____ attempted an answer in algebra class.
11. Troy and Tracey tried to trade their _____ for a tricycle.
12. Sue says someday she'll spend several semesters studying on a sleek, silver _____.
13. Anton asked the attendant to administer an _____ to the African antelope.
14. Phyllis finally found Floyd's _____ of Frank's footnotes.
15. Dalinda drew a diagram of the _____ device Donald had described.
16. Dylan's dad discovered a damaged document on Dixie's _____.
17. Robert wrote a research report on _____ for Dr. Riggs Riley.
18. Summer _____ smells somewhat like smoke.
19. David and Doris danced at the _____ during the dark, dreary days of December.
20. The alarmed Austrian ambassador was awakened by the _____.

9. **software**
10. **android**
11. **transistor**
12. **space shuttle**
13. **antibiotic**
14. **photocopy**
15. **digital**
16. **diskette**
17. **robotics**
18. **smog**
19. **discotheque**
20. **amplifier**

Skill: Students will practice spelling words that are new to English.

Home Use: Help your child practice the spelling words by having him or her complete the activities on this page. Check the completed page, and have your child practice saying and spelling any misspelled words.

Practice Master and Test Answers

257

PRACTICE A
Words Often Mispronounced

Basic Words
1. algebra
2. mathematics
3. probably
4. nuclear
5. identity
6. liberal
7. recognition
8. laboratory
9. mischievous
10. temperamental

Summing Up
Pronouncing words correctly will help you spell them correctly.

Campaign Promises Read these campaign statements made by ten candidates for student council president. Cross out the incorrect pronunciation in each statement. Then write the matching Basic Word. Use your Spelling Dictionary. Last, put a check mark next to the statement that would win your vote.

1. I'm looking for an opportunity to serve you, not just for personal (|rĕk'əg nĭsh'ən|, |rĕk'ĭg nĭsh'ən|.)
2. I may not be running on (|nōō'klēr|, |nōō'klē ər|) power, but I have the energy needed for the job!
3. You will (|prŏb'lē|, |prŏb'ə blē|) never find a more dedicated person to serve as your president!
4. As president, I will not be (|tĕm'prə mĕn'tl|, |tĕm pər mĕn'tl|), but calm and reliable.
5. Of all the candidates, I can give the school the strongest sense of (|ī dĕn'tĭ tē|, |ĭ dĕn'tĭ tē|).
6. You do not need to be good at (|ăl'jə brə|, |ăl'jə brē|) to figure out that I am going to win!
7. My political beliefs are both conservative and (|lĭb'ə rəl|, |lĭb'rəl|).
8. When I am elected president, I will work to provide better courses in (|măth'măt'ĭks|, |măth'ə măt'ĭks|).
9. My goal will be to rid our school of (|mĭs'chē vəs|, |mĭs'chə vəs|) behavior.
10. As president, I will make sure that a new science (|lăb'ər ə tôr'ē|, |lăb'rə tôr'ē|) is built by next year!

1. recognition
2. nuclear
3. probably
4. temperamental
5. identity
6. algebra
7. liberal
8. mathematics
9. mischievous
10. laboratory

Chosen statements will vary.

Classifying Write the Basic Word that fits each group.
11. electric, geothermal, solar, ___
12. studio, workshop, factory, ___
13. naughty, unruly, disobedient, ___
14. discovery, acknowledgment, notice, ___
15. possibly, certainly, supposedly, ___
16. plentiful, ample, abundant, ___
17. name, title, personality, ___
18. moody, sensitive, changeable, ___

11. nuclear
12. laboratory
13. mischievous
14. recognition
15. probably
16. liberal
17. identity
18. temperamental

Skill: Students will practice spelling words that are often mispronounced.
Home Use: Help your child practice the spelling words by having him or her complete the activities on this page. Check the completed page, and have your child practice saying and spelling any misspelled words.

Unit 34 Test: Words New to English

Each item below gives four possible spellings of a word. Fill in the letter beside the correct spelling.

Sample:
- (a) airobics
- (b) arobics
- ● (c) aerobics
- (d) aerabics

Items 1–10 test Basic Words 1–10. Items 11–20 test Basic Words 11–20.

1. ● (a) robotics (b) robootics (c) robottics (d) robutics
2. ● (a) anti-biotic (b) antibiotic (c) antebiotic (d) antibiatic
3. ● (a) diskette (b) disket (c) diskett (d) discette
4. (a) photo-copy ● (b) photocopy (c) fotocopy (d) photocoppy
5. (a) smogg (b) smoug ● (c) smog (d) smoeg
6. (a) tranzistor (b) transister (c) tranzister ● (d) transistor
7. ● (a) software (b) soft-ware (c) soft ware (d) softwere

8. (a) wordprocessor (b) word-processor ● (c) word processor (d) word processer
9. ● (a) digital (b) digitel (c) digitle (d) digitall
10. (a) androyd ● (b) android (c) androide (d) amdroid
11. (a) micrawave (b) microwave (c) micro-wave ● (d) microwave
12. ● (a) supersonic (b) supersonnic (c) super-sonic (d) super-sonnic
13. (a) amplifire ● (b) amplifier (c) amplifiar (d) amplifyer
14. ● (a) space shuttle (b) space-shuttle (c) spaceshuttle (d) space shuttel

15. (a) brunsch (b) berunch ● (c) brunch (d) bruntch
16. ● (a) calculator (b) calculater (c) calculatar (d) calcullator
17. (a) skooba (b) scooba (c) skuba ● (d) scuba
18. (a) sonnar (b) soanar (c) sonarr ● (d) sonar
19. ● (a) laser (b) lazer (c) laiser (d) laizer
20. (a) discoteque ● (b) discotheque (c) diskotheque (d) discotheqe

PRACTICE B
Words Often Mispronounced

Basic Words
1. algebra
2. mathematics
3. probably
4. nuclear
5. identity
6. liberal
7. recognition
8. laboratory
9. mischievous
10. temperamental
11. candidate
12. dinghy
13. hindrance
14. privilege
15. monstrous
16. grievous
17. preferable
18. arctic
19. similarly
20. sophomore

Crossword Puzzle   Complete the puzzle by writing the Basic Word that fits each clue.

Across
2. a second-year student
7. alike but not the same
9. the study of numbers
11. a branch of mathematics
12. a room for research
16. naughty
17. excessively sensitive
18. an obstacle
19. generous in amount
20. individuality

Down
1. more desirable
3. shocking
4. extremely cold
5. having to do with a nucleus
6. a special right
8. causing grief
10. a person who seeks office
13. the act of recognizing
14. most likely
15. a rowboat

Skill: Students will practice spelling words that are often mispronounced.

Home Use: Help your child practice the spelling words by having him or her complete the activities on this page. Check the completed page, and have your child practice saying and spelling any misspelled words.

PRACTICE C
Words Often Mispronounced

Challenge Words
1. prerequisite
2. asterisk
3. paraphernalia
4. forte
5. posthumous
Theme Vocabulary
6. equation
7. solution
8. radical
9. negative
10. variable
11. exponent
12. inequality
13. parentheses

Algebra Works   Write the Vocabulary Word that describes the underlined symbol(s) in each item.

1. $-54.\underline{2}$
2. $4\underline{x} < 2y$
3. $\underline{3}(x + 7)$
4. $5x + 7$
5. $\sqrt[3]{2}$
6. $7^{\underline{2}}$
7. $x + 2 \underline{=} 6$
8. $37{,}037 \times 18 \underline{= 666{,}666}$

1. __negative__
2. __inequality__
3. __parentheses__
4. __variable__
5. __radical__
6. __exponent__
7. __equation__
8. __solution__

Word Change   Follow the directions below to change Challenge or Vocabulary Words to other words. You may want to use a class dictionary.

9–10. Write the Challenge Word that names a star-shaped symbol. Then drop three letters to write the name of a flower.

11–12. Write the Vocabulary Word that names a symbol used to multiply a quantity by itself. Then change the prefix to write a word that means "someone who supports something."

13–14. Write the Challenge Word that means "specialty." Then change one letter to write a word that names a number.

15–16. Write the Challenge Word that means "after death." Then drop the prefix and one other vowel to write a word that names a dark-colored soil.

17–18. Write the Vocabulary Word that is a synonym for *answer*. Then add a prefix to write another word that has the same meaning.

19–20. Write the Vocabulary Word that names a mathematical root. Then replace the last three letters with two letters to write a word that names a kind of line segment.

21–22. Write the Challenge Word that means "necessary." Then replace the two prefixes with another prefix to write a word that means "of special beauty."

23–24. Write the Challenge Word that means "the equipment used in some activity." Then combine the prefix with a base word meaning "a meaningful sequence of words" to write a word that means "to restate in other words."

9. __asterisk__
10. __aster__
11. __exponent__
12. __proponent__
13. __forte__
14. __forty__
15. __posthumous__
16. __humus__
17. __solution__
18. __resolution__
19. __radical__
20. __radius__
21. __prerequisite__
22. __exquisite__
23. __paraphernalia__
24. __paraphrase__

Skill: Students will practice spelling words that are often mispronounced and words related to the theme of algebra.

Home Use: Help your child practice the spelling words by having him or her complete the page. Check the completed page, and have your child practice saying and spelling any misspelled words.

Practice Master and Test Answers

Unit 36 Review: Test A

Find the word that is spelled incorrectly. Fill in the letter beside the misspelled word.

Sample:
- ⓐ laboratory
- ● antebiotic
- ⓒ manual
- ⓓ deception

This test reviews Basic Words 1–10 in Units 31–35.

1.
- ⓐ maintenance
- ⓑ benefit
- ● dillema
- ⓓ android

2.
- ⓐ nuclear
- ⓑ pertain
- ● managment
- ⓓ monopoly

3.
- ⓐ software
- ● liberel
- ⓒ monotone
- ⓓ profit

4.
- ⓐ acclaim
- ⓑ manufacture
- ● transister
- ⓓ mathematics

5.
- ⓐ proclaim
- ⓑ monk
- ● diskette
- ⓓ mischeivous

6.
- ⓐ factory
- ● pertinant
- ⓒ duet
- ⓓ photocopy

7.
- ⓐ algebra
- ⓑ maintain
- ⓒ efficient
- ● monarck

8.
- ● probebly
- ⓑ robotics
- ⓒ decimal
- ⓓ defect

9.
- ⓐ smog
- ● decieve
- ⓒ inventive
- ⓓ recognition

10.
- ⓐ temperamental
- ⓑ digital
- ⓒ duel
- ● acclammation

Unit 35 Test: Words Often Mispronounced

Find the correctly spelled word to complete each phrase. Fill in the letter beside the correct spelling.

Sample:
a healthy _____
- ● environment
- ⓑ enviroment
- ⓒ enviorment
- ⓓ envirment

Items 1–10 test Basic Words 1–10. Items 11–20 test Basic Words 11–20.

1. the _____ child
- ● mischievous
- ⓑ mishievous
- ⓒ mischevous
- ⓓ mischievus

2. a mistaken _____
- ⓐ idenity
- ⓑ identity
- ⓒ idenntity
- ● identy

3. _____ is the best choice
- ⓐ probaly
- ⓑ probbly
- ● probably
- ⓓ probly

4. the _____ football coach
- ⓐ temprimental
- ⓑ temprimantal
- ⓒ tempramental
- ● temperamental

5. a look of _____
- ⓐ reconition
- ⓑ recognition
- ⓒ reconition
- ● recugnition

6. experiments in the _____
- ⓐ laboratory
- ⓑ labaratory
- ● laboratory
- ⓓ labratorry

7. to study _____ physics
- ⓐ nuclear
- ⓑ nuculer
- ● nucular
- ⓓ nuclaer

8. a _____ donation
- ⓐ libberal
- ⓑ liberal
- ● liberel
- ⓓ libral

9. taking an _____ course
- ⓐ algbra
- ⓑ aljebra
- ⓒ allgebra
- ● algebra

10. in _____ class
- ⓐ mathematics
- ⓑ mathamatics
- ● mathmatics
- ⓓ mathimatics

11. a _____ sight
- ● monstrous
- ⓑ monsteros
- ⓒ monsterous
- ⓓ monstros

12. a college _____
- ⓐ sophmore
- ⓑ sofomore
- ● sophomore
- ⓓ sophamore

13. right or _____
- ⓐ privlege
- ⓑ privlidge
- ● privilege
- ⓓ privelege

14. a _____ to progress
- ⓐ hindrince
- ⓑ hindrance
- ● hindrinse
- ⓓ hinderance

15. an _____ region
- ⓐ artic
- ⓑ arktic
- ● arctic
- ⓓ arctick

16. to row in a _____
- ⓐ dinhgy
- ⓑ dinngy
- ● dinghy
- ⓓ dinghie

17. a _____ for office
- ⓐ candidit
- ⓑ candadate
- ⓒ candidite
- ● candidate

18. to be _____ to
- ⓐ preferble
- ⓑ preferable
- ● preferable
- ⓓ preferable

19. to be _____ dressed
- ⓐ simmilarly
- ⓑ similarily
- ⓒ simmilarly
- ● similarly

20. a _____ error
- ⓐ greevous
- ⓑ greivous
- ● grievous
- ⓓ grievus

Unit 36 Review: Test C

Each item below gives four possible spellings of a word. Fill in the letter beside the correct spelling.

Sample:
- ● manifest
- (b) mannifest
- (c) manefest
- (d) manafest

This test reviews the Challenge Words in Units 31–35.

1. ● artefact
   (b) arrtfact
   (c) arrtefact
   (d) artifact

2. ● denounce
   (b) deenounce
   (c) denownce
   (d) denounse

3. (a) centepede
   (b) centepeed
   (c) centipeed
   ● centipede

4. ● hologram
   (b) holagram
   (c) hollagram
   (d) hollogram

5. (a) prerequisit
   (b) perequisite
   ● prerequisite
   (d) prerecwisite

6. (a) sinthesiser
   (b) synthasiser
   ● synthesizer
   (d) synthesiser

7. (a) pranounce
   ● pronounce
   (c) pronownce
   (d) pronownse

8. ● deficit
   (b) defficit
   (c) defisit
   (d) deficitt

9. (a) dipthong
   (b) diphthung
   ● diphthong
   (d) diphtong

10. (a) asteriks
    ● asterisk
    (c) asterrisk
    (d) asterisck

11. (a) airospace
    (b) arospace
    (c) aroespace
    ● aerospace

12. (a) decible
    ● decibel
    (c) decibell
    (d) desibel

13. ● circumvent
    (b) circumvent
    (c) circkumvent
    (d) circummvent

14. (a) pranounce
    (b) pronnunciation
    (c) prunounciation
    ● pronunciation

15. (a) facimile
    ● facsimile
    (c) fascimile
    (d) facsimmile

16. (a) monachrome
    (b) monocrome
    (c) monnochrome
    ● monochrome

17. (a) semi-conductor
    (b) semi-conducter
    ● semiconductor
    (d) semiconducter

18. (a) paraphanalia
    ● paraphernalia
    (c) paraphenalia
    (d) parephernalia

19. ● denunciation
    (b) denounciation
    (c) denownciation
    (d) denunsiation

20. (a) poschumous
    ● posthumous
    (c) posthumous
    (d) poschumus

Unit 36 Review: Test B

Find the word that is spelled incorrectly. Fill in the letter beside the misspelled word.

Sample:
- (a) microwave
- ● centennial
- (c) convention
- (d) perception

This test reviews Basic Words 11–20 in Units 31–35.

1. (a) sustain
   ● manuever
   (c) duplex
   (d) laser

2. (a) monstrous
   (b) sonar
   ● monalogue
   (d) factor

3. ● concieve
   (b) preventive
   (c) dual
   (d) calculator

4. (a) scuba
   ● privelege
   (c) prevail
   (d) manicure

5. (a) arctic
   (b) centigrade
   ● sustenence
   (d) effect

6. (a) candidate
   (b) brunch
   ● monarail
   (d) exclaim

7. ● discoteque
   (b) dinghy
   (c) diploma
   (d) sacrifice

8. (a) conception
   (b) feat
   (c) monogram
   ● greivous

9. ● prevalant
   (b) amplifier
   (c) sophomore
   (d) decathlon

10. (a) perceive
    (b) eventually
    (c) supersonic
    ● hindrence

Practice Master and Test Answers

261

Page 175 (left):

End-of-Year Test

Find the word that is spelled incorrectly. Fill in the letter beside the misspelled word.

Sample:
- (a) collision
- ● sosiology
- ● armada
- (d) personality

Items 1–13 test Basic Words 1–10 in Cycles 1–6. Items 14–25 test Basic Words 11–20 in Cycles 1–6.

1. (a) abstract
   (b) saute
   ● proppaganda
   (d) succession

2. (a) transperstation
   (b) counteract
   (c) pueblo
   (d) prosecute

3. ● strategy
   (b) curiousity
   (c) punctuality
   (d) pliers

4. (a) century
   (b) spaghetti
   (c) pharmacist
   (d) symbal

5. ● persperation
   (b) reference
   (c) production
   (d) cashmere

6. (a) commitee
   (b) proclamation
   (c) inventive
   ● pastuerize

7. (a) zoology
   (b) tremendus
   (c) antibiotic
   (d) algebra

8. ● mischeivous
   (b) transpire
   (c) synthetic
   (d) psyche

9. (a) intercept
   (b) choral
   (c) detention
   ● dillemma

10. ● agressive
    (b) chronology
    (c) alternate
    (d) frequency

11. (a) robotics
    (b) management
    (c) pertinent
    ● referrel

12. (a) italics
    ● mountinous
    (c) complexity
    (d) gondola

13. (a) politician
    (b) submission
    ● aquaintance
    (d) substance

14. (a) intersection
    ● abundent
    (c) exclamation
    (d) concession

15. (a) protoplasm
    (b) transfusion
    (c) indicative
    ● imaculate

(continued)

Page 176 (right):

End-of-Year Test (continued)

16. ● opake
    (b) succumb
    (c) introduce
    (d) microwave

17. (a) preferable
    (b) mosiac
    (c) dissent
    (d) theology

18. (a) prominent
    ● acomplice
    (c) pimento
    (d) symbolism

19. (a) conformist
    (b) ridiculous
    ● rinestone
    (d) harass

20. (a) decathlon
    (b) maneuver
    (c) anniversary
    ● sourkraut

21. (a) humidity
    (b) preposition
    ● prespective
    (d) syndicate

22. (a) aggravate
    (b) indigo
    ● remediel
    (d) popularity

23. (a) pneumonia
    ● rendayvous
    (c) syllabication
    (d) versatile

24. (a) trespass
    (b) amplifier
    (c) transmission
    (d) guardian

25. (a) sensor
    (b) regimen
    ● pathalogical
    (d) mentor